REPORTS

ON THE

GEOLOGICAL SURVEY

OF THE

STATE OF MISSOURI.

1855—1871.

BY G. C. BROADHEAD, F. B. MEEK AND B. F. SHUMARD.

PUBLISHED BY AUTHORITY OF THE LEGISLATURE,

UNDER THE DIRECTION OF THE

BUREAU OF GEOLOGY AND MINES.

JEFFERSON CITY:
REGAN & CARTER, PRINTERS AND BINDERS.
1873.

PREFACE.

The present volume contains all of the previously unpublished material that was transmitted to me in a condition ready for publication.

The maps were engraved, and the impressions contained in this volume were struck off, previous to 1861; therefore, they do not represent the present political geography of the respective counties. In some instances the county boundaries have changed. These maps are appended as being better than none, and as illustrating the geological descriptions contained in the reports.

RAPHAEL PUMPELLY.

ST. LOUIS, *March* 1, 1873.

CONTENTS.

CHAPTER I.

MARIES COUNTY.

BY G. C. BROADHEAD.

PROF. G. C. SWALLOW, *State Geologist:*

SIR: The following I would respectfully submit to you as a Report of a portion of my labors during the past season, not prosecuted under your immediate supervision:

GEOGRAPHY—TOPOGRAPHY.

Maries county is bounded on the north by Osage county, on the east by Gasconade and Crawford, on the south by Crawford and Pulaski, and on the west by Pulaski and Miller counties. It contains about fifteen townships and twelve sections, or about five hundred and fifty-two square miles. This county is well watered, having several large streams passing through its entire length, as the Gasconade with its branches; Little Tavern and Big and Little Maries, and the Dry Fork of Bourbeuse, in the eastern part. These various streams influence the topography very much, owing to the depth they cut beneath the general surface of the surrounding country. Little Tavern, cutting beneath the level of the surrounding country not over one hundred feet, has narrow bottoms, with hills gently sloping on either side. The bottoms of Little and Big Maries are wider; the hills are also of gentle slope, but the country between and adjacent to these streams is quite broken and hilly. The Gasconade cuts into older formations, deep down into the Third Magnesian Limestone; its hills are more abrupt—bluffs frequently precipitous, and rising to a hight of more than two hundred feet; its hills, especially in the southern part of the county, present a peculiarly wild and picturesque appearance.

The characteristics of the tributaries are very similar to those of the Gasconade itself. The country near the Gasconade, for several miles on either side, is very broken indeed. The Gasconade bottoms are wide — being frequently a quarter of a mile in width. The hills on Cave Spring Creek and Spring Creek rise up gradually from the valley, but are high. On Little Beaver the hills are neither high nor precipitous. The slopes on the Dry Fork of Bourbeuse and its tributaries are very gentle, and hills quite low — none exceeding fifty-five feet in hight.

The Prairie land in this county is limited, and there are but few extensive tracts of good timbered land, except along the streams. The Gasconade, Maries and Bourbeuse bottoms are well timbered; the other bottoms are limited in their supply. The uplands, generally, are not well timbered. The hills between the Gasconade and Maries are mostly barrens, on which but few trees grow, except a stunted growth of Black-jack and Post Oak. Nearer the Gasconade the hills support a better growth. The county, near the head waters of Little Tavern and the Maries, consists also mostly of barrens, interspersed occasionally with small tracts of larger sized trees. The hills between Little Tavern and Sugar Creek are well timbered; between Sugar Creek and Little Maries barrens occur. There is a fine body of good timber between Dry Creek and Clifty Creek. The remainder of the county consists mostly of barrens, on which very tall prairie grass* grows, causing them somewhat to resemble prairies.

SCIENTIFIC GEOLOGY.

I. QUATERNARY DEPOSITS.

The rocks found under this head in the county of Maries are, Alluvium, Bluff and Local Drift.

1. *Alluvium.*—The Alluvium occurs as a deposit, on the bottoms of all the streams in this county; also, as a very thin stratum, on the hills overlying the older formations. I noticed it three feet in thickness on Maries Creek. On the Gasconade River it is much thicker. The sands of the Gasconade River, noted for purity and sharpness, belong to this formation, and are found nearly everywhere along its banks. In these sands are found many shells, mostly bivalves; also, a very few Gasteropods. Fresh-water shells were collected from the waters of Narrows Creek, Cave Spring Creek and at Friede's Cave; from Little Tavern and from creek at Paydown. Stalagmites and stalactites occur, of beautiful form and purity of color, in Friede's Cave.

* I was informed that this grass has seed every two years.

2. *Bluff.*—The Bluff formation is limited in this county, being but thinly deposited on the uplands. Noticed it two feet in depth on the hills between Big and Little Maries, and sustaining a growth of thrifty young White Oaks. In Sec. 4, T. 39 N., R. 9 W., it is three feet in depth, as shown in a well dug on the top of a White Oak ridge. About three miles north of Clifty Dale, it is seven feet thick.

Section 79—In section 31, T. 41 N., R. 7 W.

No. 1. 10 feet Bluff.
No. 2. 10 feet Local Drift of chert and Saccharoidal Sandstone.

In Galloway's Prairie, the Bluff is about three feet deep, and in Lane's Prairie about the same, with six inches or more of soil above.

3. *Local Drift*—Local Drift is found in many places in this county, underlying the Bluff, as it appears in a well three miles north of Clifty Dale.

Section 37.

No. 1. Slope of 15 feet to a well in a depression or valley on the top of the ridge.
No. 2. 7 feet Bluff formation; upper part ashy gray soil and "Bluff," lower part reddish-gray "Bluff."
No. 3. 13 feet red indurated Clay mixed with gravel, traversed by a small vein of black ferruginous sand resembling soft Sandstone.
No. 4. 1 foot white Sandstone, part of it a brown quartzite.
No. 5. 1½ feet red indurated Clay.
No. 6. 6 inches very soft yellow coarse Second Sandstone.
No. 7. White Sand.

Noticed Local Drifts in a bench of low ground between the bottoms of Little Tavern and the adjacent hills. In the bottoms of Dry Creek observed it about three feet deep, capped by soil. The Bluff thins out on many hills, leaving the Local Drift exposed on the surface, giving rise to a rocky, gravelly soil.

The term "Local," applied to this drift, seems appropriate, for its origin may be referred to agencies in its immediate vicinity. The materials of its composition are undoubtedly from those rocks whose native position is very near. The lithological appearance of the chert is the same as that found "in place" near it.

No signs of the regular drift formation appear in this county.

Boulders of rocks, intermediate with the above and the solid rocks "in place," in this county, were found in Lane's Prairie. Rocks identical in age with these were found by Dr. Shumard, in Phelps county, and classed by him as belonging to the Chemung formation.

I think it very probable that this is the "Old Red Sandstone," as developed in Montgomery and Warren counties.

II. CALCIFEROUS SAND-ROCK.

All the rocks of this county found beneath the Quaternary deposits belong to this division of the Lower Silurian system.

I. Saccharoidal Sandstone.

This is the highest division of the Calciferous Sand-rock found in this county. I was able to identify it only in the eastern part of the county. I first observed it on Spring Creek, in Sec. 16, T. 39, R. 8 W., where it occurred on the summit of a very high ridge as a small patch of about three feet in thickness. Near this, on Sec. 14 of the township lying north, I found fragments of coarse, brown Ferruginous Saccharoidal sandstone, lying loose on the highest parts of the ridge between the Gasconade and Bourbeuse. Eastward, I found it on the Bourbeuse, and in large masses dispersed over Lane's Prairie. On the two forks of Pea Vine it is found in large masses resting on Second Magnesian Limestone.

In Sec. 30, T. 41, R. 7 W., I observed it several feet in thickness, resting on Second Magnesian Limestone, and also in very large masses, from 20 to 35 feet in thickness, lying at every angle with the horizon, many of them gorging a ravine. At this place it presents almost all the appearances peculiar to Saccharoid Sandstone. Some of it was very ferruginous; some beautifully banded pink and white; some very white saccharoidal, and some brown. Mr. Price found Saccharoidal Sandstone between Maries Creek and the Gasconade, on the ridge lying east of Maries P. O.

The only fossil that I have found was the fragment of a large *Orthoceratite*, in a peice of very ferruginous Sandstone on the hills between the Gasconade and Bourbeuse. This specimen was about 5½ inches in diameter.

I have found specimens of the same fossil as much as 30 inches in diameter and 10 feet long, near the line between Gasconade and Franklin counties, about one mile from the Missouri River.

II. Second Magnesian Limestone.

From 70 to 100 feet of the lower beds of this formation are found in that part of the county lying west of the Gasconade. The Cotton rock is found in place in only two localities, and loose fragments of it at a few other localities, resting on the lower cellular beds of the Second Magnesian Limestone. A thin bed of Sandstone, belonging to the Second Magnesian Limestone, is frequently found as the top rock. It resembles Saccharoidal Sandstone very much, and if it were not for its position with regard to the other rocks, it might very easily be mistaken for Saccharoidal. The Magnesian beds below are always a sure guide. These beds are generally heavy, and easily known even before we get close to them. They frequently stand out from the side of a hill like walled terraces, in strata of a foot in thickness, presenting a rough, weather-worn appearance on the top surface and on the face. Tracts of land called "glades" are frequently sure guides to this formation; they are small tracts, containing not often more than half an acre of ground, sustaining scarcely any vegetation and no trees, except sometimes a few thorny bushes, on which the Magnesian Limestone outcrops. Sometimes there is a very little dark soil formed, probably from disintegration and decomposition of the Magnesian Limestone.

Of the lower beds of the Second Magnesian Limestone, the upper part is of an ashy gray or drab, sometimes a buff color, having numerous small cells, containing generally a whitish powder, and sometimes vacant. The lower beds also contain a powder, which is very often coarser, and of a brown color; the beds are also very silicious. Lower down we find very thick beds of a close-grained hard Silico-Magnesian Limestone, of a bluish drab color. The lowest beds pass into a chert rock, sometimes oolitic and sometimes approaching breccia. In many places found fragments of the lower beds partaking of the nature of a Buhr-stone, being essentially a cellular quartz rock, having numerous small cells, varying from a quarter of an inch in diameter to lesser dimensions. These cavities are lined with crystallizations of limpid quartz, showing points of crystals under the magnifying glass. The cells are frequently separated by partitions, formed of a fine oolite, the oolitic grains themselves being frequently hollow, which can sometimes be distinctly perceived with the naked eye.

This Buhr-stone passes by sensible gradations into a conglomerate or breccia, and also into an oolite, and sometimes a compact chert rock. As a Buhr-stone, I did not find it in place in this county. In Cole county, on South Moreau Creek, I found it in place, and on the Pacific Railroad above Jefferson City, it occurs as a Silicious Limestone. In Maries and Osage counties, it occurs as a Silicious Buhr-stone in small fragments, and I almost invariably found it on slopes just above the Second Sandstone. Beautiful specimens of this rock are found in Webster county, where some varieties have been used with very good success as a mill-stone.

Some of the upper beds of the Second Magnesian Limestone were found on the Dry Fork of Bourbeuse and on Pea Vine, a fork of that stream. The Cotton rock was found on the same stream.

I subjoin the following descriptive section near the northern part of Sec. 5, T. 39, R. 9:

Section 23.

No. 1. 30 feet slope; oolitic chert; some of it, when water-worn, presents a beautiful oolitic appearance in relief; when broken it is frequently reddish, as if cemented by oxyd of iron. Other fragments more compact present only the iron rust appearance near the surface, with interior passing into a quartzite; on some pieces noticed a minute crystallization of quartz on the surface; some fragments eminently a quartzite, and retaining but little of the oolitic structure; sometimes it passes into a horn-stone; noticed chert passing from a horn-stone into a rotten, drab-colored flint; from that it passes into a reddish, earthy rock.

No. 2. 8 feet—Second Magnesian Limestone; upper 6 feet drab Cotton rock, breaking with an irregular fracture; glistens in the light; when lying exposed seems much water-worn, sometimes into holes several inches in depth; when weather-worn presents a curled appearance on the upper surface; broken by vertical fissures; many fragments lying loose.

No. 3. 4 feet—bluish-gray Magnesian Limestone; more crystalline than the last.

No. 4. 11 feet slope.

No. 5. 1 foot—ashy-gray Limestone; highly Magnesian; breaks with a rough fracture; numerous small cells containing a white powder.

No. 6. 6 feet—like the last, but more crystalline; lower part coarse; brownish cells, containing a drab powder, often as compact as the containing rock.

No. 7. 12 feet slope.

No. 8. 1 foot—bluish-gray, semi-oolitic Sandstone, somewhat banded.

No. 9. 8 feet slope.

No. 10. 8 feet—Magnesian Limestone like No. 5.

No. 11. 2 feet slope.

No. 12. 4 feet—coarse gray Magnesian Limestone like No. 6.

No. 13. 26 feet slope; outcrops of coarse crystalline blue Magnesian Limestone.

No. 14. 15 feet slope.

No. 15. Second Sandstone in valley; large masses of chert over-lying it; Sandstone appears sub-saccharoidal; many gray specks disseminated; silicious particles limpid; some a pinkish color; surface sometimes iron gray and sometimes brownish ferruginous streaks.

The above section was on a long slope of 15° to 25°, with over-scattered fragments of Sandstone and chert. Found one fossil in Section 23. In slope of Section 35 found fossils in chert.

These were the only localities where I found any fossils in this formation.

III. SECOND SANDSTONE.

The Second Sandstone I first noticed in the north-western part of this county, where it forms the bed of Sugar Creek for three or four miles from its source; lower down, this stream cuts through it into the

Third Magnesian Limestone. In crossing over from Sugar Creek to Little Tavern, we find it near the upper part of the hills, and near Rowden's Mill it is ten feet in thickness, cropping out about fifteen feet below the hill-top, with twenty-six feet lower slope; following this creek up to its head, we find it stretching across the bed of the creek, and Second Magnesian Limestone on the hill-top. On Big and Little Maries Creeks, it was found in some places as the lowest rock. West of Vienna, on Big Maries, it appears about twenty feet above the bottoms; lower down, near the north-east corner of Township 40, Range 10, it occurs near the base of the bluffs, and again near Maries P. O., about twenty feet above the bottoms. Near Sec. 29, T. 40, R. 10, it occurs on Maries Creek as the lowest rock. Going toward the Gasconade, the Second Sandstone appears near the hill-tops in the northern part of the county, generally capped with Second Magnesian Limestone. At Vienna, it is found in the bed of Narrows Creek at its head. Traveling southward, the rocks continue to rise, and in the south-east, Sec. 4, T. 39, R. 9, it is the highest rock. Its western boundary seems thence to take nearly a due south-westwardly direction, crossing Dry Creek, and thence curving a little more to the west for a few miles, thence southwardly toward the corner of the county in the middle of T. 38 N., R. 10 W. East of the Gasconade to Cave Spring Creek, it crops out near the hill-tops, and is sometimes found on the summit of the highest ridges. On the same side of the Gasconade, and as far down as Paydown, it is mostly found near or on the hill-tops. East of this line, it dips under the Second Magnesian rocks. It lies in the bed of Cave Spring Creek, near its head, and is the principal rock on Beaver Creek, capped by Second Magnesian Limestone; and at the head of Beavor Creek it occupies the bed. Its thickness is variable—ranging from a few feet in thickness to as much as fifty-five feet, which latter thickness I found on the Gasconade and on Spring Creek; some of the beds on Spring Creek were as much as ten feet in thickness. On the Gasconade, its beds are thinner and easily cleaved, breaking into flags. Its thickness on Beaver Creek I suppose to be about twenty feet.

The Second Sandstone is often a coarse, somewhat Saccharoidal Sandstone formed of grains of limpid quartz cemented. Generally, it is a coarse brown and sometimes Ferruginous Sandstone; often a buff, thinly laminated, and frequently a soft, white Sandstone; sometimes it is pinkish and flesh-colored. Some beds of it are frequently a hard, compact quartzite. Some of it has a reticulated, cellular appearance on the upper surface, as if broken when soft, and then laterally pressed, forcing up soft matter between the edges, leaving a ridge over the broken part. These ridges are sometimes an inch in hight, and, crossing each other, cover the surface with a beautiful network of small chambers. The Second Sandstone is frequently beautifully ripple-marked. On the Gasconade River and on Spring Creek, I found two heavy beds of Sandstone, separated by thin beds of Silicious Magnesian Limestone, alternating with chert—all of which I am disposed to class with the Second Sandstone, the two beds being much alike indeed in their lithological appearance. I subjoin the following descriptive section:

Section 25—West side of the Gasconade, in S. E. quarter Sec. 4, T 39, R. 9 W.

No. 1. 26 feet covered with silicious Buhr-stone and indurated Sandstone (quartzite.)

SECOND SANDSTONE:

No. 2. 5 feet Second Sandstone—color brownish.

No. 3. 8 feet slope.

No. 4. 21 feet Magnesian Limestone, interstratified with chert. Upper part irregularly bedded buff and gray, with thin layers of chert; lower more heavily bedded coarse gray, with particles of chert disseminated; lowest part buff drab, imperfectly Magnesian, and breaking with a sandy fracture.

No. 5. 10 feet slope—outcrops of Sandstone and chert.

No. 6. 7 feet thinly bedded Sandstone; part quite Saccharoidal, part of a coarse buff color.

THIRD MAGNESIAN LIMESTONE:

No. 7. 61 feet Third Magnesian Limestone.

No. 8. 70 feet slope to the Gasconade bottoms.

Section 36—Gasconade Bluffs, one mile S. W. of Clifty Dale.

No. 1. 25 feet slope, covered with fragments of Second Sand-stone, with gray specks disseminated.

SECOND SANDSTONE:

No. 2. 6 feet Second Sandstone; upper part resembling coarse, brown sugar; lower finer and whiter, and having buff gray specks disseminated; lowest resembling a quartzite, white, with gray specks.

No. 3. 5 feet; upper part coarse brown Sandstone; lower part cherty, with a little Sandstone.

No. 4. 5 feet slope.

No. 5. 1 foot gray Silicious Limestone.

No. 7. 11 feet slope; chert outcropping.

No. 6. 3 feet coarse gray Magnesian Limestone,

No. 8. 21 feet slope—debris of rocks above.

No. 9. 1½ feet very coarse, buff-brown Sandstone.

THIRD MAGNESIAN LIMESTONE:

No. 10. 19 feet; upper part light gray Silicious Limestone; lower part coarse, brown Magnesian.

No. 11. 6 feet slope.

No. 12. 6 feet gray Limestone; lower part Magnesian.

No. 13. 22 feet heavily bedded (slightly Magnesian) Limestone—white gray to flesh-colored.
No. 14. 20 feet slope.

Section 61—On Spring Creek.

No. 1. 10 feet Sandstone.
No. 2. 4 feet coarse, brown Magnesian Limestone.
No. 3. 7 feet slope; outcrops of gray Magnesian Limestone.
No. 4. 4 feet flesh-colored Magnesian Limestone.
No. 5. 7 feet slope.
No. 6. 12 feet whitish Sandstone—soft, coarse, like No. 1. Upper two feet brownish, resembling No. 1.

I found no fossils that I could positively refer to the Second Sandstone, but I found fossils contained in loose chert lying on Third Magnesian slopes.

IV. THIRD MAGNESIAN LIMESTONE.

This formation is seen thickest in the bluffs of the Gasconade River, which stream cuts into it very often to the depth of two hundred feet—forming in many places bold, perpendicular bluffs, studded with occasional cedars growing out of the crevices, and presenting frequently wild and beautiful scenery.

The Third Magnesian Limestone is generally found capped with Second Sandstone. In tracing it out, we have more often to depend on its stratigraphical position with other known rocks; but it is often known before getting close to it by the peculiar, weather-worn appearance of its upper surface, which has a very rough appearance—the softer part being washed away, leaving irregular furrows, and also the softer particles of each separate piece washed out, leaving a rough exposed surface, causing the rock to appear like a close-grained Sandstone. Much of it, also, when broken, has a vitreous luster, breaking with a rough, sandy fracture; it is frequently a clear-grained, flesh-colored Magnesian Limestone.

The beds near the Second Sandstone seem insensibly to pass into a drab Sandstone; but we more often find the upper part of this formation consisting of thin beds of gray, finely crystalline, Silicious Limestone. A little lower in the series we find coarse buff, with small cells containing a brownish buff powder. The middle part is generally in very thick beds of buff and flesh-colored Silicious Limestone, breaking with an even fracture. Caves are numerous in the middle part of this formation, occurring generally in bed mentioned in Sec. 21, a description of which I subjoin:

Section 21.

No. 1. 26 feet slope; Indian mound on top; some fragments of Sandstone and chert.
No. 2. 20 feet Magnesian Limestone.
No. 3. 8 feet slope; chert and Sandstone.
No. 4. 66 feet Third Magnesian Limestone; in the lower part, for a quarter of a mile along the hill, occur several small caves; an efflorescence of white powder occurs in small crevices.
No. 5. 10 feet chert bed; some of the white powder of No. 5 occurs in the upper part.
No. 6. 80 feet slope to the river Gasconade; Magnesian Limestone at top; also outcropping at the foot of the hill a little beyond.

Making 184 feet Third Magnesian Limestone.

On Clifty Creek found the chert bed of Sec. 21–5 occurring about sixty feet from the top of the Third Magnesian Limestone, with a road passing over its upper surface, presenting it very favorably for observation. It seemed here to be broken by vertical cracks into large rhomboidal blocks. Further up this creek, in a wild and secluded spot, observed a Natural Bridge, with about six feet of this chert bed at its base, and Silicious Magnesian Limestone above. The span of this bridge is about thirty feet, and elevation of opening about fifteen feet above the water; the thickness of the rock above is about twelve feet, and width on top about fifteen feet. Two small streams come together, one from the west and another from the south-west. A point of the bluff on the south-west fork spans the northern fork, and terminates about sixty feet beyond in a sharp point; a few large masses of rock lie near the termination of the promontory, and fifty feet beyond, the bluffs of the opposite hills rise abruptly from the bottoms. The bluffs, both above and below, are very precipitous, the middle and lower beds of the Third Magnesian Limestone forming perpendicular escarpments, frequently studded with cedar, some occurring on the top of the bridge. A perfectly clear stream of water courses through this valley. The bottoms near are overspread with a dense growth of trees and vines, among which latter I noticed the Muscadine grape. The valley at this part, being shut in by its perpendicular cliffs, with not a path to guide the traveler through the dense thickets, is wildly picturesque and romantic in its loneliness.

Friede's cave, in north-east quarter of Sec. 21, T. 38, R. 9 W., is in Third Magnesian Limestone, and probably occupies nearly the same relative position as the caves in Secs. 24 and 25, T. 41, R. 9 W., or a position a little lower in the series. This cave is a quarter of a mile east of Cave Spring Creek, and has a wide and elevated entrance; passing into it a hundred yards or more, the passage narrows, and in order to go further a stream of water has frequently to be waded through; this passage has been followed by some persons several miles without finding any object of interest; but, a few hundred yards from the entrance, by diverging to the right, we enter a large chamber, studded with stalactites and stalagmites, many uniting and forming solid columns of support. Many of these are very beautiful, and often as white as alabaster. There are other large rooms, but they possess no peculiar interest. Found large deposits of earth on the floor, having a saline taste. Found some gasteropod mollusks in the branch outside, a short distance from the cave.

The lower beds of the Third Magnesian Limestone are sometimes flesh-colored, but more often bluish gray and silicious, with disseminated angular fragments of chert. The lowest beds found were very coarsely crystalline, having a sub-vitreous luster.

I subjoin the following descriptive sections:

Section 27—East side Gasconade, opposite mouth of Dry Creek.

No. 1. 20 feet slope; chert.
No. 2. 10 feet Second Sandstone; colored much with oxyd of iron.
No. 3. 5½ feet slope; debris of rocks above.
No. 4. 3 feet light gray finely crystalline Magnesian Limestone.
No. 5. 11 feet buff gray Magnesian Limestone, containing disseminated particles of chert.
No. 6. 10 feet chert bed.
No. 7. 68 feet Magnesian Limestone; upper part fine light gray; lower, coarse buff.
No. 8. 5 feet chert and Magnesian Limestone.
No. 9. 16 feet Magnesian Limestone, buff gray.
No. 10. 67 feet slope to Gasconade River.

Section 43.

No. 1. Slope, thickness not known.
No. 2. 40 feet perpendicular bluff of Magnesian Limestone, interstratified with thin layers of chert, appearing of a greenish color at a little distance.
No. 3. 17 feet slope; outcrops of chert.
No. 4. 12 feet coarse gray Magnesian Limestone.
No. 5. 14 feet slope.
No. 6. 28 feet slope; in upper part outcrops of chert; lower part fine-grained and slightly flesh-colored gray Magnesian Limestone.
No. 7. 48 feet slope to level of Gasconade bottoms.

The following section, taken one mile north of the mouth of Little Piney, and on the east side of the Gasconade, is more descriptive:

Section 47.

No. 1. 50 feet slope; Sandstone on top; also found chert and some pieces of altered Sandstone resembling quartzite; water-worn on upper surface, and surface also reticularly chambered—result of mud-cracks.

No. 2. 6 feet Second Sandstone; upper part indurated, approaching quartzite; lower, coarse buff brown.
No. 3. Slope; outcrops of gray Limestone.
No. 4. 6 inches coarse gray Calcareous Sandstone.
No. 5. 1 foot coarse gray Limestone; buff specks in minute cells.
No. 6. 16 feet coarse, gray, somewhat bluish Limestone.
No. 7. 10 feet gray, tolerably coarse Magnesian Limestone.
No. 8. 6 feet slope.
No. 9. 7 feet flesh-colored Magnesian Limestone, with chert.
No. 10. 15 feet tolerably fine gray Magnesian Limestone, with disseminated angular particles of chert.
No. 11. 20 feet slope; outcrops of coarse Magnesian Limestone.
No. 12. 10 feet gray and finely crystalline Magnesian Limestone.
No. 13. 7 feet coarse buff Magnesian Limestone, with calc. spar, and thin beds of chert interstratified.
No. 14. 27 feet coarse gray Magnesian Limestone.
No. 15. 6 feet slope to Gasconade bottoms.

Section 51.

No. 1. 20 feet slope; Sandstone and chert.
No. 2. 12 feet slope; chert; outcrops of Sandstone.
No. 3. 5 feet flesh-colored Silicious Limestone slightly Magnesian, part greenish, and alternating with coarse greenish Sandstone.
No. 4. 5 feet coarse, and some flesh-colored Magnesian Limestone.
No. 5. 3 feet coarse and somewhat greenish Sandstone.
No. 6. 1 foot gray flesh-colored coarse Limestone, with green streaks.
No. 7. 2 feet flesh-colored Limestone.
No. 8. 5 feet like No. 6; lower part Magnesian.
No. 9. 7 feet slope, fragments of above, and also some cellular chert.
No. 10. 10 feet flesh-colored, slightly Magnesian Limestone.
No. 11. 7 feet slope; fragments and outcrops of green and flesh-colored banded Limestone and flesh-colored Magnesian Limestone.
No. 12. 35 feet slope; some chert with fossils.

Chincapin and Rock Chestnut Oak, Black and Black Jack on No. 1; other small trees growing on lower slopes.

ECONOMICAL GEOLOGY.

The soils of this county may be divided as follows:

I. The Bottom Lands.

Which may also be subdivided as to their extent and depth—

First Class—Including those of the Gasconade with Big and Little Maries and the Dry Fork of Bourbeuse; producing luxuriant corn crops. Saw no crops of tobacco growing, but was informed that tobacco had been produced with success on Little Maries bottoms. The principal native growth is Burr, Laurel, Red, Rock Chestnut, Swamp

White Oak, with Shell-bark and Pig-nut Hickories, Hackberry, Black and White Walnut, American and Red Elm, Sycamore, Linden, Red-bud, Pawpaw and Vines.

Second—The soils of Little Tavern, Spring Creek, Sugar Creek, Cave Spring Creek and Dry Creek. These bottom lands produce fine crops of corn; also wheat and oats, but the latter too luxuriantly. From fifteen to forty bushels of wheat per acre are raised. In 1855, Mr. Abram Rowden raised forty-two bushels of wheat per acre on the bottoms of Little Tavern, and he informed me that a tolerable crop of corn was from thirty to fifty bushels per acre; the bottoms produce vegetables well, especially potatoes. Mr. Solomon Hawkins' (residing on Cave Spring Creek) statement with regard to the bottoms of his neighborhood was about the same. He also informed me that he even thought that this year he would raise seventy-five bushels of corn per acre.

The trees most abundant on these bottoms are Pig-nut Hickory, Chincapin Oak, Rock Chestnut Oak, with sometimes Laurel and White Oak; also Hazel, American and Red Elm, Elder, Iron-wood, Horn-beam, Red-bud, Pawpaw; and the Muscadine Grape very frequently abounds.*

II. Uplands.

The uplands may be divided into three distinct classes of lands suitable for cultivation.

First—The lands of Lane's Prairie and Galloway's Prairie, and part of the adjacent country, producing fine crops of wheat, corn, oats and tobacco. Fruit trees also seem to thrive very well, viz.: the Apple and Peach. We here find Laurel Oak, Shell-bark and Pig-nut Hickory, Mulberry, Black Walnut, Red and White Elm, Plum, Sassafras, Ash and Vines.

Second—Other timbered uplands, such as that mentioned in the geographical description of the county, based on a thinner Bluff deposit than the last, and limited in their extent. Mr. Henry Barnhart, living in the north-west part of the county, in 1855 raised twenty-five bushels of corn per acre, on upland soil resting on a Bluff deposit of two or three feet.

Third—Barrens. This soil sometimes produces well. Mr. Rowden told me that he considered the "Barrens" soil better for wheat and oats than any other lands they have. There is a very tall prairie grass growing on the Barrens, which is said to be very nutritious for

* Found a few Gum trees on Dry Creek; also a few on Cave Spring, and on Dry Creek found the Chincapin Oak three feet high bearing acorns.

stock. Mr. Thomas Anderson, residing near Vienna, informed me that during the winter of 1856–57 all his horses had to subsist on was the grass of the Barrens; he fed them none, but suffered them to range on the Barrens. When I saw them, during the month of August, they looked as fat and well as any corn-fed horses. It is seldom we find any other trees excepting Black Jack and Post Oak, always of small size and thinly scattered over the hills; occasionally, we also find a small Black Hickory. The Rosin-weed (*Silphium laciniatum*) and the Prairie Burdock (*Silphium terebinthinaceum*) are very common plants on hill slopes.

Springs.

Good springs are numerous on the Gasconade and on most of its tributaries, and also on the Little Tavern. There are not so many springs on Maries Creek. All the streams flowing into the Gasconade contain the purest waters, both cool and refreshing, that could be desired. The Gasconade, itself, is one of the clearest streams I ever beheld.

Mill Sites.

Spring Creek, and several other small streams flowing into the Gasconade, afford good mill sites. The small stream on which Kinsey's mill is situated, in T. 40, R. 8, W., presents fine localities for manufacturing operations. There is a carding mill not over a quarter of a mile above the grist mill, yet it does not affect the supply of water for the other mill in the least. The stream is very bold and rapid, and many more mills might be built on it without any injury to each other. Little Tavern has also some fine mill sites.

BUILDING MATERIALS.

Stone.—There is an abundance of good stone for building in this county. The lower beds of the Second Magnesian Limestone make strong and durable masonry, and some of them, when not too silicious, are excellent material for making quick-lime. They take long to burn, are tolerably hard to slack, but when made into mortar become very hard within a few weeks.* The cellular Silicious rock, often closely resembling a breccia, at the lower part of the Second Magnesian Limestone, when found of suitable dimensions, would probably afford an excellent material for mill stones.

A fragment of indurated Sandstone or quartzite was shown me as making a good scythe stone. I supposed it to belong to the Second

* The last is the result of my own observation on the Pacific Railroad.

Sandstone, as it resembled it very much, and occupied a position which would induce such a conclusion; but there are also some beds in the lower part of the Second Magnesian very similar in appearance. The Second Sandstone is a good building stone.

Grind-stones. — I saw a grind-stone that had been made of Second Sandstone, and was informed that it was very well adapted for sharpening coarse-edged tools.

The Third Magnesian Limestone I suppose would make an excellent building material, as many of its beds break freely under the hammer, and it also seems to possess qualities of durability; but I did not find that it had been used at all for building purposes. The reason, probably, is because it generally occurs capped by other formations more accessible.

Sands. — The Gasconade River affords quantities of clean, sharp sand, much used for making mortar.

Good clay for bricks is not as abundant in this county as in some others; there is frequently too much gravel commingled; yet there is much of it to be had.

It is probable that some of the whiter, softer beds of the Second Sandstone, as those found on Spring Creek, would afford a good material for making glass.

Timber. — Gasconade and Maries bottoms afford excellent timber for most building purposes.

ROAD MATERIALS.

There being no macadamized roads in this county, I had no opportunity of testing any of the several rocks as road materials, but I would suppose that the extensive chert beds of the Third Magnesian Limestone formation would afford an excellent material for paving, as the chert seems to possess the hardness and durability so desirable.

MINERALS.

Sulphate of Baryta was found in only one locality, in Sec. 20, T. 41, R. 11, W., in irregular fragments of a massive form.

METALLIC ORES.

Iron ore is abundant in this county, occurring as a Hematite, and also as a Sulphuret. The Sulphuret is more abundant, and is found in many places in this county. In Sections 28 and 30 of T. 38, R. 9, W., Sulphuret of Iron is found in large masses in ravines, the exterior often changed from a Sulphuret to an Oxyd. Large masses of the same kind of ore are also found on Pilot Knob. The Hematite was found in large masses in Sec. 5, T. 39, R. 11, W., associated with very red ferruginous clay. Iron ore is found at Vienna. In Sec. 2, T. 40, R. 9, the oxyd is found associated with Iron pyrites and Copper ore. The mine had been explored, but, proving unprofitable, had been abandoned. In Sec. 30, T. 41, R. 7, the Hematite and "red chalk" are found at the same place, and I was told that the latter had been used very successfully as a dye-stuff for cloth.

I found a few fragments of good Iron ore on Bourbeuse, and on the hills between that stream and the Gasconade, and also east of Lane's Prairie, on Pea Vine branch.

LEAD.

In south-east quarter of Sec. 20, T. 41, R. 11 W., found fragments of Lead ore in the bed of a branch, along with Sulphate of Baryta; was informed that pieces as large as a hen's egg had been picked up. Then I was informed that only a few pounds had been found; saw no rocks outcropping, but found Second Magnesian Limestone on the hill-top, at an elevation of seventy-five feet above the bed of the branch.

In N. W. quarter of Sec. 34, T. 40, R. 11, Mr. Chrisman had found Lead in a vertical opening between two walls of Second Magnesian Limestone. The walls are about four feet apart, and the fissure runs nearly east and west, a little N. E. and S. W. Lead occurs in small cubes with Oxide of Iron. I was told that the Iron ore was found in two thin vertical sheets, with Lead between. Ore to the amount of 100 pounds had been gotten out, but the mine was not worked at the time I visited it. The reason given was that the yield seemed too small.

In N. E. Sec. 8, T. 39, R. 9, Lead has been found. I saw some good Iron ore, in very small fragments, at that place, but found no Lead. The rocks found there were fragments of cellular Buhr-stone, with Second Sandstone lower down, in a neighboring ravine. Was informed that there had been quantities of Lead ore found on Spring Creek, but on one could show me the locality.

ANTIQUITIES.

Indian mounds are found on the summits of the highest bluffs of the Gasconade River. Most of them in this county are erected on bare, rocky bluffs, and constructed solely of stones piled around human remains. It seems that these "sons of the forest" had a fondness for burying their dead on the summits of the highest hills they could find, and generally in sight of some large water-course.

COLUMBIA, MO, *December 8, 1857.*

Section from East to West, through middle of Maries County.

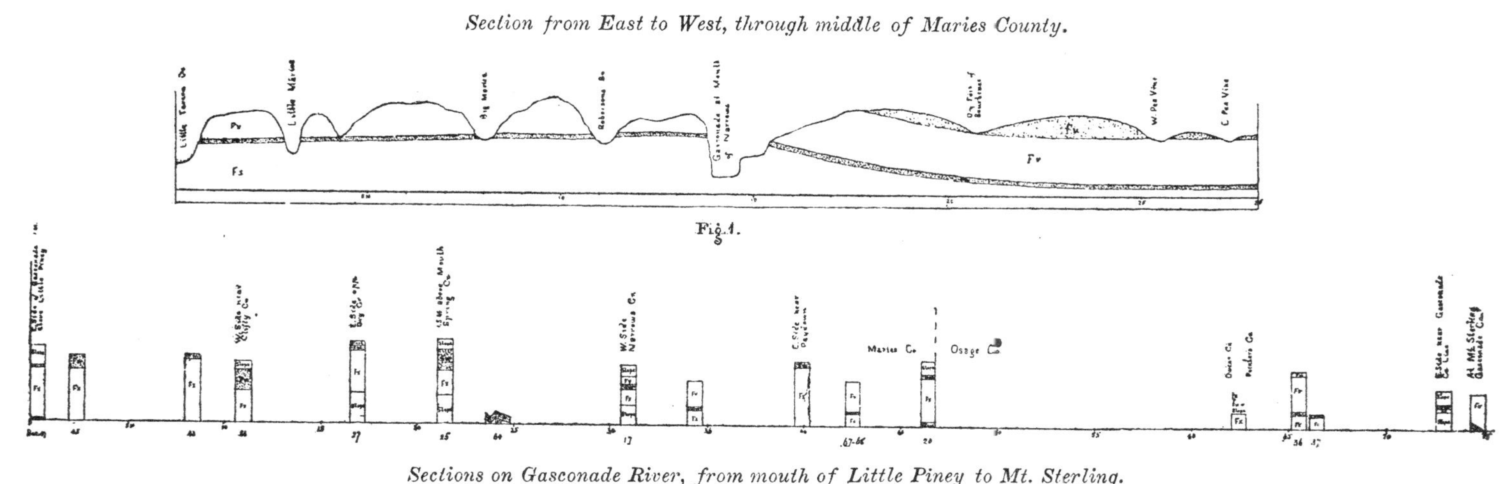

Fig. 1.

Sections on Gasconade River, from mouth of Little Piney to Mt. Sterling.

CHAPTER II.

OSAGE COUNTY.

BY G. C. BROADHEAD.

GENERAL DESCRIPTION.

Osage county is bounded on the north by the Missouri River, which washes its borders for 24 miles, separating it from Callaway county; on the east by Gasconade county; on the south by Maries; on the west by Miller and Cole. The Osage River, one of the largest tributaries of the Missouri, winds along the greater part of its western border; the Gasconade, one of our clearest streams, meanders through the south-eastern part of the county, in a general north-east direction. The other principal streams are, Maries Creek, in the western, L'Ours Creek, the center, and Bailey's Creek, the eastern part of the county. These streams cut deeply into the formations; have wide bottoms, high bluffs, and the county is very broken. The Missouri River bottoms are often a mile or more in width; the Gasconade bottoms about a quarter of a mile, and those of the Osage are also quite wide.

There are no prairies of any great extent in this county. In southern part of county, near Maries Creek, and east of the Gasconade, near Third Creek and Mistaken Creek, there are "Barrens." The county is mostly heavily timbered.

GEOLOGY.

QUATERNARY DEPOSITS.

Alluvium is found on all the river and creek bottoms. It is more fully developed and deeper on Missouri bottoms. There are probably nearly 11,000 acres of Missouri bottom lands in this county.

The tributaries of the Missouri are often difficult and dangerous to cross at their mouths, owing to the deep deposits of mud left by the Missouri River at its annual spring rise. The alluvial deposits on the Osage and Gasconade Rivers are gravelly. The Osage bottoms in Secs. 28 and 33, T. 43, R. 11 W., consist of two terraces—the upper being 10 feet above the lower. On the lower terrace, at about 15 feet above low water, a marly bed was exposed, abounding in decomposing fluviatile shells.

The *Bluff* occurs in nearly every part of the county; it is rather thin in the south, but is deeper near the central portion; observed it 15 feet deep at Linn, and well developed along the St. Louis road. It is thicker on the Missouri bluff; observed it 25 feet thick on Bailey's Creek. Where the Bluff is deep, we find generally a heavy growth of White Oak, Pawpaw, Linden, Hazel, Sugar-tree, Ash, Pignut, Hickory and Red Oak abounding on the richest soils, based on the "Bluff." The "Bluff" reposes uncomfortably on the Second Magnesian Limestone, on the Missouri River hills.

In many places where the "Bluff" thins out, a *Local Drift* of mostly chert is exposed. This is particularly the case near the Osage and Gasconade—particularly east of the latter.

LOWER SILURIAN.

The rocks of this formation in the county all belong to the Magnesian Limestone Series, and may be referred to the Calciferous Sandrock of the New York Geologists, and include the Saccharoidal Sandstone, Second Magnesian Limestone, Second Sandstone and Third Magnesian Limestone.

F. *u.* SACCHAROIDAL SANDSTONE.

This formation is found only in the eastern part of the county, capping most of the hills as far west as Linn and Chamois. Farther west it was not observed. It is 10 feet thick on Galloway's Prairie. It abounds between Galloway's Prairie and the head of Third Creek, but is not again seen in any large mass until we cross the Gasconade and reach the interior of T. 43, R. 7 W. About Sec. 28, T. 43, R. 7 W., it is 10 feet thick. It crops out near the summit of the ridges, between Bailey's Creek and the Gasconade River. Mr. Price observed it 25 feet thick near the head of Bailey's Creek. It is generally a white, soft, pure Sandstone.

F. *v*. Second Magnesian Limestone.

This formation is found in every part of the county. It is the highest rock in Ranges 9 and 10. Between the Osage and Little Maries Creek the lower thick beds, capped by the lowest Cotton rock, are the highest strata, as shown by the following section, taken on Little Maries Creek, three miles above its mouth:

Section 17.

No. 1. 15 feet cherty slope.

No. 2. 15 feet of Cotton rock, the lower part having, on the upper surface, a weather-worn, curled appearance.

No. 3. 95 feet outcrops of Second Magnesian Limestone; the upper part coarse buff; 20 feet below the top is a thin bed of coarse gray Sandstone; lower down is a coarse, ashy-gray cellular Magnesian Limestone; eight feet from bottom is 2 feet outcrop of chert, and at bottom is a dark ash-colored Magnesian Limestone.

These beds are also the highest rocks between Gasconade River and Third Creek. Descending the Gasconade the strata dip, and below Mt. Sterling no older rocks than the Second Magnesian Limestone are seen. Along the Missouri bluffs it is found from their base to their summit, sometimes capped by the Bluff formation, and, as observed along the Pacific Railroad, the strata rise and fall by gentle undulations.

The upper beds seen along the Missouri River consist of from 60 to 70 feet of Silicious Magnesian Limestone, with beds of Calcareous Sandstone, and bands of Silicious oolites. These beds often are seen projecting out near the upper part of the bluffs in bold, perpendicular escarpments. Toward the lower part I was enabled to trace out Silicious strata, containing disseminated green specks, sometimes oolitic, and often resembling a conglomerate; sometimes containing nodules of decomposing chert, and some nodules resembling Cotton rock — the whole a rock of fine texture. Beneath the last is a bed of Calcareous Sandstone, of a light buff color, sometimes porous, and very easily traced along the bluffs. It was often seen projecting from the bluffs, proving it to be a very durable rock. These beds all lie beneath those of Sec. 17, quoted above. The lower beds are often concealed by debris from those above.

The following sections of the Missouri River bluffs were made along the Pacific Railroad:

Section 50—Three-fourths of a mile from east county line.

No. 1. 10 feet bluff.
No. 2. 3 feet Magnesian Limestone, Cotton rock and chert.
No. 3. 4 feet coarse white Sandstone; some buff specks.
No. 4. 8 feet Silicious Magnesian Limestone, like No. 6.
No. 5. 8 feet drab Magnesian Limestone (Cotton rock.)
No. 6. 4 feet Silicious Magnesian Limestone; brown, with black specks; contains irregular deposits of chert.
No. 7. 8 feet coarse Magnesian Limestone; upper part has cells of gray pulverulent powder; lower part gray, with numerous green specks disseminated.
No. 8. 10 feet Cotton rock.
No. 9. 10 feet irregularly bedded buff and drab Magnesian Limestone, with round chert concretions at bottom, and green shale partings.
No. 10. 10 feet slope; tumbling rock from above.
No. 11. 2 feet chert bed.
No. 12. 7 feet Cotton rock; green shaly partings between the beds.
No. 13. 2 feet drab Magnesian Limestone, with cells containing white powder; green shaly partings between the beds.

One and three-fourths mile west we find No. 3 of Sec. 50, 20 feet above the railroad. Section here is

Section 52.

No. 1. 30 feet slope.
No. 2. 2 feet thin beds of Cotton rock and Magnesian Limestone.
No. 3. 5 feet chert and silicious beds, with thin beds of Sandstone.
No. 4. 4 feet Sandstone, like No. 3 of Sec. 50.
No. 5. 20 feet Cotton rock and Magnesian Limestone, with thin beds of chert.
No. 6. 8 feet slope to Missouri bottoms.

A quarter of a mile east of Chamois we have

Section 53.

No. 2. 25 feet thick-bedded Magnesian Limestone, interstratified with chert; has small cavities, some a foot in diameter.
No. 3. Thin bedded Cotton rock and green shale, with some irregular chert beds interstratified.
No. 4. 4 feet very irregular bed of Cotton rock and chert.
No. 5. 20 feet outcrops of buff Silicious Limestone, interstratified with chert and green shale.
No. 6. 2 feet green specked, gray Silicious Limestone.
No. 7. 6 feet silicious rock, with some chalcedonic particles and part oolitic; contains some decomposing cherty nodules.
No. 8. 4 feet silico-calcareous Sandstone, like Sec. 50–3.
No. 9. 50 feet slope to bottoms.

Section 54—Just west of Chamois.

No. 2. 15 feet Cotton rock, chert and green shale.
No. 3. 15 feet Silicious rock and some chert; lower part passing into a Sandstone; Sec. 53–8.
No. 4. 10 feet slope.
No. 5. 15 feet Cotton rock and cellular Magnesian Limestone.
No. 6. 12 feet slope.

A quarter of a mile west, the lower part of No. 3 is 20 feet above the bottoms. A half mile west, the rocks are 25 feet higher, and are nearly horizontal for the next one and a-half miles.

Section 55—A quarter of a mile east of Deer Creek.

No. 1. 40 feet yellowish buff Cotton rock near top; below is Silicious Magnesian Limestone, interstratified with chert and thin partings of green shale.
No. 2. 25 feet Silicious rock and chert.
No. 3. 2 feet Silicious rock, like Sec. 53, No. 7.
No. 4. 2 feet.
No. 5. 3 feet Sandstone.
No. 6. 110 feet slope to Missouri bottoms; on slope is gray Silicious Limestone, with numerous minute oolitic cells; some are empty and some contain vitreous quartz.

Section 56—East of St. Aubert. Indian mound on top.

No. 2. 25 feet Silicious Magnesian Limestone.
No. 3. 3 feet green-specked Silicious Limestone.
No. 4. 2 feet slope.
No. 5. 3 feet Silicious rock.
No. 6. 4 feet Calcareous Sandstone.
No. 7. 8 feet Silicious rock and chert.
No. 8. 100 feet to railroad, and 20 feet more to Missouri River.

A little further west found Cotton rock below No. 7, and Magnesian Limestone and Cotton rock below it.

One and a-half miles above Buchanan, No. 7 of last section is 90 feet above the railroad.

Section 58—A quarter of a mile further west.

No. 2. 10 feet chert, Silicious rock, Magnesian Limestone and Cotton rock.
No. 3. 2 feet blue shales.
No. 4. 5 feet chert and Cotton rock.
No. 5. 2 feet Silicious rock.
No. 6. 8 feet bluish Cotton rock, with shaly partings.
No. 7. 2 feet Silicious Magnesian Limestone.
No. 8. 7 feet blue Cotton rock.

Section 59—At L'Ours Creek Station.

No. 1. 5 feet Cotton rock, with chert marked like septaria.
No. 2. 2 feet green shales.
No. 3. 8 feet Cotton rock, interstratified with chert.
No. 4. 6 feet Cotton rock, with bluish spots.
No. 5. 3 feet Magnesian Limestone.
No. 6. 2 feet chert bed.
No. 7. 11 feet Cotton rock, with spheroids of Sulphuret of Iron; Cotton rock sometimes blue.
No. 8. 5 feet mottled gray Magnesian Limestone, with irregular and round concretions of chert.

Section 60—Three-quarters of a mile above L'Ours Creek.

No. 1. 60 feet Sandstone and Magnesian Limestone.
No. 2. 2 feet Sandstone; Sec. 55, No. 5.
No. 3. 45 feet slope to railroad.

A half mile east the Sandstone is 25 feet above the railroad, and green shale at the railroad.

From Sec. 60 for three miles west observed the Sandstone of Sec. 60, No. 3, preserving about same horizontal position as Sec. 60. At Bonnot's Mill observed a heavy-bedded gray cellular Magnesian Limestone near base of hill, resembling No. 8 of Sec. 59.

Section 62—Just west of Bonnot's Mill.

No. 1. 35 feen "Bluff" slope.
No. 2. 66 feet of gray cellular Magnesian Limestone, with some chert.
No. 3. 4 feet of Sandstone; Sec. 55–5.
No. 4. 33 feet.
No. 5. 2 feet Silicious Magnesian Limestone.
No. 6. 16 feet slope; outcrops of Cotton rock.
No. 7. 25 feet Cotton rock to railroad. The lower 10 feet coarse heavy-bedded Magnesian Limestone.

Strata continue nearly level for two miles west. Three and a-half miles west, and near the Osage, we have 180 feet of Magnesian Limestone, interstratified with Silicious rock, chert, Cotton rock and green shale.

On Osage bluffs, a quarter of a mile north of Caddy's Creek, observed 25 feet of very thick-bedded gray cellular Magnesian Limestone, some Silicious beds near the upper part. The lower bed is about 15 feet above the "bottoms." The thickness of this formation on the Missouri River bluffs is from 180 to 200 feet, and from all the data I could obtain its total thickness in the county is from 230 to 240 feet.

Fossils were obtained at only two localities.

Buhr-Stone Beds.

Lying at the base of the Second Magnesian Limestone, and over the Second Sandstone, are found silicious beds, generally cellular, which very much resemble the French Buhr-stone. The cells are somewhat oval or spheroidal in shape, their general size about that of an ordinary bean—some are larger and some much smaller—and, under a magnifier, their interior appears as if studded with minute quartz crystals.

The exact thickness of these beds could not be ascertained, but we may assume them to be at least six feet, and probably much more. These rocks were generally found in tumbling masses overlying those in place below.

Three-quarters of a mile south-east of Westphalia, the following Section:

No. 1. 50 feet slope; in upper part is cellular chert.
No. 2. 10 feet slope; irregular masses of Sandstone and chert.
No. 3. 8 feet Sandstone (Second), whitish.
No. 4. 30 feet masses of Sandstone, cellular chert, and outcrops of blue chert.
No. 5. 50 feet outcrops of Third Magnesian Limestone, flesh-colored; much chert mingled.
No. 6. 15 feet slope to water in Maries Creek.

This section indicates the "Buhr" Stone beds as beds of passage to the Second Sandstone, if they may not be even members of the Second Sandstone.

F. *w.*—Second Sandstone.

On the Osage, this formation first appears near the water's edge, one mile below the mouth of Lake Branch; gradually rising, it becomes the highest rock near the mouth of Prophet's Creek. Eastward, it occupies a lower horizon. On Maries creek, it first appears a mile above its mouth. It continues gradually rising southward to Westphalia; it then dips to the south, and near the south county line is found very near the base of the bluffs. The head-waters of Sugar Creek repose in its beds, but lower down the creek it appears high in the bluffs. We observed it, on the Gasconade, capping the Third Magnesian Limestone, and at Mt. Sterling it dips beneath the Second Magnesian Limestone.

It is generally overlaid by masses of Buhr-stone. On the Osage, it was observed ten feet in thickness. It is generally a coarse white or buff-tinged.

Fossils were found in chert of lower part of No. 4 of section 5. This chert occupies a position above the Third Magnesian Limestone, and is probably of same geological age as the Second Sandstone.

F. *x.*—Third Magnesian Limestone.

This formation is thicker and better developed on the Osage River. Below the mouth of Lake Branch, it does not appear; here it is first seen at the base of the bluffs. Rapidly rising for eight miles, we find it more than one hundred feet thick, often forming perpendicular escarpments of one hundred feet hight, composed of very thick beds, often from four to ten feet in thickness. Its greatest exposed thickness on the Osage is one hundred and thirty feet, and its maximum thickness in the county about one hundred and eighty feet. It is found on Maries Creek from near Westphalia southward, and on the Gasconade, from south county line northward to Mt. Sterling, where it dips beneath the Second Sandstone. Its characteristics are similar to the corresponding beds in Maries county—its thick beds being generally flesh-colored. No fossils were found in it.

ECONOMICAL GEOLOGY.

BUILDING MATERIAL.

Most of the Sandstones afford an excellent building material. That interstratified with the Second Magnesian Limestone furnishes a very good article. The light-colored, soft Magnesian Limestones, or "Cotton rock," are easily worked with the chisel, but do not often possess durability. They are generally too easily affected by frost; from one winter's exposure, it will often be completely reticulated with cracks. The Limestones, more granular and silicious, furnish a good building stone. Especially may this be said of the Third Magnesian. The thick beds of Third Magnesian Limestone found along the Osage, of a beautiful flesh-color or gray, break freely with a somewhat even fracture, and will doubtless be useful for building purposes at some future day. Whilst the Third Magnesian Limestone is even bedded, has no shale beds and is very durable, the Second Magnesian Limestone, on the other hand, is very irregularly and roughly bedded, often containing many chert concretions and shale beds, and contains but few beds suitable for building.

Lime.—It is often difficult to get agood stone for lime; still some of the beds of Second Magnesian Limestone furnish a very good article. Some of the hard, close-grained Magnesian Limestone beds near the base of the series, when they can be burned into lime, make a very superior mortar, which, when exposed, soon becomes very hard.

Other Building Material.—The "Bluff" formation affords a good clay for brick. The chert, so abundant everywhere, is an excellent material for "gravel roads."

Clays.—In S. W. quarter Sec. 17, T. 41, R. 11 W., is a paint bed of Red Clay. It is found on a gentle hill-slope, associated with iron ore. Mr. Price collected Red Clay in S. W. of N. E. Sec. 20, T. 44, R. 7 W. It was dug from a pit about fifty feet up hill and one hundred and twenty-five feet below the top. Large masses of Saccharoidal Sandstone are seen all along the upper slope. This clay has been successfully used in painting. A half mile north of this place, there is an extensive bed of White Clay, which is much used for white-washing. Near the last is a bed of variegated Red and Purple Clay.

MINERALS.

Iron Ore.—Both the Sulphuret and Hematite ores occur at many places in the county. The principal localities where the former was found are: In Secs. 33 and 34, T. 43, R. 7 W.; in Secs. 4 and 5, T. 41, R. 7 W., and at Rich Fountain. In Sec. 15, T. 44, R. 7 W., we found a quantity of the Sulphuret in upper portion of Second Magnesian Limestone. It was also found on Little Maries Creek, two miles above its mouth. Both Sulphuret and Hematite ores are found in S. E. quarter Sec. 34, T. 43, R. 7 W. Brown Hematite, of stalactitic form, lies loose on Second Sandstone slope, in N. W. Sec. 20, T. 42, R. 11 W., on the Osage River. In S. W. quarter Sec. 17, T. 41, R. 11 W., is a pit of deep red clay in which iron ore, sulphuret of zinc and quartz crystals, including amethyst, are found. On the hill above, I observed Second Magnesian Limestone capped with loose, thin layers of Sandstone.

Mr. Price found considerable quantities of iron ore in Secs. 7 and 12, T. 43, Rs. 8 and 9 W., forming a breccia with angular fragments of chert. He also found large quantities of the same kind of ore in southern part of T. 44, R. 7. "Jackets" mine, in Sec. 34, T. 43, R. 8, was first examined by the projectors of the Meramec Iron Works, with the view of opening works there. The ore occurs in Second Magnesian Limestone.

Mr. Price's section shows:

No. 1. 50 feet slope, with large bed of iron ore.
No. 2. 5 feet Sandstone.
No. 3. 75 feet slope, on which are many large masses of iron ore.

Lead has been discovered near junction of Second Sandstone and Third Magnesian Limestone, near middle of Sec. 17, T. 41, R. 11 W. Also, just north of Westphalia.

SOILS.

The richest soils are those of the bottom lands, which, considered also as to their extent, may be further subdivided into: 1st. The Missouri, Osage, Gasconade and Maries Rivers, with portions of Bailey's Creek, L'Ours Creek, on which are grown luxuriant crops of corn, vegetables and melons. The principal trees are, on Missouri bottoms, Ash, Box Elder, Black and White Walnut, Sycamore, Hackberry, Cottonwood, Shell-bark and Pig-nut Hickory, Burr, Red and Pin Oak, Laurel Oak, Pawpaw, Buckeye, American Elm and Grape-vines. The trees sometimes grow to a very large size, Cottonwoods often seven feet in diameter, and very tall and straight. The Cottonwood furnishes the principal source of fuel to steamboats, and many cords can be cut from a single tree. The Burr Oak also grows very large, and makes a very tough and durable timber. Grape-vines were noticed eight or ten inches in diameter at lower part.

Nearly the same kinds of timber were observed on the Osage, but Cottonwood and Pin Oak are rather scarce. White Oak and Swamp White Oak abound on second bottoms of the Osage. Cottonwood was not found on the Gasconade bottoms.

Dr. Thornton, living in Sec. 21, T. 43, R. 11 W., informed me that his corn on the first or lowest bottom would yield an average of twenty barrels per acre, and the second bottoms thirteen barrels. Mr. Clark cut, on the same place, three tons of hay per acre off of second bottoms.

These soils are very deep, and based on a deep alluvium.

The second class of bottom lands includes those adjacent to the smaller streams. The yield of most crops is good.

Second Class—Uplands.

First—Those based on a deep bluff deposit. This probably includes a very large portion of the uplands in the county. It is well developed in T. 41, R. 7 W., T. 42, R. 10, T. 43, R. 8 and 9, and part of R. 10, the western part of T. 42, R. 11, and most of the hills for a few miles from the Missouri River, with the hills near the Osage as far up as Lisle. The principal native trees are White Oak, Scarlet Oak, Red Oak, Spanish Oak, Black Oak, and where the "Bluff" formation is deepest, as near the Missouri, are found Hazel, Linden, Sugar tree, Pawpaw, Ash, Pig-nut Hickory, Shell-bark Hickory and vines.

This soil produces pretty good crops of corn, potatoes, turnips, etc. Mr. Clark, in Sec. 28, T. 43, R. 11 W., raised, in 1855, thirty bushels of wheat per acre, without estimating what was wasted; he also stated that oats will yield thirty to fifty bushels per acre.

This soil seems well adapted to fruits, especially the vine, which flourishes in all its luxuriance. When properly cultivated, it yields an abundant grape crop, from which is made a delicious and refreshing wine.

Second—Includes the poorer soils, where the "Bluff" is thin, and soil has intermingled gravel. It is confined principally to the southern tier of townships, most of T. 42, R. 7 W., hills near the Gasconade and in T. 44, R. 7, and part of T. 45, R. 7 W., the country between Maries and Sugar Creek and westward near the Osage, besides occasional tracts in other parts of the county. The principal growth is stunted Post Oak and Black Jack on the barrens, Post Oak, Black Oak and Black Hickory and White Oak on other lands.

This description of country is poorly adapted to general farming, but the Grape flourishes well on rocky slopes. The soil of the "barrens" is often quite sandy. The "barrens" mostly occur in the southern part of the county.

TIMBER.

There is an abundant supply of good White Oak, Burr Oak, Hickory, Walnut, Sycamore and Cottonwood in the county.

Good *Springs* are often seen. The Gasconade furnishes a never-failing supply of water for milling purposes.

ANTIQUITIES.

Indian mounds are often found on the highest bluffs, erected as monuments over their dead. On the hill east of St. Aubert Station several have been explored. They are about six feet high. Among the remains exhumed I saw some fragments of skull bones and a clay pipe. Several other pipes and some stone beads were said to have been found.

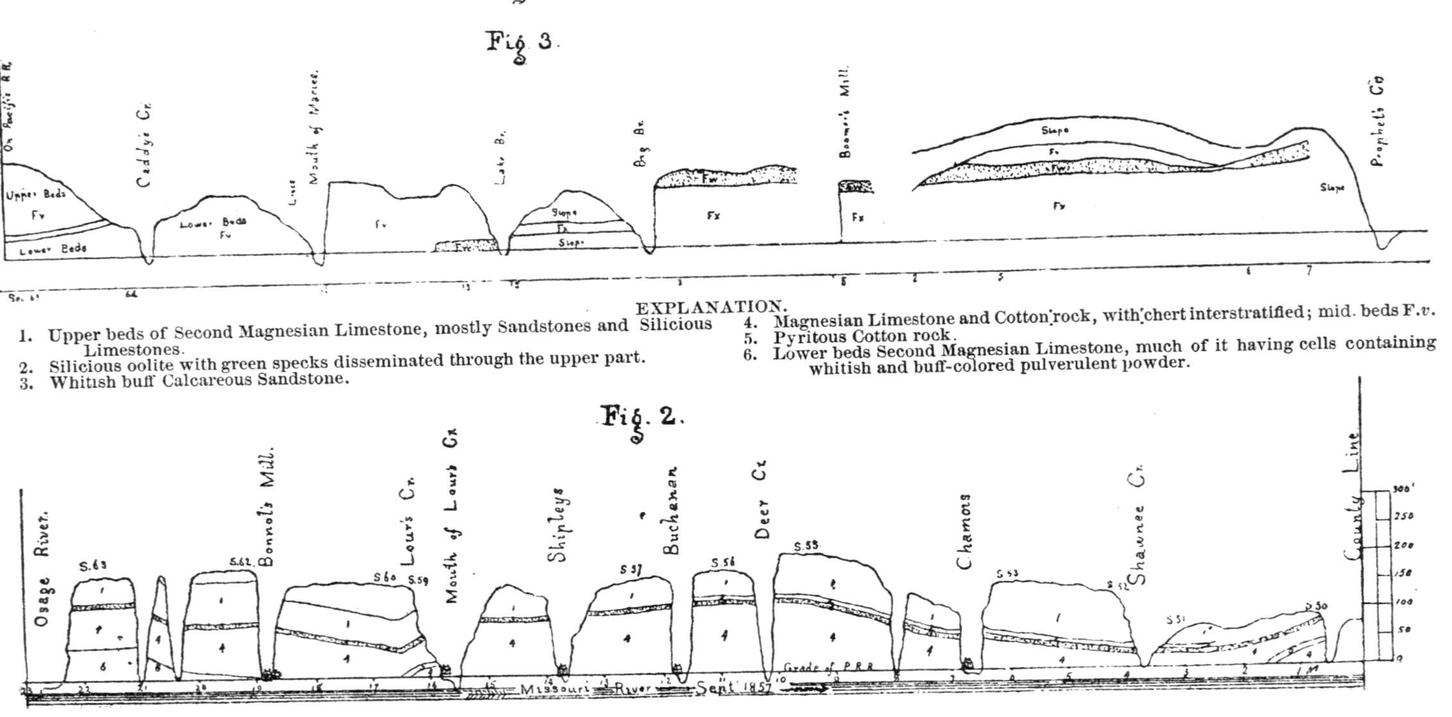

Fig 3.

EXPLANATION.

1. Upper beds of Second Magnesian Limestone, mostly Sandstones and Silicious Limestones.
2. Silicious oolite with green specks disseminated through the upper part.
3. Whitish buff Calcareous Sandstone.
4. Magnesian Limestone and Cotton rock, with chert interstratified; mid. beds F.v.
5. Pyritous Cotton rock.
6. Lower beds Second Magnesian Limestone, much of it having cells containing whitish and buff-colored pulverulent powder.

Fig. 2.

Geological Section along the Pacific R.R. through Osage County

CHAPTER III.

WARREN COUNTY.

BY G. C. BROADHEAD.

GEOGRAPHY, TOPOGRAPHY, HYDROGRAPHY.

Warren county is bounded on the north by Montgomery and Lincoln counties; on the east by Lincoln and St. Charles; on the south by the Missouri River, separating it from Franklin, and on the west by Montgomery county.

It has an area of about 406 square miles, or 11 townships and 10 sections. It occupies an important geographical position, being traversed in a somewhat devious south-east and north-west course by the main dividing ridge separating the waters flowing into the Mississippi from those flowing to the Missouri. This ridge enters the county in the north part of Sec. 17, T. 47, R. 3 W., winding south-east and east to the south-east of Sec. 24; it then passes nearly southward to Sec. 6, T 46, R, 2 W.; thence passing eastward for a short distance, it bends off to the northward to north-east of Sec. 28, T. 47, R. 2 W.; thence nearly eastward to south-west corner of Sec. 28, T. 47, R. 1 W.; from which place it deviously bends, preserving a south-east course to south-east of Sec. 24, T. 46, R. 1 W, where it leaves the county.

We thus perceive that this ridge separates the county into two unequal portions, the characteristics of which are different. About one-fourth lies to the north and three-fourths south of the "divide."

The northern portion is a little more than one-half prairie land, mostly gently undulating. None of the hills are high, being not over a hundred feet in hight on the larger streams, and away from them the slopes are very gentle, particularly on the prairies.

The largest and most beautiful prairie in this county is that near Camp Branch; occasionally a wet spot or pond is found, around which are clustered a few shrubs, including *Amorpha fruticosa* and *Ceph-*

alanthus occidentalis. The other prairies are small and gently undulating.

The woodlands on these northern slopes are generally well timbered, the soil sustaining a heavy growth, of mostly Black, White, Scarlet and Red Oak and Hickory, with some Post Oak. This land is very well adapted to growing Tobacco.

The slopes on Peruque Creek are more gentle than those of any other stream, being often so much so that it is difficult to perceive the line of demarcation between hill and bottom land. The highest bluff measured on this creek was at the county line, where I found it to be 93 feet. Two miles up stream the bluffs are not over 50 feet high, and further up become less.

The hills and valleys of Indian Camp, Big Creek and Camp Creek are very much alike, (the streams cutting through similar geological formations,) but Indian Camp bottoms are wider than the other two. The hills preserve a corresponding elevation on each stream, rather low toward the head, and with gentle slopes, becoming more abrupt near the county line, where they are about 75 feet high.

The valleys on Camp Creek toward its head, and for several miles, are often a half mile wide; as we follow down stream they diminish very much in width, and in the middle of T. 48 are narrowed down to about 200 yards wide. In T. 49 they again widen, and the slopes are more gentle.

On South Bear Creek the bottoms are mostly narrow, bluffs steep, and attain an elevation of 100 to 130 feet.

Nearly the same remarks would apply to Massey's as to Lost Creek. Running southward they cut deep into the older rocks, and a few miles from their origin the hills are as much as 200 feet high; the bottoms are also narrow, being not more than 200 or 300 feet wide. Passing down stream, the hills increase in hight, and the scenery becomes wildly beautiful and picturesque. Within about three miles of the Missouri, the hills are as much as 375 feet high; they then gradually decrease in hight toward the river; the bottoms become wider, being as much as a quarter of a mile wide.

The bottoms of Smith's Creek are not very wide, but there is generally on one side a long, gentle slope, covered with a deep "Bluff" formation, and supporting a good productive soil.

The bottoms of Charette are narrow and hills high, until we get within six miles of its mouth, where the bottoms widen. Those of Dry Fork are also wide — the second bottom often a quarter of a mile or more in width. Three or four miles above its mouth they become narrow.

The valleys of Tuque Creek for seven miles from its mouth expand into a wide second bottom or terrace, covered with a heavy growth of timber.

The Missouri bottoms, from the east county line to the mouth of Clay's branch, are generally more than a mile wide, and contain 23½ square miles, or 15,149 acres. Above this we find the river hugging the bluffs for about six miles, to the mouth of Loutre slough.

The bottoms of Loutre Island, lying in this county, amount to about 4.87 square miles or 3,120 acres, thus showing of Missouri River bottom lands a total of (in this county) 28.54 square miles, or 18,269 acres.

Most of the smaller streams flowing into the Missouri, after they reach the "Bottoms," seem to take an eastern or south-eastern course along the bluffs, often for a mile or so, and, flowing on sluggishly, are lost in swamps and lakes. With regard to the bluffs on the streams running southward, we find that for several miles from the Missouri River bottoms they are all on the east bank, and on the west side are found gentle slopes, with a deep "Bluff formation."

The depth cut into the varions geological formations by these natural water-ways, of course very much affects the topography of the country lying between; for we indeed find the Missouri hills very broken, as we find the country north of the main "water-shed" very gently undulating, and generally suitable for the production of most crops peculiar to this country, while the former is sometimes too rocky and broken to admit of successful cultivation. Although the hills are high and broken, still many of them are not so much so as to prevent their cultivation. These ridges often extend into broad "flats," on which we sometimes find small ponds. They are generally well timbered, with a growth of White Oak and Post Oak, with some Black Oak and Hickory.

The hills near the Missouri are very heavily timbered. The whole county lying south of the "Divide" is well timbered, and Warren may be said to be as well timbered as any county in the State.

GEOLOGY.

QUATERNARY.

The Quaternary deposits in this county include *Alluvium*, *Bottom Prairie*, *Bluff* and *Drift*.

Alluvium.—The deposits in this county belonging to this formation comprise soils, pebbles and sand, clays, vegetable mold and stalactites and stalagmites. It is best developed as an extensive deposit on the Missouri River, where its characteristics are about the same as described in the Second Annual Report. Pebbles abound in all the streams; beautiful stalactites are found in a cave two miles north of Marthasville. The soil in most of this county is of a dark color; red plastic Clay, very ferruginous, is found on hill-tops, near head of Ritter's Branch, and on some of the hills near Lost Creek; also, on some of the Charette hills. On Tuque Creek all the soil seems impregnated with ferruginous matter, imparting to it a very red tinge, which is apparent at a distance. This is probably owing to a disintegration of the Red Sandstone, (which is here found on the hill-tops,) and a separation therefrom of the ferruginous matter. Some of it may be derived from the Black River beds, and some from the Chouteau Limestone, for they all contain ferruginous matter.

Some quite pretty land shells are found on the slopes of the Trenton Limestone. Fresh-water shells are not very abundant. In Camp Creek and South Bear Creek are found univalves, and a very few *Unionidae*. Cyclas was found in Camp Creek, Unio and Anadonta in Charette. A few shells in some of the other streams.

Bottom Prairie.—On Lake Creek we have the following Section, which is probably older than the Alluvium:

No. 1. 1 foot Soil and Subsoil; upper 6 inches very dark.
No. 2. 2 feet yellowish mottled brown Clay.
No. 3. 3 feet brown Iron streaked Clay.
No. 4. 4 feet dark Clay, interstratified with Sand, some Iron streaks.
No. 5. 6 feet beds of stratified brown Sand, lower part very dark.
No. 6. Blue Clay.

Bluff.—The upper part of this formation is scarcely recognizable in the northern part of the county, although it is probable that there are a few feet capping the older "Bluff" in most places. But in the southern part of the county, it imparts a character to the country; it is here deep and well developed. There is a strip of country parallel to the Missouri bluffs, and varying in width from one to 2½ miles, and extending the whole length of the county, covered with a deposit which will probably average ten feet in depth, and supporting a heavy growth of fine timber, including Sugar, Ash, White Oak, Scarlet Oak, Laurel Oak, Red Oak, Dog-wood, Red and American Elm, Red-bud, Common and Shell-bark Hickory, Pig-nut Hickory, Pawpaw and Vines.

In western part of T. 45, R. 2 W., there is exposed, on a small branch, 21 feet of "Bluff," composed mostly of brownish-red Clay near the top, becoming more red below; the lower 8 feet seems to gradually become of a deeper red, especially near the bottom. The lower four or five feet is sandy, and is nearly all Sand at bottom.

Prairie Clays.—These Clays are scarcely recognized at all in the southern part of the county, but in the northern half are very extensive and deep. They are found on the head-waters of all the streams flowing both ways from the main water-shed, and the main ridge, as developed in the railroad cuts, shows quite thick deposits. On Tuque Prairie it is only two feet to these Clays, and they are quite impervious to water. On Lost Creek, near its head, these ("boulder?") Clays are 10 feet thick, the upper part yellowish; the lower part includes gravel and large boulders of chert, with some Granite. On Charette a few feet of "Bluff" overlies a drift of about 15 feet, consisting of Clay and Boulders.

In Sec. 13, T. 48, R. 3 W., a well 12 feet deep passes through thin soil at top, with yellow Clay below, which is black, spotted at bottom. On North Missouri Railroad, near county line, we have—

No. 1. 1 foot dark soil.
No. 2. 1 foot reddish sub-soil, bed of passage to No. 3.
No. 3. Hard yellow Clay.

In the woods, the Clay-bed corresponding to No. 2 of last Section contains many roots, as exhibited in the following Section, taken near Wright City:

No. 1. 3 inches black soil.
No. 2. 6 inches dark soil, passing into yellow sub-soil.
No. 3. 1½ feet red soil and Clay, with roots of trees.
No. 4. 4 to 5 feet yellow Clay.
No. 5. 3 feet yellow Clay and cherty gravel—Boulder formation.

This formation is well developed in the Railroad cut east of Warrenton, as follows:

About 2 inches of dark soil on top; below of an ash brown; at 10 inches from top is more brown, presenting a somewhat mottled appearance of light drab and red. Below, 4 feet from top, the Clay is harder; at 6 feet it is hard, bluish, with brown streaks; at 20 feet, is very hard, and contains numerous rounded Silicious pebbles, evidently belonging to the Drift period, and showing attrition. The character remains the same to a depth of 30 feet, showing a hard, brownish, buff Clay, containing small rounded pebbles. A line 4 feet from top seems to separate the Clays into two distinct Geological periods of deposit.

The greatest observed thickness of this formation was about 40 feet; it may be 50 or 60 feet. In a well in Montgomery county, near Warren line, a soft white chalky rock was dug out; also a brownish, very light, soft rock. When these Clays approach near the surface, a decided character is imparted to the country. The Clays being very compact and tenacious, water lying on the surface does not readily permeate; consequently, after a great fall of rain, farmers are prevented from plowing for some time. I was told that on Loutre Prairie, in Montgomery county, after penetrating 18 inches, we come to stiff Clay, or hard-pan, and that in cisterns no cement is used. Near the head of most of the streams flowing southward is found a deposit, consisting of cherty pebbles, loosely adhering together, imbedded in an olive or white Silicious Clay, often unctuous to the touch; some of the pebbles were recognized as Carboniferous; they evidently show a "Drift" agency, but to what particular period they should be referred, I am not able to say.

Beds of stratified red, cream, blue and purple colored Clays were found at various localities. They may belong to the "Drift," or may be "Coal measure" Clays.

CARBONIFEROUS.

Coal Measures.

I was only able to recognize the true coal measure formation at Camp Branch, in N. W. of S. W. quarter Sec. 10, T. 47, R. 3 W. I found here a drab Limestone, exposed at low water in the bed of the creek, containing *Spirifer lineatus*. The Drift formation in this neighborhood, being very thick shuts, from view further exposure of this rock.

Fragments of coal were dug out of several wells at Camp Branch. A well on Mr. Taylor's place was sunk forty-five feet, passing through Drift clays, with some shale, to a six-inch bed of coal. The water reached was so strongly impregnated with sulphur as to prevent its use, showing the coal to be pyritous. This formation does not extend over a mile north and probably two miles south, and to the southward it is probably about two miles in width. There are several other circumscribed areas containing coal within this county, but they are mere patches, not extensive. They are found in Sec. 31, T. 47, R. 3 W., two and a-half miles south-east of Warrenton, and on Sec. 31, T. 48, R. 2 W. Blue and purple clays are found on Camp and Little Lost Creeks, which may belong to coal measures.

F. *f*—Sandstone.

This formation, known in Missouri Reports as Ferruginous Sandstone, as observed in this county, is quite limited in extent. It is found on the head-waters of Massey's and Lost Creeks, and on one of the branches of West Fork of Charette. It is generally a fine-grained Sandstone, sometimes white or of a dirty white color, but more often white, with numerous red, ferruginous grains disseminated, sometimes in streaks and sometimes irregularly, through the mass. Sometimes it contains a buff, pulverulent powder. On Lost Creek it is twenty-two feet thick and cavernous.

ENCRINITAL LIMESTONE—SWALLOW.

BURLINGTON LIMESTONE—HALL.

This formation is found outcropping on all the streams in the northern part of the county. The upper beds are found on Indian Camp and Camp Creeks, the middle beds on Camp and Big Creeks, and the lower on Peruque and the head waters of Charette. It is also found on head of Massey's, Bear and Lost Creeks. Its southern limit winds across the southern part of T. 47, R. 3 W., outcropping at the head of the branches; from thence winding around the head of Massey's Creek, it is found in Sec. 31, T. 47, R. 4 W.; thence passing south-east toward Little Lost Creek; thence bending northward, it crosses it in south part of T. 47, crossing Lost Creek near Sec. 25, T. 47; thence south-east to Sec. 7, T. 46, R. 2 W. We next find it on Charette, in north part of T. 47, R. 2 W.; thence following a devious east and north-east course, it is found on Peruque, in Sec. 27, T. 47, R. 1 W. East of the last locality, it was not found south of the creek.

Its greatest observed thickness, at any one place, was about fifty-five feet; its total thickness probably about one hundred and ten feet, of which the upper part, of about forty-five, is mostly of a gray color, with some buff strata and some hornstone layers interstratified. Below, we have about forty or fifty feet of brown ochery-colored Limestone containing a very few fossils; next below are gray beds, and at bottom from thirteen to sixteen feet of brown, ferruginous Limestone. This formation is mostly even-bedded, and sometimes the beds are quite thick, especially toward the lower part, affording a good building material. Crinoid columns are numerous, especially in the upper part. Some of the upper beds are suture-jointed. The texture is more often coarse, but there are some tolerably fine-grained strata.

In following down Camp Creek, we find the upper beds to be of thinly-stratified, coarse gray Limestone, some of it inclining to flesh-color and containing *Chonetes Shumardana*, and interstratified with thin beds of chert; some beds are thin, shaly and of a greenish color.

In N. W. Sec. 23, T. 48, R. 3 W., on Camp Creek, I obtained the following section:

No. 1. 20 feet cherty slope.

No. 2. 10 feet outcrops of gray Limestone, inclining to buff; contains also some Crinoid columns of both round and elliptical cross sections.

No. 3. 5 feet outcrops of brownish-drab compact Limestone.

No. 4. 24 feet Limestone; upper part, buff; lower, gray.
No. 5. 4 feet brown Limestone.
No. 6. 2 feet gray Limestone.
No. 7. 8 feet light-buff, Encrinital Limestone.

Following down the creek we find gray beds on the hill tops, and in T. 49 they give place to about 50 feet ochery-colored, mostly thick-bedded Limestone, in some of which are numerous crinoid columns. On Big Creek, toward its head, we find the lower ferruginous beds. Toward the county line the ferruginous beds are about 35 feet thick, showing a dip toward the north. The upper beds on the western tributaries in Sec. 30, T. 48, R. 2 W., will show:

No. 1. 15 feet Cherty slope.
No. 2. 1 foot brownish gray Limestone.
No. 3. 1½ feet crumbling Limestone; brown, soft and sandy.
No. 4. 5 inches white hornstone.
No. 5. 5 inches brown Limestone.
No. 6. 2 feet, 6 inches buff Limestone.
No. 7. 5 inches hornstone.
No. 8. 4 feet like No. 6.

The upper gray beds are founnd on Indian Camp Creek, of which the following Section was taken, about a mile from the east county line:

No. 1. 6 feet slope, with some chert.
No. 2. 24 feet coarse, but mostly tolerably fine-grained gray Limestone; sink hole on top.
No. 3. 1 foot Limestone, somewhat brown or chocolate-colored, with crinoid stems.
No. 4. 1 foot like No. 3, but finer.
No. 5. 2 feet gray, shelly Limestone, containing *Orthis Mitchellina, Chonetes Shumardana*, and a small *spirifer*.
No. 6. 11 feet light brown or rather buff, with crinoid stems.
No. 7. Gray shelly Limestone, containing *Chonetes Shumardana.*

On Peruque Creek the lower beds are well developed at the quarries in Section 27, where the following section was made:

No. 1. 15 feet slope; some chert.
No. 2. 1½ feet soil thin on top; below, red clay and cherty drift.
No. 3. 1 foot Gray Encrinital Limestone.
No. 4. 14 feet brown ferruginous limestone, containing brown spar and crystals of of oxide of iron, and having drusy cavities with quartzose and ferruginous crystallizations; fossils scarce; in some of them the outer part of the shell is composed of milky quartz, and the central part has a nucleus of the same composition, surrounded by ferruginous crystals and brown earthy limestone.

The stone from this quarry was used extensively for building culverts on the North Missouri Railroad.

The best section of the lower Encrinital beds was obtained at the quarries south of Warrenton.

Section 30.

No. 1. 12 feet slope.

No. 2. 1 foot thin soil, brown clay and comminuted cherty gravel.

No. 3. 2 feet brown Limestone, abounding in white crinoid stems.

No. 4. Coarse brown, rather soft limestone, in one bed of 5½ feet, with drusy cavities containing quartz crystals, brown and pearl spar and red oxyd of iron; some beautiful crystals. Some of the cavities have an outer shell of oxyd of iron, and inner of beautiful pearl spar. A few fossils and a few crinoid stems.

No. 5. 6½ feet fine grained, soft, yellowish-brown Limestone, with cavities containing crystals of quartz and red Hematite; more especially cavernous at top. Contains some beautiful crystals of pearl spar and ferro-calcareous crystals; many beautiful dendritic markings, and lower part contains large quantities of calc. spar, with some nail-head spar. We also find, at the lower part, a little green carbonate of copper, and iron and copper pyrites.

Chouteau Limestone.

Next below the Encrinital beds we have not over 30 feet of non-fossiliferous beds, of which Sec. 30 continued, shows No 6. Nine feet of light drab compact Limestone, interstratified with thin bands of shale and intersected by small veins of calcite. Below this was found three feet of red, yellow and green clay; lower bed sandy, resting on six feet of greenish Calcareous Sandstone, resting on two feet of soft yellow black specked Limestone, passing into three feet of yellow clay below. A drab Limestone, resembling that above described, crops out on head of West Fork of Tuque Creek, overlying a brown bed; beneath which are thin shaly beds of red compact Limestone.

On head of Massey's Creek, Sec. 13 exposes the rocks next below the Encrinital Limestone.

No. 4 is four feet of fine grained bluish drab Limestone—Chouteau Limestone.

No. 5, brittle, compact drab Limestone, with purple shades; rests on dark blue Limestone containing *Favosites reticulata*, etc.—*Hamilton.*

On head waters of Charette in Sec. 7, T. 46, R. 2 W., we find six feet of thin-bedded drab Limestone; then four feet of purple and drab, beautifully mottled and banded fine-grained Limestone. Below this we find the coarse gray "Charette" Limestone. On head waters of Dry Fork of Charette, Sec. 25, T. 46, R. 3, W.

Section 54.

No. 1. Earthy slope.
No. 2. 20 feet fragments of Sandstone.
No. 3. 6 inches fine-grained and banded brown Calcareous Sandstone.
No. 4. 1 foot dark Ferruginous Limestone, traversed by black veins.
No. 5. 2 feet thin shaly beds, like No. 4.
No. 6. 6 inches compact Limestone, red and drab mottled.
No. 7. 6 feet drab earthy Limestone.
No. 8. 1 foot brown Limestone, conchoidal fracture, and has dendritic markings.
No. 9. Heavy bed of Limestone, like No. 7, may be of the Hamilton group.

DEVONIAN SYSTEM.

Although covering a limited area, and of no great thickness, yet three distinct groups, belonging to the Devonian age, are recognized in this county, viz:

"The old Red Sandstone."

Hamilton Group and Onondaga? Limestone.

The "Red Sandstone," which, in Montgomery county, was found forty feet in thickness; in Warren, is not seen presenting a greater exposed thickness than about seven feet, showing a thinning out toward the eastward.

This deposit is more often found in tumbling masses lying unconformably on the lower rocks; it is found reposing on both Devonian and Lower Silurian rocks. At its southern limit was found generally on Black River Limestone. Its most characteristic features are those of an even-grained, sometimes irregularly bedded Ferruginous Sandstone, presenting a beautiful mottled red and brown. The mottled appearance analyzed, presents a combination of light or yellowish brown, whitish deep brown, reddish brown and red, brownish black, brown, yellow ochery and white; sometimes brownish with small white spots or nuclei encircled by black ferruginous sand. On Lost Creek it is red, and also a beautiful reddish drab mottled with white; on head of Smith's Creek masses occur of a ferruginous cherty character, which I refer to these beds, although not observed anywhere else presenting similar characteristics.

On head waters of Dry Fork of Charette a concretionary fragment was observed, having the appearance of its edges folded over. The interior is soft and crumbly, of a brownish color, a deeper brown toward the center, and buff toward the outer part; one portion shows the outer part of a beautiful pink shade. The outside is hard, close-grained, ferruginous, with a vitreous luster; the outer brown and red banded; exposed surface of a black brown.

When exposed, the prevailing color is black or reddish brown often weathering to a nodular and somewhat botryoidal surface, and is often covered with beautiful mosses and lichens, presenting, in the distance, that beautiful greenish gray appearance of all moss-covered rocks.

This formation occupies an irregular zone, extending across the southern part of the county, outcropping or lying in tumbling masses on the hillsides. The southern limit is generally from two to four miles from the Missouri bluffs, and about four or five miles wide, thinning toward the northern limit. Outside of this zone I only found it at one locality, viz: on bluffs of Peruque Creek, at county line, there is six and a-half feet of a dirty white Sandstone containing fine-grained indurated white nodular masses of Sandstone.

Although the area covered by the "Old Red" is small, the influence exerted is important, for the adjacent soil is generally very ferruginous, resulting probably from disintegration and subsequent decomposition of the rock, and the soil, both on the adjacent hills and valleys, partakes of this character. No fossils were found.

Hamilton Group.

This formation is but sparingly developed in Warren, and is only important as a connecting link between the rocks above and those below.

A heavy bed of brown Limestone at lower part of Sec. 54 may belong to this group.

LOWER DEVONIAN.

The exact Geological position of the beds below, we are not able to place with certainty. On waters of Massey's Creek we have—

Section 13.

No. 1. 50 feet chert slope.
No. 2. 12 feet coarse gray Encrinital Limestone.
No. 3. 10 feet brownish Limestone.

Chouteau Beds:

- No. 4. 4 feet fine grained bluish-drab Limestone.
- No. 5. 1 foot brittle, variegated, compact Limestone.

Devonian:

- No. 6. Dark-blue Limestone, contains *Favosites reticulata.*
- No. 7. 6 feet dark, coarse Limestone, contains *Spirifer eruteines, Orthis tulliensis* and a large *Spirifer.*

No. 8. 8 feet coarse, Crinoidal Limestone.
No. 9. Trenton Limestone.

On Bear, Massey's and Lost Creeks, beneath the Hamilton (?) beds as above described, we find about 20 feet, mostly of a coarse gray, and sometimes of a dark-bluish drab Limestone. In the upper part, fossils are sometimes quite numerous, belonging to the genus *Merista* and *Rhynchonella*. At some places a fine close-grained, bluish drab Limestone occurs near the top, containing *Favosites reticulata*, *Alveolites Verneulana*, *Spirifer eruteines* and an *Orthis* resembling *Tulliensis*, or *Iowensis*, near the base. *Cyathophyllum rugosum* (?) occurs in a brownish Limestone in N. E. part of T. 46, R. 2 W. The Geological position of the above described rocks is probably above (?) that of the Coralline bed of the Callaway section. The Coralline beds were not seen in this country, but a specimen of *Zaphrentis gigantea* was found separated from its parent bed. These beds may probably belong near the Onondaga Limestone.

The following Section of Devonian rocks was taken on Peruque, at county line:

Section 19.

No. 1. 55 feet slope, mostly White Oak growth.
No. 2. 6½ feet dirty colored, whitish Sandstone, with indurated masses of the same.
No. 3. 11 feet slope—no rocks seen.
No. 4. 6 inches Olive shales.
No. 5. 4 feet coarse drab granular Limestone.
No. 6. 2 feet brownish Limestoue, with fossils—contains *Cyathophyllum rugosum*, *Crinoid* stems, etc.
No. 7. 4 feet heavy bed of drab Linestone, argillaceous or shaly, with lenticular and reniform masses of chert; contains *Atrypa reticularis*, *Megistocrinus latus*, large Corals and Crinoid stems.
No. 8. 4 feet dark drab Limestone.

Nos. 5 to 8 inclusive, probably belong to the Hamilton group.

The total thickness of Devonian rocks, exclusive of the red Sandstone, is probably about 50 feet.

CRINOIDAL LIMESTONE.

The area occupied by this rock is small; it was recognized at a few localities on Massey's and Lost Creeks, and outcrops on nearly all the bluffs of Bear Creek. It is generally about 11 feet thick, and uniformly a coarse gray Limestone, often crumbly, and generally containing many Crinoid stems. Fossils are rare; *Atrypa reticularis* is sometimes found. Its total thickness in this county is probably about 15 feet. It is extensively used in Montgomery county (where it is better developed) for chimney fire-places. It probably belongs to a division of the Upper Silurian system.

LOWER SILURIAN.

Referring to the map, it will be perceived (by the part colored yellow) that the *Lower Silurian* rocks cover quite an extensive area in the southern portion of the county. The rocks belonging to this system, in descending order, include here the Trenton Limestone, Black River, which may include the Birdseye, and the Magnesian Limestone series. The Trenton and Black River groups are seldom the top rocks, being mostly covered by the Devonian.

The Magnesian Series, almost exclusively, occupy the southern main east and west belt parallel to the Missouri River, the Black River Limestone only being found on the tops of the higher ridges, near the northern limit of this belt. The Trenton Limestone extends up the streams nearly to their heads. The Black River Limestone reaches within one or two miles of the north limit of the Trenton; the First Magnesian Limestone to within half a mile of the Black River Limestone.

TRENTON LIMESTONE.

Charette Limestone.—The upper Trenton beds, of about 34 feet, are distinctly marked, both lithologically and paleontologically, from those below, and are subdivided lithologically into two several groups, the upper gray, the lower brown. The upper 26 feet is mostly a coarse gray Limestone, sometimes quite white, and having pink tints; often contains *Orthis testudinaria* in great quantities, which shell out easily from the containing rock; a Coral resembling *Chætetes lycoperdon* also sometimes abounds. It thins out toward the west, and was found only four inches thick on Bear Creek, containing numerous *Orthis* weathered in relief. On Massey's Creek it is 9 feet in very thick beds, and coarsely crystalline. Being better developed on Charette, where it is easily recognized, I have, for the sake of distinction, applied the term "Charette Limestone." It is the equivalent of the Receptaculite Limestone of Shumard. On Charette it occurs about 26 feet in thickness; most of the beds thick, but some thin and crumbly. The texture is uniform, and the color a uniform light gray or white. On Tuque Creek, near its head, the lower beds partake somewhat of the character of the underlying brown beds, as the following section will show:

Section 42.

No. 1. Slope.
No. 2. Devonian.

CHARETTE LIMESTONE:

No. 3. 20 feet gray Limestone, mostly soft; toward the middle are many dark specks, which impart an iron-gray appearance; 8 feet from bottom it is coarse gray, with *Chætetes lycoperdon ?*

CHARETTE LIMESTONE:

No. 4. 8 feet Limestone; upper part a red or brownish gray; next below is dark reddish-brown, with numerous Corals, probably *Chætetes;* at bottom is a brown sandy Limestone.

TRENTON LIMESTONE:

No. 5. 1 foot of dark brown Limestone, containing *Leptæna.*

No. 6. Fifty yards down the creek is found a thin bedded drab Limestone, containing well-marked Trenton fossils, including *Orthis subæquata, Subulites elongata, Lingula, Murchisonia, Leptæna, Trilobites*, etc.

The brown Limestone (No. 4) was only found on Tuque and Charette, and is easily recognized; it preserves an even thickness of six feet, and has drusy cavities, containing beautiful crystals of quartz and calc-spar.

Middle and Lower Trenton.—We next have about eighty feet of mostly thinly-stratified, even-bedded Trenton Limestone. The upper few feet generally a light-drab, with numerous fossils. The beds below are generally of a darker color, and sometimes brownish. While these beds in this county are nearly always of a dark color, in Montgomery and Callaway they are of a light drab. On Charette, this division of the Trenton is altogether a thin-bedded, brownish drab Limestone. At twenty-two feet below the top we find, on Bear Creek, three feet of a brown Magnesian Limestone interstratified. On Charette, Sec. 33, No. 4 exhibits two feet of a close-grained, crystalline, dark blue Limestone.

The lower beds of the Trenton are more often traversed by numerous winding, reticulated and anastamosing fucoids, causing the rock at times to present a beautiful mottled appearance. These beds are often fine-grained, and when solid enough, would make a very pretty marble.

BLACK RIVER LIMESTONE.

The rocks classed as Black River, in the upper part so nearly resemble the Trenton that it is only by a careful examination of the contained organic remains that the line of demarcation can always be defined. Organic remains being so often difficult to find, we are apt, in our description, to run the beds into each other. The upper bed is a fine-grained, brittle, compact drab Limestone, traversed by veins, specks and bands of calc-spar. This bed, when found, is easily recognized, as it seems to preserve its color and texture very uniformly from Callaway county to the eastern part of Warren. It corresponds to Nos. 5 and 6 of Sec. 12, to top of No. 7, Sec. 58, and to Sec. 34, No. 4. It is represented by the upper part of No. 23 of Sec. 46 of

Prof. Swallow's section on Hobson's Branch, Callaway. The following sections will serve to show most of the various beds observed in this county:

Section 36.

No. 1. 7 feet bluish drab Limestone, thin-bedded, containing *Orthis*, *Murchisonia*, etc.
No. 2. 4 feet bluish drab Limestone; beds thicker.
No. 3. 40 feet thin-bedded Limestone; drab and blue, rather thin, shelly.
No. 4. 1½ feet bluish drab Limestone; veins and specks of calc-spar.
No. 5. 2 feet buff Limestone, tinged green; contains *Leptæna Deltoidea*(?)
No. 6. 3 feet buff-colored, irregularly-bedded, silicious Limestone.
No. 7. 9 feet close-grained, even-bedded, compact, silicious Limestone, white and buff; so hard that it almost seems like an altered rock. Fracture sometimes shows a vitreous luster.
No. 8. 4 feet buff Limestone traversed by occasional striæ of calc-spar. The lower part is more of a drab color.
No. 9. 21 feet drab, shelly Limestone; *Leptæna* in the upper part.
No. 10. 34 feet First Magnesian Limestone; lower twelve feet very dark drab and in heavy beds; contains *Cythere.*

On Lost Creek we have the following:

Section 61.

No. 1. 25 feet slope, with fragments of Devonian Red Sandstone and drab Limestone.

Charette Limeseone:

No. 2. 5 feet coarse gray Limestone.

Trenton Limestone:

No. 4. 2½ feet heavy bed of brown Magnesian Limestone, with winding, fucoidal ramifications.
No. 5. 10 feet. At top two feet slope; fragments of yellow Limestone, with some dendritic markings; below there is eight feet of brown Magnesian Limestone.
No. 6. 1 foot compact, thin-bedded Limestone.

Black River Beds—33 feet:

No. 7. 4 feet fine-grained, mottled drab and gray Limestone; good marble.
No. 8. 16 feet slope; fragments of drab Limestone, with brown windings.
No. 9. 13 feet Limestone. Like Sec. 36, No. 9; same fossils—*Cythere*, etc.

No. 10. 4 feet First Magnesian Limestone.

On Tuque Creek, there is thirty feet of drab Limestone; upper part brittle, has numerous vermiform windings; below, a shelly, and the lowest a somewhat buff-drab Limestone. Some beds are slightly mottled, and would make a tolerably good marble; makes excellent lime; fossils from about the middle. These beds were found at other places presenting the same characteristics as last mentioned. On Charette, in Sec. 1, T. 45, R. 2 W., it is a flesh-colored, light gray-colored, reddish and brown, with dark windings; colors somewhat wavy. On Lake Creek there is twenty feet, of which the lower six or eight feet are marble; the upper bed mottled gray, and somewhat resembling a conglomerate. Below, we have a reddish, greenish gray, compact, fine-grained Limestone, fracture conchoidal; then a reddish drab, with deeper red specks disseminated, presenting a graphic appearance, (this bed is sometimes greenish); lowest bed a greenish white, brittle, crystalline Limestone—seems to have been altered. On Lost Creek occurs a very hard, silicious Magnesian Limestone; color drab, and with many minute, vermiform cavities. It closely resembles some beds of First Magnesian Limestone.

The following sections were obtained on waters of Smith's Creek:

Section 53.

No. 1. 40 feet slope; some Sandstone.

BLACK RIVER LIMESTONE?:

- No. 2. 3 feet waxy-looking Limestone, with black, horizontal veins; pretty marble.
- No. 3. 2½ feet gray, shelly Limestone.
- No. 4. 6 inches dark, waxy-looking, brittle Limestone, with black dendritic markings.
- No. 5. 1½ feet drab, shelly Limestone.

BLACK RIVER LIMESTONE:

- No. 6. 1½ feet; upper half like No. 4; lower more brown: contains *Leptæna* and *Cythere.*
- No. 7. 33 feet slope; tumbling masses of Ferruginous Sandstone and gray Limestone.
- No. 8. 6 inches drab Limestome; marble.
- No. 9. 8 feet slope; some Limestone; mostly shelly.
- No. 10. 6 inches drab Limestone; containing calcite, and having many brown windings; will make a fine marble; contains fossils.
- No. 11. 3 inches fine-grained drab Limestone; a good marble.
- No. 12. 1½ inches brownish Limestone, with black and drab spots.
- No. 13. 5 inches drab Limestone, with brown spots; fine grained, compact; contains some calcite.
- No. 14. 11 feet slope.
- No. 15. 50 feet First Magnesian Limestone.

On the road from Warrenton to Pinkney, near the head of Smith's Creek, we have fifteen feet; the upper part gray. Eight feet from bottom is a bed of compact brown Limestone, with calcite veins, and traversed by dark, dendritic veins. In Sec. 53, No. 13, the lower part is gray. Thus we see that this formation presents very desirable shades of color. The total thickness of the group in this county is probably about fifty feet; it may be as much as fifty-five feet, but not more.

The Lower Silurian rocks near the Missouri River comprise the First Magnesian Limestone, Saccharoidal Sandstone, Second Magnesian Limestone and Second Sandstone. In following down its various tributaries from their heads, we find, after the first exposure of F. *t*, that on Charette we have to go one mile to the first outcrop of (*u*), near the western part of the county, about a-half mile. About one and a-half miles more will take us to F. *v*.

F. *t*. First Magnesian Limestone.

The following section was made on Charette, in Sec. 18, T. 46, R. 1 W.:

Section 35.

No. 1. Slope.
No. 2. 5 feet buff Limestone, traversed by occasional striæ of calc-spar; lower part more drab.

Black River Beds:

No. 3. 21 feet drab, shelly Limestone; upper part contains a small *Leptœna* bed six feet from bottom.
No. 4. 2½ feet ashy-colored, slightly olive-tinted, drab, Magnesian Limestone; brittle, breaks angularly.
No. 5. 3 inches drab, argillo-calcareous shale.

First Magnesian Limestone:

No. 6. 2 feet dark bluish Magnesian Limestone; closely crystalline and traversed by darker veins of calcite; would make a pretty marble.
No. 7. 2½ feet like No. 4.
No. 8. 5 feet slope.
No. 9. Light drab, earthy Magnesian Limestone.

The above section will serve to show what I suppose to be the upper part of the Second Magnesian Limestone; similar strata were observed on Lost Creek. But it more often a buff color, sometimes a brown or drab Magnesian Limestone. Its beds are generally of uniform thickness. Calc-spar is sometimes abundant, and often occurs in small veins or striæ, traversing the rock; it also sometimes contains iron pyrites. An oolitic bed is generally found near the base.

The following section was observed in Sec. 1, T. 45, R. 2 W., on Charette, east side:

Section 47.

No. 1. Slope.
No. 2. 25 feet slope; outcrops of Black River Limestone; upper part reddish; below of various shades; brownish flesh color; marble.
No. 3. 38 feet buff Magnesian Limestone; some veins of calc-spar.
No. 4. 10 feet blue Magnesian Limestone; some drab and green shale.

No. 5, 8 feet soft buff Magnesian Limestone; contains calcite; some black specks are disseminated.
No. 6. 2 feet yellow, shaly bed.
No. 7. 1 foot yellow and green sandy Magnesian Limestone.
No. 8. 70 feet Saccharoidal Sandstone.
No. 9. 2 feet Silicious rock, mostly oolitic.
No. 10. Slope.
No. 11. 20 feet Second Magnesian Limestone.

This formation is more often evenly bedded, and affords a beautiful and durable building rock. Its greatest observed thickness was 84 feet on Tuque Creek. Section 47 shows the least observed thickness.

F. *u*. SACCHAROIDAL SANDSTONE.

This deposit is generally a uniformly white, fine-grained Sandstone. Some of the beds are sometimes, but rarely, brownish. Near the upper part it is often very white or greenish and soft, disintegrating, and can be scraped up with the hand.

On Massey's Creek, in Sec. 1, T. 46, R. 4 W., it shows a beautiful cross lamination; a solid bed of two to four feet is seen overlying a series of very thin beds of cross laminated Sandstone.

On Charette, in Sec. 25, T. 46, R. 2 W., we have 84 feet, of which the upper is white and lower brown; a small ravine has here worn out a deep and perpendicular gorge or canon into the Sandstone for about 200 feet in length, sloping from the upper to lower end, where it is about 25 feet deep and 8 feet wide at the top, by four at the bottom. The bluffs on this creek are very picturesque, the Sandstone often rising 60 feet perpendicularly, and covered with numerous ferns, mosses, lichens, hanging, as it were, in rich green festoons.

On Tuque Creek it presents a beautiful appearance, rising into bold mural escarpments, covered with mosses and ferns, and sometimes capped with cedars.

Wherever this Sandstone is well developed, it affords charming scenery to those who love the beauties of nature; is best developed on Tuque, Charette and Massey's Creeks. Springs are apt to be found at its base; caves also abound, especially toward the lower part. There is one two miles north of Marthasville, called "Devil's Boot." Its entrance from the top of the ground is 25 feet across and nearly circular. Descending about 30 feet, we are on the floor. A large chamber reaches off to the north-east for about 150 feet, about 8 feet high in the middle near the entrance, and increasing in all its dimensions to the further end, where it is 25 feet high and 60 wide. The Sandstone is pure white; stalactites and stalagmites are found, some of them quite pretty.

At Ritter's Store, in Sec. 3, T. 45, R. 3 W., the overhanging Sandstone forms a shelter 100 feet wide, 10 feet high in front, and sloping back to an acute angle at 20 feet.

The cave on head-waters of Dry Fork of Charette has an entrance from the northward; passing in southwardly we wind around to the north-east, and descending about 60 feet over tumbling masses of Sandstone, enter a large chamber, the roof formed of broad slabs of Sandstone, sometimes showing 10 feet square of beautiful ripple marks. At many other localities it was observed beautifully ripple-marked.

Its total thickness in the county is probably about 130 feet; the greatest observed on Tuque Creek, 127 feet. On Lost Creek, fragments of Columnar Sandstone were found, but not in place. The position of the Columnar beds must be near the top, and constitutes a stratum of from one to four feet, formed of columns, often porous, and perpendicular to the place of deposit.

No fossils were observed, but on the roof of the cave near Marthasville, circular rings about 8 inches in diameter, resembling the cross section of an *orthoceras*, were observed.

Just beneath the Sandstone was found a stratum of two feet in thickness, of a Silicious and sometimes oolitic rock, viz.: at Sec. 47, No. 9, on Charette; Sec. 44, No. 2, on Lake Creek, and lower part of Sec. 46, No. 2, on Missouri Bluff. (See Sec. 18, Montgomery county.)

F. *v*. Second Magnesian Limestone.

The Second Magnesian Limestone has been so often described that it seems almost useless for me now to attempt a description. Its characteristics are about the same as in Montgomery, Callaway and Boone. It forms steep bluffs along the Missouri, often rising nearly a hundred feet perpendicularly. The following section exhibits some of its beds, taken two miles east of Marthasville:

Section 46.

No. 1. 40 feet Saccharoidal Sandstone.
No. 2. 27 feet Silicious Magnesian Limestone, in thick and thin beds; the lower two feet a Silicious rock, color drab and buff.
No. 3. 21 feet thin-bedded drab Magnesian Limestone.
No. 4. 2 feet white Sandstone.
No. 5. 3 feet yellow Magnesian Limestone; a thin bed of Hornstone appears in the lower part.
No. 6. 4 feet Magnesian Limestone and very hard Sandstone, interstratified with shale.
No. 7. 3 feet Magnesian Limestone, with lenticular and irregular concretions of chert.

On Missouri bluffs, a half mile below mouth of Lost Creek, the following section was taken:

Section 56.

No. 1. 10 feet slope.
No. 2. 9 feet rough-looking drab Magnesian Limestone, interstratified with chert; a 6-inch bed of dark drab oolite about the middle.
No. 3. 2 feet drab Magnesian Limestone.
No. 4. 6 feet drab Cotton rock, in thin beds.
No. 5. 1 foot brown Silicious Magnesian Limestone.
No. 6. 6 inches drab Cotton rock.
No. 7. 4 inches close-grained, light-colored, banded Magnesian Limestone.
No. 8. 1 foot slope.
No. 9. 8 feet Magnesian Limestone and Cotton rock, with some chert; in middle part a very thin stratum of Sandstone.
No. 10. 4 feet Cotton rock.
No. 11. 3 feet cherty Magnesian Limestone, having a rough brecciated appearance; in the middle part a Sandstone is sometimes interstratified.
No. 12. 1 foot dark drab Magnesian Limestone.
No. 13. 1 foot of Cotton rock.
No. 14. 2 feet banded buff and white Sandstone.
No. 15. 4 feet rough-looking hard Silicious Magnesian Limestone; lower part buff and softer.
No. 16. 5 feet drab Magnesian Limestone; in middle part there is five inches of cherty oolite.
No. 17. 2 feet white and buff Sandstone.
No. 18. 4 feet mostly blue Magnesian Limestone, in upper part some beds of chert and much calc-spar; the spar containing pseudomorphous pyrites; lower part oolitic.
No. 19. 8 feet rough drab, cherty Magnesian Limestone; some beds cellular; some Cotton rock.
No. 20. 6 inches rough, coarse, hard Silicious Magnesian Limestone.
No. 21. 5 feet buff Cotton rock; some partings of green shale.
No. 22. 8 inches cherty bed; some oolitic.
No. 23. 5 feet cherty Magnesian Limestone. The chert predominates, is cellular, presenting a very rough face.
No. 24. 10 feet slope; at bottom is two feet of a drab earthy Magnesian Limestone.

SECOND SANDSTONE:

No. 25. 4 feet coarse brown Sandstone.
No. 26. 5 feet thin cherty beds of impure Magnesian Limestone; one bed of banded chert.

The total thickness of the Second Magnesian Limestone formation in this county is probably about 210 feet.

F. *w*. SECOND SANDSTONE.

With the exception of Nos. 25 and 26, of the above section, the Second Sandstone was not observed at any other locality in this county.

SOILS.

The richer bottom lands may include those of the Missouri River and Charette and Tuque for about five or six miles from their mouths, and the lesser streams for one or two miles from the Missouri. These lands are exceedingly productive, being nothing less than a deep alluvium, capable of producing very fine crops of corn, which will average most seasons about seventy-five bushels per acre. The growth of timber is very luxuriant, the trees growing to a very large size, and it is not uncommon to find a Cottonwood seven or eight feet in diameter. The Burr Oak, Elm, Sycamore, Black Walnut and Red Oak also grow to a very large size.

The bottom lands on the other streams, although very rich, are deficient in the luxuriance of vegetation which we here find. I, therefore, place them as subordinate.

In passing northward from the Missouri, we ascend the bluffs and find ourselves on the "Bluff" land, a strip of country covered by a deep "Bluff" formation, supporting a very rich soil. This is the richest upland in the county. It will produce, on an average, twenty-five to thirty bushels of wheat per acre;* is scarcely inferior to the richest bottom land. Corn and most other crops succeed very well. The vine seems to do very well, and has been successfully cultivated here, yielding an abundance of excellent grapes, from which is made an excellent wine. The natural "Bluff" growth seems to be mostly Sugar Tree, Ash, Linden, Red, Scarlet and White Oak, Dogwood, Shell-bark and Pig-nut Hickory, etc. At a distance of from two to three miles from the bluffs we leave this "Bluff" land, and ascend a rocky slope for a short distance, when we find that we are passing across poor and deeply broken and often rocky ridges. This is probably the poorest land in the county, but it still has its uses; it is said, by some, to be the most suitable for grape culture. Passing on northerly for one or two miles, we reach the table lands, separating the various streams, broken at their margin by ravines. This tract of country extends northward for five or six miles, and in the county west of Lost Creek entirely to the "prairies." This land is poor, soil thin; growth principally Post Oak, Black Oak, White Oak. It is capable of producing tolerably good crops of corn and wheat, and in good seasons will produce fine tobacco.

Nearer the prairies (especially Tuque) the land is generally a little better and more productive than the last mentioned.

* According to Mr. J. Wyatt and others.

The land around Warrenton and on hills near Indian Camp and Big Creek is rather better than the table lands southward; the soil is more productive, for it is well adapted to the growth of fine tobacco. It is principally covered with a growth of Black Oak, White Oak, Spanish Oak, Scarlet Oak, Post Oak and Shell-bark Hickory. It produces good crops of corn and wheat.

The country near the streams, which cut only through the lower carboniferous formations, near their various sources, is of very gentle slope, and the land is more often rich, as for example near Camp Branch and for two or three miles north; also on and near the head of Indian Camp Creek in T. 47, R. 1 W. Of similar character is the country adjacent to the head waters of Peruque. The natural growth is principally Pin Oak, Laurel Oak, Swamp White Oak, Elm, Hickory, Walnut, Honey Locust, Thorn, Crab Apple, Red bud, etc. It often produces heavy crops of corn and tobacco.

The prairies adjacent and between Camp and Big Creeks embrace the most productive prairie lands in the county; they lie well for cultivation. Other prairie lands are inferior in quality. The Camp Creek hills in T. 48 and 49 being quite broken, the land is therefore not very fertile.

The "Drift" clays being so deep, and at the same time so stiff and impermeable to water, and the overlying soil so thin, renders the prairie soils of this county somewhat objectionable from their capacity to hold water. After heavy rains it is often a long time before the soil is in a suitable condition to plow. The timbered lands are therefore to be preferred; they having generally sufficient porosity for drainage. The railroad cuts show that roots abound for a depth of upward of two feet, and that at three or four feet the clay is quite hard and compact. We thus see that in the timber lands we have a natural porous system of drainage, extending to over two feet below the surface, with clay below, which prevents the water from percolating very deep. The prairie shows, on top, about one foot of dark soil, beneath which there is about a foot of yellowish or reddish subsoil, resting on a substratum of hard clay. Whilst in the woods we find roots extending through the subsoil, on the prairies the roots appear as only slender filaments confined to the upper two or three inches of recent alluvium, showing the natural drainage capacity of the prairie as compared to the woodland, if we regard the depth, to be about as one to twelve; but the size of pores being taken into consideration will make the ratio still greater.

The thin deposit of dark light soil, often found overlying the first Magnesian Limestone, seems to be well adapted to fruit-growing. Grape-vines often abound and seem to flourish, and it was here I found some of the largest and richest Black Haws that I ever tasted. A fine peach orchard at Mr. Muench's, on First Magnesian Limestone, bears fruit nearly every year.

TIMBER.

That portion of Warren county adjacent to the affluents of the Missouri is generally very well timbered. The ridges afford a good quality of Black Oak, White Oak, Post Oak and Hickory. The bottoms abound in Sugar tree, Burr Oak, Red Oak, Walnut, etc. Leatherwood is found on bottoms of Lost Creek. In size and quantity of timber the Missouri River bottoms can not be surpassed by any in the State; the Burr and Red Oak often attain a diameter of six feet, and the gigantic Cottonwood is often found six or eight feet in diameter, and towering aloft above all other trees. The Walnut, Hickory and Sycamore often attain a very large size. The uplands adjacent to Big Creek in T. 47, R. 2 W., afford a good supply of good Red Oak, Black Oak and White Oak timber. Quantities of similar kinds of timber abound near Indian Camp Creek in north-east part of T. 47, R. 1 W.

WATER POWER.

Water mills do not pay in this county. The streams running into the Missouri River, during the summer season, too often sink, and those to the northward evaporate; therefore, the chief dependence is on steam and horse mills.

SPRINGS.

In the northern part of T. 48, on Camp Creek, are some fine springs; also on South Bear Creek. Persons living on the prairies have to depend on cisterns for a supply of water, without which provision, in a dry season, they would be sorely troubled. No cement is necessary to line them, as the stiff clays of the drift formation do not readily absorb water.

AGRICULTURE.

Wheat, corn and tobacco are the staple crops of this county. Most vegetables peculiar to the State are here raised. In the southern part of the county the vine is cultivated, and excellent wine made from the Catawba grape; the soil best adapted to its cultivation is either that underlaid by deep "Bluff," or else the slopes of First Magnesian Limestone; the latter is better adapted. The Chinese Sugar Cane has been cultivated and molasses made from it. The Maple Sugar tree abounds on all the streams running into the Missouri, and on the hills near the Missouri, and on Camp Creek; formerly, a great amount of sugar was made from it, but during recent years not much; the principal reason assigned being the increased facilities of procuring sugar from the South. Some families residing near Marthasville have formerly, during one season, made from 300 to 1,000 pounds of the sugar. From the best information I could obtain it seems that at one time great quantities of sugar were made on Bear Creek. Some families would sometimes make as much as 1,000 pounds per year, and with but little labor, and they would generally average 400 or 500 pounds; this was exchanged, at ten cents per pound, for dry goods. Since the year 1845 it has gradually declined, until at this time but little is made, and the whole annual amount now made (1859) on Bear Creek does not exceed 400 or 500 pounds.

BUILDING MATERIALS.

The lower brown beds of the Encrinital Limestone have been quarried out, and extensively used in the construction of culverts on the North Missouri Railroad. It is easily worked, and is procured in thick strata, and furnishes a good building material; but, on account of some strata being cellular and often crumbly, and also containing much oxide of iron, I do not esteem it a superior material; but for all common practical purposes to which applied, I do not deem these defects decidedly objectionable.

Good quarries have been opened near the North Missouri Railroad, on Massey's, Charette and Peruque Creeks. At Truesdale's quarry, near Warrenton, it is easily excavated and in very thick strata. Good beds of building rock can be easily obtained on Camp Creek, in townships 48 and 49, and at some places on Indian Camp.

The Red Sandstone affords a good building material, but is not sufficiently abundant to be of economic value. The Devonian beds below are also not sufficiently extensive in this county to be of much use. There is a good quarry on Peruque, near the county line.

Trenton Beds.—The gray "Charette" Limestone affords an excellent building material. A quarry on Massey's Creek, one and a-half miles from the railroad, shows very even-grained, thick strata. Good quarries can also be opened on Charette. The brown beds, lying just below, would doubtless make good building materials. The other Trenton beds, just below, are inferior.

The "Black River Limestone" beds afford an excellent building material. It is often even bedded, and breaks with an even fracture. The buff beds are often fine-grained and would give a pleasing architectural effect. But the First Magnesian Limestone, for beauty and durability and freeness under the chisel, can not be surpassed by any other stone in the county. Missouri College is built of it. Good quarries might be opened on the bluffs of every stream where it occurs.

The Saccharoidal Sandstone is generally too soft to use in buildings, but it is sometimes hard enough.

The Second Magnesian Limestone is inferior for building; the effects of frost on it are often too apparent, but the intercalated beds of Sandstone possess strength and durability.

LIME.

The Encrinital (Burlington) Limestone affords a good material for lime. Kilns of it are burned on Indian Camp Creek, near Wright City. The Upper Trenton or "Charette Limestone" makes good lime. It is so used near Warrenton. The mottled Marble beds of the Black River Limestone make good lime. On Lost and Tuque Creeks are lins of it.

Good clays for bricks abound everywhere.

MARBLE.

This county affords good quarries of excellent marble, some of it fine-grained and quite beautiful. It is mostly from the beds of the Black River Limestone. The principal localities where found, are: On Lake Creek, in Sections 23 and 24, T. 45, R. 1 W., where about eight feet of marble beds is exposed. In the upper part there are alternations of fine and coarse-grained sub-crystalline Limestone, presenting a somewhat brecciated appearance; it glistens when broken, and if polished would look well; below is a 6-inch bed of red, compact, fine-grained Limestone, with some veins of calc-spar and many ferruginous stains; some of it is of a reddish drab, the lowest bed a very fine-grained light-colored Limestone, with a light greenish tinge.

On Charette, in Sec. 18, T. 46, R. 1 W., there are several strata of Limestone, that would make pretty marble. No. 6 of Sec. 35 would make a pretty variety of dark marble. No. 7, of Sec. 36, is a fine-grained buff.

In Sec. 1, T. 45, R. 2 W., we find a variety similar to that found on Lake Creek, besides other varieties. Some of it is of a somewhat flesh color, with calc and brown spar disseminated, and has a soft luster; some is brown, with windings of a darker color traversing it. On the head of Ritter's Branch and Smith's Creek we find on the hills outcrops of various colored marble, drab, buff, and red; their aggregate thickness from 10 to 15 feet. On Lost Creek, in the northern part of T. 46, R. 3 W., are beds of Limestone that would make beautiful marble; also on Massey's Creek, in Sec. 1, T. 46, R. 4 W.

CLAY.

On Camp Creek, in Sec. 34, T. 48, R. 3 W., is a thick bed of shaly clays — drab, blue and purple. A thickness of 15 feet is exposed at the mouth of a ravine. Encrinital Limestone crops out on the neighboring hills, and it appears that the clay occupies a valley in the Limestone probably not less than 100 feet wide. A bed of similar clays, mostly of a purple color, occurs on the head of Little Lost Creek. Ferruginous Sandstone and Encrinital Limestone crop out in the bluffs, 200 yards down stream. These beds may probably be of use in the arts. Clay of a beautiful light shade of green occurs in the cave "Devil's Boot."

In Sec. 16, T. 46, R. 1 W., on a stream running northward, is a bed of hard purplish chay. A similar bed occurs in north half of northwest quarter Sec. 25, T. 46, R. 3 W., on head-waters of Smith's Creek; at this place it seems to be about 7 feet in thickness, but may probably be much thicker; it is exposed at the head of two ravines 30 feet apart, is quite hard and even-textured, of a purple and buff color. It has not been applied to any economical purpose, but it is very probable that it may become useful. About 15 feet above this is a bed of plastic Clay.

There is another bed of reddish Clay in Section 6, T. 45, R. 1 W.

The Chalk or "Keel," as it is commonly called, is found at several places in this county. A good quality of it is found on Lost Creek, in T. 46, R. 3 W., and it is very much used for marking purposes.

SAND FOR GLASS.

The Saccharoidal Sandstone, so well developed on the streams running into the Missouri, would afford a superior article for the manufacture of glass. Its beds are often pure white, mostly free from earthy impurities; and it is often so soft that it can easily be scooped up. The sand is often hauled twenty miles, to be used in plastering, it being much valued on account of its beautiful white color, for when mixed with lime and plastered on walls, no additional whitewash is needed. I might say, with confidence, that Warren county could supply the world for ages to come with excellent sand for glass.

MINERALS.

In Section 27, T. 47, R. 1 W., in Encrinital Limestone, we find crystals of brown spar and massive quartz. At Truesdail's quarry, near

Warrenton, the lower Encrinital beds afford beautiful crystals of quartz, brown spar, pearl-spar, calc-spar and nail-head spar.

At Grabb's Spring, Marthasville, I observed two inches of a black and brown sand, resembling ore of Manganese. I was informed that it is found to a depth of five or six feet, and is also found several hundred yards off. Two miles from this place, in the cave "Devil's Boot," a similar sand is associated with black, decomposing chert.

IRON ORE.

No extensive deposits of this mineral have as yet been found in this county. Small crystals are found at several localities, and I noticed a few fragments of massive Hematite. But in the southern part of the county are many signs of its presence; the soil is often highly colored by it, showing that deposits are here, or have existed to some extent.

LEAD.

No mines in this county. I was informed that particles of Galena had been found on Tuque Creek and Lake Creek.

MINERAL SPRING.

A spring half a mile north of Wright City is strongly impregnated with Sulphur.

COAL.

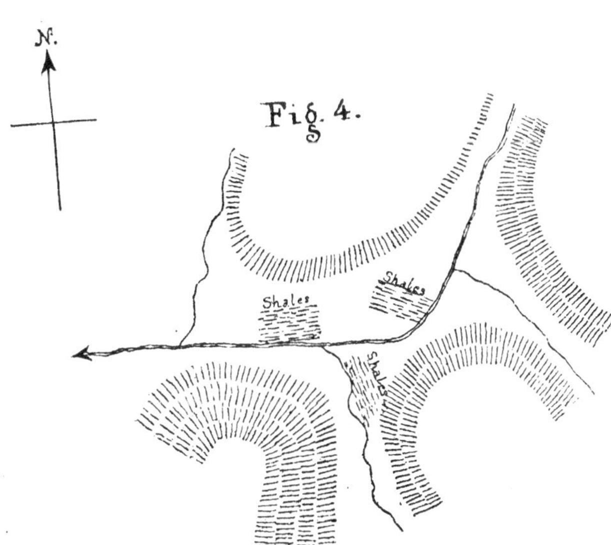

In Sec. 31, T. 47, R. 3 W., a few fragments of Bituminous Coal have been thrown out. Drab colored shales are found for 50 feet up and down the branch, dipping at the east end toward the west, and at west end about 30° E. The valley is not over 50 feet wide, and from surrounding appearances it is evident that about 50 feet square is the greatest extent of this patch. Encrinital Limestone is found on the hill adjacent. (See Fig. 4.)

Fig. 5.

About 2½ miles south-east of Warrenton, on the waters of Charette, I noticed another patch which evidently contains a less area than the one last mentioned. Encrinital Limestone is found on all the adjacent hills, and Devonian in the valleys. It is evident, therefore, that the Coal can not extend into the surrounding hills, and must even occupy a limited space in the valley, as shown by Fig. 5.

The thickness of Coal in these patches is unknown; it may be several feet, or as much as 8 or 10 feet.

The Coal of Warren county all occurs in "pockets;" some of these pockets may be extensive, but as yet none have been discovered sufficiently extensive to justify much outlay of time and money in mining. Future investigations may develop other deposits than those now known; they may especially be looked for in the northern part of the county.

Similar patches have been worked in Lincoln county, and some money spent, but developments prove them also to be limited.

The true Coal measures occur in the county west — Montgomery. An outlier of Coal measure slates is found near High Hill, but it is barren of Coal. Outliers of Limestone also occur eight miles north; they are also barren. Further west they contain the Coal, as found at various places near Wellsville. These patches may therefore be driftings from the true measures.

CHAPTER IV.

SHELBY COUNTY.

BY G. C. BROADHEAD.

Shelby county is bounded on the north by the counties of Lewis and Knox; on the east by Marion; on the South by Monroe, and on the west by Macon. The area is equal to fourteen townships or 504 square miles. The streams all flow south-eastwardly, and the general course of the main ridges is to the north-west and south-east. The streams are tributaries of Salt River, excepting those of North River and Fabius, in the north-east.

This county is essentially a prairie region, the timber being confined to the immediate vicinity of the streams, and from the appearance of the country I suppose it has not been many years since it was all prairie, for the timber is generally small and interspersed with that class peculiar to prairie thickets, and the prairie grass is also found everywhere.

The bottoms are wide, those of the larger streams being from one-half to a mile in width; they are often prairie, and are generally flat and marshy. The uplands are rolling, undulating, the larger prairies flat on the summit of ridges. None of the hills are very high, not often more than from 50 to 70 feet, and often less in hight; they are not often abrupt.

In township 56 the slopes are gentle; near Crooked Creek, for a half mile, the hills are somewhat broken, but the highest are not over 50 feet in hight, and are covered with a deep bluff and drift deposit, The prairie in townships 57 and 58, R. 9 W., slopes gently on the east, south and west, and is quite flat on the summit, expanding into a wide-level plain. On the northern slope, toward North River, and for several miles, the country consists of "barrens," covered with grass and a sparse growth of scrubby Post Oak and White Oak, with some Hazel. These rounded hills attain a hight of 60 feet, are steep, sloping from 35° to 45°, the contour seeming to form a graceful waving outline of sand hills of altered drift, with beautiful coves between. On the south-west side of the prairie are rolling White Oak hills.

Toward the Western part of the county, and on the south side of the North Fork of Salt River and adjacent to that stream, the country is rather broken, but the hills are not high. The topography is similar in the vicinity of Peyton's Branch and Ten Mile Creek, near which streams the timber is scattering, the growth consisting of Post Oak, White Oak, Black Oak, and sometimes groves consisting almost entirely of Shell-bark Hickory. None of the timber is very large, being mostly of convenient size for log houses and cross ties. Near the edge of prairie is Hazel and Pin Oak.

The prairies between North Fork of Salt River and Black Creek and the latter and North River are very gently undulating. The slopes on the north side of the North Fork of Salt River are very gentle.

The bottoms of the North Fork of Salt River are wide, generally from one to one and a half miles wide, until we reach the vicinity of Walkersville, where they become narrower. They are flat and wet, with often ponds and marshes; and adjacent to the river there is a fringe of open woods, with but little undergrowth. Outside of this fringe we have prairie bottom, extending to the foot of the bluffs, and often connected with the upland prairie.

The country adjacent to Eaton's Branch consists of hilly White Oak ridges, with some Post and Black Oak.

The south side of Black Creek is somewhat hilly, but the hills are low. On the north side the slopes are more gentle, and are separated from the hills to the south by wide, flat bottoms, often a half-mile in width. The growth near the edge of prairie is Laurel Oak and Pin Oak.

In T. 58, R. 10, near Perry's Creek, the land is good, with Hazel, Laurel Oak and Pin Oak, and Pin Oak near the edge of the prairie. In T. 59, R. 12, the slopes toward all the streams are gentle, and near the heads of the branches are small Hazel thickets, accompanied with *Amorpha fruticosa* and a small willow, which extend away up into the prairie. Pin Oak and Hazel occur mostly at the edge of the prairie. In T. 59, R. 11, the slopes are gentle. T. 59, R. 10, slopes are very gentle and no high hills. In T. 58, R. 9, on the north side of North River, are White Oak ridges. T. 59, R. 9, is mostly hilly and the land often poor; near Tiger Fork are occasionally broken tracts, but no hills are more than 50 feet in hight; the Drift sometimes is very deep; some good White Oak timber; some Post Oak, Black Oak and Shell-bark Hickory. Other timbered lands in the north-east consist of a small growth of mostly White Oak.

The "Barrens" are confined to the hills lying on the south side of the main stream. I would mention the north part of T. 58, R. 9, lying south of North River; a part of T. 58, ranges 10 and 11, on south side of Black Creek, and north part of T. 59, R. 9, west of Fabius. At some places the bluff and drift deposits are deep, and many round pebbles appear near the surface, and the soil is often quite sandy and land not very rich. The "Barrens," when apparent, being on the south side of streams, the hills on the south are also more broken and abrupt than those on the north side. Where no solid rocks are seen, but only bluff and drift clays, the slopes on the north of the larger streams are always long and gentle, whilst those on the south side are more abrupt

SCIENTIFIC GEOLOGY.

QUATERNARY SYSTEM.

Alluvium.—This includes the soils and deposits in progress of formation at the present time, as the sands and detritus of the streams. Shells are found in the streams, including species of *Unio*, *Anadonta* and *Cyclas*.

Bottom Prairie.—This is found on the bottoms of the larger streams. In T. 59, R. 12 W., on bank of North Fork of Salt River, observed the following section:

No. 1. 1 foot soil, covered with growth of grass, etc.
No. 2. 5 feet dark Clay, slightly brownish stained; contains small dark concretions.
No. 3. 5 feet Clay, mottled, ash colored and brown; some slightly sandy.

The bottom prairies are often flat and marshy. A tall grass is very abundant, and is often cut and used for hay.

Bluff.—Throughout the county the "Bluff" is found lying on the hills, just beneath the soil; it is often in sight, and frequently not more than six inches beneath the surface. It is mostly a brownish buff, stiff, jointed clay, with dark stains, and often has many small, rounded pebbles at the lower part. In S. W. Sec. 21, T. 57, R. 9 W., the following section was observed:

No. 1. 6 inches dark soil.
No. 2. 7 feet reddish brown, jointed, sandy clay, with some dark stains, and contains minute, rounded pebbles.
No. 3. 8 feet like the last, but the pebbles are larger and more numerous.

On Tiger Fork, in Sec. 27, T. 59, R. 9, I observed the following:

No. 1. 2 feet reddish brown clay.
No. 2. 30 feet stiff, yellowish brown clay, containing many small, rounded pebbles; at ten feet from the top occurs a bed of white, calcareous concretions, which effervesce very freely with nitric acid.

Between North River and Tiger Fork, small, round pebbles occur a few inches from the surface, and sometimes are directly on the surface. In T. 57, R. 9 W., east of Black Creek, clay with pebbles approaches within six inches, and often less, of the surface. Small, round, dark concretions were observed in the "Bluff" at several places. The following section was observed on Clear Creek near Miller's mill:

No. 1. Slope.
No. 2. 2 inches soil.
BLUFF:
No. 3. 8 feet coarse, reddish brown, jointed clay.
No. 4. 8 feet clay like the above, but contains round pebbles; lower part is dark-stained and bluish.
No. 5. 2 feet olive drab clay, vermilion stained. No. 5 I suppose to be altered Drift.

From the above sections, there appear to be two divisions of the "Bluff" in this county—the upper part jointed clay, free from pebbles, and the lower division, clay with small, rounded pebbles.

I did not observe a greater thickness than fifteen or twenty feet at any place, but was informed that a well had been dug at Hunnewell, passing fifty feet through "Bluff," which I suppose to be about its greatest thickness in this county.

Drift.—The Drift formation occurs beneath the Bluff throughout the county. It seems to consist of two distinctly defined groups, viz.: the upper portion (which is probably an altered Drift, and I have so classed it,) of beds of mostly ferruginous sand and clay, with rounded pebbles; and the lower mostly of blue clay and boulders. The following section was observed on Black Creek, south of Shelbyville:

Section 11.

BLUFF:

No. 2. 11 feet of hard, stiff, jointed clay; silicious; color brown and drab, or bluish variegated; has brown and black stains; the black stains seem especially to occupy the place formerly occupied by roots; contains soft, ferruginous concretions, brownish on outside and black within.

ALTERED DRIFT:

No. 3. 3 feet finely pulverized, drab sandy clay.

No. 4. 5 feet like the last, but whiter, and presents more the appearance of stratification; some portions seem quite sticky, whilst others seem to be almost entirely sand.

No. 5. 7 feet bed of mostly brown sand, formed in great part of coarse sand and coarse rounded quartzose pebbles, semi-cemented with ferruginous matter; has the appearance of stratification, and hardens on exposure.

No. 6. 11 feet alternations of beds equivalent to No. 5 with beds of dark clay; the clay is olive brown and stratified, and contains small round pebbles, together with hardened blue clay, also containing round pebbles; at the bottom lie larger boulders of Greenstone, Quartzite, Ironstone, etc.

Boulders of various kinds of igneous rock are found which indicate an origin many hundred miles off. One granite boulder was seen measuring in feet 5x5x4. Quartzose porphyry was also found, similar in appearance and composition to porphyry of Lake Superior.

Near the edge of the prairie, on south side of North River, in T. 58, R. 9 W., I observed rounded hills of altered Drift. Those near the head of Clear Creek seem to be formed mostly of coarse, ferruginous sand, some of it stratified and semi-indurated; the hills present a waving, undulating outline, sloping at from 35° to 45°, and forming coves of graceful contour. Good springs of water occur at their base.

The total thickness of the Drift formation I was unable to obtain; noticed it twenty-five feet in thickness on Tiger Fork.

CARBONIFEROUS SYSTEM.

Owing to the thickness of the Drift deposits, it is rather difficult to define the boundaries of the Geological formations in this county. In the west half of the county no rocks are seen outcropping. The western limit at which rocks were observed was at the following places: On Sanders' Branch, at county line, Coal Measure rocks;

Lower Carboniferous outcrop on North Fork of Salt River, as far up as Sec. 11, T. 57, R. 11; on Eaton's Branch to its head, and on Black Creek up to Sec. 2, T. 57, R. 10 W.; on North River, in Sec. 29, T. 59, R. 10; on Tiger Fork, about Sec. 17, T. 59, R. 9. Westward of this limit no rocks were observed, nor did I hear of any outcroppings; but it is highly probable that Coal Measure rocks may exist in the hills to the west, and Lower Carboniferous Limestone in the hills toward the center and western part of the county.

COAL MEASURES.

The Coal Measures underlie the surface of a part of T. 56, R. 10, and the south part of T. 57, R. 10, as observed by Mr. Wheeler and myself outcropping in branches—tributaries of North Fork of Salt River. In S. W. of N. E. Sec. 19, T. 57, R. 10 W., observed an outcrop of coal, underlaid by clay and seemingly in place. T. 56, R. 9, and T. 57, R. 9, are mostly underlaid by the Coal Measures, and also a part of T. 58, R. 9. Micaceous Sandstone outcrops in Sec. 18, T. 58, R. 9; also, in Sec. 36, T. 57, R. 9, and in E. half S. E. Sec. 33, T. 57, R. 9, observed Coal Measure Limestone, containing *Chonetes mesoloba*, *Productus* ——— and *Lingula* ———. Shales and fire clay were also observed, and some coal has been excavated.

F. *f.* FERRUGINOUS SANDSTONE

Appears in Sec. 36, T. 57, R. 9, and in Sec. 6, T. 57, R. 9. It is hard and white. But a few feet in thickness was observed.

F. *h.* ARCHIMEDES LIMESTONE.

Quantities of geodes were found in ravines running northward toward the North Fork of Salt River, in T. 57, R. 10, indicating the probable existence of the Geodiferous beds in the ridge to the southward. Bluffs of gray Limestone, interstratified with chert, were observed near Walkersville, and also near Bethel. East of this, F. *h* seems to thin out and give place to F. *i*, which rises to the surface. Near Walkersville appears an upper bed of very hard, brown, Silicious Limestone, containing Chalcedonic Geodes; some of the upper beds seen are light buff. The greatest observed thickness was only twenty feet. Fossils.

F. *i.* Encrinital Limestone.

This formation outcrops on North Fork of Salt River, above the mouth of Eaton's Branch, on North River near Miller's mill, and north-east of the last on Tiger Fork; a line drawn through these points is about its western boundary. It appears on the principal streams south-east of this line. In Sec. 9, T. 57, R. 10, on the North Fork of Salt River, it occurs in thin beds of gray Limestone, with much chert about the middle, and forming a Limestone bluff of 35 feet, with 27 feet of cherty slope above. Half a mile north-east of this, at a quarry on Eaton's Branch, it appears thus:

Section 4.

No. 1. 10 feet—5° slope.

No. 2. 1 foot chert and reddish clay; local drift.

No. 3. 16 feet gray Limestone, separated mostly by chert in lenticular forms; the upper one-half is thin-bedded and tinged with green; the lower one-half is thick-bedded and suture-jointed. The Sandstone is intercalated with the Limestone, having Limestone both above and below it.

No. 4. 15 feet—40° slope.

The thickness of this formation, in this county, is about 50 feet, and the beds belong to the upper divisions of the formation.

ECONOMICAL GEOLOGY.

COAL.

A little coal has been excavated in the N. E. quarter, Sec. 19, T. 57, R. 10 W., and more extended explorations may prove the bed of more worth than heretofore supposed.

In E. half S. E., Sec. 33, T. 57, R. 9 W., on Mrs. Deer's land, some coal has been dug out, but at the time I visited it, the coal was covered by debris; I was informed that the bed was one foot thick; in the absence of thicker beds of coal, this would be worth mining for.

MINERALS.

Beautiful quartz geodes were collected by Mr. Wheeler and myself in Sec. 20, T. 57, R. 9 W., and at a few other localities.

BUILDING ROCK.

There are good beds of gray Limestone (F. *h*) at Walkersville, and a good quarry of Limestone (F. *i*) on Eaton's branch, in Sec. 9, T. 57, R. 10. This quarry supplies Shelbyville with much of its building rock. Quarries of very good Limestone could also be opened on North River, near the mouth of Clear Creek. The Limestone quarries near Bethel supply the county for 15 miles west.

GRINDSTONES.

The micaceous Sandstone is sometimes used for grindstones, and answers the purpose very well. There is a good quarry of it on Mr. C. H. Hubbard's land, in Sec. 36, T. 57, R. 9; also on Clear Creek, near Miller's mill, in Sec. 18, T. 58, R. 9 W.

CLAYS.

On Mr. Hubbard's land, in Sec. 36, T. 57, R. 9, there occurs a bed of cream-colored clay, associated with carboniferous chert, which makes a beautiful white-wash.

TIMBER.

Good timber on the hills is rather scarce in this county; it is to the bottom lands that we must look for supplies, and we there find Pin Oak, Swamp White Oak, Elm, Hickory, Red Oak, Burr Oak, Ash, Hackberry, with some Red Birch, White Maple, Buckeye, etc.

STREAMS.

Clear Creek is a pretty and clear stream, and is fed by many springs. North River seems to afford a good supply of water. Black Creek is a very dark, sluggish stream. North Fork of Salt River affords a good supply of water, and in some places is quite swift; but the stream is generally deep, banks steep, and fording difficult.

SOILS.

Generally speaking, most of the land in this county is good; the prairies all comprise good land. Near Shelbina, I collected soil from flat, uncultivated prairie, at the several depths of—No. 1, 2 to 6 inches, No. 2, 10 to 12 inches, and No. 3, 15 to 20 inches beneath the surface.

No. 1 is dark, loose soil, with grass-roots; No. 2, dark-colored, crumbles somewhat, but is more compact than No. 1; No. 3 is dark, tough and clayey, and with brownish stains.

Mr. E. J. King says that the prairie near Shelbina does not often yield over 5 barrels of corn per acre, but by careful cultivation 10 could be produced. I am inclined to think that by judicious management 10 could be produced every year.

Mr. G. W. Leonard, in Sec. 9, T. 58, R. 11, says: 5 barrels of corn per acre, and sometimes more, are produced in his neighborhood. Wheat is not worth raising; Hungarian grass succeeds well, and makes good feed; other grasses do well; most vegetables, especially potatoes, (sweet and Irish), succeed well.

Mr. Perry, in T. 59, R. 12, says: The ground is too wet for wheat, but wheat succeeds better on timbered than on prairie lands. The prairie produces from 6 to 10 barrels of corn per acre.

The land between Fabius and Tiger Fork only averages 10 to 12 bushels of wheat per acre, and corn 6 to 8 barrels, and but rarely 10 to 12. The rolling lands stand wet seasons very well. Most vegetables succed well in this county. My opinion is that the only thing wanting to make the lands produce well in this county is a judicious and scientific system of farming. There is very little land but could be made to produce at least 10 to 12 barrels of corn per acre every year, and we hope yet to see the day when Shelby will be behind but few counties in the State in the production of cereals.

In making my Geological examinations in this county, I am indebted to the assistance of Mr. C. G. Wheeler.

CHAPTER V.

MACON COUNTY.

BY G. C. BROADHEAD.

GEOGRAPHY, TOPOGRAPHY, HYDROGRAPHY.

Macon county is bounded on the north by Adair and Knox counties; on the east by Knox and Shelby; on the south by Randolph and Chariton, and on the west by Chariton and Linn. Its area is about 813 square miles.

This county is mostly prairie; the timber being confined to the hills adjacent to the streams, and to a strip lying near the streams; the outer portions of the bottom lands consisting often of prairie. The bottom lands are generally flat, and often wet prairie. On Grand Chariton the bottoms are quite extensive, being from two to three miles wide, and consist mostly of prairie, upon which there is a tall growth of grass, which seems to be peculiar to the bottom prairie; tracts of marshy ground or ponds often occur on these bottoms. Strips of timber fringe the banks of the streams, and often extend across the bottoms. A similar description would apply to nearly all streams in this county. The bottoms of Muscle Fork, Brush Creek, Walnut and Bear Creek are about a quarter of a mile wide; those on Middle Fork of Chariton, East Fork of Chariton, and on Middle Fork of Salt River, are from a quarter to three-quarters of a mile wide. The slopes from bottoms to the hill tops are gentle, seldom exceeding from 30° to 40°.

Near Chariton, wherever the bluffs approach the stream, the hills are very much broken for a mile back. Where the bluffs are distant, the hill slopes are often gentle. West of Chariton, and north of the

Hannibal and St. Joseph Railroad, the country consists mostly of "Barrens," a very hilly region covered with tall grass and occasional clumps of stunted Post Oaks. On east side of Chariton the "Barrens" seem to be confined to the east part of T. 60, R. 16, which is quite broken to the county line; hills are high and rounded, with a few scattering Post Oak or Black Jack trees of small growth, and the valleys or "draws" between are often destitute of trees, and, in place of the reddish prairie grass which grows on the hills, have the "Bottom Prairie" grass. The country near the Muscle Fork is quite hilly; between Muscle Fork and Brush Creek especially so. On East Fork of Chariton, lying south of T. 59, it is also quite hilly; also on Middle Fork of Salt River, as far north as T. 58. The south-east township in this county is quite broken. The remainder of the county can not be said to be very broken; slopes are mostly gentle; the highest hills are on Grand Chariton and the Muscle Fork, where they attain a hight of not over 100 feet. On the other streams they are much less, being at the greatest not over 75 feet, and within twelve miles of their sources not over 40 or 50 feet high. The "Grand Divide," separating the waters of the Missouri and Mississippi, passes in a line nearly due north and south through the middle of R. 14 W. East of it we have the Middle Fork of Salt River with its braches, Narrows Creek, Winn's Creek and Hoover's Creek; also Bear Creek and Ten Mile Creek flowing into the North Fork of Salt River. West of the "Divide" the streams run in a southerly course, flowing into Chariton, and thence to the Missouri. The course of all the main ridges is thus seen to be north and south.

QUATERNARY DEPOSITS.

Alluvium.—This includes the soils, river deposits, sands, etc., and occurs everywhere in the county. North-west of McGee College, on a depression betwen slopes, noticed 2½ feet of dark soil supporting a rich growth of timber. In streams, fresh-water shells are found, of species of *Unio*, *Anadonta* and *Cyclas*. They are numerous in Chariton.

Bottom Prairie.—This formation is quite extensive, and is found on all the bottom lands, and to them it gives a decided character. It is a dark clay, which is sometimes slightly ferruginous stained. On bottoms of Grand Chariton noticed it fifteen feet in thickness. In this county it seems to be free from beds of sand, thus giving it considerable capacity to hold water, and where this formation prevails there often occur marshy tracts of ground, and sometimes ponds; these ponds seem to be a favorite resort for muskrats, and their huts on the larger ponds often number several hundred, and present the appearance, at a short distance, of a meadow covered with hay-shocks. The bottom prairies are mostly covered with a tall grass, which is cut and cured, and very much valued for hay, and is said to winter cattle well, and leave them in good order at commencement of spring. It is different from the upland prairie grass, being whiter when dry, and finer in appearance.

Bluff.—I was not able to recognize this formation in Macon county.

Drift.—This formation is quite extensive. It consists of beds of marly clays, sands and rounded pebbles and boulders. The following Section was made in railroad cut, just east of Macon City:

Section 7.

No. 1. 6 inches dark soil; a few Hazel, Laurel Oak, Pin Oak bushes.

No. 2. 1½ feet dark clay, with brownish stains. This may be the equivalent of the Bluff.

No. 3. 5 feet clay; slightly variegated; mottled brown, with bluish drab; weathers to light yellowish brown; contains a few rounded pebbles.

No. 4. 5 feet, somewhat like No. 3, but of a deeper brown, more jointed, and weathers to a deeper color.

No. 5. 12 feet brown jointed clay; dark stained on joints; is quite compact; contains many rounded pebbles; also contains white calcareous concretions; these concretions are sometimes found in flat perpendicular sheets like dykes, extending upward several feet, and of 2 inches thickness; pebbles are found adhering to them. The angle of excavation is about 45 deg., and the action of frosts causes Nos. 3 and 4 to laminate parallel to the same.

At Stoddard and Newsom's mill, on Chariton, the following Section was made:

Section 19.

No. 1. 2 feet soil and subsoil.

No. 2. 25 feet drift to water's edge in Chariton; at 8 feet from the top occurs a 2 foot bed of brown Sand, which indurates on exposure, forming a ferruginous Sandstone; below are beds of drab and brown Sand; lower down are many large boulders.

The Drift includes boulders of rock of all ages, but mostly of igneous rocks, as Granite, Greenstone, Quartzite, Porphyry. The Drift or Boulder formation is found all over the county; near Macon City it often lies directly on the surface, and in the N. W. part of the county lies strewn over the surface of the "Barrens," undoubtedly showing why these regions are so barren and destitute of large growth of trees. I am unable to give its exact thickness, but it is probably at least 60 feet. Local beds of Sand seem to prevail in the Drift.

Mr. Johnson, in Sec. 18, T. 57, R. 16, dug a well 13 feet through Clay, struck a bed of Sand which reposed on one side, but on the other side was Clay; the Sand was fine and golden colored.

Mr. Thompson dug a well 18 feet through Clay, but saw no Sand; but a short distance off he dug an ice-house, and at 10 feet came to a bed of Sand which offered effectual drainage.

COAL MEASURES.

The Coal Measures are the only Paleozoic rocks seen in this county, and extend over its whole area. In N. E. part, on Bear Creek, and also on Ten Mile, no rocks at all are seen in place, but from the topography of the country, I am disposed to place that portion among the Coal Measures. I found it difficult to get a connection of the different beds, owing, partly, to the great thickness of the overlying drift. Beds of Limestone occur on most of the streams where any rocks are found, but their proportion is small when compared with the shales and Clays. On Muscle Fork, the proportion of Limestone to shales and Sandstone is less than one-fourth, and on Chariton it is scarcely a twentieth. The Coal formations belong to the middle and lower Coal series. The Micaceous Sandstone is found in S. E. part of the county, and also on Grand Chariton and south part of Muscle Fork. The middle Coal series is found nearly everywhere. Sandstone belonging to the Micaceous Sandstone of Lower Coal series, is found on the East Fork and Middle Fork of Chariton. The highest rocks are probably on Muscle Fork, of which the following is a correct section. (Red Clay is found above No. 1):

No. 1. Near New Boston we have from 1 to 2 feet fine-grained, light-gray, or dove-colored Limestone, sometimes sligthly greenish tinged, splitting freely, and with a somewhat conchoidal fracture; even bedded; particles of calc-spar often disseminated; would polish well. Contains *Productus costatus*, *P. œquicostatus*, *Spirifer cameratus*, *Allorisma terminalis*, *Meekella striato—costata.*

No. 2. 13 feet—the upper 7 feet of Clay and calcareous shales, and next below 6 feet Clay or shales and nodular masses of Limestone. Contains many fossils, *Meekella striato-costata*, *Hemipronites*, *Athyris subtilita*, and a large *Athyris*, *Spirifer lineatus*, *Athyris decussata*. Under this we have several feet of shelly and nodular gray Limestone. These beds continue as far as the south part of T. 59.

No. 3. 4 feet of close-grained silicious ferruginous Limestone, brownish-gray, and weathering to brown; shows brown powder or rust on the surface; is thick-bedded and very hard; freshly broken, shows a buff, inclining to flesh color.

No. 4. 10 feet thin bedded Sandstone, or shaly Sandstone; color drab. Contains a little Mica, some beds of argillaceous shales interstratified. This bed is first seen in north part of T. 58; no fossils seen.

No. 5. 2 feet of dark blue Limestone, fine and close-grained; breaks vertically in right lines; recognized it as equivalent to that seen in Randolph county, where it was easily recognized by its breaking into rhomboid masses. It is used at abutment of bridge on Hannibal and St. Joseph Railroad, over Muscle Fork.

No. 6. 6 inches olive and drab shales. This is one foot thick on Chariton.

No. 7. 2 feet Bituminous shales.

No. 8. 6 to 8 inches Bituminous Coal; exposures do not show good quality.

No. 9. 5 feet Fire Clay, dark at top, brownish and blue below.

No. 10. 10 feet mostly bluish Clay and calcareous shales, containing nodular masses of blue Limestone, and sometimes a regular bed of Limestone is seen.

No. 11. 25 feet shales, drab and greenish, micaceous, argillaceous and sandy; more argillaceous toward the lower part; contains brown ferruginous concretions. South of H. and St. Jo. R. R., noticed at top 8 feet of olive and drab sandy shales, with one or two thin beds of Sandstone of 2 or 3 inches in thickness.

No. 12. 6 feet dove-colored argillaceous shales.

No. 13. 17 inches of Bituminous Coal—good quality.

No. 14. Fire Clay.

Most of the rocks seen on Grand Chariton occupy a lower geological position than those on Muscle Fork. Tumbling masses of No. 2 of the Muscle Fork section, containing a large species of *Athyris*, are found on slope at Perrin's Mill, and apparently near the parent bed, which is covered by Clay and boulders of the Drift period. The bluff is 85 feet high (50°) and the section shows:

No. 2. 1 foot coarse, dark bluish gray Limestone.

No. 3. 1½ feet bituminous shales; Coal is wanting.

No. 4. 5 feet dark olive laminated clay; contains concretionary calcareous nodules.

No. 5. 4 feet slope.

No. 6. 5 inches dark, coarse, thin-bedded Limestone; contains *Productus*.

No. 7. 2 feet slope.

No. 8. 2 feet red laminated clay.

No. 9. 3 feet fine grained buff, Silicious Limestone.

No. 10. 6 feet green shaly Sandstone.

The last is probably equivalent to the upper part of No. 11 of the Muscle Fork section.

On Cottonwood Creek we have an outcrop of buff or brown Limestone, resting on 20 feet of light blue or greenish shales, with Sandstone at bottom.

In Sec. 11, T. 59, R. 16, the following section was made:

Section 27.

No. 1. 40 feet slope; many round pebbles of drift are seen; at bottom outcrops a blue concretionary Limestone, containing large *Productus equi-costatus*, *Chonetes mesoloba*, etc.

No. 2. Snuff-brown argillaceous shales, weathering to brown. Many coal plants are found in a bed of brown ochery shale.

No. 3. 1 foot thinly laminated impure coal.

No. 4. 12 feet blue and drab argillaceous shales; some are silicious and micaceous; is probably equivalent to the Muscle Fork bed No. 11. Fossil wood is found.

On Rock Creek we have about thirty-five feet of drab shales; some are blue and some micaceous, and contain very large concretions of *Septaria.* These concretions are calcareo-silicious, and are reticulated very regularly and beautifully by veins of calc-spar. Some of them are four or five feet across and two feet in thickness; appear like a flattened Spheroid. This is also probably equivalent to No. 11 of Muscle Fork section. The same beds appear at McCulloh's Mill, and three-fourths of a mile south-east from it we have Nos. 4, 5, 6, 7 and 8 of Muscle Fork section. The equivalent of No. 11 is also seen at Hammock's Mill.

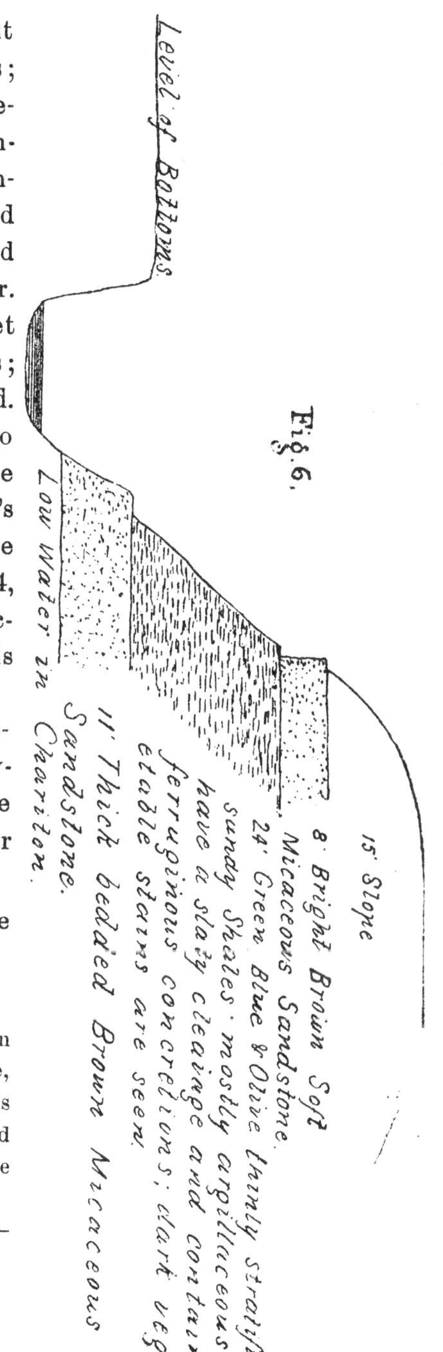

The Sandstone of the accompanying section may be the equivalent of the micaceous Sandstone on Middle Fork of Salt River, near Woodville.

In Sec. 18, T. 57, R. 16, we have the following section of rocks:

No. 1. 1 foot bluish gray Limestone.

No. 2. 12 feet sandy shales, with brown and gray calcareous Sandstone, slightly micaceous; some beds very hard, seem indurated, and of a greenish drab color. The scales of mica are few.

No. 3. 1 foot bluish drab Limestone—weathers to brown.

No. 4. 3 feet bituminous shales.

No. 5. 2 feet drab shales.

No. 6. 1 foot blue clay and shales.

No. 7. 1 foot bituminous coal.

No. 8. 9 feet slope; clay is seen at bottom and a bed of blue concretionary, pyritiferous Limestone.

On Brush Creek Mr. Wheeler observed no rock in passing down stream until he got to south part Sec. 3, T. 57, R. 17 W., when he observed ten inches of blue Limestone weathering to brown; it is quite hard and the abrasion by water is but little. In north-west of north-east Sec. 32, T. 57, R. 17, Mr. W. made the following section:

No. 1. 10 feet, 80° slope.
No. 2. 6 feet sandy micaceous shales.
No. 3. 2 feet slope.
No. 4. 1 foot hard blue Limestone; weathers to brown—No. 5 of Muscle Fork section.
No. 5. 8 feet, 60° slope.
No. 6. 2 feet very dark blue Limestone—splits easily.
No. 7. 15 feet, 60° slope.

On East Fork of Chariton, in northern part of the county, the highest rock *in situ*, observed by Mr. Wheeler, was a thick bedded, brownish drab sandstone, somewhat micaceous and often quite soft. A thickness of four feet was exposed, but it is very probable that there may be as much as twenty or thirty feet of it. Next in position below the last, we have in Sec. 22, T. 60, R. 15, about twelve feet of olive and drab argillaceous shales, containing ferruginous concretions. The connexion of this with next stratum below is not visible, but after a slope of about ten feet we have in Sec. 1, T. 59, R. 15, an outcrop of ten feet of rather irregularly bedded bluish Limestone.

Following down stream, Mr. W. made the following section in Sec. 24, T. 59, R. 15:

No. 1. 17 feet, 30° slope.
No. 2. 2 feet hard thick-bedded bluish gray Limestone, splitting readily and weathering to a grayish drab; is traversed by small veins of calc-spar; contains small ferruginous concretions.
No. 3. 1½ feet bituminous shales; argillaceous at top; contains small concretions.
No. 4. 10 inches bituminous coal.

The following Section was observed in N. W. 36, T. 59, R. 15:

No. 1. 8 feet, 75° slope.
No. 2. 1½ feet of hard dark blue Limestone, thickly bedded, but shelling off on exposure; contains *Athyris*. This bed is probably the equivalent of No. 5 of Muscle Fork section. The rocks appear about the same for several miles.

In S. W. of Sec. 30, T. 58, R. 14 W., Mr. Wheeler has the following:

Section 26.

No. 1. 29 feet, 10° slope.

No. 2. 2 feet fine-grained, thick bedded, bluish-gray Limestone, traversed by small veins of calc-spar; weathers to a ferruginous brown; contains a species of *Syringapora* (?)

No. 3. 8 feet, 60° slope.

No. 4. 15 feet Sandstone, mostly thick bedded; is calcareous; contains *Fusulina cylindrica*, *Productus* —— and concretions.

No. 5. 2 feet, 50° slope.

No. 6. 3 feet irregularly bedded, brownish Sandstone, in thick beds; —— to water in E. fork.

On Long Branch, west of Atlanta, I observed the following:

No. 1. Blue Limestone, fine-grained, mottled, silicious; rings under the hammer.

No. 2. 6 feet slope.

No. 3. 10 feet coarse ferruginous Sandstone, brown and dark-specked.

No. 4. A few feet slope.

No. 5. 1½ feet light-colored, greenish-blue argillaceous shales.

No. 6. 2½ feet of Bituminous shales.

No. 7. 10 inches Bituminous coal.

No. 8. 2 feet fire-clay.

No. 9. 10 feet slope.

No. 10. 4 feet thick bedded greenish drab Limestone, rough looking and nodular on upper part, with greenish shaly partings; contains *Spirifer plano-convexus*, *Athyris decussata* and *Hemipronites crassus.*

In Sections 29 and 31, T. 57, R. 14, we have:

No. 1. 1½ feet of Limestone.

No. 2. 15 inches bituminous shale.

No. 3. 13 inches bituminous Coal; observed at Fox's bank in Sec. 33.

No. 4. 6 to 10 feet slope, showing clays and shales.

No. 5. 5 feet drab inclining to olive argillaceous shales.

No. 6. 3 feet bluish-drab Limestone, weathering to brownish.

No. 7. 6 inches buff shales or clay.

No. 8. 11 inches shales; olive at top, dark blue at bottom.

No. 9. 4 feet bituminous shales, containing at the lower part a local bed of indurated pyritiferous shales, containing many fossils, viz.: *Productus muricatus, Pr. æqui-costatus, Machrocheilus, Selenomya, Orbiculoidea, Chonetes Smithi, Teniopteris.*

No. 10. 22 inches bituminous coal.

No. 11. Bluish fire-clay.

The above section is seen at Reese's coal bed, on a small branch flowing into East Fork of Chariton. It is further continued at Smith & Goddin's Mill, thus:

Section 11.

No. 1. 75 feet slope, 45°; two feet of drab shales are seen at bottom.

No. 2. 2½ feet Limestone; same as S. 10–6; contains *Fusulina cylindrica* and *Chætetes Milleporaceus.*

No. 3. 4 feet shales; argillaceous at top, bituminous at bottom.

No. 4. 22 inches bituminous Coal; S. 10-10.

No. 5. 7 feet fire-clay.

No. 6. 8 inches dull bluish-gray Limestone; weathers to a brownish; contains *Chonetes mesoloba* and *Fusulina cylindrica.*

No. 7. 5 feet olive clay or shales.

No. 8. 2 feet blue argillaceous Limestone, nodular and decomposing; weathers to a buff.

No. 9. 2½ feet bluish clay.

No. 10. 1½ feet ash-blue laminated clay.

No. 11. 28 inches of bituminous Coal. Down the creek found it 3 feet in thickness; one-half way from bottom appears an inch stratum of blue clay.

No. 12. 2 inches blue-black clay.

No. 13. 6 inches 30° slope.

No. 14. Blue Limestone; rough surface; in creek.

Fig. 7.

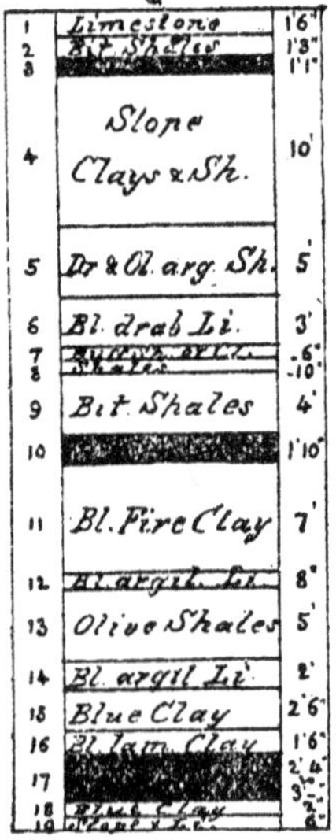

Coal beds near Macon City Macon Co.

One mile down the creek, we find six feet of bluish drab Limestone, weathering to a yellowish drab, and interstratified with it are some shaly calcareous beds, containing *Chonetes mesoloba*, etc.

On East Fork, near the south county line, Mr. Wheeler made some sections which I am disposed to place near the base of the Lower Coal series. I quote the following in S. E. of N. W. Sec. 31, T. 56, R. 14 W.:

No. 1. Slope.

No. 2. 8 feet Micaceous Sandstone; cream-colored, brown, greenish brown and banded; of greatly varying hardness.

No. 3. 11 feet nodular Limestone with clayey partings; color mottled or spotted flesh and drab; weathers to drab with brown tinge.

No. 4. 5 feet 60° slope; on upper part occur fragments of grayish-drab Limestone (S. 4, No. 7 of G. C. B.) containing *Chonetes mesoloba, Productus* ——.

No. 5. 4 feet brownish-drab argillaceous shales, with Limestone concretions containing Carbonate, Sulphuret, and Oxyd of Iron.

No. 6. 6 feet bituminous shales with concretionary beds of greenish, drab and black Limestones, interstratified with some brownish-drab, traversed by calc-spar veins; the dark Limestone contains much Sulphuret of Iron in minute crystals.

No. 7. 2 feet argillaceous shales; color dove, with yellow stains, with concretionary masses of ferruginous stained argillaceous Limestone, coated with crystals of selenite. Fossils found are *Productus muricatus* and *Rhynconella Osagensis*.

No. 8. 10 feet 30° slope; a bed of 18 inches of Coal has been worked here.

No. 9. 4 feet green, drab, grayish-white and yellow argillaceous shales; contains fragments of hard, black ferruginous Limestone, similar to that of No. 6.

No. 10. 1 foot micaceous sandy shales; greenish and brown ferruginous stained.

On Claybank Creek is 16 feet of sandy shales, resembling No. 11 of Muscle Fork section; resting on 4 feet 7 inches bituminous Coal. Nodular Limestone is found on slope above the shales.

But little rock is seen on the Middle Forks of Salt River; Sandstone mostly abounds. Near Vienna, we have the following:

No. 1. Drab shales, containing *Chonetes mesoloba*.

No. 2. 1 foot bluish drab Silicious Limestone; weathers to brown ferruginous; is probably equivalent to Sec. 26–2 of Mr. Wheeler; contains *Fusulina cylindrica*.

No. 3. 12 feet calcareous Sandstone; at bottom more sandy; contains *Fusulina cylindrica* and *Chonetes mesoloba,* as observed in Sec. 25, T. 58, R. 14. On Salt River, near Vienna, it is of a greenish color, with brown specks, and highly calcareous; contains very little mica; found *Pr. æqui-costatus* and *Athyris subtilita;* it is quite fucoidal; equivalent to No. 3 of Long Branch section.

No. 4. 22 feet coarse calcareous conglomerate is the next lowest rock seen. No. 3 was not seen resting on it; contains *Spirifer*.

Next below are 12 feet slope, with shaly outcrops. Coal has been found below the shales. Down the branch, a few hundred yards, we have four feet grayish nodular Limestone, containing *Hemipronites crassus*. This is probably the equivalent of Long Branch, Sec. No. 10.

At Carbon, on the Hannibal and St. Joseph Railroad, we have, with its accompanying rocks, the coal of Sec. 10–10.

In Sec. 16, T. 56, R. 13, I made the following Section:

Section 4.

No. 1. 40 feet, 25° slope. White Oak growth.

No. 2. 3 feet bituminous shales.

No. 3. 18 inches bituminous Coal; is of good quality, but contains some Iron pyrites. Probably=Sec. 10–10.

No. 4. Fire-clay; unknown thickness.

No. 5. 15 feet, 10° slope.

No. 6. 5 feet coarse, drab Limestone; weathers to brown on the outside. Contains *Fusulina cylindrica*, Crinoid stems, etc.

No. 7. 4 feet argillo-calcareous shales and shaly Limestone; fossils are, *Chonetes mesoloba*, *Chonetes* ———, *Productus æquicostatus*, numerous *Productus Spines*, *fucoids*, *Athyris subtilita* and *Rhombopora.*

No. 8. 4 feet greenish and olive shales; contains some round silico-calcareous concretions.

No. 9. A short distance down the creek, found a blue pyritiferous Limestone, striking fire readily, and containing *Spirifer lineatus*, *Productus æquicostatus*, *Rhynconella Osagensis.*

The next rock below this I was unable to see. Near Woodville, we have about 40 feet of micaceous Sandstone; contains ochery concretions and fossil plants; is mostly a quite soft, brown or buff Sandstone.

ECONOMICAL GEOLOGY.

COAL.

In the following list of Coal mines I shall, as far as possible, place similar beds together.

The thickest strata of Coal seen in this county are those in T. 56, R. 15 W. On Claybank Creek, in S. E. of Sec. 33, T. 57, R. 15 W., on land belonging to Mr. Nineveh Summers, I observed the following:

No. 1. 12 feet olive and blue sandy and micaceous shales.

No. 2. 3 feet of bituminous Coal.

This outcrops at the foot of the bank of creek; but little has been taken out at any time.

In S. E. corner Sec. 15, T. 56, R. 15, and on land of Basley Powell:

No. 1. Soil with Drift clays underneath.

No. 2. 3 feet sandy shale, and brown or yellow and cream-colored Sandstone; micaceous.

No. 3. 2 feet dark shales; bituminous and pyritiferous; contains *Productus æquicostatus.*

No. 4. 5 feet 9 inches bituminous Coal.

No. 5. A few inches of dove-colored, fine Clay.

No. 6. Blue, nodular Limestone in creek.

The bed of Coal here varies from 3 to 6 feet in thickness, and is exposed along creek for 200 feet. Considerable Coal has been mined here, and it is easy of access.

Mr. Wheeler observed on E. S. Gibson's land, in N. E. S. E., Sec. 22, T. 56, R. 15, the same bed of Coal, separated in middle by a stratum of a grayish blue, sandy and earthy, pyritous rock, with four and a half feet Coal above and three feet below it.

On Sand Creek, on land of Jno. B. Truitt, in N. E. of S. E., Sec. 36, T. 60, R. 16, we have—

No. 1. 15 feet of blue shale.
No. 2. 18 inches of bituminous Coal; good quality.

On west side of Muscle Fork, one and a half miles north of Hannibal and St. Joseph Railroad, there are two excavations, one owned by Thos. Burke, the other by Nutter & Cutter. The Coal is 17 inches thick, and is capped by 6 feet of dove-colored argillaceous shales. Three or four men were at work at each excavation. Messrs. Nutter & Cutter had drifted under about 40 feet. The adit is several feet above the water in the creek, so that the work is not apt to be impeded by water. The Coal is hauled to Bucklin — two miles; and from thence shipped on railroad.

The bed of Coal, 28 inches to 3 feet in thickness, which occurs at Smith & Goddin's mill, and two or three miles south, I am inclined to suppose is the equivalent of the above, but I say so with hesitation.

The following are important beds: Reese's, in Sec. 28, T. 57, R. 14 W. It has been described above. Nine men are constantly employed at work, and a face, several hundred feet in length, is exposed; no drifting has yet been done here. The thickness of stratum is 22 inches.

In S. W. of N. W., Sec. 33, T. 57, R. 14, on land of Judge Fox, the same bed of Coal crops out. Also at Smith & Goddin's mill; but at neither place has any work of consequence been done. The same stratum of Coal probably crops out on Gilstrap's land, near the crossing of the Hannibal and St. Joseph Railroad over East Fork. The Coal taken from this place is pronounced by some a superior article; but at the time Mr. Wheeler visited it, the excavation was covered with debris.

At Peter Spaulding's Coal bank, in Sec. 23, T. 57, R. 14, we have—

No. 1. Blue Limestone, 1½ feet.
No. 2. Shales, 6 feet.
No. 3. Bituminous Coal, 20 inches.

At Baxter, Bro. & Co.'s mine, near Carbon, we have the following:

No. 1. Slope.
No. 2. 2 feet blue Limestone.
No. 3. 1 foot drab shales, or Fire-clay.
No. 4. 1 foot blue shales.
No. 5. 3½ feet bituminous shales.
No. 6. 19 to 22 inches bituminous Coal.
No. 7. Grayish and blue argillaceous Clay.

The lower portion of the bituminous shales, in 50 feet, increases from 0 to 2 feet in thickness, is indurated, and contains calcareous and silicious matter; is fossiliferous. The Messrs. Baxter & Co. got out about 500 bushels per day.

At John Clifton's bank, (the "Almeda,") on east side of the creek, they were getting out about 20 tons per day. They have drifted under at one place for 100 yards, and at another 45 with sid e-driftings. They had thirteen miners at work when I visited it. The floor of the mine is 15 or 20 feet above low water in Salt River; the Baxter mines about the same; length of main adit 240 feet, with side entries about every 45 feet. The Coal here is of good quality, and easy of access. It is sent off on railroad to Hannibal.

Coal bank near Smith & Lester's mill shows the following Section:

No. 1. 20° slope.
No. 2. 18 inches dark-blue Limestone.
No. 3. 2 feet bituminous shales.
No. 4. 20 inches bituminous Coal.

No mining done here.

In Sec. 16, T. 56, R. 13, on Lewis Cox's land, the Coal is 18 inches thick; but little work has been done here.

In S. W. of Sec. 20, T. 56, R. 15, on land of Johnson Summers, Mr. Wheeler observed the following:

No. 1. 6 feet 45 deg. slope.
No. 2. 1½ feet bituminous shales; lower part has imbedded round masses of iron pyrites inclosing a few fossils; some fossil wood. Argillaceous concretions abound.
No. 3. 1½ feet of bituminous coal.

At a quarry in S. E. Sec. 27, T. 58, R. 16 W., I made the following:

Section 24.

No. 1. 50 feet 20° slope.
No. 2. 12 feet drift, of which the upper six feet is brown clay; below, it is jointed, and at bottom is two feet of coarse sand and rounded pebbles.
No. 3. 12 feet thinly stratified Sandstone; micaceous, brown and bluish drab. Fossils are, *Productus costatus*, *Spirifer cameratus*, *Athyris subtilita.*
No. 4. 16 inches blue Limestone. When broken it presents a rough, coarse-looking fracture, but it is in reality fine-grained. Contains *Spirifer cameratus*, etc.
No. 5. 1 foot dark blue argillaceous shales.
No. 6. 2½ feet bituminous shales.
No. 7. 1 foot bituminous Coal.
No. 8. 10 feet slope to bottoms.
The bed of coal here is not worked at all.

In N. E. Sec. 33, T. 56, R. 14, on Newton Switzer's land, Mr Wheeler observed the following:

No. 1. Slope.
No. 2. 5 feet Limestone.
No. 3. 6 feet shales; argillaceous at top, bituminous at bottom.
No. 4. 2 feet bituminous Coal; thickness is variable, and was informed that it ranged from fourteen to twenty-six inches in thickness.

At Stanfield's coal mine, in E. half S. W. Sec. 24, T. 56, R. 15, Mr. Wheeler observed the following:

No. 2. 2 feet Limestone; blue, brown-specked, weathers to brown.
No. 3. 8 inches bright yellow clay.
No. 4. 4 feet shales; argillaceous at top, bituminous at bottom. Contains concretions.
No. 5. 12 inches bituminous Coal, thirty-five or forty feet above water in East Fork.

On S. E. N. E. Sec. 24, T. 56, R. 15, at Mr. Walter's bed, the following section:

No. 1. 3 feet slope.
No. 2. 2½ feet thick-bedded, bluish gray Limestone; breaks into nodular masses.
No. 3. 12 feet slope.
No. 4. 4 feet bituminous shales; contains a bed of Limestone.
No. 5. 16 inches bituminous Coal.
No. 6. 1 inch blue clay.
No. 7. 2½ feet slope.
No. 8. 1½ feet bituminous shales.
No. 9. 14 inches Coal.
No. 10. 1 inch yellow clay. Level of East Fork.

In N. W. corner of Sec. 3, T. 56, R. 13 W., on land of A. Harris, I made the following:

Section 1.

No. 1. 40 feet 10° slope.
No. 2. 6 feet drab, earthy shales. A bed of brownish Limestone, traversed by veins of calc-spar, occurs toward the lower part.
No. 3. 2 feet blue-black shales, containing small, earthy concretions.
No. 4. 1 foot bituminous shale, containing a five-inch stratum of white, soft botryoidal concretions.
No. 5. 1 foot shales or fire clay; olive, brown and blue.
No. 6. 4 feet blue, argillaceous shales; thin ferruginous partings toward the lower part.
No. 7. 18 inches bituminous coal.
No. 8. 12 feet 45° slope. A little coal has been excavated here, and has proved good.

The above are the principal exposures of Coal in this county, from which we see that Macon county is well supplied with Coal.*

IRON ORE.

Brown, ocherous, hollow concretions occur in the Sandstone and shales on Middle Fork of Salt River, in T. 56, R. 13 W.; also in similar shales on Grand Chariton, in Sec. 2, T. 59, R. 16 W. At the latter place, there is a thin stratum of two or three inches of brown Oxide of Iron. Sulphuret of iron is intercalated with most of the beds of Coal and bituminous shales.

Quartz crystals are found adhering to Limestone. Carbonate of lime is found in the beds of bituminous coal, adhering in thin sheets between the perpendicular joints; it also is often found with the Limestones.

GYPSUM.

Selenite is found at Carbon in argillaceous shales. Near Atlanta, in the fire clay underlying the coal, Mr. Atterbury found some beautiful crystals, which he presented to the State collection. Among them was a twin crystal.

FIRE-CLAY.

None of the clay in this county has yet been tested as to its utility for making fire-brick, but the beds are extensive, and would doubtless answer that purpose very well. It underlies the coal nearly everywhere.

*Since the survey of this county, some valuable Coal mines have been opened. I would mention those at Bevier, where large quantities of Coal are mined. This Coal is probably the equivalent of the thick seam seen in bed of East Fork of Chariton, south-west of Macon City.

BUILDING ROCK.

This article is scarce in some parts of the county, more especially the northern part. In fact, there is very little rock suitable for building north of the Hannibal and St. Joseph Railroad. Near the head of East Fork of Chariton, there occurs a Sandstone which is used for common building purposes. Rock is very scarce on Middle Fork of Chariton. The Limestone equal to No. 2 of section at Carbon is much used on Hannibal and St. Joseph Railroad and North Missouri Railroad. Good quarries of this rock are also found on East Fork of Chariton. In the neighborhood of Woodville, there are good beds of Sandstone. The only good quarry on Grand Chariton is in S. E. Sec. 27, T. 58, R. 16 W.; it is a blue Limestone sixteen inches in thickness, and is used for abutments of bridge over Chariton at McCulloh's mill. The same rock is quarried on Brush Creek and Muscle Fork, and used in railroad bridges. The Limestone (No. 1) at New Boston forms a beautiful and durable building rock.

Red Clay, highly ferruginous, is found near New Boston; also, at Perrin's mill. If developed and properly tested, it may prove valuable for ordinary painting.

WATER POWER.

Springs are scarce in this county; but by sinking wells, good streams of water are often reached. Cisterns are depended on mostly for drinking water. Grand Chariton is a tolerably clear running stream, having sufficient water for mills at all seasons. Mr. McCulloh informed me that he had owned his mill for eleven years, and had never stopped running it for lack of water. There are three water mills on this stream, which grind and saw the year round.

Muscle Fork is a clear, swift-running stream, but the water power is not sufficient to propel machinery the whole year. There are several water mills on this stream.

The other streams of this county are mostly quite sluggish.

SOILS.

As soils are apt to vary in all counties, it is very natural to suppose that in a county as large as Macon, there would be considerable difference in the character of the soils. They may be divided as follows:

1. Bottom Lands, which include all the low grounds along the streams. The soil is from one to three feet deep, and capable of yielding abundantly; but as yet none of the bottoms have been much cultivated, owing to their being so flat and holding much water. By ditching, any of them could be made valuable. On Grand Chariton there are upward of sixty square miles of exceedingly rich bottom land, very little of which is at present cultivated. The ditching of this would not cost a great deal, and the yield to the farmer would be great. The same may be said of the bottoms on the other streams. The principal growth on Chariton bottoms is Pin Oak, Swamp White Oak and Shell-bark Hickory, which fringe the edge of the bottom prairie. Cottonwood, Elm and White Maple also abound. Other trees, not quite as abundant as the last, are Black Walnut, Burr Oak and Box Elder. Along the banks of the streams, Sycamore and Birch abound. The bottoms on other streams are similar to those of Grand Chariton.

Upland Soils.

1. The best that came under my notice was that portion of the county including most of T. 56, R. 15 W., and lying south and east of Claybank Creek. Soil is rich, and growth of timber Pin Oak, Laurel Oak, Wild Cherry, Red and Am. Elm. Similar land was noticed in Secs. 9 and 10, T. 60, R. 16 W.

2. Portions of this are but little inferior to the first-named, and it includes a large portion of the county. We find good land throughout most of R. 13, beginning at the southern part of T. 57, and spreading across T. 60 as far as Newburg; thence southward along the divide between the Middle Fork of Salt River and East Fork of Chariton, but is here mostly confined to the prairie and immediately adjacent; near the edge of the prairie are found Laurel Oak, Black Oak, Cornus, Crab Apple, Hazel and Post Oak. This class of land also extends over R. 15, beginning at south part of T. 57. We here find Black Oak, Laurel Oak and Hazel, sometimes Shell-bark Hickory, Swamp White Oak and Pin Oak. Similar land occurs on west side of Claybank Creek; also east of Chariton, in T. 57. On slopes near Muscle Fork, in T. 60, the land is not quite as good as some above mentioned, but is still tolerably good, as is also some lying between Brush and Puzzle Creeks.

3. Poorer land we find on hills near Billy's Creek, Long Branch and East Fork and on Middle Fork of Salt River. The growth con-

sists mostly of White Oak, Post Oak and Black Oak, with sometimes a little Hickory.

4. Land more broken and poor is found between Newburg and Cottonwood Creek; between Brush Creek and Muscle Fork; most of T. 60, R. 17; hills east of Chariton in Ts. 58 and 59, and west of Chariton, near Hammack's Mill.

AGRICULTURE.

The prairie near Macon City produces eight to ten barrels of corn per acre, but with proper care twelve could be raised. The richest lands in the county could, if properly cultivated, produce twelve barrels of corn per acre.

Wheat has not yet succeeded well; it sometimes freezes out, and very often not more than half a crop is produced; thirty bushels per acre has been produced on the prairie between Grand Chariton and Middle Fork. Most vegetables succeed well. Grasses grow well. Clover has not been tried much as yet, but it succeeds tolerably well; it is said that it does not often withstand the frosts of winter.

Most fruits succeed well, but as yet little attention has been paid to their culture. Peach trees are liable to be killed by the cold winters, but, when not killed, bear good crops of fruit. Wild grapes are rare on the hills; winter or "coon" grapes grow on the bottoms. There are some wild plums. The persimmon does not grow in this county.

The mingling of the marls of the Bluff (?) or Drift with the soil seems to improve it very much, as we see exemplified near the railroad excavations, where these clays have been thrown out, and, mixing with the soil, produce a very luxuriant vegetation. I was further informed that it was sometimes even more rank than on Chariton bottoms. I was also informed that a gentleman in Chariton county hauled out the clay and scattered it over his meadow, which was thereby very much improved. This clay is generally very calcareous.

Query: Would not subsoiling improve the lands of Macon county?

TIMBER.

The principal bodies of good timber found in this county occur on the bottom lands. There is but little good timber on the hills. The principal localities of good timber are the following: On the bottoms of Grand Chariton we have Cottonwood, Sycamore, Elm, White Maple, Burr Oak, Swamp White Oak, Pin Oak, Red Oak, Black Walnut, Linden, Laurel Oak. The above trees are found on most of the bottoms. On Walnut Creek there is a good deal of Black Walnut; also on Muscle Fork. On the latter we find Ash. White Walnut is only found on Cottonwood Creek and Muscle Fork. Near McGee's College we have good timber, including Pin Oak, Laurel Oak, Elm. Near Claybank Creek there is good timber, including Laurel Oak, Swamp White Oak, Pin Oak, White Oak. The woods around Bloomington afford some good timber, such as Black Oak, Swamp White Oak, Hickory, White Oak. There is some good timber on the hills near Ten Mile Creek.

CHAPTER VI.

RANDOLPH COUNTY.

BY G. C. BROADHEAD.

GEOGRAPHY—TOPOGRAPHY.

Randolph county is bounded on the north by Macon, on the east by Monroe and Audrain, on the south by Boone and Howard, and on the west by Chariton county. Its area is about 463 square miles. The proportion of timbered lands exceeds the prairie.

The Grand Divide between the waters of the Missouri and those of the Mississippi passes in a northerly course through the eastern part of the county, leaving more than one fourth on the east drained by streams flowing off eastward to the Mississippi; west of this divide, the streams, mostly pursuing a south-west course, flow onward to mingle their waters with the Missouri. The slopes east of the divide, and near the prairie, are generally quite gentle; but as the streams enlarge and pass onward into the timber, the hills gradually become of greater hight; but at their greatest elevation, none of the bluffs exceed 75 feet.

The slopes adjacent to Flat Creek are very gentle, and the hills not much over 50 feet in hight. The southern part of T. 52, R. 14 W., is very broken, especially near Moniteau and Perche Creeks. Westward, toward Roanoke, the country is rolling; near Silver Creek, from near its source, and as far as R. 16, the country is quite hilly, and near the streams the bluffs are about 75 feet high. Westward, and extending northward into T. 54, the slopes are gentle, undulating and rolling, with bluffs not over 45 or 50 feet high, and oftener much less. Eastward, between Chariton and Sweet Spring Creek, the country is rolling. Between Dark Creek and East Fork, it is gently rolling; slopes adjacent to Dark Creek and Muncas Creek are gentle; more hilly near the Middle Fork of Chariton, and still more so near the

East Fork. In the northern part of the county, between the East Fork and Middle Fork, the country is undulating — rolling. Near the East Fork, Walnut and Sugar Creeks, the country is quite hilly.

The valleys of the streams are generally pretty wide--the bottoms of Middle Fork about one-fourth of a mile; those of East Fork at least one-fourth, and often one-half mile in width, and are very flat; those of Sweet Spring Creek, Sugar Creek, Flat Creek and Mud Creek are narrower; those of Moniteau and Perche are quite narrow--the Moniteau bottoms being not often over 200 yards wide.

SCIENTIFIC GEOLOGY.

The Geological formations seen in this county are the Quaternary, Coal Measures, Ferruginous Sandstone and Archimedes Limestone.

QUATERNARY SYSTEM.

Alluvium.—This includes the soil, humus or mold, sands and Local Drift in and near streams, and all formations now in progress.

Bottom Prairie.—This is confined to the flats or low grounds near the principal streams. It is well developed on East Chariton, where I noticed it 10 feet in thickness, and mostly a dark blue stiff Clay, with brownish concretionary spots, which harden on exposure, forming roughly-shaped botryoidal concretions of brown Oxide of Iron.

Bluff.—These Clays more often occur on the hills, and generally of a brown-ash color, and mostly stiff, tenacious and jointed. Sec. 23 shows No. 2, 4 feet of reddish-yellow or brown Clay, with a few small pebbles; No. 3, 36 feet yellowish and yellow and blue mottled, jointed Clay, with many small, round pebbles.

Sec. 55, on Flat Creek, appears thus:

No. 1. 10 inches soil and subsoil.
No. 2. 1 foot brown jointed Clay.
No. 3. 9 feet yellow Clay, blue and drab variegated; contains rounded pebbles; the escarpment is worn by abrasion of water into recesses, causing it to present a constellated appearance.

The total thickness of Bluff observed was about 40 feet; but it is probably 60 or 70 feet in all.

Drift or Boulder Formation.—Underlying the Bluff, of Sec. 23, appear beds of Sand and blue Clay, with many pebbles and boulders. Beds of very coarse ferruginous Sand occur; boulders of Granite, Greenstone, Quartzite, etc., are occasionally found strewn over the surface.

CARBONIFEROUS SYSTEM.

COAL MEASURES.

The Coal Measures occupy near the whole county. The thickness of the various strata, as shown in accompanying section, is correct:

I. 1 foot coarse gray oolitic Limestone.

II. 5 feet slope.

III. 8 feet mostly thin beds of fine-grained grayish or light drab Limestone, with particles of calc-spar disseminated; the beds are separated by green shaly partings; the Limestone is sometimes greenish tinged—is often nodular and very rough on the upper surface. The fossils mostly abounding are: *Productus costatus, P. splendens, P. semireticulatus, Spirifer cameratus, S. lineatus, Sp. Kentuckensis, Chætetes milleporaceus, Hemipronites crassus, C. Flemingi, C. mesoloba, C. Smithi, Athyris subtilita, Rhynconella Osagensis.*

IV. 4 feet fine-grained blue or dove-colored Limestone; lower part somewhat nodular, and with clayey partings. Fossils are, *Spirifer cameratus*, etc.

V. 3 feet blue Clay.

VI. 8 feet mostly a nodular or concretionary heavy bedded Limestone; very rough looking, breaks into nodules with clayey partings; when broken it seems a compact, grayish or bluish-drab, with a somewhat mottled appearance; this resembles No. III. Fossils are: *Spirifer cameratus, Sp. lineatus, Sp. plano-convexus, Productus muricatus, Pro. costatus, Pro. splendens, Athyris subtilita, Chonetes mesoloba, Chætetes milleporaceus, Allorisma hiatula, Holopea (?), Hemipronites crassus, Meekella striato-costata.*

Fig. 8.

System	No.	Stratum	Thickness
Quarternary		Bottom Prairie	10'
		Bluff	40'
		Drift	10'
Coal Measures	1	Oolitic Li.	1'
	2'	Slope	10'
	3	Li & Marlite	8'
	4	Dove col. Li	4'
	5	Blue Cl.	3'
	6	Nodular Li	8'
	7	Ferruginous Li.	2 6
	8	Drab & Brown Sandst. & Shales slightly mic.	22
	9	Rhomboidal Li.	5
	10	Bit. Shales	2 6
	11	Bit. Coal	1
	12	Fire Clay	2'
	13	Marlite & Li.	13'
	14	Clay	1
	15	Bit Shales	5
	16	Bit. Coal	2 0
	17	Fire Clay	4
	18	Clay with Nod. Li.	5
	19	Cal. Conglomerate	1
	20	Drab Sandst.	10'
	21	Mic. Sd.st. & Sh.	18'
	22	Argill Shales	17'
	23	Ochreous Sh.	1'
	24	Bit. Coal	4
	25	Laminated Cl.	1
	26	Marlite	1
	27	Bl. Drab Li.	2
	28	Fucoidal Sd.st.	3
	29	Bl. drab Li.	2
	30	Argill Shales	20
	31	Bit. Shales	3
	32	Bit Coal	1 5
	33	Shale & Fire Cl.	16'
	34	Slope	15'
Lower Carbon.	35	Ferruginous Sd.st.	15
	36	Chert	3'
	37	Archimedes Li.	20'

Randolph Co.

VII. 2½ feet buff or blue mottled Limestone; weathers to brown, and rings under the hammer. Fossils are *Productus costatus*, *Spirifer lineatus*, etc.

VIII. 22 feet of buff or light drab Sandstone and shales, somewhat micaceous; the Sandstone, of which there is from 4 to 8 feet, more often occupies the middle, with shales above and below. The upper shales and also those at bottom are generally olive-green or blue; the Sandstone is often ferruginous stained; the strata are generally thin.

IX. 3 feet, and sometimes only 2½ feet of *Rhomboidal* Limestone. This is a dark blue Limestone, weathering to ash-brown; fine-grained, silicious, and rings under hammer; the upper part is shelly, below which there is 1½ feet breaking with even, perpendicular planes into fragments, whose upper and lower surfaces are rhomboids. In the bed of Moniteau I noticed it extending across the bottom of the stream, causing it to appear as if paved with regular lozenge-shaped flags.

X. 2 feet to 32 inches bituminous shales.

XI. 1 foot bituminous Coal; varies from 8 inches to 19 inches, and Sec. 29 shows it to be absent.

XII. 2 feet blue fire-clay; in some places it is much thicker.

XIII. 13 feet, including bluish-drab Limestone and Marlite. The Limestone weathers to a brownish, and rings under the hammer. Fossils are *Athyris subtilita*, *Productus Hildrethianus*, *Pr. Portlockianus*, *Pr. punctatus*, *Pr. æquicostatus*, *Pr. Boonensis*, *Pr. muricatus*, *Spirifer cameratus*, *Spirifer lineatus*.

XIV. 1 foot Clay.

XV. 5 feet bituminous shales; contains small, round, dark concretions.

XVI. 20 inches bituminous Coal.

XVII. 4 feet yellow fire-clay.

XVIII. 5 feet bed of Clay, containing small, nodular concretions of Limestone.

XIX. 1 foot calcareous conglomerate—not persistent.

XX. 10 feet Sandstone; at Huntsville this bed is found containing indurated nodules, which sometimes weather out, leaving irregular, vermiform, winding cavities; is not persistent.

XXI. 18 feet shaly Sandstone and shales; brown and drab micaceous, and sometimes speckled with ferruginous stains.

XXII. 17 feet argillaceous shales, mostly blue, especially the lower 6 or 7 feet, and often light dove or gray color; contains ocherous concretions, and sometimes concretions of carbonate of Iron. The partings between the strata are sometimes yellowish, and the shales often contain a little mica.

XXIII. 6 inches to 1 foot; Sec. 24 shows indurated bituminous and pyritous shale; at Sec. 6, 3 inches of brown ocherous shale. Bituminous shales were only observed capping the Coal at two localities, at one of which they were 2 inches in thickness.

XXIV. 4 feet bituminous Coal; varies in thickness; is sometimes more and often much less than 4 feet in thickness.

XXV. 2 feet mostly blue laminated Clay, often ferruginous, and at Sec. 6 the upper portion consists of 8 inches of a brown ocherous conglomerate.

XXVI. 2 feet Marlite, or nodules of concretionary Limestone, imbedded in Clay; fossils are *Spirifer* ——, *Athyris subtilita*, *Productus æquicostatus*, *Pr. punctatus*.

XXVII. 2 feet bluish-drab Limestone, rough looking on the surface; contains *Chonetes mesoloba* and a fucoid.

XXVIII. 3 feet mostly calcareous sandy shales, containing a fucoid resembling the *Cauda-Galli—Caulerpites*. This rock is micaceous, and may be denominated "Fucoidal Sandstone." Fossils are *Spirifer plano-convexus*, *Athyris subtilita*, *Chonetes mesoloba*, *Productus Hildrethianus*.

XXIX. 2 feet bluish-gray or drab Silicious Limestone, mostly in even beds; contains *Fusulina cylindrica*, *Spirifer cameratus*, *Sp. lineatus*, *Chonetes mesoloba*, *Productus costatus*, *Pr. muricatus*, *Pr. Portlockianus*.

XXX. 20 feet argillaceous shales; contains a few thin calcareous concretionary beds, some concretions of septaria, and some ferruginous concretions; and a few thin calcareous strata, abounding in *Chonetes mesoloba*, *Athyris subtilita*, and *Productus muricatus*, are present.

XXXI. 3 feet bituminous shales; sometimes they contain concretions of black Limestone; lower part is sometimes indurated and very pyritiferous, and contains many fossils—*Chonetes mesoloba*, *Chonetes* ——, *Athyris subitlila*, *Productus muricatus*, and *Spirifer lineatus*.

XXXII. 17 inches bituminous Coal.

XXXIII. 16 feet shales and fire-clay.

NOTES AND OBSERVATIONS ON THE ABOVE GENERAL SECTION.

VII. In Macon county this is a very ferruginous and silicious Limestone.

VIII. In Sec. 35-3 the Sandstone occurs with shales below; the color is brown, with a greenish tinge; ferruginous stains and spots are disseminated.

XIII. Sec. 52 shows 4 feet of Limestone resting on bituminous shales. At Sec. 67-3 we have 8 feet outcrops of bluish drab Limestone and nodular masses of Limestone in Clay. No. 4, bituminous shales outcrop. [See Moniteau section.]

XVI. The Coal is of variable thickness: Sec. 47-6 = 11 inches; 49-8 = 14 inches; 50-5 = 20 inches and sometimes 2 feet; 52-8 is 18 inches and 54-4 is 20 inches thick.

XIX. This was only observed at Huntsville; it is formed of coarse pebbles cemented together and resting on XX.

XX. Was only observed at Huntsville.

XXIV. This bed of coal is generally 4 feet in thickness, but it sometimes varies very much: Sec. 3, 12-3, 67-8, are all 4 feet thick; 19-4 is 4′ 3″; 24-5 is 18 inches; 25-4 is 16 inches; 30-4 is 20 inches; 31-2 is 3½ feet; 50-7 is 18 inches thick.

XXVI, XXVII, XXVIII and XXIX are better developed at Sec. 12 than at any other locality, which section is as follows:

No. 3. Bituminous Coal.
No. 4. 4 feet slope.
No. 5. 6 inches ocherous ferruginous shales, becoming indurated on exposure.
No. 5½. 4 feet grayish drab Limestone, rough looking on the upper surface.
No. 6. 3 inches buff calcareous Clay containing concretions and fossils.
No. 7. 2½ feet calcareo-silicious shales, sandy; with markings resembling *Fucoides Cauda-Galli*, (*Caulerpites marginatus*.)
No. 8. 8 inches Limestone, resembling No. 5, and containing *Caulerpites*.
No. 9. 1 foot olive shales.
No. 10. Bluish drab Limestone, even bedded.

XXX. I am inclined to refer the lower part of Sec. 3 to XXX. It appears thus:

No. 2. 1 foot Limestone = XXIX.
No. 3. 9 feet slope.
No. 4.—
- a = 2½ feet drab and olive shales.
- b = 5 inches dark bluish drab limestone; contains Septaria.
- c = 3 feet drab and blue shales; contains *Ch. mesoloba* and Septaria.
- d = 5 inches—similar to b.
- e = 6 inches blue and drab shale.

No. 5. Bituminous shales, containing black calcareous concretions traversed by veins of calc-spar.

In sections 8, 11 and 13 there occurs a concretionary bed of dark bluish black, compact earthy pyritiferous Limestone, variegated with ash blue, black and brown spots and bands. The shales of sections 13 and 62, and some other sections, contain ferruginous concretions.

XXXI. In Sec. 13-6, at bottom, is 1½ feet of dark indurated shales. very pyritiferous and containing many fossils.

Sec. 64 shows the connection of some of the lower beds :

No. 1. 15 feet—10° slope.
No. 2. 9 feet ochery ferruginous shales, with some concretions = XXIII.
No. 3. 2 feet slope, showing black smut.
No. 4. 2 feet nodular bluish drab Limestone = XXVII.
No. 5. 3 feet greenish fucoidal Sandstone = XXVIII.
No. 6. 3 feet drab Limestone, bluish tinged = XXIX.
No. 7. 18 feet drab argillaceous shales, containing ferruginous concretions, Septaria and thin calcareous strata, containing *Chonetes mesoloba* = XXX.
No. 8. Black smut.
No. 9. 9 feet like No. 7 = XXXIII.
No. 10. 10 feet blue Clay = XXXIII.

The following is a vertical section, including all the rocks seen on Moniteau Creek:

Section 68.

No. 1. 1 foot coarse gray oolitic Limestone.
No. 2. 5 feet slope.
No. 3. 4 feet fine-grained grayish drab sub-crystalline Limestone, weathering roughly; occurs in 6-inch strata, separated by buff marly shales, containing nodules of Limestone; contains many fossils = III.
No. 4. 2 feet fine-grained dove-colored Limestone.
No. 5. 4 feet slope.
No. 6. 3 feet blue Clay.
No. 7. 7 feet Limestone; fracture shows a dove color, mostly a nodular or concretionary heavy-bedded Limestone; noticed it at a few localities lying in large tumbled masses on the hill-side.
No. 8. 6 inches blue and buff sandy shales.
No. 9. 1 foot olive micaceous sandy shales.
No. 10. 10 inches olive and brown micaceous sandy shales.
No. 11. 4 feet olive and blue shaly micaceous Sandstone.
No. 12. 1 foot thin-bedded grayish micaceous Sandstone.
No. 13. 1 foot sandy and argillaceous shales.
No. 14. 3½ feet Rhomboidal Limestone, blue color; rings under the hammer.
No. 15. 20 inches to 32 inches bituminous shales.
No. 16. 8 inches to 10 inches bituminous Coal = XI.
No. 17. 1 foot blue Clay = XII.
No. 18. 1 foot yellow Clay = XII.
No. 19. 3 feet 4 inches heavy-bedded bluish drab Limestone; colors arranged in spots, showing light and dark shades of blue shading into each other = XIII.
No. 20. 2 feet buff argillo-calcareous shales, containing in the upper part many concretions of Limestone in round and oblong cylindrical forms = XIII.

The following is a vertical section on Sweet Spring Creek:

Section 69.

No. 1. 3½ feet fine-grained dove-colored Limestone; the lower part nodular, with clayey partings.
No. 2. 2 feet olive Clay=V.
No. 3. 1 foot slope.
No. 4. 5 feet dove-colored Limestone; separates into nodular masses by clayey partings; rough looking.
No. 5. 10 feet Sandstone.
No. 6. 3 feet blue Limestone—"Rhomboidal."
No. 7. 2 feet bituminous shales.
No. 8. 1 foot bituminous Coal.
No. 9. 15 feet slope.
No. 10. 1 foot drab Limestone.
No. 11. 1 foot bituminous shales.
No. 12. 11 inches bituminous Coal.
No. 13. 2 feet yellow Clay.
No. 14. 1 foot nodular calcareous clayey bed.
No. 15. 10 feet brown and bluish sandy shales.
No. 16. 5 feet olive-colored sandy shales, with an occasional thin one-inch ferruginous stratum.
No. 17. 7 feet mostly sandy shales, argillaceous at bottom.
No. 18. Bituminous Coal.

Similar sections to the above were observed on Silver Creek and Walnut Creek, and Mr. Wheeler made the following general section on Sugar Creek from near its head-waters to north-east of Sec. 15, T. 54, R. 14 W.

No. 1. 5 feet irregularly bedded, fine grained, bluish drab or dove-colored Limestone, in thick beds and contains veins of calc-spar.
No. 2. 10 feet Sandstone and shales.
No. 3. 2½ feet blue and yellow argillaceous shales.
No. 4. 3 inches brown ferruginous shales.
No. 5. 2 feet dark blue hard Limestone, thick bedded, traversed by small veins of calc-spar and abounding, on upper surface, in *Chætetes milleporaceus*, forming large mammillary protuberances; breaks into rhomboidal masses.
No. 6. 2 feet bituminous shales.
No. 7. 12 inches Coal.
No. 8. 3 feet slope.
No. 9. 1 foot hard blue Limestone; weathers to brown.
No. 10. 5 feet yellow and bluish drab argillaceous shales.
No. 11. 2½ feet hard blue Limestone; upper part concretionary; has a pot-metal ring.
No. 12. 4 feet shales, argillaceous at top, bituminous at bottom.
No. 13. 1 foot bituminous Coal.
No. 14. 10 feet slope.
No. 15. 4 feet hard, blue and buff Limestone, traversed by small veins of calc-spar; pot-metal ring.
No. 16. 6 feet blue, olive and yellow argillaceous shales.

No. 17. $1\frac{1}{2}$ feet blue Limestone, in thick beds, but laminates on exposure; weathers to brown; is traversed by small calc-spar veins.

On Hoover's Creek I observed the rocks from III to XVI inclusive.

LOWER CARBONIFEROUS.

FERRUGINOUS SANDSTONE

Was only observed at and near Fray's Mill, on East Fork of Chariton, in Sec. 12, T. 54, R. 15 W. The upper part is highly ferruginous, quite red and very coarse-grained; the lower beds are whitish and hard; its total thickness is probably about fifteen feet.

ARCHIMEDES LIMESTONE.

This formation was observed at the same locality where the Ferruginous Sandstone was seen and immediately underlying it; the upper portion is a three foot bed of chert; and next below are beds of gray Limestone, interstratified with chert. At Sweet Spring, in Sec. 17, T. 53, R. 15 W., observed about twenty feet of coarse gray Limestone, interstratified with chert; some of the beds make a good building rock; fossils contained are *Bryozoons*, *Cyathophyllum* and *Productus punctatus*, etc., supposed to be equivalent to Prof. Hall's Keokuk Limestone. This rock extends only a short distance up and down the stream, and as no dip of strata was observed, we are induced to believe that this rock formed the nucleus of an island in the seas previous to the deposition of the upper Archimedes or Warsaw Limestone, and remained so until the close of the epoch immediately preceding the deposition of the Coal Measure rocks.

ECONOMICAL GEOLOGY.

COAL.

I subjoin the following notice of the principal localities where Coal was observed, and would add that but little mining has been done at any of them; only enough Coal taken out at different times to supply the immediate necessities of the neighboring people. Coal is so abundant in this county, and is seen outcropping at so many localities, that the inhabitants do not place a proper estimate on its value. The quality is generally good, but we find more or less Sulphuret of Iron accompanying it. At some future time the Coal of Randolph county will be a valuable article of commerce.

On land of J. B. Mitchel, in Sec. 3, T. 55, R. 15, excavations have been made at several localities, but little Coal has been taken out; the thickness of the stratum is about 16 inches, and corresponds to XXXII. XXXII also crops out on the land of M. Richmond, in southern part of Sec. 8, T. 55, R. 15 W.

In Sec. 7, T. 55, R. 15, on land of Robt. H. Jackson, the Coal is 17 inches thick, and may be referred to XXXII.

A. J. Hunt's Coal bed in N. W. S. E., Sec. 10, T. 54, R. 15, is four feet thick, and is equivalent to XXIV; 300 yards west, and on land of R. Mitchell, it appears of the same thickness. These outcrops are situated very favorably for working.

On T. T. Vroom's land, in N. E. Sec. 6, T. 53, R. 15, the four foot bed occurs very favorably for working.

At Huntsville, several driftings have been made, and considerable Coal taken out; the thickness is generally about four feet, and corresponds to XXIV; the quality is good. Messrs. Carlyle and Rothwell have drifted under about 140 feet, with 15 feet width at terminus. Mr. W. R. Samuels has also drifted in some distance.*

North-east of Huntsville, three-quarters of a mile, XI crops out 15 inches thick, and is exposed very favorably for working; XVI has been worked near by, but when I visited the locality it was covered up by debris, so that I could not observe the thickness.

South-east of Huntsville a short distance there is an outcrop of 10 inches Coal, which is probably equivalent to XVI.

In Sec. 36, T. 53, R. 16, on land of Jno. D. Bowcock, XXIV is worked, but it lies at great disadvantage, being partly in the creek, and often covered by water.

One-half mile east of last, XXIV is 16 inches thick, and is 9 feet above the water in creek; but little Coal has been taken out at either of these places.

In Sec. 33, T. 53, R. 15 W., on land of L. C. Fullington, XXIV appears in the bed of Silver Creek, generally 20 inches thick, but its thickness varies. Some work is done here, but the water is quite an impediment.

On Coal Bank Creek XXIV appears 3½ feet in thickness, with outcrops at several places. On land of John Viley, in N. E. N. W., Sec. 3, T. 52, R. 15 W., XXIV is finely exposed at the base of the bluff, appearing at intervals for several hundred yards along the stream. The following Section was made:

* Shafts on railroad extend to the same Coal. This has been opened since the survey was made.

Fig. 9.

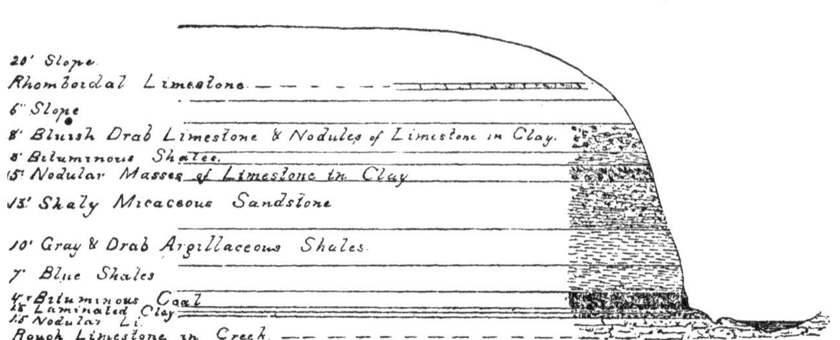

On land of John Fray, in N. E. Sec. 7, T. 52, R. 15 W., we have the following Section :

No. 2. 5 feet dove-colored argillaceous shales.
No. 3. 11 inches bituminous Coal ; lower part shaly.
No. 4. Clay.
No. 5. 8 feet slope ; sandy shales crop out at the lower part; down the branch a hundred yards we find a nodular Limestone. This bed of Coal I was unable to make agree with my general Section ; it may occupy (as I think it does) a higher stratigraphical position.

In Sec. 30, T. 52, R. 13, on the land of Wm. Lewis, XXIV is 4½ feet thick. It is situated favorably for working, but as yet it has scarcely been noticed.*

In N. E. S E., Sec. 23, T. 55, R. 15 W., on Jas. Roberts' land, Coal, equivalent to XXIV, crops out at base of hill 4 feet thick, with thinly stratified brownish and cream-colored Sandstone resting unconformably on it.

On Tetereau Creek, in Sec. 35, T. 55, R. 15 W., Coal crops out, varying in thickness from 15 to 19 inches, and I refer it to XXXII.

In the N. W., Sec. 6, T. 52, R. 14 W., XI appears 11 inches thick. On head of Sweet Spring Creek it is one foot thick.

On Moniteau Creek, about a mile from the county line, XI is 19 inches in thickness; one and a-half miles north it is 13 inches thick, and two miles further up stream it is 8 inches thick ; thus showing a gradual thinning as we go north.

In S. E. of S. W., Sec. 22, T. 55, R. 14 W., XI is one foot thick. At the same locality XV is 18 inches thick, and crops out 22 feet below XI. Some of this Coal has been used.

* Since the survey was made a shaft has been sunk at Rennick nearly a hundred feet deep, reaching this Coal. From this mine it is shipped off to many places.

On Hoover's Creek, S. E. of Jacksonville, XI is 13 inches thick, and one mile further down stream XVI is 20 inches thick.

At Huntzman's mill, in Sec. 20, T. 55, R. 13, we have an outcrop of Coal of variable thickness; it is seen for several hundred feet along the stream, and in thickness averages about 15 inches. The bituminous shales also vary somewhat in their thickness; the following Section was observed:

No. 1. 8 feet soil and clays.
No. 2. 2 feet drab Limestone, containing *Chonetes*.
No. 3. 5 to 8 feet bituminous shales, containing small concretions.
No. 4. 15 inches bituminous coal; probably=XXXII.
No. 5. 14 inches fire-clay; the upper ten inches greenish with buff striæ; below there are four inches blue clay, ferruginous stained.
No. 6. 4 feet nodules of Limestone in clay.
No. 7. 5 inches drab, earthy Limestone.
No. 8. 2 feet greenish clay.
No. 9. 1 foot bluish green, earthy Limestone.

The following localities were examined by C. G. Wheeler:

N. W. Sec. 9, T. 55, R. 14, on land of Hugh McCann, is a 15-inch bed of bituminous coal, with bituminous shales above, fire-clay beneath. Coal crops out at several places in this neighborhood. A quarter of a mile down stream, the following section was made:

No. 2. 1 foot hard blue Limestone.
No. 3. 15 inches bituminous shale.
No. 4. 13 inches bituminous Coal; probably=XI.
No. 5. 10 inches blue clay.

On left bank of East Fork, a-quarter of a mile above the mouth of Gun Creek:

No. 1. 9 feet slope; some Sandstone near the upper part.
No. 2. 3 feet purple and blue argillaceous shales.
No. 3. 6 feet shales; drab argillaceous at top, and passing below into bituminous.
No. 4. 2 feet somewhat laminated clay, containing pyritiferous concretions.
No. 5. 1 foot bituminous Coal; fracture shows a brilliant reflection; probably=XXXII.
No. 6. 2 inches hard dark blue clay.

N. E. N. W. Sec. 28, T. 54, R. 14, Sebrin Jones' coal bank: Coal is four feet thick, and the bed has been opened at intervals for the distance of a mile along the stream.

At Moore's coal bed, in N. E. N. W. Sec. 19, T. 54, R. 14, the following section appears:

No. 2. 1½ feet yellow and drab sandy shales.
No. 3. 1 foot bituminous Coal; not very good=XXIV.

No. 4. 2½ feet good Coal=XXIV.
No. 5. 5 inches blue, bituminous sandy clay, of irregular thickness=XXIV.
No. 6. 6 inches bituminous Coal=XXIV.
No. 7. 2 inches blue clay.

In N. E. of N. W. Sec. 26, T. 53, R. 15, Tilman Oliver's coal bank, XXIV appears thus:

No. 5. 3 inches impure Coal, with partings of iron pyrites.
No. 6. 3 feet Coal.
No. 7. 5 inches hard blue clay, varying in hardness and thickness.
No. 8. 1 foot bituminous Coal.
No. 9. 2 inches blue clay.

At Mr. John Head's Coal bank, on E. half N. W. Sec. 35, T. 53, R. 16, the Coal is one and a-half feet thick and capped by three and a-half feet of argillaceous and bituminous shales, and underlaid by blue fire-clay. This bed is probably the equivalent of XI.

Mr. Cross' bank, in N. W. N. W. Sec. 35, T. 53, R. 16, shows the following:

No. 2. 28 inches Limestone.
No. 3. 2 feet shales; argillaceous at top, bituminous at bottom.
No. 4. 18 inches bituminous Coal.
No. 5. Clay.

Center of E. half S. E. Sec. 15, T. 52, R. 15, J. B. Hudson's bank:

No. 2. 15 inches blue and buff Limestone.
No. 3. 3 inches yellow and grayish colored clay.
No. 4. 2 feet shales; argillaceous at top, bituminous at bottom.
No. 5. 1 foot Coal.

S. W. S. E. Sec. 24, T. 52, R. 14, the following section shows:

No. 2. 2 feet bituminous shales.
No. 3. 1 inch yellow shales.
No. 4. 1 foot Coal.
No. 5. 17 feet slope to creek.

S. E. S. W. Sec. 19, T. 52, R. 13, the following section appears:

No. 1. 30 feet slope; fragments of Limestone.
No. 2. 2½ feet black bituminous shales, containing small, rounded concretions.
No. 3. 3 inches clay.
No. 4. 18 inches Coal.
No. 5. 16 inches stiff, blue clay.
No. 6. 7½ feet 40° slope.
No. 7. 6 inches bituminous shales.
No. 8. 15 inches Coal.
No. 9. 15 inches light drab and yellow clay.

In N. W. of N. W. Sec. 8, T. 52, R. 13, J. R. Alexander's coal bed, Coal is about three feet thick, and suppose it to be equivalent to XXIV. This also crops out in N. E. of N. E. Sec. 7, T. 52, R. 13. The quality of Coal is good. S. W. Sec. 13, T. 52, R. 14, Mrs. Eliza Lewis' Coal bank: thickness of stratum, twelve to fifteen inches.

W. half of N. W. Sec. 6, T. 52, R. 13 W., at Joel Hubbard's, we have:

No. 1. 15 feet slope.
No. 2. 4 feet thick-bedded, buff Limestone; good for building purposes, and is much used on the railroad in the construction of culverts.
No. 3. 1 foot clay.
No. 4. 3½ feet shales; argillaceous at top, bituminous at bottom.
No. 5. 2 feet Coal.
No. 6. Blue clay; becomes bleached on exposure, and is used for white-washing. The same bed is seen outcropping about seventy-five feet up stream, and is fifteen inches in thickness.

On S. E. S. E. Sec. 26, T. 54, R. 13, at Tennessee Matthews' Coal bank, we have:

No. 1. 18 feet 10° slope.
No. 2. 3½ feet bituminous shales.
No. 3. 2 feet good Coal.
No. 4. Blue clay.

The following section appears in S. E. Sec. 23, T. 54, R. 13:

No. 1. 8 feet 5° slope.
No. 2. 2 feet blue and buff Limestone.
No. 3. 1 foot yellow clay.
No. 4. 4 feet shales; argillaceous at top, bituminous at bottom.
No. 5. 20 inches bituminous Coal.
No. 6. Fire-clay.

There are many other outcrops of Coal in this vicinity, but all seem to belong to the same bed as the above. They vary in thickness from fifteen to eighteen inches.

S. E. Sec. 16, T. 54, R. 13, the following:

No. 2. 3½ feet hard blue and dove-colored Limestone.
No. 3. 28 inches bituminous shales.
No. 4. 12 inches Coal.

S. W. Sec. 16, T. 54, R. 13, bituminous Coal crops out sixteen inches thick, and appears to be the same as the bed of last section.

S. E. Sec. 19, T. 55, R. 13, the following:

No. 2. 1½ feet light blue argillaceous shales.
No. 3. 1 foot bituminous Coal.
No. 4. Fire-clay.

N. W. N. W. Sec. 19, T. 55, R. 13, John Darby's Coal bank:

No. 2. 2½ feet bituminous shales.
No. 3. 22 inches good Coal.
No. 4. Blue clay. Length of excavation, about 200 feet.

S. E. S. W. Sec. 10, T. 55, R. 13:

No. 2. 2 feet Limestone.
No. 3. 7 feet slope.
No. 4. 7 feet shales; micaceous and sandy at top, argillaceous in the middle, bituminous at bottom.
No. 5. 1 foot slope.
No. 6. 6 inches bituminous shales.
No. 7. 1½ feet hard, blue Limestone, traversed by veins of calc-spar.
No. 8. 2½ feet bituminous shale.
No. 9. 4 inches bituminous Coal.

N. W. Sec. 11, T. 55, R. 13, Mrs. Riding's Coal bank has—

No. 2. 2 feet dove-colored Limestone; weathers to brownish buff.
No. 3. 4 feet slope.
No. 4. 2½ feet bituminous shales.
No. 5. 14 inches bituminous Coal, in bed of branch flowing into Mud Creek.

N. W. Sec. 9, T. 53, R. 13, Thos. Coates' Coal bank, Coal is said to be eighteen inches thick.

IRON ORE.

Nos. XXI and XXII contain ocherous concretions and concretions of brown Hematite, which are often hollow; the same bed in Sec. 64–2, shows at the lower part several feet of shaly, yellow ocher. In Sec. 6, No. 8 is an 8-inch bed of bog Iron ore, corresponding in position to XXV. No. XXX contains ferruginous concretions. A shaly ore of red Hematite occurs in No. 4 of Sec. 26, corresponding in stratigraphical position to VIII; traces of it were also observed in the same group of rocks on Moniteau.

Sulphuret of Iron is found in every coal bed, and sometimes is quite abundant; and the bituminous shales are often highly impregnated with it, and sometimes quite large pyritous concretions are interpolated.

The ferruginous Sandstone (F. *f.*), at Fray's Mill, is highly charged with red Oxyd of Iron.

Copperas is collected by the citizens from the vicinity of Coal mines; is used in dyeing, and said to be as good as any used.

OTHER MINERALS—NOT ORES.

Quartz Crystals.—In S. E. Sec. 13, T. 53, R. 13 W., Mr. Wheeler found crystals of quartz adhering to black Limestone.

Carbonate of Lime.—Nail-head spar was found by Mr. Wheeler, in S. E. Sec. 13, T. 53, R. 13, in a mass of Septaria, associated with quartz crystals. Whitish fibrous carbonate of Lime was found in S. W. of Sec. 15, T. 54, R. 13, and dark, olive-green, fibrous carbonate of Lime in the N. W. S. E. Sec. 24, T. 52, R. 14. The concretions of dark Limestone, forming Septaria, are often beautifully traversed by veins of calc-spar, as noticed in No. 3 of Sec. 25.

Selenite is sometimes found in the shales and clays of Coal Measures.

Fossil wood occurs at many places, but always in loose fragments, so that I am unable to say where its proper geographical position is; it is always silicified.

Fire-clay.—The Clays lying below the Coal would undoubtedly make good fire-brick, but as yet they have not been tried.

MINERAL SPRINGS.

Sweet Spring is situated on the south side of Sweet Spring Creek, in the west half of Sec. 17, T. 53, R. 15 W., and belongs to Mr. G. B. Dameron, who informed me that the water is very good for dyspeptic diseases, being a good tonic and cathartic. I detected a sulphurous taste; may also contain salt.

Goreham's Lick.—This spring is about 12 feet deep and 10 feet square at top; the ground immediately adjacent is quite marshy; the water has a strong saline taste; on stirring it many bubbles of Sulphureted hydrogen arise. The ground near by seems to have been much resorted to by cattle, and the buffaloes of old, who have worn quite a space by licking and tramping. In former years there was much salt made here, and the ruins of the old works may be still seen; some posts yet remain; the trenches in which the kettles were arranged (of which there are two rows, extending for fifty feet,) are nearly filled up with ashes and rubbish. Dr. Fort, of Fort Henry, esteems this water for its valuable medicinal properties. He recommends drinking and bathing in it regularly for diseases of the lungs; and he says that course is an effectual cure. He says that it will cure the chills if you drink it and bathe with it early in the morning; for diseases of the chest he says it is the best remedy he has ever tried.

There are a few other springs in this county impregnated with a small proportion of Sulphur, but they are scarcely worthy of notice.

At Jacksonville is a very fine spring; it is the main source of Hoover's Creek; it gushes out very boldly, and affords water for the steam-mill located there, and also for all the stock in the neighborhood. Mr. John McCann informed me that in very dry seasons, when Flat Creek and other streams dried up, and many persons had to send a great distance for water, this spring afforded an abundant supply. The taste of the water is pleasant, and it seemed to be slightly chalybeate, and after flowing out it presents a slight iridescent appearance. I was informed by Mr. McCann that it is very healthy for both man and beast, and a horse when very much heated could drink as much as he wanted without injury. It is said to be very healthy for dyspeptic persons.

STREAMS.

Silver Creek is a beautiful, clear, running stream. Big Sugar Creek is a clear stream, and flows gently along. Dark Creek, Muncas Creek, East Fork and Middle Fork of Chariton are very sluggish streams, and the water in them is quite dark. The other streams preserve a medium, being neither very sluggish nor swift.

BUILDING ROCK.

The Sandstones are generally too soft for building purposes, and the only quarry of it worthy of notice is at Huntsville, where it occurs in very good thick beds, but owing to a portion being very much indurated, it is diffiucult to work.

Many of the Limestones are too brittle, and shell off too much when exposed to the action of frost, to make a good building material.

The Rhomboidal Limestone, No. IX, is often very good for building; a good quarry of it is exposed on Silver Creek, in the north part of Sec. 3, T. 52, R. 15, in a good, thick, even bed. A good bed of it also crops out on head-waters of Walnut Creek, in Sec. 16, T. 55, R. 14. It crops out near the head of most of the streams flowing both ways from the Grand Divide.

The blue or dove-colored Limestone, No. IV, is good for building, but it was only noticed on Moniteau and Silver Creeks near their sources.

No. XXIX affords a good, thick bed of building rock, of which there is an outcrop in Secs. 2 and 11, T. 54, R. 15.

Grindstones and Scythestones.—The micaceous Sandstone is used for these purposes, and is found to answer well.

Lime.—Most of the Limestones will make good lime.

SOILS.

There is much good land in Randolph county, and some large tracts of very rich land. The bottom lands, of course, are rich; but those of East Fork, Middle Fork and Sweet Spring Creek are rather flat, and have many small ponds and tracts of marshy ground, which are sore hindrances to the farmer who, in order to cultivate them every season, would have to resort to ditching and draining. The soil is a very dark, rich loam, reposing on stiff, dark clays of the Bottom Prairie formation.

The best uplands may include most of T. 52 and T. 53, R. 16; supporting a growth of Ash, Redbud, Elm, Mulberry, Hickory, Laurel Oak, vines, etc.; a portion of T. 53, R. 15, and nearly all of T. 54 and T. 55, R. 15. The timbered part of the latter consists mostly of a large growth of Swamp White Oak, Shell-bark Hickory and Pignut Hickory, Ash, Coffee-bean, Honey Locust, White Oak, etc. Other good bodies of land, but not quite as good as the last, may include that region near the head of Silver Creek, and the prairie lands not heretofore mentioned, with the timbered land for half a mile from the prairie. In T. 52, R. 13, T. 53, R. 13, the land is tolerably good. T. 54, R. 13, includes some good land; but this township has also much land that is poor. The same will apply to T. 55, R. 13. The northern part of T. 52, R. 14, and in T. 54, R. 14, there is some good land. There is good land in N. W. part of T. 52, R. 15. Other third and fourth rate and poorer lands include the hills lying between Perché and Moniteau, supporting a growth of White Oak and Black Oak and Post Oak; in N. W. part of the county, near the Middle Fork; the hills adjacent to East Fork, and north of Huntsville; the hills near Silver Creek, east of the range line of 15 and 16. After leaving the Grand divide, and entering the timber for a half a mile to a mile, the country becomes somewhat broken, the growth mostly Black Oak and White Oak, and the soil thin.

TIMBER.

Nearly all the western half of the county is heavily timbered. The bottom lands afford much good timber, including Elm, Cottonwood, Shell-bark Hickory, Linden, Burr Oak, Sycamore, Birch, Hackberry, White Maple, Black Walnut, Swamp White Oak, Red Oak, Pignut Hickory, Pin Oak. On Walnut Creek there is much good Black Walnut timber. I saw only White Walnut on Hoover's Creek. On Sugar Creek and Moniteau there are many Sugar trees. On Silver Creek the Cottonwood grows to a large size. On the hills in the western part of the county, near Silver Creek, we have Red Oak, Ash, Hickory, Elm, Black Walnut, etc. On the ridge between Sweet Spring and Silver Creek, there is much fine timber. T. 54, R. 15, contains much very good timber, including Swamp White Oak, White Oak, Black Oak, Laurel Oak, Hickory, Elm and Wild Cherry.

AGRICULTURE.

Randolph county is adapted to the producing of most crops of grain and vegetables peculiar to the State. Fine crops of corn and tobacco are raised. It is not as good for wheat as some other counties. Fruits succeed very well; apples are very fine.

MILLER, MORGAN AND SALINE COUNTIES.

STATE GEOLOGICAL ROOMS,
COLUMBIA, MISSOURI, *February, 1859.*

PROF. G. C. SWALLOW, *State Geologist:*

DEAR SIR: In the reports herewith respectfully submitted, you will find the results of examinations made by me, as Assistant Geologist, during the summer and fall of 1855, in Miller, Morgan and Saline counties. In making out the report on Saline county, I have, in accordance with your instructions, used observations made by you in portions of some of the south-eastern townships not visited by me. I am also under obligations for valuable aid in the field-work to Mr. Warwick Hough, of Jefferson City, who accompanied me as assistant in the survey of Morgan and portions of Miller counties.

I would likewise avail myself of the present opportunity of returning my thanks to the citizens generally of the counties examined by me, for important information and assistance, as well as for the kindness and hospitality with which I was everywhere received while prosecuting the survey.

Very truly yours, etc.,
F. B. MEEK,
Assistant Geologist.

CHAPTER VII.

MILLER COUNTY.

BY F. B. MEEK.

This county occupies a position a little south of the center of the State, and embraces a superficial area of about 572 square miles. Its surface varies in elevation from some 40 or 50, to over 600 feet above the level of the Missouri at the mouth of the Osage—the lowest portions being in the valley of the latter stream, and the north-western and south-eastern townships. Near the Osage and its larger tributaries, the country is generally very broken and rocky, excepting immediately in the valleys; but further back, slopes usually become more gentle, with fewer exposures of rock, until we reach the higher districts, more remote from the streams, where the surface is comparatively level, or but slightly undulating.

STREAMS.

The largest stream in the county is the Osage River, which passes diagonally through it near the middle, in a north-easterly direction. Being navigable for small steamboats, at high stages of water, as far up as to Osceola, in St. Clair county, it is of much value to the country as an outlet for its surplus products, and for the return of such freights as the trade of the interior demands.

The Grand Auglaize and Tavern Creeks are rivulets too small for navigation, but large enough, as are several of their principal branches, to furnish valuable water power. The first heads in Camden county, and flows northward, so as to meander through the south-western corner of Miller county, where it receives some tributaries, soon after it crosses the county line, and north-westward, through Camden county, to the Osage. That portion of it in Miller county has, at ordinary stages of water, an average breadth of about 120 feet from bank to bank, and a mean depth of about 2½ feet. It has a rapid current, and its water is very clear.

Tavern Creek* heads in Pulaski county, and flows northward through the eastern township of Miller county, entering the Osage about one and a-half miles north of the line between Cole and Miller counties. It is almost as large as the Auglaize, near its mouth, and receives several large branches in T. 39 and 40, R. 12 and 13. As the water backs up five or six miles above the mouth from the Osage when the latter is high, the best sites for mills are further up. Like the Auglaize, its water is very clear, excepting when it is high.

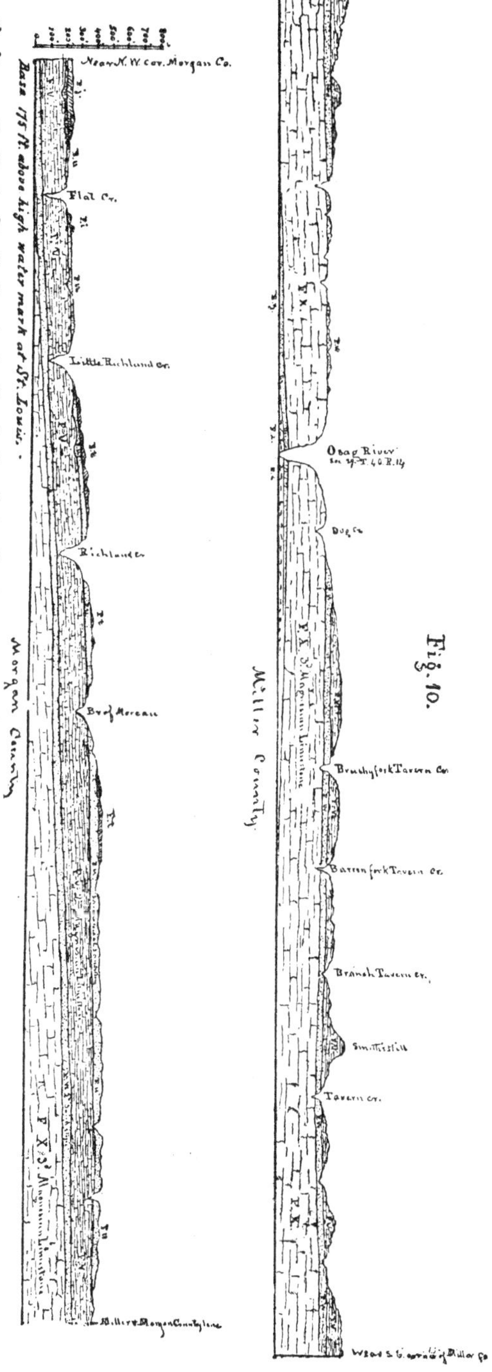

Dog and Bear Creeks are much smaller streams, (not being more than eight or ten miles in length,) which head in T. 39, R. 14, and flow at first north-westward, then north and north-westward, falling into the Osage in T. 40, R. 14.

On the north side of the Osage there are two small streams—the Saline and Little Gravois. The first is about 12 miles in length, and near its mouth has an average breadth of 80 or 90 feet. It heads up near the

*This is probably a corruption of the name *Cavern Creek*—there being several large caverns on this stream, and a large one on the Osage, near its mouth.

north-west corner of T. 41, R. 15, and flows south-westward, entering the Osage about three miles below Tuscumbia. It is a clear, rapid stream, and has fall enough to furnish good mill-sites.

Little Gravois Creek is about the size of the Saline, and heads near the same place. It runs at first to the south-west, into Morgan county, but soon turns to the south-east and passes through two or three miles of Miller county, to the Osage.

Some small branches head in the north-western townships of the county, and flow northward and north-westward to Moniteau Creek, in Cole county. These streams are generally more sluggish, and not so clear as those on the south side of the divide between the Osage and Moreau Creek.

SPRINGS.

Perhaps no county in the State is better supplied with good water than this. In addition to the many clear streams already mentioned, fine never-failing springs of cool, clear water abound in all parts of the county. Many of these springs afford extraordinary quantities of water—so much, indeed, as to be of great value for the purpose of driving machinery. As these great springs generally continue to flow at nearly the same rate, independent of rains or drouth, and of course never freeze, mills driven by them can be in constant operation the year round, and are never subject to any of the usual annoyances caused by drouths, floods or freezing, and require no expensive dams.

One of these large springs in Sec. 2, T. 39, R. 15, runs a small mill, but discharges water enough to drive a much larger establishment. I found the temperature of this spring to be 62°. A similar spring was observed in Sec. 27, T. 41, R. 14, which also runs a small mill; another in S. W. quarter Sec. 15, of same range and township, drives a mill owned by Mr. John W. Johnson; the temperature of this latter spring was 58°. Another similar spring, with a temperature of 56°, was observed on Mr. Simeon Brackman's place, in N. E. quarter Sec. 17, T. 41, R. 14.

No Sulphur or Chalybeate springs were met with in the county, nor were any seen strongly enough impregnated with any kind of mineral matter to impart a perceptible taste. In S. W. quarter Sec. 23, T. 41, R. 14, I saw a fine, bold spring of very clear water, boiling up in the middle of a small stream, and discharging considerable quantities of gas. As this had not the peculiar odor of hydro-sulphuric acid, and extinguishes the flame of a candle, it is most probably carbonic acid gas. The water of this spring does not mix readily with that of the small stream into which it flows; and although both are as clear as crystal, the water from the spring can be seen running like oil through that of the stream, excepting that its greater specific gravity causes it to flow at the bottom. It is said to possess slight purgative properties when drank in large quantities, and persons afflicted with ophthalmia have experienced relief from frequently bathing their eyes in it. This latter effect, however, I attribute more to the temperature of the water, which I found to be 54°, than to anything it holds in solution. A large demijohn of this water carefully sealed up for analysis was, unfortunately, broken before I left the county.

TIMBER.

This county is well supplied with fine timber of various kinds, the only prairie land in it being of comparatively small extent, nearly all of which is located on the high country in the north-western townships. Some portions, however, south of the Osage, partake more or less of the character of prairie lands, the trees being so scattering as to cause a dense growth of tall grass over the high country and along the slopes. In the valleys of Osage River, and Auglaize and Tavern Creeks, as well as in those of nearly all the other streams of any extent, there is a fine growth of large timber. It generally consists of Red, Burr and Black Oak, American and Red Elm, White and Black Walnut, Sugar and Soft Maple, Ash, Sycamore, Hickory, Honey Locust, Hackberry, Basswood or Linden, Wild Cherry, Buckeye, etc.

In the districts known as the "Big and Little Rich Woods," in the southern part of the county, the large growth of timber is not everywhere confined to the valleys, but at many places extends up on the higher country. The growth in most of the more elevated districts, not included in the "Big and Little Rich Woods," is generally Post, Black-jack and Laurel Oak, Hickory, Crab Apple, Persimmon, etc

GEOLOGICAL STRUCTURE OF MILLER COUNTY

By reference to the map of this county accompanying this report, it will be seen that with the exception of a few small isolated spots of carboniferous rocks, and the usual alluvial deposits of the country, its entire area is occupied by an extensive series of Magnesian Limestones and Sandstones, representing the Calciferous Sand rock, and possibly also the Potsdam Sandstone of the New York system; or, in other words, the lower part of the Lower Silurian of the Old World.

Whether or not the great thickness of rocks composing the middle and upper portions of the Silurian System, and the whole of the Devonian, known to hold positions between the lower part of the

Silurian and the base of the Carboniferous, ever existed here, is a problem it is by no means easy to solve. They may possibly have been, at least in part, deposited here, and subsequently swept away by powerful denuding agencies; or, as is more probable, those portions of the country where they are wanting may have been elevated by great oscillations and changes above the sea, and remained dry land during the whole of the long periods of time these rocks were elsewhere forming, to be again sunk beneath the sea at the dawn of the Carboniferous epoch.

That Carboniferous formations were once spread over considerable areas now occupied by these older Silurian Magnesian Limestones and Sandstones in Miller, Moniteau and Morgan counties, is attested by the numerous thin isolated patches and outliers of Encrinital Limestone and Coal, scattered over the country here far south of any continuous deposits of that age. Yet it is by no means probable that the whole, or any considerable portion, of the Carboniferous system of rocks ever existed here at any one time, for if this had been the case, and all but the remnants now found scattered over the country were subsequently worn away, these remaining outliers should all belong to the *lower* part of the great Carboniferous system. This, however, is not the case, for although many of them do belong to the Encrinital Limestone, which occupies a position at the base of the Carboniferous system, many others, especially in Moniteau and Morgan counties, are composed entirely of Coal and shale, belonging to the Upper Carboniferous series.

It is also manifest that between the deposition of the Encrinital Limestone, and that of the outliers of Coal already mentioned, the surface of the country here must have been modified to some extent by erosive agencies; for, as a general thing, these deposits of Coal are found in valleys which must have been worn in the old Silurian rocks long after the deposition of the Encrinital Limestone; while we almost always find the outliers of this latter rock on the summits of the higher elevations, excepting in a few cases where it is manifest they have been undermined and thrown down long since their consolidation. Now, had these valleys in which we find these local deposits of Coal existed at the time the Encrinital Limestone, which is older than the Coal, was deposited, we should now find them filled, or at any rate partly filled with this Limestone, and the Coal reposing upon it, instead of resting directly on the Silurian rocks.

To the eye, the rocks of Miller county, with the exception of a few local undulations, appear to be nearly or quite horizontal, but by observing the various elevations at which certain beds are met with, in passing from this into some of the adjoining counties, it will be at once seen that there is a general dip of all the rocks throughout at least much of the middle and northern portions of the county, in a northerly or north-easterly direction.* This will be better understood when it is borne in mind that the Second Magnesian Limestone, which occurs near Rocky Mount, in the north-western part of the county, at an elevation of about 464 feet above the Missouri, at the mouth of Osage River, sinks gradually as we proceed northward, so that near the north-east corner of Moniteau county, a distance by an air line of 42 miles, we find it down nearly on a level with the Missouri at that place, or about 34 feet above the Missouri at the mouth of the Osage. Hence, supposing the thickness of all the beds of the Magnesian Limestone series to be uniform, the dip would be a fraction over ten feet per mile.

A general vertical section of all the formations seen in this county would be, in descending order, as follows:

QUATERNARY SYSTEM:

No. 1. Alluvium from Osage, to perhaps as much as 30 to 40 feet.

CARBONIFEROUS SYSTEM:

No. 2. 12 feet Argillaceous Cannel Coal and Clay.
No. 3. 20 feet Encrinital Limestone.

SILURIAN SYSTEM—LOWER PART:

No. 4. 30 feet Saccharoidal Sandstone.
No. 5. 150 feet Second Magnesian Limestone.
No. 6. 70 feet Second Sandstone.
No. 7. 300 feet Third Magnesian Limestone.
No. 8. 6 feet Third Sandstone.
No. 9. 27 feet Fourth Magnesian Limestone (above the Osage.)

QUATERNARY SYSTEM.

ALLUVIUM.

The only alluvial deposits observed in this county, out of the valleys, consist of the soils, subsoils and yellowish and sometimes reddish clays, with more or less fragments of flint and other rocks. These clays, as well as the fragments of rocks embedded in them, appear to have been derived, for the most part, from the disintegration of the rocks upon which they repose, or at any rate they do not seem to have been transported from a distance, as no boulders or water-worn pebbles of foreign rocks were met with among them; nor were any Drift deposits of any kind observed in this county. The Bluff formation, so common in the counties bordering on the Missouri, appears to be also wanting here.

* Along the Osage, near the west side of the county, there is a slight dip toward the west or south-west.

In the valleys of the Osage and other streams the alluvial deposits possess the usual mixed and finely comminuted characters common to those of other portions of the State—being more arenaceous, and containing more organic matter than the clays on the higher country.

CARBONIFEROUS SYSTEM.

As already stated, this system of rocks is only represented in this county by a few very small outliers of Encrinital Limestone and impure Cannel Coal, together with a little Clay associated with the latter The Limestone is found on the high country near the northern limits of the county in T. 42, R. 14, and does not appear to be at any place more than 20 feet in thickness; while the Coal was only seen in T. 39 and 40, R. 13, reposing directly on the older Silurian rocks.

LOWER SILURIAN ROCKS.

Saccharoidal Sandstone.

This member of the Magnesian Limestone series was only recognized on the higher country in northern part of the county. The furthest point toward the south at which I observed it is in the north-west quarter of S. 2, T. 41, R. 14, where it crops out on a small branch of Saline Creek, showing a thickness of about 16 feet. At another place about 2½ miles further north-west, and near the Cole county line, large masses of this rock were seen on a ridge, under circumstances indicating a thickness of over 25 feet. Similar bodies of it were likewise observed on the summit of the highest part of the country in the north-east quarter of S. 11, T. 42, R. 14; it also occurs at another place about one mile north of this outcrop, at about the same elevation.

Second Magnesian Limestone.

This formation underlies areas of considerable extent in the more elevated portions of the county, especially in the north-western and south-eastern townships. North of the Osage it extends throughout the whole of T. 42, ranges 14 and 15, passing southward also into some parts of T. 41, ranges 13, 14 and 15. It attains a greater thickness in the high country comprised in the two northern townships, than in any other part of the county. Not being all exposed at any one place, and having generally no well-marked subdivisions, preserving their peculiar lithological characters throughout areas of much extent, by which the same beds in the absence of organic remains can always be identified at different localities, I have no means of determining, with much precision, its maximum thickness in this part of the county; but from the various elevations at which I saw it cropping out along slopes, I think it may safely be estimated at as much as 150 feet.

In most cases the upper and middle beds here consist of the fine-grained, softer, light drab and whitish varieties of Magnesian Limestone, known by the local name of "Cotton rock," alternating with thin layers and beds of harder light grayish and flesh colored, coarser grained Silicious Magnesian Limestones, containing more or less chert. These harder beds are often concretionary, and sometimes the cherty portions are oolitic. At a few places a thin bed of Sandstone was observed intercalated between the harder beds.

The lower portions of this formation generally consist of the coarser light grayish and flesh-colored Magnesian Limestones, with much less "Cotton rock." These gray granular layers, when free from chert, have been found well adapted to the construction of back walls and jambs of common fire-places, in consequence of which they have been termed "Fire rock."

The following section, taken in descending order, on a branch of Moreau Creek in Sec. 1, T. 42, R. 15, at the northern boundary of the county, illustrates the nature of the beds a little above the middle of the formation, as developed in this part of the county:

No. 1. 9 feet "Cotton rock."
No. 2. 5 feet hard, granular, light flesh-colored Magnesian Limestone.
No. 3. 6 feet "Cotton rock."
No. 4. 12 feet hard, rough, gray, granular, somewhat cherty, Magnesian Limestone.
No. 5. 8 feet "Cotton rock."
No. 6. 3 feet same as No. 4.
No. 7. 1 foot "Cotton rock."

At another locality, about one mile and a-half due west of the place where the above section was taken, I saw a bluff 50 feet in hight composed of nearly the same kind of beds.

Near the highest part of the country, about two miles east and south and east of the last-mentioned locality, and as much as 100 to 120 feet above its level, beds of beautiful "Cotton rock" were struck in sinking wells, at depths varying from four to ten feet below the surface.

In Sec. 2, T. 41, R. 14, some of the harder granular beds crop out along slopes 150 feet above an exposure of Sandstone I suppose to be the Second Sandstone, seen in the valley of a small branch of Saline Creek, while outliers of apparently the Saccharoidal Sandstone were observed on the higher country further back, not much above the elevation of the Magnesian Limestone. Consequently, if I am not mistaken in the identity of one or the other of these Sandstones, the thickness of the Second Magnesian Limestone must be here near 150 feet.

On the south side of the Osage, back from that and the other principal streams, the lower beds of this formation occupy much of the higher country in T. 40, ranges 13 and 14; also in townships 38 and 39, ranges 12, 13 and 14; but in all this area, all the larger streams have excavated their valleys down through it and the Second Sandstone, far into the third Magnesian Limestone.

At most of the localities where I saw the second Magnesian Limestone, on the south side of the Osage, it consists of the light grayish and mottled, harder, coarse beds, with whitish softer spots, though at some places there are interstratified beds of "Cotton rock," and occasionally a thin intercalated bed of Sandstone was seen. The coarser granular beds, with softer white spots, are often exposed in rather thin layers on the surface of the higher parts of the country, where they frequently form naked glades. Being usually seen only on the more elevated country, and along gentle slopes, some distance from the larger streams, good exposures of this formation are rarely met with in this part of the county.

The beds composing the following section, taken on Brushy Fork of Tavern Creek, in T. 39, R. 13, belong, I suppose, to the lower part of this formation, though they may possibly belong to the upper part of the Third Magnesian Limestone:

No. 1. 20 feet slope, with loose cellular chert.
No. 2. 5 feet light grayish Sandstone.
No. 3. 15 feet "Cotton rock."
No. 4. 12 feet very hard, compact, light brownish and mixed, more or less concretionary, Magnesian Limestone.
No. 5. 12 feet slope; no rocks seen in place.
No. 6. 21 feet mixed, irregularly stratified, concretionary, flesh-colored and grayish Magnesian Limestone, with seams and concretions of flint.

At several places in T. 40, R. 14, east and south of Tuscumbia, exposures of this rock were seen as much as 60 to 70 feet above outcrops of the second Sandstone observed in the valleys and along slopes. Near the south-east corner of the county, ledges of it crop out of slopes, some 35 feet above the elevation of any exposure of the Second Sandstone seen in a small valley near. As the highest hills near here rise as much as 50 to 60 feet above the horizon of this Limestone, it may attain at this place a thickness of near 80 feet. The same beds also occur at several places from 6 to 12 miles farther west, near the county line.

Organic remains are generally very rare here in this rock. I only saw in it a few fragments of apparently one or two species of *Euomphalus.*

SECOND SANDSTONE.

This formation varies much, as well in thickness as in its lithological characters, at different localities, being usually a fine-grained, regularly stratified, quartzose Sandstone, of a light grayish brown color, but sometimes passing suddenly into a heavy-bedded light gray or white Sandstone. At other places there is much chert in it, and at a few localities it seems to pass almost entirely into beds of rugged chert. On the south side of the Osage I only recognized it at a few localities on the high country near the river, but below the elevation of beds of the Second Magnesian Limestone seen farther back. I first observed it in the south-west quarter Sec. 15, T. 41, R. 13, where I found large masses of it occupying areas of 30 to 40 yards across, and rising from 6 to 8 feet above the soil.

On some high ridges, two miles due west of the above-named locality, I again observed exposures of this rock rising 12 to 15 feet above ground. Other outcrops were also seen, indicating that it must be the surface rock here over an area of several acres. About 10 miles a little south of west from this, exposures, consisting of large masses, were met with in Sec. 2, T. 40, R. 15, on the summits of the highest hills, near the Osage, and as much as 280 feet above it.

South of the Osage this formation occurs at many localities, though near that stream it was generally observed only on the summits of the highest hills, in the form of remnants and outliers. Near the north-east corner of the county some masses of it occur on the tops of the bluffs about 200 feet above the Osage, and similar bodies of it were met with near the mouth of Tavern Creek, at an elevation of 230 feet above the same horizon. Between these localities it occurs at several places, and seems to be the surface rock for some distance, forming, by its disintegration, a very sandy soil.

Near the county line, in Sec. 12, T. 40, R. 12, outcrops of this rock, consisting of coarse, gray, heavy-bedded Sandstone with distinct lines of deposition, occur at several places along slopes above exposures of the third Magnesian Limestone.

Due south of the last mentioned exposure, this Sandstone was seen at many places quite to the southern limits of the county. At one of these localities, on Tavern Creek, in Sec. 16, T. 39, R. 12, it is found reposing on the older rocks, as represented in the following section:

No. 1. 20 feet; no rock seen in place.

SECOND SANDSTONE:

No, 2. 33 feet heavy-bedded, grayish-yellow Sandstone, with distinct horizontal and oblique lines of deposition.

THIRD MAGNESIAN LIMESTONE:

No. 3. 66 feet rugged chert, alternating with beds of hard, gray, granular Magnesian Limestone.

No. 4. 22 feet heavy-bedded, bluish-gray, hard sub-crystalline Magnesian Limestone.

The Sandstone is probably either not all exposed, or partly worn away here, as it is known to be much thicker a short distance southeast of this outcrop; and on Bolin's Creek, only one mile and a quarter farther east, it forms, for some distance, a continuous bluff from 30 to 60 feet in hight.

Another Section, taken on Sandstone Creek, in Sec. 34, of same township and range, presents the following beds—descending:

No. 1. 30 feet slope; no rocks seen on place.

SECOND SANDSTONE:

No. 2. 35 feet heavy-bedded, yellowish and gray Sandstone, with distinct horizontal and oblique lines of deposition.

THIRD MAGNESIAN LIMESTONE:

No. 3. 26 feet slope, with many large, loose masses of the overlying Sandstone.

No. 4. 9 feet hard, light-bluish, gray, sub-crystalline Magnesian Limestone, in thin layers.

No. 5. 25 feet grayish and flesh-colored Magnesian Limestone and chert, variously mingled, so as to form a very rugged mass.

No. 6. 5 feet light-grayish and bluish granular or sub-crystalline Magnesian Limestone.

No. 7. Rugged mixture of chert and gray Magnesian Limestone.

Of this section, No. 2, and possibly portions of the slopes above and below it, belong to the Second Sandstone, and all below, to the Third Magnesian Limestone.

West of the localities where the above-mentioned exposures were examined, this formation occurs at numerous places throughout much of the county lying south of the Osage. It is usually seen either cropping out along slopes from beneath the Second Magnesian Limestone, or where that rock has been denuded, as a surface formation. Near the Osage and other large streams, where not protected by overlying beds of the Second Magnesian Limestone, it has generally been entirely worn away, or is only represented by isolated masses, on the summits of higher hills.

One of the localities where it may be seen exposed on a slope beneath the Second Magnesian Limestone, is in Sec. 19, T. 40, R. 13, near a small branch of Dog Creek. Here, as much as 70 feet below the summits of the highest country near, a thickness of forty feet of it is exposed, while ledges of the Second Magnesian Limestone crop out at several places within a short distance along the slopes above.

Near the county line, about 10 miles in a direction south of west from the exposures just mentioned, and 2 miles north-west from the Auglaize, outcrops of this rock, consisting of masses of light-colored Sandstone, 25 feet in diameter, and rising 2 to 3 feet above the ground, were seen on the summit of a high ridge. Other similar exposures were also observed at about the same elevation, 2 miles south of the Osage, in Sec. 5, T. 39, R. 15.

As it is probable a formation disintegrating so readily as this under the influence of atmospheric agencies would rarely present its whole thickness at any one exposure, and I saw as much as 60 feet of it at one place, I have estimated its maximum thickness in this county at 70 feet. It is evidently, however, much thinner than this at most places.

In the pure Sandstone of this formation, I never saw any fragments, even, of organic remains, but toward the lower part, where there are, at some places, many cherty, and mixed sandy and cherty layers, I observed a few casts of *Euomphalus*, and species of one or two other genera of *Gasteropoda*, in a bad state of preservation.

Third Magnesian Limestone.

Of all the rocks in Miller county, this is by far the thickest and most important. It underlies all the foregoing formations throughout the whole county, and is exposed along all the larger streams, excepting in the north-western townships. The Osage has generally excavated its valley near 300 feet down into it, and at one place, owing to a slight uplift, down even into the Fourth Magnesian Limestone.

It is seen at numerous places along that stream, in the form of bold mural escarpments, some of which rise almost perpendicularly from the water's edge, to elevations varying from 50 to 200 feet high.

There are also numerous high cliffs of this rock on the Auglaize and Tavern Creeks, and their tributaries, as well as on the Saline and Little Gravois. As a general thing, it is the only rock exposed immediately on these streams, the higher rocks being usually worn away for some distance back, though we sometimes find it at such places crowned by the Second Sandstone.

As seen in this county, the Third Magnesian Limestone generally consists of heavy, massive beds of hard, very light-gray, bluish-gray and flesh-colored, granular Magnesian Limestone, with seams, layers and concretions of flint. Often 40 to 50 feet, or more, of the upper part consists of alternations of these Limestones, with beds and layers of rugged brecciated chert, and sometimes intercalated beds of Sandstone.

Weathered surfaces of these hard, massive, more crystalline beds resemble coarse, quartzose Sandstones, and even the face of fresh fractures often feel as harsh as, and have much the granular appearance of, a hard silicious Sandstone. Under a lens, however, they are found to consist almost entirely of an aggregation of small rhomboidal crystals of dolomite, cemented apparently by silicious matter.

Although, like the other members of this series, the Third Magnesian Limestone is by no means a very fossiliferous rock, I think, as a general thing, organic remains are more frequently met with in its upper cherty beds, than in any part of the other rocks of this series; at any rate, this appears to be the case in Miller and Morgan counties. Those observed by me in it, in Miller county, belong to two or three species of *Euomphalus*, one or two species of *Pleurotomaria*, and a small *Turbo*-like shell, similar to species I have seen in some of the cherty portions of the Second Sandstone, and apparently identical with species found in the Lower Magnesian Limestone of Dr. Owen's Minnesota series.

A remarkable peculiarity of this rock is its tendency to weather into caverns, tunnels and natural bridges. These natural bridges usually span little side-valleys, or deep ravines near their outlets into the main valleys of larger streams. They seem to have been formed by the surface-waters first finding their way down through fissures in the rocks, some distance back from the brink of precipices, and then passing through caverns, beneath heavy bodies of strata, out into the valley below. In cases of this kind, water, aided by other atmospheric agencies, in the course of ages, wears away the rock, so as to form small valleys or ravines, extending back, perhaps, in some instances, a considerable distance, and receiving the surface-waters from comparatively large areas, all of which must find outlets through these subterranean passages into the main valley. Such a passage, after being widened and deepened by the wearing power of running water, probably long continues to resemble, in some respects, an artificial tunnel, but gradually the rock above crumbles, under the "tooth of time," until at last nothing is left but a narrow arch, spanning the outlet of a small valley.

Natural bridges of this kind are not so common in Miller as in Morgan county. Caverns, however, are frequently met with in this rock along the streams in both counties; and one of the most extensive natural tunnels observed by me is in Miller county, on Tavern Creek, Sec. 34, T. 41, R. 12. In approaching this, by descending a valley on the east side of Tavern Creek, I was surprised to find the valley I was descending suddenly terminated by nearly as high land as the hills on either side. As I drew near this barrier, however, I found that the small brook flowing down the valley, without any sudden fall or change of its course, entered what appeared to be a large cavern. On going into this, I discovered that instead of an ordinary cavern, it was a natural tunnel, about 100 yards in length, having a slight descent, and terminating, at the other end, in a high precipice, bounding the east side of the main valley of Tavern Creek.

The upper or east entrance of this tunnel measured 30 feet in hight, and about 50 feet in breadth, and the other extremity is nearly 70 feet in hight, and 160 feet wide; though the passage at some points between the two extremities is smaller than at either end. The solid rock and loose material above is about 70 feet in thickness, and overgrown by large forest trees.

Some of the caverns in this rock are quite large at the entrance, but they do not appear to be so extensive generally as those frequently met with in the Lower Carboniferous rocks of the West.

The numerous large springs, already mentioned, in various portions of the county, issue from this formation. The water of all these springs, as well as that of all the streams heading in this rock, is remarkable for its clearness.

The best sections of the Third Magnesian Limestone were seen along the Osage and on Tavern and Auglaize Creeks. The following section, showing the nature of the beds comprising this formation, was taken, in descending order, on the Osage, in Sec. 2, T. 41, R. 12, near the Cole county line:

No. 1. 22 feet slope, with loose mass coarse gray and brownish Sandstone.

No. 2. 44 feet mostly covered with loose, rugged, sandy, more or less brecciated chert, with exposures, near the base, of alternations of light gray granular Magnesian Limestone and chert.

No. 3. 27 feet, very light gray or whitish hard granular Magnesian Limestone, in rather thin layers below.

No. 4. 87 feet heavy bedded, hard, light gray and flesh-colored Magnesian Limestone, with irregular beds (2 to 6 feet in thickness) of rugged, bluish brecciated chert.

No. 5. 30 feet talus; no rock seen in place.

The loose masses seen on the summit of the bluff here are evidently remnants of the Second Sandstone. This rock also probably composes the whole of the slope upon which these masses repose, as well as much of the 44 feet of slope strewed with chert below. The larger portion of the slope No. 2 is, however, evidently occupied by the upper beds of the Third Magnesian Limestone, consisting of alternations of Limestone and chert, with more or less Sandstone. No. 3 and No. 4 are more massive beds of the same Limestone, and other exposures near this locality show that the slope No. 5 is also composed of this rock, making altogether a thickness of 130 to 140 feet of it above the Osage at this place.

The dip of the rocks here being toward the north, or a little east of north, we find, on ascending the Osage, that the Third Magnesian Limestone gradually rises, so that along near Sec. 28, T. 41, R. 13, bluffs entirely composed of this rock rise as much as 220 feet above the river; and near the western side of the county, the top of this formation is elevated more than 300 feet above the Osage.

The following section, taken on the right shore of the Osage, three miles from the Morgan county line, at the highest bluff seen in the county, includes, I think, the entire thickness of this rock, as developed here:

No. 1. 2 feet coarse Sandstone, with some angular fragments of chert.

No. 2. 110 feet slope, strewed with masses of rugged, sandy and brecciated chert, some portions of which appear to be *in situ*.

No. 3. 157 feet hard, light gray and bluish-gray, semi-crystalline Magnesian Limestone, in heavy beds, alternating with more finely-grained flesh-colored Magnesian Limestone in thinner layers—the whole passing upward into very cherty and sandy beds.

No. 4. 7 feet fine-grained, light flesh-colored Magnesian Limestone, in thin, undulating layers, with seams and concretions of chert.

No. 5. 22 feet hard, light bluish-gray, heavy bedded, sub-crystalline Magnesian Limestone, having a granular or sandy structure.

No. 6. 6 feet light grayish and flesh colored, granular Magnesian Limestone, with softer, bluish spots, and a little calc-spar; is inclined to weather into thin layers.

No. 7. 30 feet slope; no rocks seen in place.

No. 1 of this section is a part of the Second Sandstone, which doubtless also composes some of the upper part of the slope No. 2. All other beds, down, including, perhaps, a portion of the slope 7, at the base of the section, belong to the Third Magnesian Limestone. It is probable, however, from some other exposures seen near here, that the Third Sandstone, and possibly a few feet of the Fourth Magnesian Limestone, are above the level of the Osage at this place, but covered by the slope No. 7. Consequently the entire thickness of the Second Magnesian Limestone is probably not more than about 300 feet here, though it may be thicker in other parts of the county.

There are many good sections of this formation seen on the Auglaize and Tavern Creeks, but as they are generally similar to those already given on the Osage, it is perhaps unnecessary to present them here.

THIRD SANDSTONE.

The bed I suppose representing this formation, was only seen at one locality in this county. This was on the Osage, about four and a half miles east of the place where the section given on the preceding page was taken. As it was only 6 feet in thickness, and there can not be more than about 300 feet of space between it and the outcrops of the Second Sandstone, seen on the summits of the hills near here, I am left in some doubt whether it may not be a local bed of Sandstone intercalated near the lower part of the Third Magnesian Limestone, instead of the Third Sandstone. Yet, as I am not aware of such a bed of Sandstone having been anywhere seen in the lower part of the Third Magnesian, I am inclined at present to regard it as probably an attenuated representative of the Third Sandstone. The section given below shows its relation to the other beds at the locality mentioned:

THIRD MAGNESIAN:

No. 1. 130 feet of slope, with much rugged chert, some of which appears to be in place, near the top.

No. 2. 90 feet hard, heavy bedded, rugged, yellowish and light-grayish Magnesian Limestone, with some chert at intervals.

THIRD SANDSTONE:

No. 3. 6 feet white Sandstone, composed of rounded grains of quartz, cemented in part by calcareous matter.

FOURTH MAGNESIAN:

No. 4. 27 feet hard, gray, and light flesh-colored Magnesian Limestone, in rugged, irregular beds from 5 to 8 feet in thickness.

FOURTH MAGNESIAN LIMESTONE.

I am equally in doubt whether or not this formation is exposed in Miller county. If the bed No. 3 of the foregoing section represents the Third Sandstone, No. 4 of the same section must represent the upper part of the Fourth Magnesian Limestone. This rock (the Fourth Magnesian) was only seen at one place in this county, and it here only rises about 27 feet above the level of the Osage. All the beds at this place appear to have a slight dip toward the west, but this bed and the overlying Sandstone, although hidden by the slope at all the other localities examined west of here in this county, probably do not pass below the level of the Osage east of the Morgan county line, as apparently the same Sandstone was seen near the water's edge, five miles west of the county line in Morgan county. I saw no fossils in either of these beds.

ECONOMICAL GEOLOGY.

SOIL.

In the valleys of the Osage, and those of all the other streams of Miller county, there is a rich alluvial soil, unsurpassed in fertility by any of the best bottom lands in the State. In the higher districts there are also areas of considerable extent, of fine, arable land, especially in the north-western and south-eastern townships. South of the Osage, in Townships 38 and 39, Ranges 12 and 13, there is a district of about 23 square miles, and another in Townships 38 and 39, Ranges 12 and 13, of about 46 square miles, which are known as the "Big and Little Rich Woods." In both of these the soil is of excellent quality, and the growth of timber much larger than in much of the surrounding country, though they by no means embrace all the good land in this part of the county.

On the north side of the Osage, in the region of Mount Pleasant and Rocky Mount, on the high divide between the streams flowing north-eastward to the Moreau, and those flowing to the Osage on the south, there is a fine district of good land, much of which was well improved when I visited that region. In various other parts of the county there are smaller areas of good land, and even those districts too hilly and rocky for the plow, are admirably adapted to stock-grazing and the grape culture. Indeed, I saw at many places along the rocky bluffs near the Osage, wild native vines bearing larger and better flavored grapes than I have elsewhere observed growing without cultivation.

CLAYS FOR THE MANUFACTURE OF BRICKS.

Most of the clays seen by me in this county contain too many fragments of chert and other rocks to be well adapted to brick-making, though by proper care in selecting from beds most free from this objection, good brick clay can generally be found.

BUILDING STONES.

Rocks suitable for almost every kind of building purposes abound throughout the whole of Miller county. At several places in the northern townships already mentioned, the variety known as "Cotton rock," belonging to the Second Magnesian Limestone, crops out or is known to exist so near the surface as to be easily accessible. It is usually found in layers of very convenient thickness, and can always be quarried and dressed with great facility, while it's fine even texture and pleasing drab color make it a very desirable material for most building purposes.

The Third Magnesian Limestone, although generally having a coarser texture, also furnishes excellent building rocks. For heavy masonry, such as large abutments, bridges, etc., it is perhaps the best material in the county. Being often in heavy, massive beds, it can be quarried in blocks of almost any desired size. It is not compact enough to receive a polish, but would dress well under the hammer, and by selecting from such beds as are free from flint, it could probably be sawed. The fact that it is so frequently seen forming bold, precipitous bluffs along the streams shows that it must be a very durable rock.

ROAD MATERIAL.

The Third Magnesian Limestone, being much harder and tougher than the common pure Limestones, would make fine macadamized roads. The chert from this formation, as well as from the Second Sandstone and the Second Magnesian Limestone, would also make good roads.

LIMESTONE FOR QUICKLIME.

The outliers of Encrinital Limestone previously mentioned, in the northern part of the county, will always furnish that region with a good material for the production of quicklime. Further south, where these outliers do not exist, the Third Magnesian Limestone can be made available for this purpose. Although rather more difficult to burn than the Encrinital Limestone, it has been tried and found to make a good quality of lime. Indeed, it will probably make a stronger cement than Limestones having less magnesia in their composition.

SAND.

In the northern part of the county, outliers of the First Sandstone, which are generally friable, can be made to supply that region with sand. South of this, there are, at numerous places in various parts of the county, beds and outliers of the Second Sandstone, which, although not usually so easily crushed, have in most cases, by their disintegration, formed beds of loose sand. These beds of sand are not often exposed, but by digging near outcrops of the Sandstone, they can almost always be found near the surface.

IRON ORE.

At several places on the south side of the Osage, in this county, Iron ore was observed, apparently in considerable quantities. The first locality where I observed it was in S. E. quarter of Sec. 35, T. 40, R. 15. Here, along slopes one hundred and fifty feet below the summit of the country, I saw, lying loose and partly imbedded amongst the loose chert, masses of brown Hematite varying in size from a few inches to two feet in diameter. Similar masses were seen along the slope for more than half a mile west of this.

The hills here, for as much as sixty feet above the ore, are composed of the Third Magnesian Limestone. Higher up, many large masses of sandy chert, apparently belonging to the Second Sandstone, were seen.

Loose bodies of Iron ore also occur, under similar circumstances, in Sec. 11, T. 40, R. 14, nearly opposite Tuscumbia; and at another locality about fifteen miles further south, near the county line, I saw many fragments of brown Hematite lying over the surface amongst loose chert. Some of these masses at the last locality have the peculiar stalactitic form known as "pipe-stem ore."

In Sec. 15, T. 39, R. 12, near Bolin's Creek, along slopes occupied by the Second Sandstone, many loose masses of very pure Specular Iron ore were seen—some of which would weigh several hundred pounds. On fresh fractures, this ore has a bright, metallic luster, and contains, in little cavities, numerous small, very brilliant crystals of the Specular Oxid. It appears to be derived from the Second Sandstone, and was seen at no other locality in this county.

At several places in Secs. 14, 15, 22 and 23, T. 40, R. 13, I saw large quantities of brown Hematite on land belonging to Mr. Charles Sample, of St. Louis. The ore at one of these localities in Section 23, was observed strewed along a slope about one hundred and fifty feet below the summit of a ridge, down to a little branch as much as sixty feet below. Some twelve or fourteen pits were sunk here in order to determine the extent of the ore. The deepest of these pits, I was informed, (they were all partly filled with loose materials when I saw them,) penetrated as much as eighteen feet into the ore without passing through it. One of the openings near the top of the ridge seems not to have struck the ore, there being only red clay and chert thrown out. Much of the ore seen here is the "pipe-stem" variety, and it appears, where penetrated by the openings, to be *in loco*, or as originally deposited—the little rod-like columns of which it is composed being all standing in a vertical position. I saw no rock in place near the ore, excepting an outcrop of the Second Sandstone in a little valley, as much as forty feet below the heaviest bodies of ore. All the loose rocks about the outcrops of ore are masses of chert, apparently like that belonging to the Second Sandstone, to which formation I think the ore also belongs.

One mile west of the locality above named, Mr. Sample owns another deposit of Iron ore agreeing in all respects with that just described. Here he had also sunk some pits at about the same elevation as at the other locality, and penetrated the ore in the same way.

At another place about one and a-quarter miles a little west of north from the last locality, Mr. Sample has sunk several pits amongst loose chert, on a ridge at about the same elevation as the other openings, and took out a considerable quantity of ore. It is the same kind of "pipe-stem" ore seen at the other localities, and appears to hold the same position.

As these deposits of ore evidently do not exist in the form of veins or strata, but seem to have been deposited in large cavities in a rock, which has since been worn away, leaving them embraced amongst loose chert, it is very difficult to form any definite conclusion in regard to the quantity of ore that may exist here until more extensive openings are made. The impression left on my mind, however, was that it occurs in rather extensive bodies.

LEAD.

Lead ore has been found at several localities in this county, generally on the north side of the Osage. It occurs both in the rocks *in situ*, and among the loose surface materials. Where found mingled with the loose chert, clay, etc., overlying the solid rocks, it is manifest that it has been left by the disintegration of strata in which it was originally deposited, and has not been transported from a distance, as it never shows any marks of attrition, and is not, in this county at least, associated with any kind of Drift deposits.

The first locality at which I observed any of this loose ore was in S. 6, T. 42, R. 15, just above the top of a low outcrop of Second Magnesian Limestone, on the slope of a hill. At this place some large crystals of Galena were found on the surface.

In S. 20, T. 42, R. 14, about two miles north-east of Mount Pleasant, on a slope 30 to 40 feet below the summit of the country, Mr. Wm. Greenup sunk a shallow pit in search of Lead ore, and at a depth of three feet struck a soft porous bed of the Second Magnesian Limestone, in which he discovered a fissure about eight inches wide, bearing north and south. In this he informed me he found about 100 pounds of Lead ore in excavating to a depth of two feet below the surface of the rock. As far as he penetrated, the fissure was filled with Clay and Lead ore. At a distance of about 12 feet south of this opening another was made, and at a depth of three feet a similar fissure was found bearing east and west, and containing Lead ore and Clay, like the other.

These openings were filled with water and loose earth when I examined them, but judging from what I was informed, in regard to these fissures, I would recommend further explorations here.

About four miles, a little south of east from the last locality, and near the county line, in S. 25, T. 42, R. 14, I saw in the Second Magnesian Limestone forming the bottom of a small creek, about 150 feet below the higher portions of the surrounding country, a fissure 8 to 18 inches wide, bearing east and west. On excavating a short distance into this, Mr. Belche—a gentleman living in the neighborhood—found it was mainly filled with Sulphate of Baryta, with occasional crystals of Galena. He did not penetrate more than 18 inches, and raised about sixty pounds of Lead ore. He then drilled down through the Baryta and Lead ore, about five feet, when he struck a body of Lead ore, the thickness of which he did not determine.

Near 100 yards east of this locality, and on a slope 15 to 20 feet above it, Mr. Belche made an opening in the loose surface materials, to a depth of about five feet, when he struck apparently the same fissure seen in the creek, and in a very similar rock. This fissure he also found filled with Sulphate of Baryta, with some Lead ore. From all I could see here, I should think this locality worthy of a more thorough exploration.

In the south-west quarter of S. 2, T. 41, R. 14, in the bed of a small branch of Saline Creek, about 150 feet below the summit of the country, I saw, in some gray layers of Second Magnesian Limestone, occasional crystals of Lead ore; and Mr. Belche informed me he has picked up loose, in the bed of this creek near here, several hundred pounds of ore. It does not appear to exist here in a fissure, but is disseminated in the form of isolated crystals through the rock.

On the south side of the Osage I heard of Lead ore having been found at but one place. This is in S. 2, T. 39, R. 42. Here, on a slope some 15 feet above a small branch, three pits were sunk among loose chert, clay, etc., to depths of from three to five feet, and about 15 or 20 pounds of Lead ore found.

COAL.

The only places where I met with Coal, or indications of its presence in Miller county, are on the south side of the Osage. One of these localities is in S. 9, T. 39, R. 13, near the head of a small valley about 60 feet below the summit of the higher country. At this place four excavations were made in the loose surface materials; and at a depth of a few feet below the surface a kind of impure Cannel Coal, or highly bituminous shale, was struck (*in situ*,) and penetrated about 10 feet without passing through it. I saw specimens of this Coal, and found it possessing a slaty structure, and containing a large proportion of earthy matter. When heated, it first decrepitates, and then burns freely with a bright yellow flame, leaving a large amount of white ash.

Above these openings I saw cropping out of the slopes, nearly to the tops of the surrounding hills, ledges of the Second Magnesian Limestone; and about 200 yards further down the same little valley, an exposure of the Second Sandstone was seen as much as 50 feet below the horizon of the Coal. From these facts it is manifest this Coal has been deposited in the bottom of a depression worn in the Second Magnesian Limestone, perhaps nearly or quite down to the Second Sandstone. Consequently, it can not be expected to be of great horizontal extent, though it may be quite thick.

The other locality is in S. 12, T. 39, R. 14. Here, in a small valley, some 80 feet below the summit of the surrounding country, at the base of a bluff, the lower 38 feet of which is composed of the Third Magnesian Limestone, and the upper 30 feet of the cherty portions of the Second Sandstone, some pits were sunk to a depth of four or five feet into loose chert, clay, etc., among which numerous masses of loose Cannel Coal were found. These have evidently been transported by water to their present position, from a bed originally deposited somewhere, perhaps not far above the place where these pits were sunk.

Other local deposits of Coal will probably be found in this county, but the geological structure of the country shows that such beds can not be of any great extent. Some of them may contain Coal enough to be of use to the immediate neighborhood in which they are found, but any expensive preparations to mine it on an extensive scale would certainly result in loss. The great abundance of good wood in Miller county, however, renders the absence of extensive Coal beds a matter of no great consequence.

SULPHATE OF BARYTA.

Considerable quantities of this mineral occur at several places in this county, in the form of fine large transparent crystals, generally having a slight bluish tinge. In S. 2, T. 40, R. 14, I collected some beautiful specimens of these crystals along a slope about 70 feet below the summit of the country. It appears to occur here either in the

Second Sandstone or the upper part of the Third Magnesian Limestone. I also found fine crystals of it at another place, among loose chert, belonging to the Third Magnesian Limestone, in S. 13, T. 38, R. 14. A large number of valuable specimens for mineralogical cabinets might be collected at the localities mentioned above.

Sulphate of Baryta has been used to some extent as a pigment, ground and mixed in various proportions with White Lead, which it is supposed to improve for some kinds of painting.

CHAPTER VIII.

MORGAN COUNTY.

BY F. B. MEEK.

This county contains a superficial area of about 640 square miles, and lies immediately west of Miller and Moniteau counties. Its more elevated portions rise from 400 to 550 feet above the Osage, and from 600 to 700 feet above high water mark at St. Louis. This high country trends in a nearly east and west direction through the county, a little south of the middle, and constitutes the divide or water-shed between the streams flowing northward to the Lamine, and those flowing into the Osage on the south.

North of this divide, there is a general slope of the surface, so that the higher country near the northern boundary of the county is not elevated more than 260 feet, and the lower (in the valley of Lamine Creek) not more than about 40 feet, above the level of the Osage. South of the divide, the general slope toward the Osage, following the highest country between the streams, is at near the same rate; but the descent of the streams on the south side is much more rapid than that of those on the north.

The surface of the elevated region near the middle of the county is beautiful, comparatively level, or undulating prairie land. South of this, the slopes are at first gentle, near the head branches of the Gravois, but as we descend these, the face of the country becomes more hilly; and almost everywhere near that, and the other main creeks, as well as their principal tributaries, and especially near the Osage, it is very broken and rocky.

North of the main divide, the high, nearly level prairie land extends, with a slight descent, for some distance northward between the streams flowing in that direction; but near most of the larger streams the surface is more or less broken, and sometimes rocky, but generally not so much so as on the south side.

SPRINGS.

Almost every part of this county is bountifully supplied with good water, excepting some portions of the higher districts; and even there it can generally be obtained by sinking wells. The largest springs, however, are on the south side of the divide. Some of these, like those described in Miller county, discharge such enormous quantities of water as to afford valuable power for driving grist mills and other machinery. In T. 42, R. 17, I saw a large mill belonging to Mr. F. L. Ross, driven entirely by the water flowing from one spring. Another affording water enough to run a good mill was observed near the Benton county line, some 12 miles north of the Osage.

In T. 41, R. 17, two large grist mills (known as the Gravois Mills,) and a carding machine, are run by one spring, without using more than half of the water flowing from it. As near as could be ascertained from measurement of the average breadth and depth of the aqueduct leading to these mills, and the mean rate at which the water flows, there can not be less than 2,000 gallons per minute passing through it; and when it is borne in mind that apparently as much more water passes off in another direction, some idea may be formed of the quantity afforded by this spring. I was informed that the longest drouths produce scarcely any perceptible decrease in the quantity of water discharged here, but that heavy falls of rain sometimes cause an increased flow, and make the waters turbid, though it always runs down to its usual quantity and clearness in a few hours after the rains cease. At the time I visited this spring it was very clear, and had a temperature of 56° — that of the air being 80°. Numerous other smaller springs of cool, clear water were seen in the southern part of the county.

I met with no mineral springs of much strength in any part of Morgan county; though I saw, in Sec. 9, T. 43, R. 18, a large spring slightly impregnated with Sulphur. It boils up in a nearly circular marshy spot, and affords a considerable quantity of clear water, with a temperature of 57°. After leaving the county, I also heard of a Sulphur spring near Versailles; but not knowing of its existence when near there, I did not visit it.

STREAMS.

Osage River—the largest stream in this region—does not enter this county, but forms its southern boundary, excepting near the middle, where it makes an extensive bend to the south, into Camden county. So far, however, as it can be made available for purposes of navigation, it is conveniently accessible to all the middle and southern portions of Morgan county.

South of the main divide, the largest stream within this county is Big Gravois Creek, which heads in T. 42, R. 18 and 19, and flows south-eastward to the Osage. Although only about 20 miles in length, it has a fall, from the head branches of its connection with the Osage, of about 400 feet, and an average breadth of about 70 yards near the mouth. It has several large branches, all of which (as well as the main creek) are clear, rapid streams, furnishing fine water-power. Proctor, Little Buffalo and Minna's Creek are much smaller streams, flowing southward to the Osage, in the south-west part of the county. They are all clear streams, having considerable fall, and probably afford water enough to be made available to some extent, for water power.

Big Buffalo is a larger stream, heading in T. 42, R. 19, and running south-westward, so as soon to cross the county line into Benton county. One branch of Little Gravois Creek heads in T. 41, R. 16, and runs southward and south-westward some four miles, after which it forms a junction with the other main branch, and flows eastward through a part of Miller county, to the Osage. Like all the other streams in this county south of the middle elevated portion, it is a clear, rapid stream.

On the north side of the central elevated country, the principal streams are, Big and Little Richland, Haw and Flat Creeks. All of these, excepting the last, head in T. 42, R. 18 and 19, and flow northward, so as to unite with Flat Creek in T. 45, R. 19, to form the Lamine. These, as well as nearly all the streams north of the divide, present a marked contrast with those on the south, being more sluggish and not near so clear as the latter. This is due to the fact that they have less fall, and are mainly fed by surface waters, while those on the south have a rapid descent, and are chiefly supplied by deep-seated springs. It is true, in each case the quantity of surface-waters discharged in proportion to the areas drained is the same, but the more rapid descent on the south causes it to pass sooner away after the rains cease, leaving the streams clear; while on the north it runs more slowly, and, when gone, leaves the streams very low, or sometimes entirely without water; consequently, the streams in the northern part of the county do not furnish as good water-power as those further south.

Flat Creek is much the largest stream in the northern part of the county, though it only passes through the north-western corner, and connects with Richland Creek to form the Lamine, near the county line. A short distance north and east of Versailles, some small head branches of North Moreau take their rise and flow in a north-easterly direction, but cross the line into Moniteau county, before becoming streams of much importance.

TIMBER.

Most of the southern part of this county is woodland, and contains—especially in the valleys—extensive forests of fine, large timber, of the best varieties for building purposes. North of Versailles, nearly one-third of the county is occupied by prairies; but they are so distributed with relation to the intervening woodlands, that an abundant supply of wood for fuel, and good timber for the construction of houses, fences, bridges, etc., can always be found at convenient distances. The growth is the same as in Miller county.

GEOLOGICAL STRUCTURE.

The formations in this county are the same as those already described in Miller, with the addition of the First Magnesian Limestone, and, in the north-west corner of the county, of a small patch of Chouteau Limestone. In other words, almost the whole county is occupied by the great Magnesian Limestone series belonging to the older Silurian epoch. The same general inclination of the strata toward the north, or a little east of north, also prevails here; at any rate, from a point somewhere south of Versailles. Near the west side of the county, north of Versailles, the dip appears to be west of north. In the southern part, near the Osage, there is a general dip toward the south, with local undulations and flexures, causing sudden changes from a south-eastern to a south-western dip. These undulations, and the scarcity of organic remains on these rocks, which are so variable in their lithological characters, make it very difficult, sometimes, to identify the same formations at different localities.

The formations in this county occur in descending order, as follows:

QUATERNARY:

No. 1. Alluvium, from 0 to perhaps as much as 40 feet.

CARBONIFEROUS:

No. 2. Coal from a few inches to more than 14 feet.
No. 3. 10 feet Encrinital Limestone.
No. 4. 35 feet lower beds of Chouteau Limestone.

LOWER SILURIAN:

No. 5. 20 feet First Magnesian Limestone.
No. 6. 40 feet Saccharoidal Sandstone.
No. 7. 175 feet Second Magnesian Limestone.
No. 8. 40 feet Second Sandstone.
No. 9. 300 feet Third Magnesian Limestone.
No. 10. 30 feet Third Sandstone.
No. 11. 153 feet Fourth Magnesian Limestone (above the Osage.)

QUATERNARY SYSTEM.

ALLUVIUM.

The alluvial deposits of this county, out of the valleys, consist of the surface and subsoils, and various yellowish and reddish clays, with imbedded fragments of flints and other rocks. These clays appear to have been chiefly formed by the disintegration of the subjacent strata, as no fragments of rocks differing from those of this region were anywhere observed in them; nor were any beds of water-worn pebbles or sand, such as are usually attributed to Drift agency, met with, and but a single erratic of any kind was seen in the county, this was a solitary granite boulder, about 18 inches in diameter, observed in the valley of Gravois Creek. As it presented no marks of attrition, it was most probably transported here by floating ice from some locality far north of this, during the Glacial period.

The Alluvium of the valleys is composed of the usual mixed materials left by the overflow of the streams and washed by the rains from the adjacent high lands. As in Miller, the Bluff formation seems to be entirely wanting in this county.

CARBONIFEROUS ROCKS.

Coal Measures.

This member of the Carboniferous system only exists here in the form of very small, isolated local deposits of coal, scattered at intervals over the county.* There may, however, also be at some places small outliers of clays and shale belonging to the same epoch, as a local bed of dark bluish shale, 30 feet in thickness, containing much pyrites, was penetrated in sinking a well in Cooper county, near the northern line of this county, though no such beds were anywhere observed within its bounds.

Encrinital Limestone.

Like the deposits of coal above mentioned, this Limestone, which is the only representative of the Lower Carboniferous series found in this county, occurs here only as outliers of very limited extent, resting, at least in one instance, on the Upper Devonian, but more frequently directly upon the Lower Silurian rocks.

The first exposure of it seen in this county is in Sec. 2, T. 45, R. 19, where, on a ridge composed of the Second Magnesian Limestone, at an elevation of about 65 feet above the valley of Flat Creek, large masses of this rock—some of which would measure as much as 50 feet in length and 10 feet in thickness—were seen lying tilted and dipping at various angles beneath the soil and loose materials.

At several other localities, in the same township and range, a little west of south from that last mentioned, outliers of this formation were observed under similar circumstances, but usually resting on the older Silurian rocks. Near the same place it was also seen reposing upon the Chouteau Limestone beds, as represented in the following section:

No. 1. 50 feet slope, no rocks seen.
No. 2. 6 feet Encrinital Limestone.
No. 3. 36 feet slope, with occasional exposures of Chouteau Limestone.
No. 4. 40 feet slope to bottom of Flat Creek valley.

East of these exposures, along near the county line, a few very small outliers were met with on some of the higher points, and at a

*A more detailed account of these outliers of Coal will be given under the head of Economical Geology in the subsequent pages of this report.

few distant intervals south-west and south of this, similar masses of it were observed, even to within a few miles of Versailles.

Chouteau Limestone.

This formation occupies but a very small area in the northern part of T. 45, R. 19, where it crops out at several places along Flat Creek, and has been struck in sinking wells on the higher country back from the bluffs. None of these exposures show very clearly its thickness, but at the point where the above section was taken there appears to be as much as 35 feet of it. The beds seen here are chiefly the lower part of the formation, containing great numbers of a peculiar *Cauda-Galli*-like *Fucoid.* The other fossils noted were *Leptæna depressa, Productus Murchisonianus, Rhynchonella Missouriensis*, and fragments of a large *Orthis* or *Leptæna.*

SILURIAN SYSTEM.

First Magnesian Limestone.

The difficulty of distinguishing this rock from the Second Magnesian Limestone is so great that it is often almost impossible to determine to which we should refer a given exposure. Being very variable in their lithological characters, and generally destitute of any organic remains by which they can be distinguished, we are compelled to decide the question, in most cases, by determining whether the Saccharoidal Sandstone exists above or below the horizon of an outcrop under examination. Now, when it is borne in mind that this Sandstone is very variable in thickness, and may in some cases thin out entirely, while there are sometimes local beds of Sandstone *in* the Second Magnesian Limestone, of even greater thickness than the Saccharoidal Sandstone itself where attenuated, some idea may be formed of the uncertainty of such a guide in a district where the strata are more or less undulating.

The only outcrop of this formation examined by me, where it could be seen reposing directly upon the Saccharoidal Sandstone, is in T. 45, R. 19, on Richland Creek, at which place the section given below was taken:

No. 1. 20 feet slope, with occasional outcrop of the First Magnesian Limestone, consisting of hard, very fine-grained drab-colored layers.

No. 2. 25 feet Saccharoidal Sandstone, of grayish color, with small particles of flint.

No. 3. 50 feet rugged, bluish gray beds of Second Magnesian Limestone, with more or less chert.

No. 4. 15 feet white, rather hard Sandstone, with small fragments of chert; probably a local bed in the Second Magnesian Limestone.

I also saw some exposures of beds I supposed to belong to this formation at a few elevated localities south-east of that where the above section was taken, both in the same township, and in T. 43, R. 17. It may also occur at some of the high places toward the west side of the county, in townships 42, 43 and 44, but I did not recognize it there. I had no opportunity to determine the thickness of this rock, though I do not think it more than 25 or 30 feet in this county. No fossils were seen in it.

Saccharoidal Sandstone.

Exposures of this Sandstone were seen in almost every township north of Versailles, and at a few places south-east of there, in T. 42, R. 16. It generally crops out on or near the more elevated portions of the country, and rarely forms continuous exposures of much extent. Sometimes it thins out quite suddenly to only a few feet in thickness, and in other cases swells very abruptly from 10 to 15 feet to as much as 50 or 60 feet. This seems to have resulted from inequalities of the surface of the Second Magnesian Limestone upon which it was deposited. A remarkable instance of this kind was observed in the north-western part of the county near Flat Creek, where this rock suddenly swells out from a thickness of only 10 or 12 feet to as much

Fig. 11.

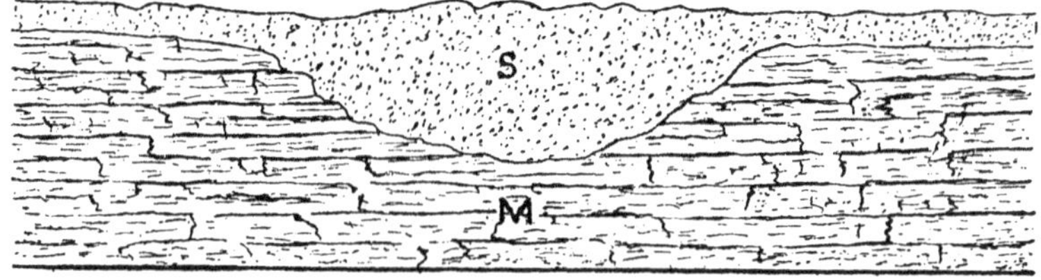

as 60 feet, as represented by the annexed cut; S being a bed of the Sandstone filling a cavity 240 feet long and about 60 feet in depth, in the Second Magnesian Limestone M.

At other localities in this part of the county, this rock usually presents a thickness of from 15 to 25 or 30 feet. Coming southward, it is observed at several places, gradually rising with the swell of the country, and often showing itself in the form of isolated, shapeless masses of grayish color, rising from five to ten feet above the soil, near the summit of the country. At Versailles, near the middle of the county, it has been struck in wells, and crops out along a branch just east of the town, showing a thickness of 20 to 25 feet. About two miles a little north of east from Versailles, it was observed along a small stream forming bluffs from 15 to 20 feet in hight, and indicating an entire thickness here of near 40 feet. At this place it assumes almost exactly the lithological characters of the Second Sandstone, being a coarse-grained reddish mass containing large quanties of chert, in the form of angular fragments, and even appears to pass into a rugged brecciated mass of chert and Sandstone.

At a few localities south-east of this, in T. 42, R. 16, thin outcrops of Sandstone, probably belonging to this formation, were seen; and near the southern part of this township, in Sec. 35, I observed a very peculiar bed of about 20 feet in thickness, which appears to belong to it. This bed is composed of extremely fine silico-argillaceous matter, of a light buff color, with numerous slender parallel stripes of bright delicate carmine. It is almost light enough to float in water when dry, and can be easily cut with a knife, but is not compact enough to receive a polish.

Excepting where deposited in depressions, this formation seems not to attain in this county a thickness of more than about 40 feet, and its average is probably not more than 15 or 20 feet. I observed no organic remains of any kind in it.

Second Magnesian Limestone.

The Second Magnesian Limestone underlies all the rocks previously mentioned, and is exposed along the streams at many places throughout nearly all the northern and middle portions of the county, extending southward to Versailles, and some distance beyond, especially on the higher parts of the country.

The upper beds of this formation, here as elsewhere, consist of light grayish and flesh-colored mixed more or less concretionary layers, with, at some places, beds of Sandstone and "Cotton rock." The middle and lower beds, however, consist of more heavy bedded, harder and more coarsely-grained strata than I have elsewhere seen in any part of this formation, being scarcely distinguishable by their lithological characters from the Third Magnesian Limestone. Indeed, where outcrops of the Second Sandstone are not seen, it sometimes becomes very difficult to distinguish these two Limestones, especially in a district where either may have been abruptly elevated or depressed by undulations of the strata, much above or below the horizon at which we would otherwise expect to find it.

Good exposures of the middle and upper beds are seen in the northern part of the county, where Lamine and Flat Creeks have excavated their valleys near 150 feet down into them; though all of this thickness is not exposed at any one place. About 120 feet of the gray, flesh-colored and mixed concretionary beds were seen at the locality where the section given on page 142 was observed in T. 45, R. 19. At another place, some 4½ miles south-east of this, on Richland Creek, the following section was taken:

No. 1. 25 to 30 feet slope, with loose chert.
No. 2. 10 feet Sandstone.
No. 3. 30 feet "Cotton rock."
No. 4. 35 feet light-colored granular harder Magnesian Limestone.

No. 2 of this section is probably the Saccharoidal Sandstone, though it may be an intercalated bed of Sandstone *in* the Second Magnesian Limestone. South of the above locality the exposures seen along Haw and Richland Creeks are all hard grayish granular beds, resembling the Third Magnesian Limestone more than the Second. I saw no "Cotton rock" along these streams, nor southward, until in T. 42, R. 19, where some outcrops of it were seen along slopes, perhaps 100 feet below the highest part of the country near. Similar exposures were also observed at Versailles, and south-east of there in T. 41 and 42, R. 16.

This formation probably attains a thickness of about 175 feet in this county, and appears to be almost entirely destitute of organic remains.

Second Sandstone.

This Sandstone was only recognized toward the southern part of the county—generally near the Osage and along the Gravois, and some of the smaller streams. It was observed on the Osage near the south-western corner of the county, occupying a position as much as 240 feet above the river, near the summits of the bluffs, where it exhibited a thickness of about 40 feet. It contains much chert here, and the chert is often more or less oolitic. Similar exposures were seen at several places back three or four miles north of this.

East of these localities it again occurs at some places on the high country near the middle of T. 40, R. 17, elevated as much perhaps as 240 feet or more above the Osage. Here there appears to be a dip to the south-east, but a little north of this the strata incline to the north, so that along the Gravois this rock is seen at lower elevations. Again, near Indian Creek, in T. 41, R. 16, exposures of it showing a thickness of 15 to 20 feet were observed on elevated bluffs, perhaps 160 feet or more above that stream. South-east of these outcrops, in T. 40, R. 16, it occurs on the high country near the Osage, and was also seen on Little Gravois Creek.

The maximum thickness of this rock in Morgan county is probably about 40 feet, but it is apparently at many places less than half that thickness. It often becomes very cherty, at which places I sometimes found in the chert a few fossils belonging to the same species of *Euomphalus* and *Pleurotomaria* occurring in the Third Magnesian Limestone below.

THIRD MAGNESIAN LIMESTONE.

The Third Magnesian Limestone is extensively exposed in the southern part of the county, especially along the Osage and other principal streams. On the Osage, near the mouth of Gravois Creek, and for some distance up the latter, it forms bold, picturesque bluffs and hills, sometimes more than 250 feet in hight. In going westward from these localities, it is found to rise so that only the upper parts of the hills are composed of it at the mouth of Proctor Creek; and from near that point it dips suddenly toward the south-west.

A short distance east of the south-west corner of the county, entire bluffs, rising as much as 280 feet above the Osage, are made up of this rock and the Second Sandstone, as represented by the following section:

SECOND SANDSTONE:

No. 1. 40 feet grayish and yellowish Sandstone, with white layers and bands, and some chert.

THIRD MAGNESIAN LIMESTONE:

No. 2. 77 feet heavy bedded, light grayish, granular Magnesian Limestone.

No. 3. 3 feet whitish cherty band.

No. 4. 40 feet Magnesian Limestone like No. 2.

No. 5. 3 feet band whitish chert.

No. 6. 120 feet hard, bluish-gray, heavy bedded, granular Magnesian Limestone with little chert.

The exposures already mentioned on the Gravois, and near its mouth along the Osage, are made up of nearly the same beds composing the above section, excepting that the Second Sandstone is generally worn away near the bluffs. At one place, on a small tributary of Gravois Creek, in T. 41, R. 17, some high exposures were observed presenting the section given below:

No. 1. 20 feet slope, covered with loose chert.

No. 2. 2 feet coarse brecciated mass, composed of fragments of chert imbedded in Sandstone.

No. 3. 56 feet slope, strewed with large, loose masses of No. 2.

No. 4. 84 feet hard, heavy bedded, light grayish, granular Magnesian Limestone, with thin beds and concretions of chert.

I think No. 2 of this section belongs to the Second Sandstone, and that portions of the slopes above and below are probably occupied by the same rock; if so, there must be a considerable dip toward the north or north-east in this region, since the exposures of the Second Sandstone seen south of here, near the Osage, are elevated considerably above the top of the foregoing section.

The inclination of the strata, however, appears to be here so much to the east of north, that the Second Sandstone seems not to pass beneath the bed of the Gravois for some distance up; at any rate, all the exposures along this stream, far up into T. 42, R. 18, present much more the characters of the Third and Fourth Magnesian Limestones than those of the Second. This is also the case with all the outcrops seen along the north branch of the Gravois, as far up as Ross' Mill, and for some distance up Indian Creek.

The lithological characters of this formation are in all respects the same in this as in Miller county, and as near as I could determine it attains here about the same thickness. Although organic remains are by no means abundant in it, they are occasionally met with; and at one place, on Little Gravois Creek, I collected from a cherty, arenaceous bed, I supposed to be intercalated in this rock, (though it may belong to the Second Sandstone,) quite a number of good specimens. Amongst these there are two or three species of *Euomphalus*, allied to *E. levata*, and *E. complanata*, (*Ophileta levata* and *O. complanata* Vanuxem;) two or three others similar to *E. polygyrata*, of Roemer; one or two small species of *Pleurotomaria*, a slender annulated *Orthoceras*, and fragments of *Trilobites*, belonging to Dr. Owens' genus *Lonchocephalus*. These are probably all new species, but show close and unmistakable affinities to forms found in the Calciferous and Potsdam Sandstones of New York and Minnesota.

THIRD SANDSTONE.

I only recognized this formation at a few localities in Morgan county; these were immediately on the Osage. First, in ascending that stream, it was observed near the water's edge, at a place only about two miles below the mouth of the Gravois. The section taken here was as follows:

THIRD MAGNESIAN LIMESTONE:

No. 1. 50 feet hard, heavy bedded, rough, granular Magnesian Limestone, of light grayish color.

No. 2. 10 feet light bluish-drab, fine-grained Magnesian Limestone, in rather thin layers.

No. 3. 3 feet hard, concretionary, gray Magnesian Limestone.

THIRD SANDSTONE:

No. 4. 15 feet soft, white Sandstone, with a few very hard seams.

I could not determine the entire thickness of the Sandstone here, its base being beneath the level of the river, though it probably does not pass much below the surface of the water, as it is only six feet in thickness at a locality about 10 miles farther east, in Miller county, where its base is elevated 27 feet above the Osage. At the locality where the above section was taken, all the beds show a dip of 10° to 12° to the west or south-west, in consequence of which the Third Sandstone passes entirely beneath the river a short distance above. It must, however, rise again rather rapidly not far west of the Gravois, for after crossing the high divide between the bends of the Osage, west of the mouth of the Gravois, we find it elevated along the bluffs in T. 40, R. 18, as much as 150 feet above the Osage. After crossing the next bend, however, at a distance of only two to three miles farther west, it is brought, by a reverse dip, down within 35 feet of the surface of the river.

At the latter locality the section presented is as given below:

THIRD MAGNESIAN LIMESTONE:

No. 1. 35 feet very cherty bed, in regular strata.

No. 2. 156 feet heavy beds of light gray, granular Magnesian Limestone, alternating with thin beds and layers of chert, the whole becoming very cherty above.

THIRD SANDSTONE:

No. 3. 30 feet white Sandstone, composed of rounded grains, partly connected by calcareous matter.

No. 4. 35 feet slope; no rocks exposed above the water's edge.

The dip of the strata must take this Sandstone beneath the level of the Osage at no great distance above the point where the foregoing section was taken, as it was not again seen at any of the exposures further west in this county. Not being all exposed at that locality, where it attains a greater development, perhaps, than in any other part of the county, I was unable to determine its greatest thickness here, though I do not think it much more than 30 feet.

It evidently increases in thickness toward the west, there being 30 feet of it exposed where last seen, while at another place about 2½ miles farther east, it measures 5 feet less; and at the point where first seen, below the mouth of Gravois Creek, about 14 miles farther east, it crops out under circumstances indicating a thickness of not much over 16 or 18 feet; while as already stated, about 10 miles east of there, in Morgan county, it only measures 6 feet. From these facts, I am inclined to believe that they, as well as the other Sandstones of the Magnesian Limestone series, may, in some instances, thin out entirely, in which case we would be liable to greatly over-estimate the thickness of one or the other of the Magnesian Limestones. I met with no organic remains in this rock.

FOURTH MAGNESIAN LIMESTONE.

This Limestone appears to differ from the Third, chiefly in being almost entirely free from chert. It was only recognized in the southwest part of the county, in T. 40, R. 18, where, in consequence of a rather sudden uplift, it rises, so as to form bluffs as much as 150 feet in hight above the Osage.

At one of these places, the section exposed is as represented below:

THIRD MAGNESIAN LIMESTONE:

No. 1. 3-foot bed of coarse, rough chert.

No. 2. 75 feet slope, with occasional exposures of hard, gray, granular Magnesian Limestone.

No. 3. 30 feet slope, with occasional exposures of rough, cherty Magnesian Limestone.

THIRD SANDSTONE:

No. 4. 25 feet white Sandstone, with some seams near the top, of very hard, compact Sandstone.

FOURTH MAGNESIAN LIMESTONE:

No. 5. 150 feet heavy, massive beds of hard, light-gray, granular Magnesian Limestone, with scarcely any chert.

Due north of the above locality, on the upper Gravois, as already stated, exposures were seen very similar to the Fourth Magnesian Limestone, at several places; and, as it is possible the axis which has so abruptly elevated this rock at the point where the above Section was taken may continue that far north, these outcrops may belong to this formation. It probably also rises a little above the Osage, near the south-east corner of the county, though I did not see it exposed there. I saw no organic remains in it, either in this or Miller county.

ECONOMICAL GEOLOGY.

SOILS.

In the elevated central and northern portions of this county there are large areas of beautiful, level or undulating prairie lands, possessing a soil scarcely inferior in fertility to that of any uplands in the State. Much of the more elevated forest land of this part of the county is also of good quality, especially for the growth of wheat, while in the valleys there is some first-rate bottom land.

The southern part of the county, excepting in the valleys, is generally too broken and rocky for the plow, but well adapted to stock-grazing and, probably, to the grape culture. In the valleys and along the more gentle slopes, there is a fair proportion of good, arable land in this part of the county.*

COAL.

Beds of this useful and important mineral have been found at many places in this county, though, like those described in Miller and Moniteau counties, they are not continuous deposits, but small, isolated outliers, occupying depressions in the older Silurian rocks. These

* Specimens of the different varieties of soils and subsoils were collected for analysis.

deposits generally consist entirely of Coal, (usually Cannel,) without any of the associated Clays, Shales or Sandstones of the Coal Measures.

The first bed of this kind examined in the county is on Mr. George Evans' land, in Sec. 28, T. 44, R. 19. Here, in a valley about 100 feet below the summit of the higher country on either side, a pit was sunk in the loose surface materials about three feet, when a bed of rather impure Cannel Coal was struck, and penetrated, I was informed, 8 or 9 feet, without passing through it. On the south side of the pit, the Coal, 3 feet below its surface, terminates abruptly against light-grayish Magnesian Limestone, but its extent in other directions was not determined. It is evident, however, that it must be confined to the valley in which it occurs, as the hills on each side, for 70 or 80 feet above, are composed of the Second Magnesian Limestone, surmounted by the Saccharoidal Sandstone.

The Coal obtained here, although compact when taken out, shows a tendency to split into thin laminæ, after being long exposed; it is quite light when dry, and burns very freely, leaving a rather large proportion of white ash.

In Sec. 7, T. 42, R. 18, a little Coal and some dark, shaly matter were thrown out of a shallow excavation made on the slope of a hill, in searching for lead ore. It is probable a small local deposit of Coal may exist here, a little above the elevation of this opening. Similar indications of Coal have also been observed in some pits sunk in a little valley about 120 feet below the summit of the country, near Versailles, in Sec. 8, T. 42, R. 17.

In another small valley, in Sec. 18, T. 42, R. 16, about 100 feet below the highest part of the neighboring country, a bed of Coal was discovered only overlaid by the loose surface materials. Its thickness was unknown at the time I visited the locality, though I was informed it had been penetrated 8 feet. As in the foregoing instances, outcrops of the Second Magnesian Limestone are here seen along the slopes above the Coal, so as to show that it can not be of great horizontal extent, though it may be quite thick.

This Coal differs from nearly all these local deposits I have seen in this county, as well as in Miller, in being a common variety instead of Cannel Coal. It appears to be of good quality for most purposes; but I was informed that it contains too much pyrites to be suitable for blacksmiths' use. The specimens I saw, however, did not appear to contain an unusual quantity of that mineral.

I heard of another coal mine in Sec. 25, T. 42, R. 17, but did not succeed in finding the locality. Some four miles from this, however, I examined a mine belonging to Mr. S. L. Ross, in Sec. 35, T. 42, R. 17. The bed here has been discovered in a small valley, and opened by sinking a pit through loose surface materials to a depth of about six feet, when the coal was struck. As in the other instances, the thickness of the bed was not determined; but it was penetrated, I was informed, fourteen feet without passing through it. The opening being filled with water and loose earth when I visited the locality, I had no opportunity to see the coal *in situ*, though amongst heaps of dark carbonaceous matter lying about the opening I found some fragments of it; but as they had been exposed to the weather for several years, they were not in a condition to convey a very clear idea of its nature. It does not, however, appear to be Cannel Coal.

I was informed about four thousand bushels of this Coal have been taken out at different times, and that it has been found to be of good quality for blacksmiths' use. Owing to the thickness of this bed, there may be enough of it to supply local demands for a long time to come, but outcrops of Magnesian Limestone in the vicinity show that it must be, as in the other instances, of limited horizontal extent; for it certainly does not pass under the strata composing the hills on either side of the valley.

At another locality, half a mile north of the above, a bed of Coal occurring under exactly similar circumstances has been opened, and some fifteen wagon-loads taken out; and about three-quarters of a mile further south-west, I saw a bed of Cannel Coal cropping out of a slope near sixty feet below the summit of the country. This latter bed was in an inclined position, having probably slidden down somewhat below its original horizon. I could not determine its thickness, though only twelve to fifteen inches of it were exposed. From outcrops seen near here, I think this bed rests either on the Saccharoidal Sandstone or the Second Magnesian Limestone, and is of small extent.

Again, in Sec. 7, T. 41, R. 16, a bed of Coal has been opened in a valley near Indian Creek. At the time I visited the locality, the pit was partly filled with loose materials, so that I could not see the Coal in place, but fragments of it were mingled with heaps of dark, carbonaceous matter lying about the pit. I was informed it burns freely, but contains too much sulphur (Sulphuret of Iron) for blacksmiths' use. It is evidently only overlaid by the superficial clays of the country, and occupies a depression in the Lower Silurian rocks.

In regard to all these deposits of Coal, I would merely state, as I have already done in relation to those of Moniteau and Miller counties, that some of them may be extensive enough to supply the demands of the immediate neighborhoods in which they occur, but I would caution those interested against the expenditure of capital in preparations to mine it extensively, or to ship it to distant markets, as the quantity will always be found insufficient to justify such outlay.

LEAD.

There is, perhaps, scarcely a township in this county in which more or less Lead ore has not been found. It usually occurs mingled with chert and fragments of other rocks, in the loose, superficial deposits of the county, where it has doubtless been left by the disintegration of the subjacent Magnesian Limestones, in which it was originally deposited. It has also, in several instances, been found filling fissures and cavities in these rocks.

The localities at which loose fragments of Lead ore have been found in this county are so numerous that it would be extremely tedious, and perhaps useless, to refer to them all in detail. I shall, therefore, confine myself to the notice of those where it is known to occur either *in situ,* or has been found loose in such quantities as to indicate its probable existence in the rocks below.

Beginning in the northern part of the county, the first Lead locality examined is on Mr. F. Lucket's land, in Sec. 20, T. 44, R. 19. Here, near Haw Creek, I was informed as much as one hundred pounds of ore have been collected at a time on the surface. I also saw fragments of it at several places in this vicinity lying loose. The Second Magnesian Limestone forms the bluffs here.

In the S. W. quarter Sec. 10, T. 43, R. 18, I saw several old shafts that had been sunk on Messrs. Wyan, Trigg and Bryant's land some sixteen years previous for Lead ore. Judging from the material thrown out, they rarely penetrated down to the solid strata, though one of them evidently struck gray beds, apparently of the Second Magnesian Limestone. I met with no person who could give me any reliable information in regard to the quantity of ore taken out, but I observed more or less of it remaining amongst the loose rocks, clay, etc., about several of the openings.

About five miles, nearly in a south-west direction from the above, in the N. W. quarter of Sec. 34, T. 44, R. 19, I saw, in a gray granular rock (probably the Third Magnesian Limestone) forming the bed of a small tributary of Buffalo Creek, several seams varying in thickness from that of a knife-blade to three-quarters of an inch, in which Lead ore occurs. These seams have an east and west bearing, and can be traced along the bottom of the creek for about one hundred and fifty yards.

Some sixteen or eighteen years since, quite a number of shallow shafts were sunk on a declivity in the N. W. quarter of Sec. 28, T. 42, R. 18, by some German miners, and eight hundred or nine hundred pounds of Lead ore taken out. None of these excavations appear to have reached solid rock in place.

Near Versailles, in Sec. 8, T. 42, R. 17, Mr. F. L. Ross sunk some six or eight pits in the valley of a small creek, amongst surface deposits, to depths varying from 8 to 12 feet, and obtained about 1,200 pounds of Lead ore. It was generally found in large masses, some of which weighed as much as 50 pounds each. The rocks forming the bluffs here are the Second Magnesian Limestone and the Saccharoidal Sandstone.

A short distance from the Gravois Mills, in N. W. quarter Sec. 17, T. 41, R. 17, in a little valley, numerous masses of Galena have been found, amongst loose chert. One of these masses shown to me contained about 18 pounds of ore, with imbedded fragments of Magnesian Limestone and calc-spar. The Third Magnesian Limestone forms the hills in this vicinity.

At Gravois village, in Sec. 2, T. 40, R. 17, on a ridge about 200 feet above Gravois Creek, numerous shallow pits and shafts have been sunk for Lead ore. On the summit of this ridge, which is composed of the Third Magnesian Limestone, several fissures were seen having a north-east and south-west bearing, and varying in breadth from a few inches to two or three feet. Crossing these at various angles, other similar fissures were also seen. The ore was mostly found in these openings, mingled with red Clay and broken rocks.

This mine was worked, according to the best information I could obtain, about 12 months, and some 50,000 pounds of ore obtained. As usual where mining operations have been suspended for some time, I found all the shafts and openings here so filled with loose materials that I had no opportunity to examine them very critically; but from all I could see, I thought the indications sufficiently favorable to warrant further explorations here.

In the south-east quarter of Sec. 18, T. 41, R. 16, on a declivity about 75 feet below the summit of the country, near Indian Creek, I examined a mine in the Third Magnesian Limestone, on Mr. Thomas V. Jones' land. The ore occurs here in a vein or fissure, filled with light buff-colored, soft silico-argillaceous matter, fragments of chert, Sandstone and Lead ore; there are also sometimes thin vertical seams of Sulphate of Baryta extending parallel to the direction of the vein, which has a bearing a little east of south. The breadth of the vein varies from half an inch to 18 inches, and in some places expands so as to form cavities three or four feet across. I am not sure that it has all the characteristics of a true vein; but it certainly resembles one very much, and has been traced across the hills for nearly half a mile south of the opening.

In 1843, Mr. Jones sunk a shaft here to a depth of 67 feet, and raised, as near as I could ascertain, about 5,000 pounds of ore. I also saw, at several places near here, shallow surface openings, from which I was informed considerable quantities of loose Lead ore, in large masses, were taken.

Another mine was opened by Messrs. Bunker & Irvin, some time back, at a locality in Sec. 4, about three miles north-east of Mr. Jones'. Several shallow pits were sunk here from 3 or 4 to about 16 feet, most of the way in "Cotton rock" of the Second Magnesian Limestone. The strata here are very much fractured, and at one place there is a fissure varying from 6 to 15 inches in breadth, filled with fragments of broken rocks and Lead ore.

I noticed amongst the broken rocks thrown out here, masses with striated and polished surfaces, showing they had formed the walls of fissures and seams, where there had been sufficient movements of the strata to produce more or less friction. No spars of any kind were seen at this mine. I could not ascertain from any reliable source the quantity of ore raised here.

Again, in Sec. 27, T. 42, R. 16, Messrs. Tole & Sketton have opened a Lead mine on a small tributary of Indian Creek. Here, in a valley perhaps 150 feet or more below the elevation of the high prairie country on the north, they sunk some six or eight shallow pits at different places, in a space extending about 300 yards up and down the valley. Although these openings had been made only three months previous, they were all filled with water at the time I visited the locality. The rock thrown out is mixed gray, granular concretionary Magnesian Limestone, with dark oolitic chert. Immediately associated with the Lead ore, I saw much of this dark oolitic chert, and gray, sandy rock, with calc-spar — the latter being in large fine crystals. These materials, together with the Lead ore, which is in large crystals, are rather confusedly mingled.

At one place, near the base of the hill, the rock has been blasted away so that I could see the ore *in situ*. It consists of numerous seams, from half to three-quarters of an inch in thickness, which ramify through the bed in every direction, horizontally as well as vertically. It also occurs in detached cubes, one to two inches in diameter, disseminated through the rock.

Immediately overlying this dark bed of mixed materials containing the Lead ore, there is a light flesh-colored concretionary bed, apparently entirely destitute of ore. From the top of this low exposure back to the summit of the highest surrounding country, the slope is so gentle that no rocks are seen in place anywhere near. The rock in which the ore occurs, however, I think, holds a position near the base of the Second Magnesian Limestone.

I did not learn what quantity of ore has been found here, but I saw, as near as I could estimate, about 1,500 pounds of it lying near the openings. At another place, about half a mile east of this, some pits were sunk amongst loose rocks, etc., in the bed of a branch, and some 40,000 pounds of ore taken out.

IRON ORE.

I only met with Iron ore in notable quantities at one locality in this county. This was in the north-west quarter of the south-west quarter Sec. 27, T. 41, R. 17, where large bodies of the "pipe-stem" variety of brown Hematite were seen along a slope about 100 feet above the Gravois. These masses, some of which would measure 8 or 10 feet in diameter, appear—at least many of them— to be *in situ*, the columns being in a vertical position. I could not determine its extent, the larger bodies of it extending beneath the loose surface materials. Considerable quantities of heavy spar were associated with it. I think it occurs in the Third Magnesian Limestone.

HEAVY SPAR.

In addition to the localities already mentioned, where this mineral was seen associated with Lead and Iron ore, it occurs in Sec. 24, T. 41, R. 17, and Sec. 18, T. 41, R. 16, in the form of fine, large, transparent crystals. At the first of these places it appears quite abundant, large quantities of it having been thrown out in making a shallow excavation in search of Lead ore. Almost any amount of beautiful cabinet specimens might be obtained here.

BUILDING MATERIALS.

Nearly every part of this county has an abundant supply of good building stones and rock for the construction of roads, conveniently accessible. In the northern portions of the county the best material for the production of quick-lime can be obtained from beds and outliers of the Chouteau and Encrinital Limestones already mentioned. Where these are not at hand, in this and other parts of the county, certain beds in the various Magnesian Limestones, although rather more difficult to burn, can generally be found pure enough to make good lime.

Sand of good quality can generally be obtained near outcrops of the different Sandstones at several localities in most of the township. Good Clays for the manufacture of bricks also occur, especially in the central and northern portions of the county.

CHAPTER IX.

SALINE COUNTY.

BY F. B. MEEK.

This county occupies a great bend of the Missouri River, a little north-west of the middle of the State, and is bounded on the south-east by Cooper county; on the east, north-east, north and north-west, by the Missouri River, and on the west and south by Lafayette and Pettis counties. It contains an area of near 740 square miles, no part of which appears to rise more than about 240 feet above the Missouri, and its average elevation is perhaps not more than from 100 to 130 feet above that stream. The most elevated positions are on the divide between the Salt Fork and the Blackwater.

Immediately north of the Salt Fork, in township 51, ranges 22 and 23, the surface of the country is from 80 to 100 feet lower than on the south side, and forms a beautiful plateau, elevated from 70 to 90 feet above the Missouri, and known as the "Petit Osage Plains." North of this plateau, in townships 51 and 52, ranges 22 and 23, there are along the Missouri immense alluvial flats or "bottoms," as they are usually termed, varying from one to four miles in breadth. Similar flats also occur at intervals along the river around most of the northern and eastern borders of the county.

The face of the country in Saline county may be described in general terms as level or undulating, there being but a very small portion of broken land, which is nearly all situated immediately along the bluffs of the Missouri and the Blackwater. Although the scenery is nowhere diversified by rugged hills or extensive escarpments of rock, it is pleasing and often highly picturesque. From some of the more elevated points, as at Mr. Bruce's residence, a short distance north-west of the middle of the county, the eye wanders in every direction over an immense expanse of beautiful prairie country, with numerous farms and neat farm-houses, interspersed with groves and belts of timber.

STREAMS.

As already stated, the Missouri River sweeps around nearly the whole of the northern and eastern borders of the county, affording great facilities for shipping to distant markets the products of the country. A farmer located, for instance, at the center of the county, can reach the river in an eastward, northward, north-westward or any intermediate direction, in from 10 to 17 miles, while a large proportion of the most productive lands lie almost immediately along the river, or only a few miles back.

The largest stream passing through any part of this county is the Blackwater, or the "Black Fork of the Lamine," as it is sometimes called. It enters the county near the south-west corner, and meanders in a direction a little north of east, through the southern townships, passing out into Cooper county on the east, in T. 49, R. 19. Although quite a rivulet, measuring near its junction with the Salt Fork about 120 feet across, it is at many places too shallow for navigation, and has generally rather too little fall to furnish very reliable water power, though there must be some good mill sites on it.

Davis Creek, one of the largest tributaries of the Blackwater, enters this county from Lafayette, in T. 49, R. 23, and soon forms a junction with the latter stream near the south-west corner of the county, receiving in its course some of the smaller branches.

Farther east, in T. 49, R. 21, the Blackwater receives a small branch known by the name of "Ferris Creek," coming from the north and northwest. Its most important tributary, however, flowing through any considerable portion of this county, is the Salt Fork, which comes in from Lafayette, in T. 50, R. 23, and flows in an easterly and south-easterly direction, through near the middle of the county, forming a junction with the Blackwater near where the latter passes out into Cooper county. It is a sluggish stream, but discharges a considerable quantity of water, and may have fall enough at some places below Marshall to furnish water power.

It is a little remarkable that this stream approaches so near the Missouri Valley at the Grand Pass, in the north-western part of the county, that it could be turned into it, if desirable, by a canal not more than about 35 feet deep and 150 to 200 yards long, and yet afterward turns and flows across the interior, where the country must rise at some places as much as 140 feet above its valley on each side.

At the narrow point mentioned above, there is a low place where water appears to have flowed across at some time, either from the Salt Fork into the Missouri Valley, or from the Missouri into the Salt Fork. As it seems scarcely possible so small a stream as the latter could ever have been swollen to such an extent as to flow through this gap, I am inclined to the opinion that at some extraordinary freshet the Missouri broke over this barrier, and some of its water found an outlet down through the valley of the Salt Fork into the Blackwater, and thence out through the Lamine below into its own valley again.

I was informed that during the great flood of 1844 the Missouri only rose to within about 25 feet of the lowest part of this gap; consequently, if it ever did break over here, it must have been when at a much greater hight than it is now subject to attain, or perhaps ever will do again, as it has probably deepened its channel some, and may have acquired an increased velocity of current in consequence of a gradual rise of the country, even within a few hundred years past.

There are quite a number of little streams flowing into the Missouri from the townships bordering upon it, and others falling into the Salt Fork on both sides, but as they are all small branches, it is perhaps unnecessary to notice them here.

TIMBER.

Although timber is not very abundant in Saline county, there is enough to supply the present wants of the country. It is true, the consumption of fuel, and of timber in the construction of houses, fences, bridges, etc., is on the increase, but not near so rapidly as the increase in the growth of the timber itself. Where the fires are kept out, it is astonishing to see how soon trees spring up on these prairies. Beautiful young forests were observed in various parts of the country, consisting of trees from 8 to 10 inches in diameter, where, it is said, 10 to 15 years previous not a single bush was to be seen.

When the Coal mines of this county are systematically worked, the inhabitants of the county can, at most places, if they wish to do so, dispense entirely with the use of wood for fuel; while hedges are being so rapidly introduced that a large proportion of the better farms will soon be thus inclosed.

The growth in this county is: Cottonwood, Oak, Black and White Walnut, American and Red Elm, Maple, Linn, Hackberry, Hickory, Birch, Buttonwood or Sycamore, Buckeye, Ash, Coffee Bean, Willow.

GEOLOGICAL STRUCTURE.

Aside from the Quaternary deposits, the rocks of this county all belong to three of the great systems or primary groups of the Paleozoic series, viz.: the Carboniferous, the Devonian and the Silurian. Of these, however, we have comparatively meager representations. The Carboniferous is the most extensively developed, the Devonian next, though consisting apparently of but two of the principal subdivisions, neither of which is complete; while of the Silurian, only two rocks occur, one of which belongs near the base of that system, and the other considerably below the middle; both were seen at but one and the same place.

These rocks have nowhere suffered much disturbance in this county, and generally appear to the eye to be nearly horizontal. At one locality, however, some six miles north of Arrow Rock, on the Missouri, there has been a local uplift, which has brought the Saccharoidal Sandstone and the Trenton Limestone, which are there overlaid by the Devonian and Lower Carboniferous beds, above the surface of the river; though at Arrow Rock below, and at Cambridge, about the same distance above, the Lower Carboniferous is again seen down at the water's edge, indicating a distinct north and south dip from this place.

In the south-eastern part of the county there is a rather gentle east or south-east dip, which continues nearly to the middle of the county, whence there seems to be a slight inclination of the strata to the westward. In the north-eastern part of the county there is a moderate dip toward the north-east.

The following is a general section, in descending order, of the rocks of this county:

QUATERNARY:

No. 1. 10 to 15 feet Alluvium of Missouri valley (above the Missouri at ordinary stages.)

No. 2. 90 feet Bluff or Loess deposit.

No. 3. 60 feet Drift.

CARBONIFEROUS:

No. 4. 200 feet Coal Measures.

No. 5. 40 feet Ferruginous Sandstone.

No. 6. 36 feet Archimedes Limestone.

No. 7. 100 feet Encrinital Limestone.

No. 8. 90 feet Chouteau Limestone.

DEVONIAN:

No. 9. 18 feet Cooper Marble.*

No. 10. 45 feet Semi-crystalline Limestone.

* No fossils have been found in this rock, and its exact relative position is doubtful.

LOWER SILURIAN:

No. 11. 25 feet Trenton Limestone.

No. 12. 15 feet Saccharoidal Sandstone (above the Missouri.)

QUATERNARY DEPOSITS.

ALLUVIUM OF THE MISSOURI FLATS.

The extensive alluvial bottoms along the Missouri, in this county, are usually elevated from about 10 to 15 feet above that stream at its ordinary stages. They vary from half a mile to three or four miles in breadth, and are all, I believe, subject to occasional inundation. These bottoms generally appear to the eye almost perfectly level, but where wide they are usually a little lower back near the bluffs than immediately along the banks of the river, and, of course, correspond to the general descent of the same.

I saw no good sections of this deposit anywhere in this county, but it is doubtless composed of the usual fine clays and arenaceous materials, characterizing it at other places along the river.

BLUFF OR LOESS DEPOSIT.

This formation occurs almost everywhere along the bluffs of the Missouri in this county, and extends back over much of the adjacent country north and east of the Salt Fork. I am not sure it exists on the highest country south-west of the Salt Fork; at any rate, if it does occur there, it is not easily distinguishable from the Drift.

The bluffs bounding the Missouri valley in T. 52, R. 22, located some distance back from the river, are chiefly composed of this formation, with probable nuclei of Encrinital and Archimedes Limestones. At this place, owing to the abruptness of the slope, and the loose, incoherent nature of the deposit, these bluffs have been worn into numerous sharp ridges and conical elevations, which are known as the "Pinnacle Hills." These hills rise about one hundred to one hundred and fifty feet above the alluvial bottoms at their base, their tops being but little below the summit of the higher country back. At this place this deposit consists, as usual, of very fine light-yellowish argillaceous and arenaceous materials.

The same line of bluffs continues, with a gradual descent, in a south-west direction for eight or ten miles, forming the boundary of the great alluvial bottoms north of the Petit Osage Plains. They are not here, however, worn into the peculiar forms characterizing the "Pinnacle Hills."

Although the deposit generally occurs at higher elevations than the alluvium of the Missouri valley, it is known to be older than that formation, as it has been found to pass under it where they come in contact at the base of the bluffs. It is not easy to determine the greatest thickness of a formation like this, but it is probably as much as ninety feet at some places in this county.

Drift.

The Drift formation is rather generally distributed in this county. It exists at many places beneath the Loess in the townships near the river, and where the Loess does not occur, it seems to be the first material struck beneath the surface and subsoils. It consists of beds of arenaceous clays, with more or less water-worn pebbles, and sometimes a few boulders. At many places, there are also, near the upper part, deposits of whitish pipe-clay. These beds are seen along many of the streams, and are struck at various places in sinking wells.

The following is a section of the beds penetrated in a well sunk on the high country, in Sec. 31, T. 52, R. 20:

No. 1. 14 feet, beneath soil, Loess, consisting of fine yellowish loam.

Drift:

No. 2. 20 feet white pipe-clay.

No. 3. 23 feet loose yellowish sand and clay, with a few pebbles.

The same beds were penetrated in a well sunk at another place about six miles south-west of the above, on Mr. Thos. Harvey's farm. They are also exposed in the bluffs along the Salt Fork, near Mr. Harvey's place. At Mr. H. H. McDowell's residence, about four miles further west, in the Petit Osage Plains, a well was sunk through—

No. 1. 3 or 4 feet soil and subsoil.

No. 2. 16 feet light yellowish fine loam (Loess) varying somewhat in the quantity of arenaceous material.

No. 3. 11 feet very fine-grained, yellowish blue sandy loam.

The lowest bed here is very peculiar, and appears at this place more like the Loess than like Drift; but as it has been seen at other places with pebbles and small boulders imbedded, it must belong to the Drift. About one mile and a-half north of Mr. McDowell's, another well was sunk on the same Plains to a depth of thirty-three feet, all the way, after passing through the soil and subsoil, in the Loess, without striking the bed No. 3 of the foregoing section.

South of the Salt Fork, on the higher country, excepting near that stream, the Drift seems to consist mainly of light-colored and whitish tough clays, with scarcely any of the lower arenaceous pebbly bed. This lower bed, however, is exposed in the bluffs of Salt Fork at numerous places, for some distance below Marshall. Near that place it was seen reposing upon Archimedes Limestone, as represented in the section given below:

No. 1. 20 feet slope, with much white clay.
No. 2. 30 feet yellowish sand, with more or less clay, and a few pebbles.
No. 3. 3 feet Archimedes Limestone (seen above creek.)

Boulders are not abundant in this county, though they were observed at a few places. One of dark Greenstone, three feet in diameter, was seen at the base of the bluff where the last section was taken. Others, composed of granitic rocks, were observed along a little stream near Arrow Rock. Boulders of Granite and dark Hornblende rock also occur on some of the streams in T. 51, Ranges 20 and 21. They all appear to have been deposited in the lower part of Drift, instead of being scattered over the surface, as is often the case.

CARBONIFEROUS ROCKS.

Coal Measures.

The Coal Measures occupy something less than one-third of the entire area of Saline county. It may, however, be proper to remark here, for the information of persons who are not familiar with the principles upon which geological maps are colored, that it is not pretended Coal can be found *everywhere* within those portions of the county colored as Coal Measures, but simply that the districts so colored are occupied by rocks belonging to the Coal series.

It is also possible that the Coal bearing rocks on the north-east side of the Salt Fork, instead of chiefly occupying one continuous, irregular area, as represented on the map, may be broken up into a number of small, isolated patches. Where the Coal Measures are as thin as they are here, and for the most part buried beneath heavy deposits of Drift and Loess, it is not possible always to define their boundaries with a great degree of minuteness.

It is likewise very difficult, for the same reason, to work out the details of their structure here, and indeed throughout the whole county, as sections showing more than a few feet in thickness at one place are rarely met with. This difficulty is greatly increased by the inequalities of the surface upon which these beds were deposited, and more particularly by the many irregularities amongst the strata of which the series is composed. These irregularities are such, that it is an exceedingly rare thing to find two sections taken at localities a few miles apart agreeing in their details. Sometimes there are such great differences that it seems scarcely possible to account for the change in any other way than by supposing that after the deposition of portions of the series, there must have occurred oscillations and changes by which they were exposed to denuding agencies, and often wholly, or in part, swept away previous to the deposition of the succeeding beds.

The heaviest deposits of the Coal Measure rocks on the south-east side of the Salt Fork, occur in T. 51, R. 19 and 20. Here, toward the head of a little stream known by the name of Fish Creek, several mines have been opened. These mines are all in the same bed, which is first seen in ascending the little valley in Sec. 16, T. 51, R. 19, where it was observed cropping out of a bluff, as represented in the following cut:

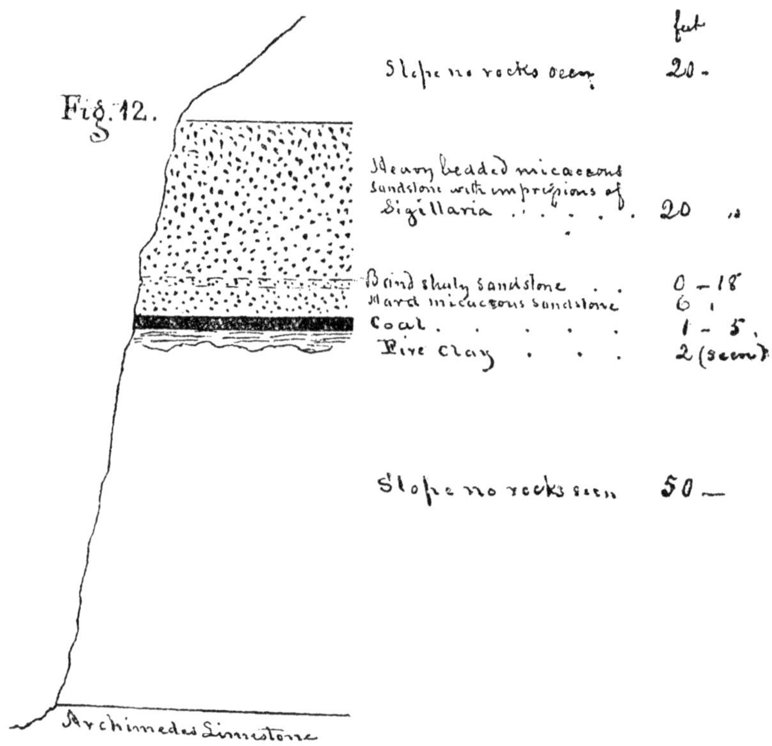

Unfortunately, no exposures were seen here giving any clue to the nature of the beds occupying the space between the Archimedes Limestone at the base of this section, and the two feet of Clay immediately below the Coal.

About two miles higher up the same stream, on Mr. H. S. Mills' land, this bed of coal again shows itself, but owing to the rise in the bottom of the valley, and perhaps in part to a local inclination of the strata toward the west, it is here seen near the base of the bluff, but surmounted by the same Sandstone. A short distance above this it passes beneath the bottom of the valley, and at several places about half a mile above, on Mr. Sappington's land, it has been opened by sinking pits through the loose materials in the valley, as represented by the following cut:

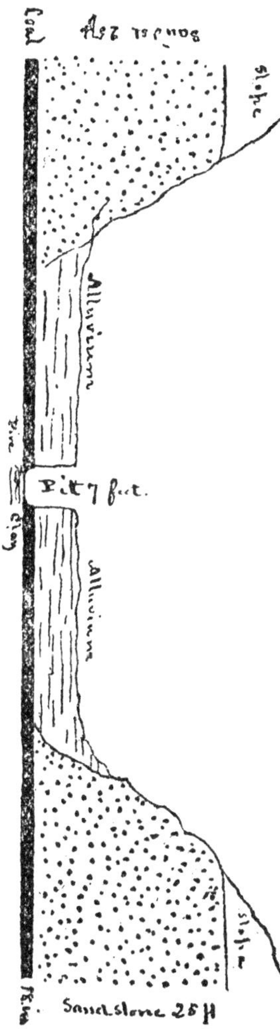

Fig. 13.

This bed has also been opened at several other places in this neighborhood, amongst which may be mentioned Messrs. Durret & Scott's mine, in Sec. 21, Mrs. Dennis' mine, in Sec. 27, and Mrs. Trigg's, in Sec. 33, of the same Township and Range.

At another locality some four miles a little north of west from Mr. Sappington's mine, a bed of Coal has been opened at several places in the valley of Rock Creek, near the middle of T. 51, R. 20. One of these mines, on Mr. Woodward's land, is located in the valley, about 70 feet below the summit of the surrounding country; and has been opened by sinking a pit first through loose surface materials 10 feet, then 3 feet through bluish laminated fire-clay, when a bed of Coal was struck, and found to be 14 inches in thickness. Less than a mile below this, on the same stream, apparently the same bed of Coal was found overlaid by 2½ feet of blue fire-clay; at this place, however, the Coal is 18 inches in thickness. A short distance farther down the branch, Encrinital Limestone was seen cropping out at the base of the bluffs; while on the higher country, less than half a mile north of the Coal mine last mentioned, and about 80 feet above its elevation, a micaceous Sandstone was struck in a well, at a depth of 38 feet.

The occurrence of this Sandstone above, and the Encrinital Limestone so near below this bed of Coal, would seem to indicate that it holds a position below the Fish Creek bed; still it may occupy a higher geological position, and be nearer the Lower Carboniferous rocks here, in consequence of the absence at this place of some of the intermediate beds.

About two miles farther north, in Sec. 4 of the same Township and Range, Coal has been found on Mr. Thos. C. Duggins' land, near a small stream. There are said to be two 18-inch beds of Coal here, though I only saw one of them. The beds of Clay, etc., associated with this Coal are not very well exposed, but as near as could be determined, a section of the rocks here would be in descending order, as given below:

No. 1. Very gentle slope, 50 to 60 feet.
No. 2. Sandstone; thickness unknown, but showing 4 feet.
No. 3. Coal, said to be 1½ feet.
No. 4. Clay, 2 feet.
No. 5. Hard, compact, gray Limestone, 1 (?) foot.
No. 6. Yellow and bluish fire-clay, 12 feet.
No. 7. Coal, 1½ feet.

The lower bed of No. 7 of this section appears to be the same as that opened at the Rock Creek mines.

In section 18, T. 52, R. 20, near the head of the west branch of Edmonson Creek, Mr. P. D. Booker opened a bed of Coal at a point 50 feet below the highest surrounding country. The Section here observed was:

No. 1. About 50 feet long, gentle slope.
No. 2. 4 to 5 feet red Clay.
No. 3. 6 inches Sandstone.
No. 4. 8 feet blue Fire-clay.
No. 5. 14 to 20 inches Coal.

This Coal is probably the same bed opened at Mr. Duggins' mine, though we can not determine very satisfactorily the relations of beds seen at different places in this way, where no better Sections can be obtained for comparison.

Near a mile west of Mr. Booker's mine, and at about the same elevation, Mr. Thomas Garnett opened the same bed; and at an intermediate, but apparently a lower, position than either of these mines, a bed of micaceous Sandstone was struck, and penetrated 4 or 5 feet, in searching for Coal.

At several places near Miami, in Secs. 4 and 9, T. 52, R. 21, a bed of Coal has been opened along a slope, some 60 feet below the higher country back. This bed is said to be from 18 to 36 inches thick; but it was not visible at the time I examined the mine, in consequence of the falling in of the loose materials about the pits.

The following is a section of the beds seen here:

No. 1. 60 feet slope, very gentle.
No. 2. 12 feet yellowish laminated Fire-clay.
No. 3. 5 inches to 1-foot layer of concretionary hydraulic Limestone.
No. 4. 4 inches black Slate.
No. 5. Coal, (said to be) from 18 inches to 3 feet.

This is probably the same bed seen in Sec. 28, T. 52, R. 19, on Dr. George Penn's land. At this place, it is said to be 26 inches in thickness, (only the upper part of the bed could be seen when it was examined,) and is known to be overlaid by a dark, sandy shale, of which a thickness of about 13 inches was seen. Numerous exposures of Lower Carboniferous rocks near this latter Coal mine show that it must belong to an isolated outlier, while the proximity of these Lower Carboniferous beds to the Coal, both here and near Miami, would seem to indicate a low position in the series for this bed, though, as already remarked in regard to other beds, this may be in consequence of the absence of some of the strata.

Nearly all the Coal found in the south-eastern part of the county also holds similar relations to outcrops of Lower Carboniferous rocks. One of these beds, opened at Mr. Marmaduke's mine, in Sec. 8, T. 49, R. 19, is 3 feet in thickness, and associated with bituminous shale, etc., as represented in the following Section:

Fig. 14.

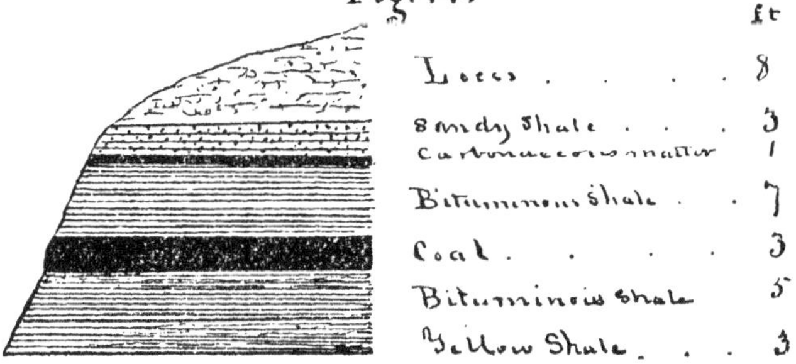

ft
Loess 8
Sandy Shale 3
Carbonaceous matter 1
Bituminous Shale . . 7
Coal 3
Bituminous Shale 5
Yellow Shale . . . 3

Near this, on Flat Creek, exposures of Archimedes Limestone are seen at several places not far below the elevation of the base of this Section.

In the valley of Flat Creek, from a half to three-quarters of a mile east of this mine, a fine bed of Cannel Coal has been opened on land belonging to a gentleman by the name of Jackson. This bed is only covered by loose alluvium, while Archimedes Limestone is seen cropping out of the bluffs above its elevation, a little further down the creek.

This mine has been opened by sinking a pit 8 or 10 feet through the loose alluvium, when the Coal was struck and penetrated, it is said, 12 to 13 feet without passing through it. From all the facts ascertained in regard to this deposit of Coal, it evidently must be one of those anomalous beds such as have been described in Miller and Morgan counties. Instead of being interstratified with the Clays, shales, etc., of the regular Coal series, it occupies a depression in the Lower Carboniferous rocks, and is only overlaid, as already stated, by the superficial deposits of the country.

It is a very difficult question to determine to what part of the Coal Measures these abnormal deposits belong. The fact that they have always, so far as my observations go, been found occupying depressions directly in the Lower Carboniferous or older rocks, would seem to indicate that they belong at the base of the Coal series of this region; but as they appear never to be overlaid by any other members of the Coal Measures, there would seem to be quite as good reasons for supposing they were formed after the deposition, and even after the extensive denudation, of such other portions of the Coal Measures, at least, as exist in this part of the country. That they have been deposited, as might be supposed, where we now find them by streams, in wearing their valleys through the Coal Measures, since the commencement of the Quaternary epoch, is rendered extremely improbable, by their fine, compact structure and homogeneous composition.

The striking similarity of these beds, wherever they are found, points unmistakably to a unity of origin. Whether observed reposing on Lower Carboniferous or Devonian rocks, near the margins of regular Coal fields, or upon Lower Silurian strata, far removed from other Carboniferous rocks, they usually consist of massive beds of Cannel Coal of limited horizontal extent, but often of great thickness.

The Coal mine opened on the estate of the late Gen. T. A. Smith, in Sec. —, T 50, R. 20, is of this kind. The bed here has been found to be 12 feet in thickness, at the north side of the opening, and thinner at the south. Like Mr. Jackson's bed, it reposes upon Archimedes Limestone.

The Section here is as follows, in descending order:

No. 1. 2 feet soil.
No. 2. 10 feet Loess.
No. 3. 25 feet Drift.
No. 4. Coal—penetrated as much as 12 feet.
No. 5. Archimedes Limestone (seen in bed of creek near.)

This and Mr. Jackson's Coal are the only deposits of this kind seen in this county, though there may be others not yet discovered.

The Coal Measures occupying the larger area of country between the Salt Fork and the Blackwater, consist, in part at least, of the same deposits as those already described; but it is very difficult to draw parallels between the subordinate beds here and on the other side of Salt Fork. We have evidently, however, some higher beds here, and altogether a greater thickness of these rocks on the higher parts of the country, especially toward the western part of the county, than occur between the Salt Fork and the Missouri.

At several places on the west branches of Ferris Creek, in T. 49, R. 22, a Coal bed varying from 18 to 20 inches in thickness has been opened and worked to some extent. At one of these mines, belonging to Mr. Nathaniel Walker, the Coal is overlaid by black Slate, Clay, etc., as represented in the section given below:

No. 1. 1 foot black bituminous Slate, (exposed.)
No. 2. 3 feet yellowish shale.
No. 3. 2½ to 3 feet blue Clay.
No. 4. 18 to 20 inches Coal.

In following down the little valleys from all the places where this bed has been discovered, stratum of micaceous Sandstone is always seen at a rather lower position. This Sandstone was observed at several localities about one mile east of Mr. Walker's mine, and at one place a little farther down the creek, it was seen, exposing a thickness of 35 feet. It looks very much like the Sandstone overlying Mr. Sappington's Coal, on Fish Creek; if it is the same bed, the Coal here on the head branches of Ferris Creek must hold a higher position than the Fish Creek bed. There does not here, however, seem to be the same amount of space between its base and outcrops of lower Carboniferous rocks seen a little farther down the creek, that was observed below the Fish Creek Coal.

The same bed seen at Mr. Walker's mine has been opened at several other places, in the same township and range, farther west. At one of these mines, belonging to Mr. J. D. Bailey, in Sec. 4, the following beds were observed over the Coal:

No. 1. 3 feet yellow Clay, (exposed.)
No. 2. 8 inches hydraulic Limestone.
No. 3. 6 inches Clay.
No. 4. 6 to 8 inches hydraulic Limestone.
No. 5. 3 feet black Slate with concretions, Iron pyrites.
No. 6. 2 feet hard blue Clay.
No. 7. 18 inches to 2 feet Coal.

Farther west, in T. 49, R. 23, Coal has been found at many places apparently holding the same position; but as the bed is generally thinner, and the associated strata do not present exactly the same section, it may hold a higher, or little lower position. The section observed at one of these mines owned by Mr. W. Johnson, in Sec. 8, is as given below:

No. 1. 18 inches hydraulic Limestone, containing *Fusulina*, and a small smooth *Spirifer* like *S. lineatus*.

No. 2. 1 foot bright yellow Clay.

No. 3. 3 feet black bituminous Slate, containing small *Discina*, and passing upward into gray Clay.

No. 4. 1 foot Coal.

Below the elevation of this and the other mines opened in this vicinity, outcrops of apparently the same micaceous Sandstone seen below the mines on the branches of Ferris Creek, are seen at numerous places.

About two miles north-east of Mr. Johnson's mine, and apparently 30 to 40 feet above its elevation, Mr. Thomas Hunter opened a bed of Coal in a small valley. The section here is very similar to that at Mr. Johnson's, being in the descending order—

No. 1. 16 inches hard gray hydraulic Limestone, containing *Productus æquicostatus*, *Chonetes mesoloba*, small *Spirifer*, like *S. lineatus*, with great numbers of *Fusulina*.

No. 2. 3 feet black Slate shading upward into lighter colored do., and containing below many concretions Iron pyrites.

No· 3. 1 foot to 14 inches Coal.

One mile nearly north of this mine, and perhaps 70 feet above it, a well was sunk on nearly the highest part of the country, which penetrated higher beds of the Coal series than are included in any of the preceding sections. The section observed in this well is as follows, descending:

DRIFT:

No. 1. 3 feet soil and subsoil.

No. 2. 14 feet very tough, yellowish Clay.

No. 3. 3 feet white Clay.

COAL MEASURES:

No. 4. 2 feet very hard gray and bluish-gray Limestone, containing *Productus æquicostatus*, with great numbers of *Fusulina*.

No. 5. 2 feet dark shelly Limestone.

No. 6. 21 feet gray shaly fire Clay.

No. 7. 2 feet dark shaly Limestone.

No. 8. 2 feet black Slate.

No. 9. Shaly bed, like No. 6.

In Sec. 30, T. 50, R. 23, on one of the head branches of Elm Creek, Mr. J. C. Clake opened a Coal bed, 18 to 20 inches in thickness, which is overlaid by almost exactly the same beds seen at Mr. Johnson's mine, three or four miles farther south; but it appears, like Mr. Hunter's mine, to be more elevated than Mr. Johnson's, and may possibly belong higher in the series.

Thin beds of Fusulina Limestone continue to be seen along the slopes east of Elm Branch, nearly all the way down, and are struck in wells at several places on the high country between Elm and Pass Branches. About one mile above the mouth of Elm Branch, in Sec. 32, T. 51, R. 23, several of these beds are seen along the slopes alternating with other beds, as seen in the Section given below:

No. 1. 25 feet slope, with loose pieces *Fusulina* Limestone, indicating a thin bed of that rock 10 to 15 feet above the base.
No. 2. 1⅓ feet hard light-colored Hydraulic Limestone, with masses of *Chætetes*, and a few *Fusulina*.
No. 3. 32 feet slope; no rocks seen in place.
No. 4. 1½ feet hard yellowish Limestone, with *Fusulina*.
No. 5. 2 feet black slate.
No. 6. 1½ feet black bituminous Limestone, with *Productus*, *Chonetes*, etc.
No. 7. 7 inches Coal.
No. 8. 6 feet whitish fire-clay.
No. 9. 1½ feet hard yellowish Limestone, with *Productus*, *Spirifer cameratus*, *Chonetes mesoloba*, *Fusulina*, etc.
No. 10. Black shale; a few inches seen.
No. 11. 57 feet slope, with loose pieces micaceous Sandstone about 30 feet above base.

From the number of loose pieces of micaceous Sandstone seen along the slope No. 11, of the above section, I am inclined to think there is a bed of this Sandstone occupying perhaps all the lower half of this slope. This is probably the same Sandstone so often seen along the streams just below Johnson's and the other mines in T. 49, R. 23; also below Walker's and the other Coal mines on Ferris Creek. If so, the same 18 to 24 inch bed of Coal may be expected to occur just above it on Elm Branch.

The several Coal mines on the head branches of Salt Creek, one to two miles east of the Big Salt Spring, in T. 50, R. 22, are in the same bed worked at Walker's and the other mines on Ferris Creek, a section of the clays, etc., overlying them being almost exactly the same, while the underlying micaceous Sandstone was seen at a little lower elevation on the little streams near all these openings. This Sandstone is also seen in a quarry near Mr. Robert Kirtley's place, about one mile east of the Big Salt Spring, and below the elevation of the Coal mines near.

It is very difficult to determine with accuracy the entire thickness of the Coal series in Saline county, where good continuous sections of more than a few feet are scarcely ever seen; but from the best estimate I could form, I should think it not far from 200 feet, though it is probably not near so thick at any one place. The greatest thickness of these strata occurring all together in this county, is in T. 50, R. 22 and 23. The fossils most frequently seen here in these beds have been mentioned in the several local sections.

Ferruginous Sandstone.

The next rock in the descending order here is a rather fine-grained yellowish quartzose Sandstone, apparently always destitute of mica. As no Coal has ever been found in or below this rock, and it has evidently suffered considerable denudation previous to the deposition of the Coal-bearing strata, it most probably belongs to the Lower Carboniferous series. Owing apparently to the erosion to which it has been subjected, it varies much in thickness at different places, and is frequently wanting. It was only recognized toward the eastern and north-eastern portions of the county, and attains its greatest thickness in the bluffs of the Missouri in the north-western part of T. 52, R. 19, extending into the north-eastern part of R. 20 of the same township. At these places it forms a continuous perpendicular bluff, varying from 25 to 30 feet in hight, and probably attains a thickness of 40 feet.

It was again seen at a quarry a short distance above Miami, in the Missouri bluffs, and apparently reposing upon the Encrinital Limestone. At this place only a thickness of about 12 feet was seen. A local bed of this rock only 8 feet in thickness was observed in S. 29, T. 50, R. 19; and in S. 27, T. 51, R. 20, it crops out on a little stream forming a bluff about 15 feet in hight.

As the Coal Measures were seen at numerous intermediate localities between those mentioned above, reposing directly upon one or the other of the Lower Carboniferous Limestones of this region, it is manifest this Sandstone must be frequently wanting here. It was not recognized on the Blackwater, though it may exist at some localities in that part of the county. No organic remains were seen in this rock.

Archimedes Limestone.

Although this Limestone was seen at numerous places in this county, it is evidently not a continuous stratum here, but must consist of numerous local patches, since the Coal Measures were frequently observed reposing directly upon the Encrinital Limestone at various places between these different outcrops. As seen in this county, this rock consists of bluish gray argillaceous Limestone, with partings and layers of blue marly clay.

It attains its greatest development in the south-eastern part of the county, along a small stream, known by the name of Flat Creek, where it forms bluffs from 10 to 36 feet in hight. Along the Salt Fork thin beds of it occasionally crop out from S. 12, T. 48, R. 20, up nearly to the mouth of Little Rock Creek, where it passes beneath Drift and the Coal Measures.

In the townships bordering on the Missouri, this formation was first observed, north of Arrow Rock, in the bed of Fish Creek, near the outcrop of Coal represented in the wood cut on page 164. At Cambridge it was seen exposing a thickness of about 8 feet above the Missouri; and thin outcrops of it also occur at several places near this, on Bear Creek. It was likewise observed a little south of the middle of T. 52, R. 20, on the east branch of Edmonson Creek, showing at one place a thickness of 15 feet.

At Miami, in the north-western part of T. 52, R. 21, some loose masses of this rock were observed on a bluff of Encrinital Limestone, indicating the presence of a thin bed of it here. This is the furthest point toward the west at which this formation was met with in this county. As it was not seen on the Blackwater, or any of its branches above the Salt Fork, it probably does not exist in that part of the county.

With the exception of great numbers of reticulate *Bryozoa*, organic remains appear not very abundant in this rock here. The other fossils found in it are a large *Actinocrinus*, similar to *A. Gouldi*, but perhaps new, an undescribed *Syringapora*, spines and plates of a *Paleocidaris*, (a delicate species with small smooth spines,) and the axis of an *Archimedes*.

Encrinital Limestone.

Succeeding the Archimedes Limestone, just described, we have in the descending order here, the Encrinital or Burlington Limestone, which is the most important calcareous mass in the county. As the lithological characters of this rock have been fully described in former reports, and it presents no new features in this region, it is unnecessary to enter into a description of it here.

This formation is most extensively exposed in the south-eastern part of the county. At Arrow Rock it forms bluffs near 80 feet in hight, and is seen at numerous places near there. Along the Salt Fork it crops out at many localities up to Sec. 29, T. 50, R. 20. On the Blackwater, just above the mouth of Salt Fork, it forms bluffs near 100 feet in hight, and continues to be seen along that stream surmounting bluffs of Chouteau Limestone up to near the west side of R. 21. Beyond this it continues to crop out in lower exposures to near the middle of T. 48, R. 23. It is also seen along Ferris Creek for five or six miles above its mouth.

In the eastern and north-eastern portions of the county this rock occurs along all the little streams flowing into the Missouri, and at many intermediate places, as far back from the river as Lower Carboniferous rocks have been colored on the map. At Miami it forms bluffs 25 to 30 feet in hight above ordinary stages of the river, and was seen showing a thickness of 12 feet above the alluvial bottoms, in the bluffs known as the Pinnacle Hills, along the east side of Sec. 52, R. 22.

This is as far west as this formation has been traced in the northern part of the county, bnt it doubtless forms the nucleus of this line of bluffs for five or six miles farther toward the south-west.

Owing to the slight local uplift in T. 51, ranges 20 and 21, this formation is brought to view along the principal branches of Cow Creek, and the northern branch of Rock Creek. West of these localities, all those portions of T. 51, ranges 21 and 22, which have been colored on the map as Lower Carboniferous, are covered by heavy beds of Drift and Loess; but these deposits probably repose there either upon Encrinital Limestone or some other Lower Carboniferous rock. This formation is characterized in this county by its usual organic remains.

Chouteau Limestone.

This rock is here a rather pure, compact, thin-bedded gray Limestone, nearly equaling the Encrinital Limestone in thickness. It occupies, however, a limited surface area in this county, being everywhere hidden by other Carboniferous rocks, excepting where a few of the streams have excavated their valleys down so as to bring it to view.

It is most extensively exposed along the Blackwater in the southern part of the county. In ascending that stream, it is first seen near the mouth of the Salt Fork, elevated but a few feet above water. About one mile higher up it was seen rising 20 feet above the creek, and two miles further west it is elevated 50 feet above the Blackwater. In Sec. 32, T. 49, R. 20, about two miles west of the last-mentioned locality, a bluff, near 200 feet in hight, is composed of this and other rocks, as represented in the following section:

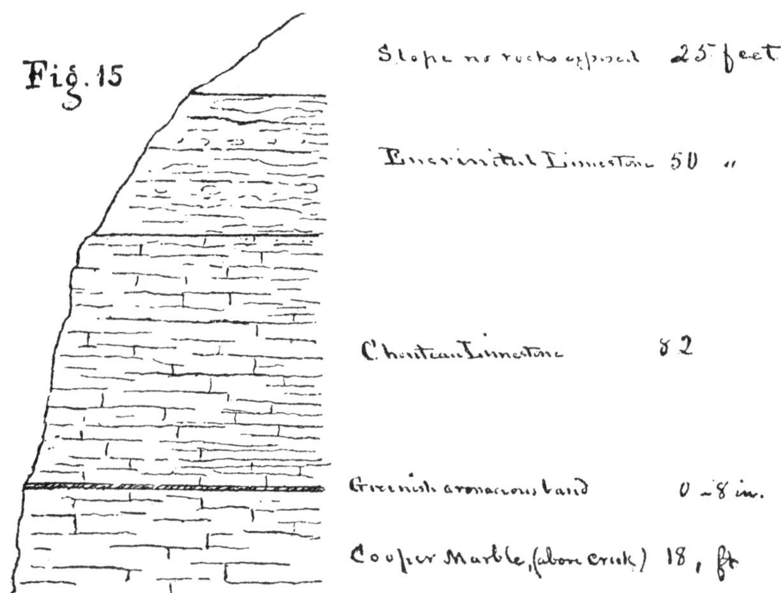

From near this point the strata all gradually incline westward, so that at the mouth of Ferris Creek, the top of the Chouteau Limestone is but 50 feet above the Blackwater, and it appears to pass beneath the surface of that stream before reaching the line between ranges 21 and 22, above which point it was not again seen in this county.

South of the Blackwater, on a stream known by the name of "Heath's Branch," outcrops of this rock were met with at several places, varying from 50 to 70 feet in thickness, and surmounted by from 20 to 50 feet of Encrinital Limestone.

The local uplift, near the center of the county, which, as already mentioned, has brought to view the Encrinstal Limestone on Cow and Rock creeks, has also exposed the Chouteau Limestone on both of these streams, in bluffs varying from 12 to 35 feet in hight. A low outcrop of this rock was also seen beneath a bluff of Encrinital Limestone near the head of Bear Creek, in Sec. 31, T. 52, R. 19, and several exposures of it were seen along Fish Creek, in T. 51, R. 19. At one of these exposures in Sec. 15 on Fish Creek, a bluff of it 38 feet in hight was observed, surmounted by 33 feet of Encrinital Limestone.

At the mouth of Fish Creek, in Sec. 24, T. 51, R. 19, a bluff near the Missouri is composed of fifty-five feet of this rock, surmounted by thirty feet of Encrinital Limestone; but, owing to the northern inclination of the strata produced by a local upheaval near here, Chouteau

Limestone dips beneath the alluvial bottoms of the Missouri, half a mile north of this.

The fossils most frequently observed in this rock in Saline county were *Chonetes ornata*, *Productus Murchisonianus*, *Spirifer peculiaris*, a small *Spirifer* like *S. lineatus*, a larger species somewhat similar to *S. cameratus*, *Rhynchonella Missouriensis*, *Leptæna depressa?*, *Avicula circulus*, *A. Cooperensis*, and a small undetermined species of *Arca;* all of which occur in greatest abundance along the Blackwater.

COOPER MARBLE.

The exact position of this rock in the series has not been determined, as no organic remains have yet been found in it, and it has only been seen in connection with the Chouteau Limestone and the Saccharoidal Sandstone. That is to say, it has been seen immediately beneath the former and reposing upon the latter. In this county it was only observed associated with the Chouteau Limestone, as represented in the section given on page 175, and is not known to occur at any other locality excepting where that section was taken, and near there on the Blackwater.

In composition it is a rather pure Limestone, and resembles some of the more compact layers of the Chouteau above. It is generally, however, more compact and heavy-bedded, and differs in always having numerous small, irregular particles of calc-spar disseminated through it.

The fact that this rock occurs so frequently immediately beneath the Chouteau Limestone in Cooper county, leads me to place it provisionally in that position in the general section, though I am aware future investigations may prove it to belong even to some part of the Lower Silurian series. It is the only bed observed in this county in regard to the relative position of which there can be any doubt.

SEMI-CRYSTALLINE LIMESTONE.

This is a light grayish, granular Limestone, which breaks with a rough, irregular fracture, and presents, on fresh surfaces, a semi-crystalline appearance. Under a lens, it is seen to consist, in part, of numerous small, whitish, sub-oolitic particles, with occasional rounded grains of quartz imbedded in a calcareous base. It also contains, at some places, great numbers of fossils belonging to three species, only one of which, *Atrypa reticularis*, appears to be identical with any described species. The others are a small, plicated

Spirifer, with a high area, and a medium-sized *Orthis*—both of which are probably new.

This rock appears to be exposed at only one place in Saline county. This is on the Missouri, about one and a-half miles below the mouth of Fish Creek, in Sec. 36, T. 51, R. 19. Here it is seen in a bluff, reposing upon Lower Silurian rocks, as represented in the section given below.

A rather sudden uplift has brought these rocks to view here, and as they were seen to dip both toward the north and south from this point, at an angle of about 15°, they must soon pass beneath the level of the Missouri, both above and below this exposure.

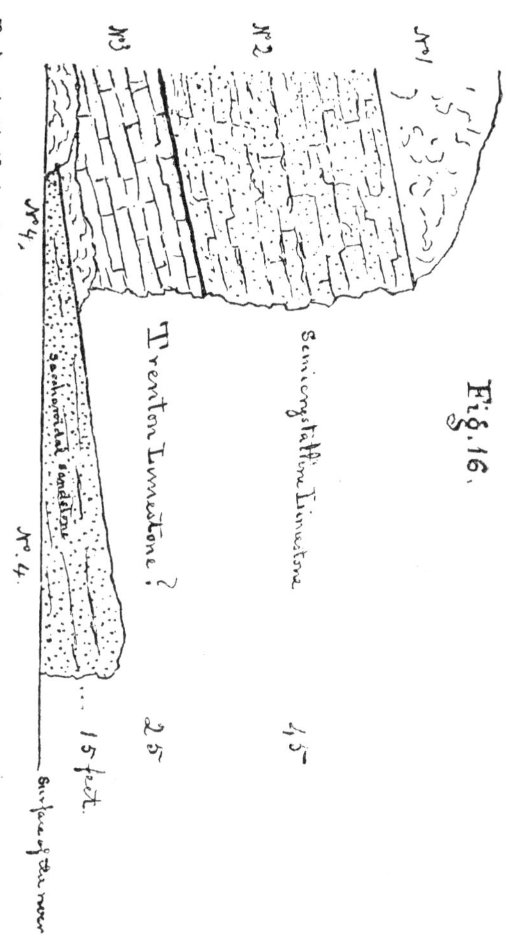

I am now satisfied this Limestone (No. 2 of accompanying section) is the same as the lower of two rocks holding a position at some places in Moniteau county just below the Chouteau Limestone.* Nearly all of the few fossils found in these two rocks in Moniteau county being new, and some of them resembling very closely Lower Helderburg forms, I was led to refer both these rocks, in my report on that county, to the Lower Helderburg series. Since that time, however, some of the same species occurring in the upper of the two beds in Moniteau having been found in Callaway county associated with well-known Hamilton Group fossils, I am inclined to the opinion that this upper bed (*a*) in Moniteau is of the age of the Hamilton Group.

*See beds *a* and *b* of section on page 104, Vol. I, part 2d, Report Geological Survey of Missouri.

In regard to the lower bed (*b*,) however, in Moniteau, and its equivalent in Saline county (No. 2) now under consideration, there is room for some doubt as to its exact age. The specimens of *Atrypa reticularis* found in it are all small, and even more like Upper Silurian varieties than those found in the Hamilton Group; while the *Spirifer* associated with these is rather nearly related to some new species found in the same beds with well-marked Hamilton forms in Callaway county. From all our present information, it seems most reasonable to refer this rock to the Devonian system, and to place it, provisionally, in association with the Hamilton Group, though better collections of organic remains may prove it to belong to an older epoch.

SILURIAN SYSTEM.

TRENTON LIMESTONE?

The rock here referred, with some doubt, to the Trenton Limestone, occurs at the same locality as and immediately under that just described, as may be seen by the section on the preceding page.

It is a reddish, impure, concretionary crystalline Limestone, with much whitish quartz and calc-spar disseminated through it. But two fossils were obtained from this rock, one of which is *Orthis lynx* and the other a cast, apparently, of *Murchisonia bellicincta*.*

About half a mile above this locality, a thickness of six feet of this bed is seen at the base of a bluff, where it is surmounted by 90 feet of the Chouteau Limestone, the intermediate rock, No. 2, of the preceding section, being wanting there. These are the only outcrops of this rock known to occur in this county.

SACCHAROIDAL SANDSTONE.

The only place in Saline county where this Sandstone rises to view is at the locality where the section given on page 177 was taken. It is here elevated about 15 feet at the highest point above the usual level of the river, and dips beneath it a short distance below. It is a little remarkable that this Sandstone should here project out some distance into the river beyond the overlying, harder rocks, as represented in the section.

It is here a pure white quartzose Sandstone, which is generally known all over the country as the "Salt Rock," from its resemblance to common salt. This is the oldest rock seen in the county.

* These fossils were collected by Prof. Swallow; and as they were mislaid at the time this report was written, I did not have an opportunity to examine them.

ECONOMICAL GEOLOGY.

SOIL.

Saline is well known to be one of the finest agricultural counties in the State. Throughout almost its entire area, there is a deep, rich, black soil, of unsurpassed fertility, and the proportion of land susceptible of cultivation is very large. Indeed, there is scarcely as much of the surface too broken for the plow, as will necessarily be allowed to remain as forest land. The ease with which these beautiful, rich, mellow prairie lands can be cultivated, almost makes the toil of the husbandman a pleasure, while their freedom from rocks, roots, stumps and other impediments, enables him to use the various sowers, reapers, mowers and other modern labor-saving agricultural implements, with astonishing effect.

The dark-colored surface soil in these prairies usually varies in depth from 8 to 24 inches, where it begins gradually to shade into a yellowish, extremely fine loam, which often continues down from 10 to 20 feet. Tbis loam, when taken from wells and other excavations, at various depths, even down as much as 20 feet below the surface, and exposed to the frosts and other atmospheric agencies for one winter, changes its color to a darker shade, and supports as dense a growth of vegetation as the surface soil.

The staple production of Saline county is hemp, which is extensively grown, and yields large profits. Some of the principal hemp-growers, it is said, sometimes sell a single crop for from $8,000 to $20,000. All the other crops usually cultivated in this climate are also produced here in great abundance. The common proverb that "hemp land will grow anything" seems to hold good here.

I saw the farmers gathering fine crops of Indian corn, and was informed that the crop of wheat had been very good. One gentleman informed me that he entered a piece of prairie land under the Graduation Act in 1854, at *fifty cents per acre*, plowed it up and sowed it in wheat that fall, fenced it during the winter, and the next season reaped a crop, which, when sacked and shipped to St. Louis, yielded *fifteen hundred dollars.*

The soil and climate here seem to be admirably adapted to the growth of fruits of various kinds. The orchards, with a few exceptions, are young and only just beginning to bear, but produce very fine fruit.

A gentleman extensively engaged in the nursery business near Rochester, New York, informed me he had seen apples grown in this and some of the adjoining counties, that were so large and finely flavored, that he was in some cases totally at a loss to identify varieties with which he had long been familiar in the East.

Saline county is rapidly improving, and everywhere gives evidences of thrift. Neat school-houses, churches, and numerous comfortable, as well as tasty farm-houses, seen in various parts of the county, not only speak well for the intelligence and refinement of the people, but tell more plainly than words can do, that capital and labor, when invested in the soil, here reap their reward.

COAL.

From what has already been said respecting the structure and boundaries of the Coal Measures in this county, it may be seen there is here an abundant supply of this highly important mineral. It is true the beds having the greatest horizontal extension are not very thick, but where overlaid, as is the case with the Fish Creek stratum, by a rock firm enough to be "timbered up," an 18-inch bed can be extensively worked by "drifts," especially by removing a few inches of the under clay.

Large quantities of Coal may be obtained at some places from even thinner beds, by stripping off the superincumbent loose materials, where they are not too heavy. The bed at Miami, if as thick as it is said to be (18 inches to 3 feet,) could very easily be worked by drifting under, there being a firm 12-inch layer of Limestone four inches above it.

The Coal obtained at the various mines in this county is generally of good quality for most purposes. Some of the beds contain too much pyrites for blacksmiths' use, but others afford a good quality of Coal, comparatively free from this objection.

The two abnormal 12-feet beds mentioned in the south-eastern part of the county (Smith's and Jackson's) can of course only be worked by means of open pits. They may contain large quantities of Coal, but should not be regarded as inexhaustible mines. Both of these deposits consist mainly of Cannel Coal. Specimens from Mr. Jackson's mine, it is said, were tried at the gas-works in St. Louis, and found well adapted to the production of gas.

BUILDING STONE.

Rocks suitable for most kinds of masonry are conveniently accessible in nearly all parts of the county, excepting the north-western townships; and in some portions of these, beds of Sandstone and Limestone of the Coal Measures can be used for such purposes. The

Encrinital and Chouteau Limestone, as well as the Cooper Marble, and portions of the Archimedes beds found here, all afford good building materials. The bed of Lower Carboniferous Sandstone mentioned in the northern and north-western parts of the county would probably be found suitable for some kinds of masonry.

Most of these Limestones, especially the Cooper Marble, and the Chouteau, would afford good material for the construction of macadamized roads.

LIMESTONES FOR MAKING LIME.

Nearly all the Lower Carboniferous and Devonian Limestones observed in various portions of this county will make good lime. Some of the Archimedes beds are rather too argillaceous, but other layers are quite pure and compact. The Encrinital Limestone makes excellent lime, and is accessible at many places along the streams, excepting in the western and north-western parts of the county. The best rock for this purpose, however, is the Cooper Marble, which makes beautiful lime, admirably adapted, in consequence of its snowy whiteness, to plastering and whitewashing. It occurs in great abundance on the Blackwater, in T. 49, R. 20.

The several thin beds of Limestone in the Coal Measures have the texture and general appearance of hydraulic Limestone, and would doubtless make good hydraulic cement.

SAND.

Sand can generally be obtained along the streams flowing through the Coal Measures, and at many places along the shores of the Missouri.

CLAYS FOR BRICKS, ETC.

Good brick Clays occur in the Drift and other superficial deposits at numerous places, in various parts of the county. One bed of whitish pipe Clay, holding a position apparently at the top of the Drift formation, would doubtless make excellent pottery.*

Several of the beds of Clay belonging to the Coal Measures would probably make good fire-bricks.

SPRINGS.

There are numerous fine springs of excellent water in the valleys along nearly all the streams, and at other low places in almost every part of this county. On the more elevated portions, however, especially the high prairies, they are scarcely ever met with; but good water can generally be obtained at such places by sinking wells.

A remarkable peculiarity of a very large number of springs in this county, is their strong impregnation with common salt. This is so frequently the case as to have suggested the name of the county, as well as those of some of the streams. I have seen no other portion of the State, nor indeed of the West, of the same extent as this county, containing so large a number of brine springs. Many of them are also more or less strongly impregnated with Sulphur, and a variety of other minerals.

When first entering upon the survey of this county, we commenced collecting for analysis, specimens of water from each of these springs, but soon found they were so numerous that it was a hopeless undertaking, unless we could devote our whole means of transportation to this one object, to the exclusion of all other specimens. It was therefore found necessary to collect specimens from only a few of such springs as are most remarkable for the quantity or strength of the water discharged, or for its supposed medicinal purposes; and even these specimens, although carefully sealed up in strong demijohns, unfortunately all failed to reach Dr. Litton's laboratory in safety.

It is evident, however, both from the strong brine taste, and from actual experience, that many of these springs are so strongly impregnated with common salt as to yield, in large quantities, by evaporation, an excellent quality of this indispensable mineral. There are also many springs in this county known to possess valuable medicinal properties, which have been much visited by invalids. Indeed, I feel quite confident Saline county will, at no very distant day, furnish some of the most noted watering places west of the Mississippi.

Nearly all the mineral springs observed in this county are found along streams which have excavated their valleys down nearly or quite to the Lower Carboniferous rocks, or through these into the Upper Devonian. On ascending these streams fairly up into the Coal Measures, some distance above where Lower Carboniferous rocks are seen, mineral springs of any kind are rarely met with here, though fresh-water springs are not uncommon at such places. I do not think from this fact, however, that the salines of this county have their origin in these Lower Carboniferous or Upper Devonian rocks, which are generally not very thick here, but that they are probably more deeply seated, and merely find more ready outlets through the fissures in these Limestones where they are not overlaid by the impervious clays of the Coal Measures.

The first of these brine springs observed in ascending the Blackwater is on the south side, near the mouth of Ferris Creek. It rises in an alluvial bottom, elevated some 15 feet above the creek, the hills on either side being composed mainly of Chouteau and Encrinital Limestones. This spring affords a considerable quantity of rather strong salt water, having a sulphurous odor, and a temperature of 54° —that of the air being 35°. Salt was formerly manufactured from this water.

About one mile and a half north-west of the last-mentioned locality, in the valley of Ferris Creek, there is another fine, bold salt spring, belonging to a gentleman by the name of Harris. This spring boils up through alluvial clays, in a marshy place, and discharges a large quantity of very clear water, having a temperature of 56°, while that of the air was 52°. It deposits a white, flocculent precipitate, has a slight odor of sulphureted hydrogen, and is kept in a constant state of ebullition by the escape of gas. Considerable quantities of salt were made here during the early settlement of the country.

Some two and a half miles above the mouth of Ferris Creek, on the south side of the Blackwater, there is a mineral spring, which has been much resorted to by invalids. It is very clear, has a saline taste and a slight odor of sulphureted hydrogen gas. I found its temperature to be 51°; that of the air being 42°. This water is said to act freely on the kidneys.

A short distance below this, on the opposite side of the creek, a strong brine spring issues from the bank, considerably below high water mark, and another boils up in the creek.*

In T. 48, R. 22, about four miles higher up the creek, on the south side, there is, in the valley, an old buffalo-lick, including an area of near half an acre. The whole of this space has been eaten and worn out to the depth of 20, and at some places, perhaps, as much as 30 feet. In this basin, which is in yellowish and ash-colored clays, perhaps of the age of the Drift, there are two salt springs, and all the clays within the basin appear to be more or less impregnated with salt.†

Brine springs also occur at a locality on the north side of the creek, about one mile below the lick, and at another place, less than a mile above it, there are two noble springs, affording large quantities

* At very low stages of water, bones and teeth of Mastodons have been found along the creek near these springs. I saw some of these, and tried to procure them for the State collection, but they were in the possession of persons who were unwilling to part with them at what I considered their value.

† On the high prairies, and down the slopes of the surrounding country, old paths of buffaloes, tramped as much as two feet in depth, are still seen radiating in various directions from this lick.

of clear, strong salt water, having a distinct odor of sulphureted hydrogen gas, which escapes in large quantities. I was informed that some salt was formerly made here.

About one mile higher up the creek, there is, on a small branch coming in on the south side, a fine salt spring, and, within a few steps of it, a sulphur spring. Both boil up in the bed of the branch among loose chert; while Encrinital Limestone occurs in the hills on either side above. The sulphur spring is much used by invalids during the warm months, and is said to act promptly on the bowels and kidneys. It affords a considerable quantity of water, so strongly impregnated with hydro-sulphuric acid, as to blacken silver in a few seconds. I found it to have a temperature of 60°, when that of the air was 42°. The salt spring has the same temperature, with a strong saline taste, and a sulphurous odor. It has been used to some extent in the manufacture of salt, and is said to yield a good article.

Higher up the creek, in Sec. 11, T. 48, R. 23, there is a spring, issuing from a low bluff of Encrinital Limestone about 16 feet above the creek, at ordinary stages of water. It discharges a considerable quantity of clear water, having a scarcely perceptible saline taste, and is known as the "Sweet Spring." I saw no gas escaping from it, nor does it appear to possess any odor of sulphureted hydrogen. I was informed, however, that a fine sulphur spring boils up at the base of the bluff near the Sweet Spring, but, being below high water mark of the creek, it could not be seen when I visited the locality. The water of the Sweet Spring, which has a temperature of 58°, is much used by invalids from the surrounding country, especially by dyspeptic persons, who, I was informed, think they derive much benefit from it. Several small houses have been erected here for the accommodation of visitors, by Mr. J. L. Yantis, the proprietor.

In a low bottom on Davis Creek, two and a half to three miles north-west of the Sweet Spring, there are two large brine springs and two sulphur springs. The salt springs here, as usual, are also impregnated with sulphureted hydrogen. The water of all these springs is very clear, and had a temperature of 58°, when that of the air was 40°. The hills on each side of the valley here are composed chiefly of the Coal Measures, but Encrinital Limestone was seen in the bed of the creek, a short distance below.

About one mile, a little east of north from the last-mentioned locality, and in Sec. 34, T. 48, R. 23, in the valley of Salt Pond Creek, a large salt spring boils up in a pool of saline water, located in a marshy place. I could not approach near enough to examine it very carefully, but it appeared to be very similar to those already described. A sulphur spring was also seen a short distance above this in the same valley. Both of these springs boil up through alluvial clays, while the hills on each side of the valley are composed of Coal Measure rocks; but it is evident the Encrinital Limestone can not be much below the bottom of the valley here. No other mineral springs were seen above here in this county, either on this or Davis Creek.

Brine springs also occur at numerous places along the Salt Fork of Blackwater and its tributaries. As it would be incompatible, however, with the necessary limits of a county report like this, to enter into a detailed description of each of these springs, I would merely remark that they are nearly all more or less impregnated with sulphur, as well as common salt, and vary in their temperatures from 55° to 58°. They also occur under very similar circumstances to those already described along the Blackwater. Several of them discharge considerable quantities of water, which has been found to yield, by evaporation, good qualities of common salt.

In ascending the Salt Fork they were first observed near the south side of S. 1, T. 49, R. 20, again near the mouth of Camp Creek, in S. 12, T. 50, R. 21, and at other localities on a small tributary of Salt Fork, in T. 51, R. 21.

The most remarkable brine spring, however, observed in this county, is known as the "Big Salt Spring," situated in a little valley in the south-east quarter of S. 17, T. 50, R. 22, perhaps as much as 80 feet below the summit of the surrounding country. The hills on either side of the valley are made up of Coal Measure rocks, while the bottom of the valley beneath the soil is composed of light-colored clays, perhaps of the age of the Drift, reposing probably on some of the lowest members of the Coal series. The general structure of the surrounding country also indicates that Lower Carboniferous Limestones exist not far beneath the surface of the deepest parts of the valley.

This spring consists of an oval or sub-circular pool, measuring in its greater diameter about 70 feet. I had no means of sounding it, but was informed it is of great depth. It is kept in a constant state of ebullition by the escape of gas, and discharges a large quantity of water; enough apparently to run a medium-sized mill. This water, which appears to boil up from the bottom of the pool, has a rather strong brine taste, and a distinct odor of hydro-sulphuric acid, and deposits a white flocculent precipitate. Its temperature was found to be 60°, when that of the air was 68°. When examined, it had a whitish milky appearance, though it is said to vary much in this respect at different times, being often quite clear.

A short distance south of this spring there are, at a little lower position in the same valley, several similar but smaller springs. One of these, however, appears to afford at least half, if not two-thirds, as much water as the large one, and is said to have been sounded to greater depths without finding bottom—from which fact it has been called the "Deep Spring." It appears to be more strongly impregnated with salt than the large spring, and was found to have a temperature of 59°. It was quite clear when examined, but is said to be milky at times like the large one, and, like it, is also strongly enough impregnated with sulphureted hydrogen gas (which was seen escaping in large quantities) to blacken silver in a few seconds.

Another brine spring near the latter is remarkable for being subject to rather sudden, irregular ebbs and flows, independent of rains or drouth. The opinion is also general among those who have frequently visited the springs in this valley, that they are all, including the large one, more or less subject to these irregularities. The same opinion is likewise prevalent in regard to some of the salt springs in other parts of the county, as well as in regard to a fresh-water spring that comes up in the Missouri valley five miles north-west of Miami.

When first informed of this fact, I was inclined to think there might be some mistake about it, but on visiting the salt spring above alluded to, I had the satisfaction to see it in the act of rising. This was so palpable as to remove all doubts from my mind on the subject, for the water was seen spreading and flowing out over perfectly dry ground. Large quantities of gas were escaping, and the temperature of the water was found to be 60°, that of the air being 68°. There had been no rain for eleven days previous, excepting a slight sprinkle that morning, which had scarcely laid the dust. It was cloudy, however, and the wind was from the south, attended by a sudden and unusual fall in the barometer; and that evening and the following night it rained quite hard.

This increased flow of water, it seems to me, may have been produced by the sudden decrease in the density of the air, indicated by the fall in the barometer, which must of course have been accompanied by a corresponding diminution of the atmospheric pressure on the surface of the fountain.*

The average quantity of water discharged by these great springs is said not to be either increased or diminished by the most protracted rains or drouth. Their united waters form quite a brook, known as the Salt Branch, which flows northward to the Salt Fork, (a distance

*See paper in Proceed. Am. As. Ad. Sci., Washington Meeting, p. 170, "On the swelling of springs and the reappearance of streams just before rain." By Prof. John Brocklesby, of Trinity College, Hartford, Connecticut.

of some five miles,) imparting to that stream, which is comparatively fresh above its mouth, a distinct brine taste below. Considerable quantities of salt were formerly made at these springs.

When we bear in mind the number of brine springs there are in Saline county, the quantity and strength of the water they afford, and reflect that they are here located in the midst of one of the finest agricultural regions in the world, we can not avoid the conclusion that they must ultimately become an important source of wealth to the county.

Their value, however, seems not to be generally appreciated, in consequence of the fact that many intelligent persons who have given no attention to the various improved methods of salt-making, think the scarcity of fuel in this region must be an insurmountable obstacle in the way of turning these salines to profitable account. Indeed, there are some persons who contend that they have already done the country more injury by the consumption of fuel they caused while the early settlers were making salt here, than the value of all that ever can be manufactured from them would repay. Such persons, however, are perhaps not aware of the fact that salt can be, and is, manufactured on the most extensive scale without the consumption of any kind of fuel, simply by the heat of the sun, which is as cheap on the prairie as in the midst of the forest, and far more available.

At the present time there are annually manufactured at the Onondaga Salt Works in New York, by solar evaporation alone, from 500,000 to 600,000 bushels of salt, requiring, during the six months' season of operations, an average daily supply of about 2,000,000 gallons of water. The annual production of salt by solar evaporation at Schönebeck, Germany, is said to be 57,500,000 pounds; while some idea may be formed of the amount manufactured in this way on the British West India Islands when it is borne in mind that there were imported into this country alone from there in 1857, 1,033,601 bushels.*

It has been found by experience that the expense of manufacturing salt by solar evaporation, at the Onondaga Works, scarcely differs from that of salt made by boiling. But the former process is known to produce a superior article, a measured bushel of it being usually about 19 pounds heavier than the same quantity of that made by boiling, while its antiseptic properties are far superior. The reputation of Turk's Island salt is well known to every one familiar with the beef and pork packing business.

The climate in Central Missouri is probably better adapted to the manufacture of salt by solar evaporation than at Onondaga, New

*See an interesting article by Wm. C. Dennis, Esq., on the "History, Commerce, Sources, Manufacture, etc.," of salt; page 133 of the Patent Office Report for 1857. *(Agricultural Department.)*

York. The warm weather here continues longer, and the air is less humid during the warm part of the season.

The French method of evaporation by "graduation," as it is termed, would probably be better adapted to making salt in Saline county, than the plan pursued at Onondaga, since the latter process requires more lumber in the construction of the fixtures. In the "graduation" process, the water is pumped up into tanks 20 to 30 feet high, and allowed to flow into troughs, provided with numerous small perforations, through which it falls in the form of a shower of separate drops. Beneath these troughs there is erected a kind of wall, built up of black thorn twigs, cut of uniform length, and placed horizontally upon each other, the whole being supported by a frame-work. In this way the drops of water falling upon the wall of twigs are retarded in their descent to the receiving tank below, in such a way as greatly to accelerate the process of evaporation.

The plan adopted at Onondaga is merely to pump the water into numerous long, narrow, shallow, wooden vats, elevated a few feet above the ground, and provided with movable covers, which can be run on or off in accordance with the nature of the weather. Here it is allowed to stand until, by slow evaporation, the water is all expelled, leaving the salt behind.

I would refer those who may wish to inquire more particularly into the details of these methods of producing salt to the able article in the Patent Office Report, cited on the preceding page.

CHAPTER X.

OZARK COUNTY.*

BY B. F. SHUMARD.

This county, with but a single exception—Oregon county—is the largest in the State. It contains nearly 45 townships, or an area of about 1,580 square miles. The surface is in general remarkably hilly and broken, although there are some districts which present the features of a beautiful and gently undulating plain. The principal streams, and, in fact, most of their tributaries, are separated from each other by dividing ridges, which sometimes attain an elevation of five hundred feet, their general elevation being from 150 to 200 feet. The highest hills are situated at the head-waters of Cane, Little Pine, Turkey and Spring creeks, and near the Big and Little North Forks and Bryant's Fork of White River, where they often assume a neatly-rounded, conical outline.

The whole county is remarkably well watered by a multitude of beautiful streams, whose waters are unusually clear, and abound in a variety of choice fishes. They are all tributaries of White River, and the largest of them are the Big and Little North Forks and Bryant's Fork. None of them are susceptible of being navigated, as their currents are very swift and rapids are of frequent occurrence throughout their whole extent.

All the principal streams furnish eligible mill sites, more than sufficient to supply the present and future demands of the county.

QUATERNARY DEPOSITS.

The alluvial bottoms of Ozark county are quite narrow, usually varying from 200 to 600 yards wide, and scarcely ever exceeding a half mile. Their soil being chiefly derived from the destruction of the

*Douglas county at present includes a part of what was formerly Ozark.

older geological formations, its characters will be better understood after these have been described.

When opportunities presented of inspecting the deposits immediately beneath the soil and subsoil, which were by no means frequent, we usually found sands and clays of a reddish or ash color, from five to twenty feet thick, frequently filled with fragments of chert, some of them of considerable size. Beneath these occur alternations of sands and clays, from five to fifteen feet thick or more, which present the lithological aspect of the bottom prairie of the general section, (F. *v*,) although no fluviatile or terrestrial shells were found in any of the beds examined.

The Bluff deposits doubtless exist in Ozark county, but owing to the extensive accumulation of *detritus*, it was not satisfactorily recognized as a distant formation.

CARBONIFEROUS SYSTEM.

The rocks of this system can scarcely be said to form a part of the geological formations of the county, since we find them represented merely by loose fragments of chert, containing *Orthis Michelini*, *Actinocrinus Christyi*, and some other fossils of the Encrinital Limestone. This chert was observed in T. 24 N., R. 16 W., sections 4 and 5, and at some other points occupying the tops of the highest hills.

CHEMUNG GROUP.†

The strata belonging to this period are very sparingly represented. I noticed their occurrence at only a single locality, namely, near the head-waters of Turkey Creek, in T. 24, R. 16 W., sections 3 and 4. At this place are some hills with an elevation of from 400 to 450 feet, and at 50 feet below their summits I found a light-colored sub-crystalline Limestone, with *Chonetes ornata*, *Cyrtia acutirostris*, and other characteristic Chemung fossils. It exhibits a thickness of 50 feet, and consists of two well-marked varieties, both, however, presenting the same paleontologial characters. One is a compact, fine-textured Limestone, of a light gray color, and would make an elegant as well as durable building material. The other is of coarser texture, more friable and crystalline, and some of the layers contain an abundance of the remains of *Crinoidea*. Either variety is remarkably well adapted for making quicklime, for which purpose it is probably superior to any rock to be found in the county.

*Since this report was written this so-called Chemung group of Missouri, represented by the Chouteau Limestone, Vermicular Sandstone and shales and Lithographic Limestone, has, by recent investigations by American Geologists of the typical fossils, been placed above the Devonian, and at the base of the Lower Carboniferous. And in these reports, wherever the word Chemung occurs it is understood to be this group.

The stratigraphical position of these beds is immediately underneath the Vermicular Sandstone and shales, as is well shown in Wright county, and they are equivalent in age to the Lithographic Limestone (F. *l*) of the general section, though their lithological characters are quite different. They repose directly on the Calciferous Sand-rock, as appears from the following section, taken at the locality under notice:

No. 1. 50 feet slope, covered with fragments of chert, containing fossils of the Encrinital Limestone.*
No. 2. 50 feet Lithographic Limestone.
No. 3. 224 feet Calciferous Sand-rock.

CALCIFEROUS SAND-ROCK.

In Ozark county, all the formations from the base of the Chemung down to the Saccharoidal Sandstone, are entirely deficient. But the Sandstones and Magnesian Limestones of the Calciferous Sand-rock are developed on a large scale. In fact, nearly all the rocks of the county belong to this geological period. The strata vary considerably in character in different parts of the county, and often the change is quite sudden. Thus, we sometimes find a heavy bed of Magnesian Limestone passing into a perfect quartzose Sandstone in the distance of a few hundred yards. The strata also differ considerably in lithological appearance from their equivalents as observed in other parts of the State, and, hence, it has sometimes been no easy task to decide to which of the divisions of the Calciferous Group certain groups of beds should be assigned.

SACCHAROID SANDSTONE.

This formation appears merely as outliers of no great extent on or near the tops of the highest ridges of the county. The descriptions you have given of it in the published report will very nearly apply to it here. It is usually a friable Sandstone, its color passing from a pure white to a reddish brown. Its thickness varies from four to eighty feet.

In T. 24 N., R. 14 W., Sec. 27, this Sandstone occupies the upper eighty feet of the divide between the head-waters of the Barren Fork of Little North Fork and Spring Creek. The strata are from six inches to as many feet in thickness, and the surface is, in places, strewn with large lichen-covered masses of this rock—some of them quite hard and semi-vitrified, and others assuming the characters of a quartz breccia, with cavities lined with small quartz crystals and chalcedony.

*It is not at all improbable that the slope of this section is underlaid by the Vermicular Sandstone and shale.

On the high mounds at the head of Turkey Creek, (T. 24 N., R. 16 W., Sec. 3,) the Saccharoid Sandstone is seen reposing on the Second Magnesian Limestone, and directly under the Chemung rocks already described. The rock at this place is soft, of a reddish brown color, and the thickness about four feet. On the west side of Bryant's Fork, a short distance south of Little Pine Creek, from thirty-five to forty feet of it appears at an elevation of three hundred and thirty feet above the bed of the former stream. It occurs again on the summit of the high range of hills which lie between Lick and Cave Creeks, and as occasional outliers on the tops of the ridges between Bryant's and Big North Fork of White River, and also on the east side of the latter stream. In fact, detached fragments of this Sandstone, sometimes of very large size, are common on most of the highest elevations throughout the county, where they are usually commingled with huge masses of semi-vitrified Sandstone and quartzite, presenting often a brecciated appearance.

Where this formation prevails, the surface of the ground is in general remarkably rough and broken, so that it is often quite difficult and sometimes impossible to travel over it on horse-back.

Fossils.—At a few localities we have found fragments of the internal casts of *Straparollus* and *Chemnitzia*, but too imperfect for accurate determination.

SECOND MAGNESIAN LIMESTONE.

This formation is remarkably well developed in Ozark county, both horizontally and vertically, entering largely into the composition of all the highest hills, and presenting sometimes a thickness of nearly three hundred feet. In general lithological appearance, it does not differ materially from the Second Magnesian Limestone observed by Prof. Swallow on the Osage River, and by myself in Franklin county. The section of it given on page 121 of the Second Report, presents a pretty fair general idea of its character in this county. The upper part consists of even-bedded layers of light buff and drab, earthy, fine-grained Magnesian Limestone, with thin layers of chert and soft, brown Sandstone interstratified. This part of the formation is often to be recognized by the occurrence of bare places or glades, on the sides of which the strata are frequently seen projecting in a series of benches or steps from base to top. At a few localities, the Cotton rock contains crystals of milk-white quartz in masses from the size of a filbert to that of a walnut, and on Bennett's Bayou, in T. 22 N., R. 11 W., Sec. 16, the beds are filled with small, smooth concretions of flint—some of them almond-shaped, some pyriform, and others branched and resembling fucoids; but they do not show any traces of organic structure. The lower part of the formation is generally a compact Calcareo-magnesian Limestone, with beds of Sandstone and chert intercalated. It generally occurs in thicker layers than the Cotton rock, and the weathered surfaces are often rough and jagged.

The best exhibitions of the Second Magnesian Limestone were observed on the Big North Fork, below Bryant's Fork, throughout nearly the whole course of the Little North Fork, at the head of Pine Creek, in T. 23, R. 13, Sec. 5, and between that stream and the head of Lick Creek. At these localities, its thickness is from two hundred to two hundred and seventy-five feet. In the south-western townships of the county, about three miles west of the Little North Fork, it presents a thickness of two hundred and fifty feet, and the different members of the formation may here be seen to good advantage. It is also well shown on the dividing ridges between the Big North Fork and Bryant, and between the latter and Little North Fork. But it is needless to particularize localities, as it appears on the higher ground in every township in the county, limited above by the Saccharoid Sandstone, and below by the Second Sandstone.

Fossils.—The explorations in Ozark county have enabled us to make some interesting additions to our catalogue of the organic remains from this division of the Calciferous Sand-rock. We find here, with *Murchisonia melaniaformis* and *Melia** (*Orthoceras*) *primigenius*, a number of new species, which I have described under the following names: *Lituites complanata*, *Chemnitzia resticula*, *C. Ozarkensis*, *Murchisonia carinifera*, *Straparollus valvataformis*, *S. bigranosus*, *Raphistoma grandis*, *R. subplana* and *Arionellus* (?) *Missouriensis*. Besides these species, we find several *Trilobites* and a number of *Gasteropods* which have not yet been sufficiently studied to permit us to refer them with certainty to their proper genera.

The best locality for the organic remains of this formation that I have seen in the county is on a branch of the Little North Fork of White River, in T. 22 N., R. 15, Sec. 34. At this place, fossils are almost as abundant and beautifully preserved as in the most favored portion of the Trenton Limestone, although we do not find such a

*I have but little doubt with regard to the identity of our species and *Orthoceras primigenius* of Mr. Vanuxem. The specimens from Ozark county, however, show clearly that the fossil must be removed from the genus *Orthoceras*, and be placed in that of *Melia*, as the siphuncle is marginal and not central, or sub-central, as in the former genus. Our specimens show also other interesting characters, which will be given in detail in the Paleontology.

variety of species. They occur at the summit of the ridges in masses of rough, dirty-looking chert, filled with cavities, the sides of which are often lined with small crystals of quartz. I have not obtained any fossils in the bottom rock, but in the intercalated chert, indurated Sandstone, and the compact Magnesian Limestone toward the base of the formation, they are frequently found.

Second Sandstone.

Beneath the formation just described occur strata which, on account of their stratigraphical position, I refer to the age of the Second Sandstone, (F. *w*) although they present some striking lithological differences from that formation in other districts of the State. It is here subject to considerable variation in character and thickness, sometimes exhibiting all the characteristic features of the Saccharoid Sandstone, occurring in thick, massive beds, made up of rounded, semi-crystalline quartz grains; at other times appearing in thin strata, with a good deal of chert interstratified. The texture of the rock varies from a close, fine-grained Sandstone, to a coarse Gritstone. In color, it passes from a pure white to a dark ferruginous brown. On Bryant's Fork, in T. 26, R. 14, Sec. 6, and at some other localities, it is elegantly variegated and ripple-marked. Near Mr. Hines' residence, in T. 25, R. 13 W., Sec. 11, it contains prominent semi-cylindroid concretions, which traverse the surfaces of the rock in various directions, frequently intersecting, and resembling fucoids.

The Second Sandstone is best developed in the northern half of the county, where it is almost constantly exposed along the water-courses, imparting to the scenery an exceedingly rough and rugged aspect. On the Big North Fork, it commences at the northern boundary line of the county, and extends for some distance below Indian Creek. At first it constitutes hills about 50 feet high; but as we descend, it is seen reposing on the Third Magnesian Limestone, exhibiting, sometimes, a thickness of 150 feet, and presenting perpendicular faces, and steep declivities to the stream.

At the mouth of Clifty Creek, we have the following section in descending order:

No. 1. 44 feet slope, covered with immense blocks of Sandstone and chert.
No. 2. 140 feet heavy beds of white and brown Sandstone, with thinner layers of the same interstratified.
No. 3. 40 feet thick bedded Third Magnesian Limestone.

At James' saw mill, a mile lower down the river, Mr. Hough obtained the following Section:

No. 1. 77 feet white and brown thick-bedded Sandstone.
No. 2. 10 feet Sandstone, moderately fine-grained, with calc-spar disseminated.
No. 3. 10 feet pure white Sandstone, made up of coarse, rounded semi-crystalline grains.
No. 4. 10 feet Magnesian Limestone.
No. 5. 2 feet Sandstone.
No. 6. 30 feet Magnesian Limestone.
No. 7. 44 feet Sandstone.
No. 8. 11 feet Magnesian Limestone.
No. 9. 20 feet slope.

This Sandstone is finely exposed on Hungry and Indian Creeks, and on the smaller confluents of the North Fork, between these streams.

Along Fox Creek, it forms the chief part of the bluffs, from the head branches to its mouth, and on Bryant's Fork occupies the upper part of all the escarpments, from the north county line until we get below the town of Rockbridge. It then dips southwardly, and in the distance of about six miles disappears beneath the level of the streams. At a point about three miles south of Rockbridge, its thickness is 160 feet by measurement.

This formation also appears in the bluffs of all the branches of Bryant's Fork, in T. 25, 26 and 27; and it is again well exhibited, for a short distance, on a small creek in T. 25 N., R. 16 W., Secs. 7 and 8.

Fossils.—In the cherty beds on Big North Fork and Bryant's Fork we obtained a large species of *Raphistoma*, *straparollus acuto-carinatus*, and the pygidium of a trilobite, perhaps belonging to the genus *Arionellus*, and very similar to one found in the Second Magnesian Limestone. Perfect specimens, however, are very rare.

THIRD MAGNESIAN LIMESTONE.

The next formation in the descending order, and the oldest in the county, I am disposed to regard as the representative of the Third Magnesian Limestone; yet I do so with some hesitation, as its lithological characters in Ozark county are usually quite different from those presented by the Third Magnesian in other parts of the State, whilst the fossils are in general badly preserved, and of too infrequent occurrence to permit us to rely solely on them as guides in determining the question of equivalency.

The following Sections, taken on the North Fork of White River and Indian Creek, will convey a pretty good general idea of the character and relative thickness of the different beds, as they appear in the bluffs of the streams in different parts of the county:

Section on the North Fork, 2½ miles below Indian Creek:

No. 1. 33 feet slope, covered with large angular blocks of white and brown, compact and friable Sandstone, and rough chert, containing *Straparollus acutocarinatus* and *Raphistoma*.
No. 2. 13 feet gray and buff Magnesian Limestone.
No. 3. 15 feet Sandstone.
No. 4. 5½ feet same as No. 2.
No. 5. 5½ feet same as No. 3.
No. 6. 14 feet compact, rather thick-bedded Magnesian Limestone, with *Straparollus*.
No. 7. 2 feet Calcareo-magnesian Limestone, with calc-spar disseminated.
No. 8. 26 feet fine-grained Sandstone; some of the beds indurated.
No. 9. 9 feet compact Magnesian Limestone.
No. 10. 18 feet slope, covered with large masses of Sandstone.
No. 11. 9 feet Sandstone.
No. 12. 2 feet buff Magnesian Limestone, containing a good deal of calc-spar.
No. 13. 8 feet Sandstone.
No. 14. Alternating layers of Sandstone and buff Magnesian Limestone.
No. 15. 2 feet Sandstone.
No. 16. 18 feet slope.

Section on Indian Creek, T. 26, R. 11, Sec. 20:

No. 1. 30 feet thick-bedded Sandstone, with thin layers interstratified.
No. 2. 2½ feet rough Magnesian Limestone.
No. 3. 10 feet thick-bedded, coarse-grained, friable Sandstone.
No. 4. 2 feet rough and broken chert.
No. 5. 4 feet compact Magnesian Limestone.
No. 6. 9 feet Sandstone, passing into chert.
No. 7. 10 feet thick-bedded Calcareo-magnesian Limestone.
No. 8. 3 feet chert and Sandstone.
No. 9. 40 feet Sandstone and slope.
No. 10. 5 feet arenaceous Magnesian Limestone, containing a good deal of chert.
No. 11. 30 feet white, soft Sandstone, in thick beds, becoming indurated on exposure to the air.
No. 12. 20 feet heavy-bedded, compact Magnesian Limestone.
No. 13. 23 feet Sandstone.

Thus characterized, the Third Magnesian Limestone prevails extensively, and constitutes one of the most important formations of Ozark county. Along the Big North Fork and Bryant's Fork, it constantly appears north of the line between T. 23 and 24, and likewise some distance up their tributaries, forming everywhere bold and perpendicular escarpments, extending from the water-level sometimes to the hight of 150 or even 200 feet, and presenting often a rude castellated appearance. It is also well seen along the bluffs of Fox Creek.

Caves are of frequent occurrence in districts where this formation prevails, and some of them are of considerable magnitude. The one most deserving of notice, that I have observed, is situated on the east side of Bryant's Fork, in T. 25, R. 14, Sec. 14. The entrance is 35 feet wide and 30 feet high, and is situated at the foot of a perpendicular cliff, and far above the water-level of Bryant. Just within the entrance, it expands to 60 or 70 feet, with a hight of about 50 feet, and this part of the cave has been used by the citizens of the county as a place for holding camp-meeting. I estimated its length at not far short of one mile and a half. The main passage is in general quite spacious, the roof elevated, and the floor tolerably level, but often wet and miry. For some distance beyond the entrance, there is not much to attract attention, but, as we proceed, at the far extremity, the chambers are quite as picturesque as the most noted of the well-known Mammoth Cave. The ceilings, sides and floor are adorned with a multitude of stalactites and stalagmites, arranged in fanciful combinations, and assuming a variety of fantastic and beautiful forms.

Fossils.—The Third Magnesian Limestone of this county has yielded a *Straparollus*, which I have characterized under the name of *S. acutocarinatus*, *Chemnitzia* and *Arionellus*. Mr. Hough discovered also a small species of *Orthis*, quite abundantly, in some loose masses, lying at the foot of the bluffs at Double Spring, which doubtless belong to this formation.

ECONOMICAL GEOLOGY.

SOILS.

The alluvial bottoms, for the most part, possess good and productive soils. In the Sandstone districts they are perhaps too arenaceous, but here also there are many excellent farms. Nearly all the settlements in the county are confined to the river bottoms, although they are very narrow, never exceeding the half of a mile in width, and generally averaging not more than three or four hundred yards.

The soils of the uplands are subject to considerable variations, depending on the character of the underlying geological formation. In places where the Second Magnesian Limestone prevails, the soil is often of excellent quality, and well adapted for cultivation. The "Oak Barrens," in the south-eastern, middle and western parts of the county, occasionally offer some very desirable farm sites, and it has been to me sometimes a matter of surprise that these have not been more frequently selected for farms, instead of the contracted valleys of the streams.

In those districts where the surface rock is Sandstone and Third Magnesian Limestone, the land is in general too rough and rocky, and the soil too thin and light to be well fitted for cultivation. There are, however, exceptions to this rule, particularly in some of the northern townships.

IRON.

This valuable ore occurs at a number of localities in Ozark county, usually in the form of brown Hematite. Near Mr. Lantz's farm, T. 22 N., R. 15 W., Sec. 34, Hematite of good quality occurs in sufficient quantity to lead to the belief that it might be worked to advantage. The ore, in masses from a few pounds to half a ton in weight, projects from the lower slope of a hill composed of Second Magnesian Limestone.

At the base of the same hill the Magnesian Limestone contains Sulphuret of Iron in large masses, and quantities of this worthless mineral have been extracted at the expense of much time and labor, under the impression that it was a rich ore of silver, or some other of the precious metals. In the south-east quarter of Sec. 36, T. 22 N., R. 12, brown Hematite, of good quailty, occurs on the top of a high ridge of Second Magnesian Limestone. The ore exists in masses varying from a few ounces to fifty pounds in weight, and is thickly strewn over a space of about one hundred square yards in extent. The surface indications are that the ore exists here in considerable quantity.

In Sec. 29, of T. 23, R. 12, an ore very similar in appearance occurs on the surface of a high glade of Second Magnesian Limestone; and in Sec. 23, T. 23, R. 12, Mr. Hough saw a rich Hematite ore near the summit of an elevated ridge of the same formation. He estimated that a hundred bushels of the ore might be gathered from the surface of the ground at this locality. Two miles south-west of James' saw-mills, in T. 26, R. 11, the surface is thickly covered with Iron ore for the distance of nearly a quarter of a mile. Brown Hematite is also of common occurrence, in greater or less quantities, over those districts where the Second Magnesian Limestone prevails, and it is highly probable that extensive deposits of this invaluable ore will be found in Ozark county.

LEAD

Has been observed at a few localities in the county, but only in small quantities, disseminated rarely through the Second Magnesian Limestone, or in the form of "float mineral" in the beds of the streams. The character of the geological formations of Ozark county would, however, lead one to the opinion that it may be found in some abundance, since the appearance of the formations is very analagous to the Lead-bearing strata of Franklin and Washington counties. All the Galena that I have observed was in the Second Magnesian Limestone. It is generally associated with calc-spar, but sometimes with Sulphate of Baryta. The localities are laid down on the map.

ZINC,

In the form of blende, was noticed at a single locality, in small crystalline masses, disseminated through the Second Magnesian Limestone, in the north-west portion of the county.

COPPER.

Minute particles of the green carbonate of this metal were found disseminated through the calc-spar which sometimes accompanies the Second Magnesian Limestone.

SALTPETER.

At the locality on Indian Creek where the section of the Third Magnesian Limestone was taken, Saltpeter occurs in a friable Sandstone, near the tops of the bluffs, (bed No. 3 of section.) There is here an opening some four or five feet deep and a couple of yards long, the sides of which are covered with a white efflorescence of this substance. The Sandstone is also pretty strongly impregnated with it for a short distance around the opening. Saltpeter was also observed incrusting this Sandstone at other points in the county, but at no place was it observed in any considerable quantity.

BUILDING MATERIALS.

Ozark county is bountifully supplied with good materials for construction. The Cotton rock, which, as I have before observed, occurs in nearly every township in the county, is a beautiful and durable building rock, possessing nearly the same characters as that used for the State House at Jefferson City. The lower part, also, of the Second Magnesian Limestone, as well as many of the beds of the Third Magnesian Limestone, furnish material of the very best kind for building purposes, and the rock may be usually obtained of any required thickness. These dolomites are especially adapted for the heavier kinds of masonry, such as the foundations of buildings and bridges. The Sandstone formations, also, furnish an excellent quality of stone for construction, but as a general rule they are inferior to the Magnesian Limestones.

On Bryant's Fork, in T. 26 N., R. 12 W., N. W. corner of section 6, is a quarry of a beautiful variety of Sandstone. The rock is made up of fine grains, and occurs in strata from six inches to three or four feet thick, and when first taken out is quite soft, but it hardens on exposure to the air. It is of a pure white color, elegantly clouded and banded with reddish-brown. This rock is used to some extent in the neighborhood for chimneys and fire-places, for which it is well adapted.

Fire Rock.

Sandstone, suitable for hearths of furnaces, may be selected from the Second Sandstone formation, and also from the arenaceous beds of the Third Magnesian Limestone.

Lime.

The beds of the Chemung Group, which I have described as occurring near the head of Turkey Creek, are the best in the county for quick-lime. But wherever the lower part of the Second or the Third Magnesian Limestone occurs, beds may be found that contain a sufficient quantity of calcareous matter to make a very good article of lime for all ordinary purposes.

Hydraulic Lime.

Some of the more compact earthy-looking varieties of the Cotton rock have the appearance of Hydraulic Limestone.

Materials for Brick-making.

Bricks of good quality can be made from the sands and clays of the Quaternary deposits, which occur in the valleys of the streams. It is also probable that excellent materials for this purpose will be frequently met with on the uplands, as the bluff formation doubtless exists, and will be found on removing a few feet of superficial detritus.

ROAD MATERIALS.

Most of the streams in the county contain comminuted chert, in the greatest abundance, and this is well adapted for the construction of roads. Smooth and durable ways can be constructed from it at comparatively trifling cost.

SAND FOR GLASS-MAKING.

The Saccharhoid and Second Sandstone will furnish inexhaustible supplies of pure silicious sand, suitable for the manufacture of the better kinds of glass.

MILL-STONES.

Large amorphous masses of silex, sometimes brecciated and containing cavities, are quite common on the uplands in different parts of the county, and these will often furnish a good variety of Buhr-stone.

SPRINGS.

Ozark county is bountifully supplied with springs of the finest water, and some of them of remarkably large size. The largest one is situated near the North Fork, in T. 24 N., R. 11 W., Sec. 32, and is known under the name of the Double Spring. It issues from near the base of a bluff of Sandstone and Magnesian Limestone, a few feet above the level of the North Fork. This spring discharges an immense volume of water, which is divided, by a huge mass of Sandstone, into two streams, with swift currents, flowing in opposite directions, to join the North Fork about one hundred and fifty yards distant from the spring. I estimated the width of these streams at not less than fifty yards. They are separated from the North Fork by a pretty wooded island, one hundred yards long. The upper stream affords a good mill-site. I am informed that the quantity of water discharged by this magnificent spring is not materially diminished during the dryest seasons of the year. The temperature of the water, measured at the edge of the spring, was found to be 56°; the temperature of the air, at the same time, 59°. Other springs, of considerable magnitude, occur in various portions of the county, giving rise to beautiful and limpid streams.

Chalybeate Springs.

A spring, strongly impregnated with iron, occurs in T. 21 N., R. 12 W., Sec. 3. It issues from the base of a hill of Sandstone, two or three feet above the level of a small branch, and deposits a copious gelatinous precipitate. A chalybeate spring was also observed in T. 26 N., R. 14 W., Sec. 31. Both of these springs are worthy of trial in cases requiring the use of tonics.

PINE TIMBER.

Perhaps no county in the State can boast of such extensive and excellent pine forests as Ozark. In fact, the size and quality of the timber will compare favorably with that of the celebrated pineries of Wisconsin and Minnesota. The largest forests are situated in the eastern and middle portions of the county. That on the east commences at the north line of the county, and continues almost uninterruptedly along the North Fork, for the distance of about twenty-two miles. On the west side of the river its width varies from a half to a mile, but on the east it is from two to ten miles wide. This pinery, according to a careful estimate, embraces a district of country probably not less than one hundred and thirty square miles in extent. The next largest body of pine land lies chiefly in T. 24, 25 and 26, of R. 13 and 14 W. The greatest length is about twelve miles, its width from two to twelve miles, and it embraces an area of about ninety square miles. A small forest of pines also exists on a small branch of Spring Creek,* in the N. W. quarter of T. 25 N., R. 16 W.

On the geological map of the county I have endeavored to lay down, with as much accuracy as possible, the general boundaries of the pine lands, as gathered from personal observation and information obtained from reliable persons residing in the county. The North Fork and Bryant's Fork, and their tributaries, furnish water-power in the greatest abundance for saw-mills. At this time there are thirteen or fourteen mills in the county, some of them capable of cutting upward of two thousand feet of lumber per day. Five of them are situated on the North Fork, and the others on Bryant's Fork and its tributaries. A large portion of the lumber is conveyed by ox-teams to Springfield, Bolivar, and even to the mouth of Linn Creek, on the Osage River.

The importance of these extensive pineries to the future improvement and prosperity of Southern Missouri is evident. At present, Ozark county can not get this valuable material to market without great cost, but when the South-western Branch of the Pacific Railroad is completed, she will be able to furnish large supplies of the very best quality of lumber to all parts of the State.

* There are at least a half dozen creeks of this name in Ozark county.

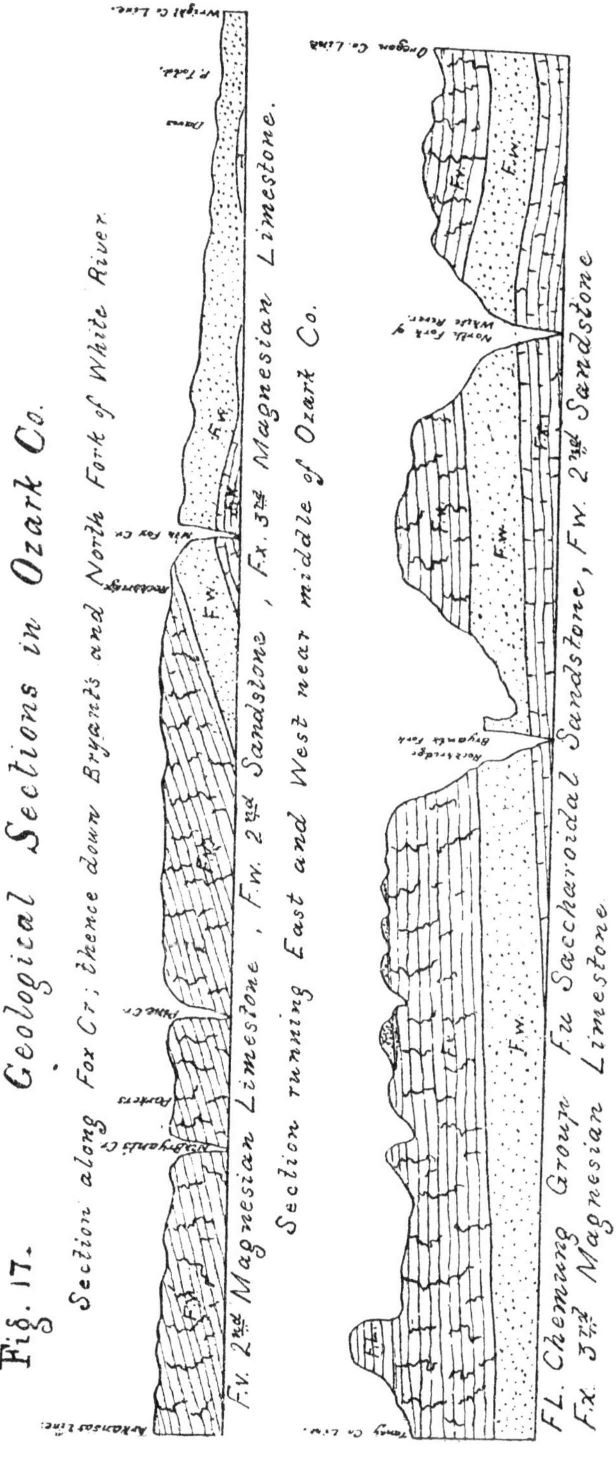
Fig. 17.
Geological Sections in Ozark Co.
Section along Fox Cr; thence down Bryant's and North Fork of White River
F.V. 2nd Magnesian Limestone, F.W. 2nd Sandstone, F.x. 3rd Magnesian Limestone.
Section running East and West near middle of Ozark Co.
FL. Chemung Group Fu Saccharoidal Sandstone, F.W. 2nd Sandstone
F.x 3rd Magnesian Limestone
Arkansas Line.
Wright Co. Line.
Oregon Co. Line
Taney Co. Line.
North Fork of White River.

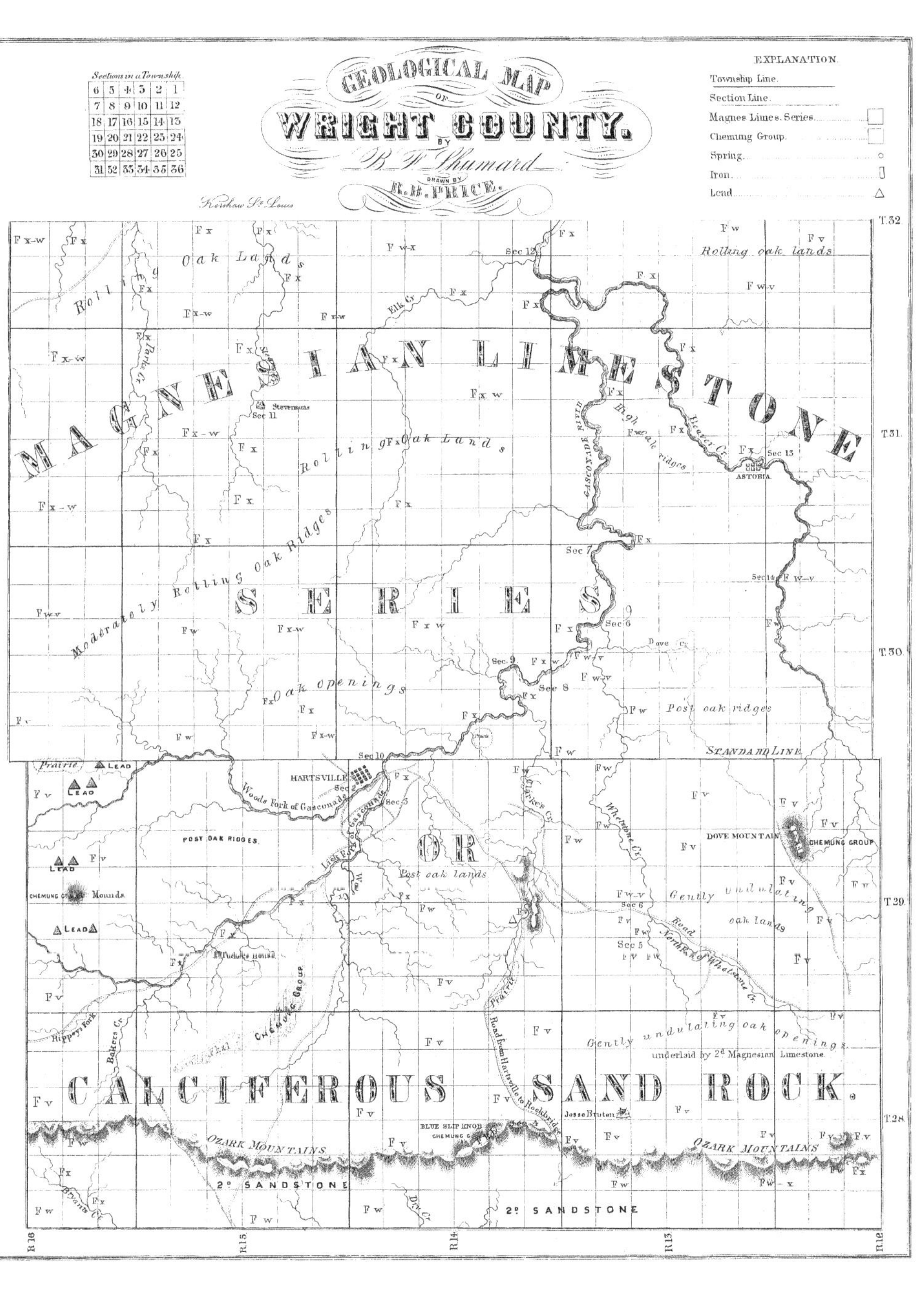
GEOLOGICAL MAP
OF
WRIGHT COUNTY.
BY
B. F. Shumard
DRAWN BY
R. B. PRICE.
Kershaw St. Louis
Sections in a Township
EXPLANATION.
Township Line.
Section Line.
Magnes Limes. Series.
Chemung Group.
Spring.
Iron.
Lead
MAGNESIAN LIMESTONE
SERIES
OR
CALCIFEROUS SAND ROCK.
Rolling Oak Lands
Rolling oak lands
Rolling Oak Lands
Moderately Rolling Oak Ridges
High oak ridges
Oak openings
Post oak ridges
STANDARD LINE
HARTSVILLE
POST OAK RIDGES
Post oak lands
DOVE MOUNTAIN
CHEMUNG GROUP
Mounds
Gently undulating oak lands
Gently undulating oak openings
underlaid by 2d Magnesian Limestone.
OZARK MOUNTAINS
2° SANDSTONE
BLUE SLIP KNOB
ASTORIA
Gasconade River
Woods Fork of Gasconade
Lick Fork of Gasconade
Elk Cr.
Beaver Cr.
Dove Cr.
Whetstone Cr.
Clarkes Cr.
Bakers Cr.
Rippeys Fork
Bryants Cr.
Road from Hartsville to Rockbridge
Road North of Whetstone Cr.
Tuckers House
Stevensons
Jesse Bruton
T.32
T.31
T.30
T.29
T.28
R 16
R 15
R 14
R 13
R 12

CHAPTER XI.

WRIGHT COUNTY.

BY B. F. SHUMARD.

This county embraces rather more than nineteen townships, or about 600 square miles. The surface is generally hilly, and occasionally rough and broken. The elevation of the hills ranges from 50 to 450 feet above the streams. Most frequently they are neatly rounded in their outlines, and present gradually ascending slopes, susceptible of a good state of cultivation. In the neighborhood of the Gasconade and some of its branches, their sides are often rough and precipitous. The Ozark Mountains (Hills would be most proper) traverse the southern tier of townships, and constitute the dividing range between the waters flowing northwardly into the Missouri, and those flowing in an opposite direction into White River. The bearing of this range is nearly east and west. From the north the ascent is rather moderate, but the southern slope usually exhibits steep declivities down to the valleys. Its general elevation may be stated at 300 feet, but in T. 28 N., R. 14 W., some rounded, conical eminences rise from it which are upward of 100 feet higher. Among these, Blue Slip Knob is the most conspicuous, and from its summit one may have a magnificent and picturesque view of Ozark connty. Nearly every part of Wright is supplied with clear streams—chiefly the Gasconade and its tributaries.

The geological formations in this county are the same as in Ozark, but we find some of them more extensively developed, and others more sparingly.

QUATERNARY DEPOSITS.

The alluvial bottoms are usually long, and vary from a hundred yards to a mile in width. The soil is, for the most part, rich and productive.

The *Bottom Prairie* is well developed in Wright county, being frequently met with in the valleys of the streams, though it is often covered with a thick accumulation of more recent deposit. The following section, taken at Mr. Stevenson's well, on Stein's Creek, T. 31, R. 15, Sec. 15, presents the usual characters of the formation :

No. 1. 4 feet dark vegetable loam.
No. 2. 20 feet reddish and yellowish clay, containing numerous fragments of chert.
No. 3. 8 to 10 feet tough, ash-colored clay, with small masses of ocher disseminated through it.
No. 4. 2 feet red clay, plastic and containing cream-colored spots.
No. 5. 9 feet red and yellowish clay, with carbonaceous stains.
No. 6. Silicious sand in bottom of well.

I have not observed any shells in the formation in this county.

The soil of the uplands is, of course, greatly modified by the character of the subjacent strata. Throughout much the largest portion of the county it is of excellent quality and produces well, while the land is just sufficiently undulating to secure the necessary amount of drainage. In places where the arenaceous and cherty beds of the Calciferous Sand-rock reach the surface, the soil is too thin and light, and is sometimes rendered unfit for cultivation by the large quantities of chert it contains.

CARBONIFEROUS SYSTEM.

On the summit of Blue Slip Knob, Dove Mount, the high divide between the Lick Fork of the Gasconade and Wolf Creek, and near Mr. Prock's, in T. 29, R. 16, we find a great deal of loose chert, filled with remains of Crinoids and Brachiopods characteristic of the Encrinital Limestone, but no regular strata of this formation have been met with in this county.

CHEMUNG GROUP?

This group is represented by the Vermicular Sandstone and shales, and the Lithographic Limestone, which occur in isolated patches only on the highest mounds of the county.

Vermicular Sandstone and Shales.

This formation occupies a narrow, crescent-shaped band, five or six miles in length, and from a-fourth to half a mile in width, on the elevated ridge between the Lick Fork of the Gasconade and Wolf Creek. It may be seen to the best advantage at a slide near the southern extremity of the ridge, where occurs an exposure of it of about forty feet. The upper part is a soft, buff Calcareo-magnesian Sandstone perforated with vermicular cavities, and contains *Fucoides Cauda-galli*, *Spirifer Missouriensis*, etc.; while the lower twenty-five feet consists of thin layers of blue and drab shale, with laminations of gray Limestone interstratified. The shales are replete with the characteristic fossils of the formation, among which the most common are *Spirifer Marionensis*, *Cyrtia acutirostris* and *Rhynconella Missouriensis*. In addition to these, we find here a pretty *Orthis* very abundant, two species of *Goniatites* and several *Gasteropods* distinct from any hitherto observed in the State. The fossils are usually casts, often composed of specular Iron ore and pyrites, and exhibiting occasionally, when broken open, perfectly formed crystals. The Vermicular Sandstone and shales, with the above characters, occur also near the top of Blue Slip and other knobs in its vicinity, and at the top of a conical mound on Mr. Prock's land, in T. 29, R. 16, Sec. 11. Mr. Hough also observed this formation at Dove Mount.

Lithographic Limestone.

Immediately beneath the Vermicular Sandstone and shales, we find a thin-bedded, light-colored Limestone containing *Chonetes ornata* and other Chemung fossils. These strata occupy the same relative position in the series as the Lithographic Limestone of the general section, to which formation I therefore refer them, although they do not possess the fine, smooth texture and conchoidal fracture of the lithographic rock on the Mississippi, but, on the contrary, are rather coarse-textured, sub-crystalline, and break with an uneven fracture. The thickness of these beds is from twenty-five to thirty feet, and they have only been observed on the high ridge between the Lick Fork of the Gasconade and Wolf Creek, but they probably exist under the Vermicular Sandstone and shales in other parts of the county.

CALCIFEROUS SAND ROCK.

The formations of this group lie directly beneath the Chemung, as in Ozark county. They are very extensively developed, forming the underlying rock of the entire county, save the few isolated patches above indicated as being occupied by the Chemung.

Saccharoid Sandstone.

This Sandstone exists on many of the higher elevations throughout the county, and its presence is generally recognized by detached masses lying over the surface. Rarely do we find good exposures of the strata. Not unfrequently we see mingled with the Sandstone large uneven masses of extremely hard silicious rock, vitrified, cellular and sometimes assuming the character of a quartz breccia. These masses probably once formed a part of this formation.

In T. 29, R. 14, sections 34 and 35, the Saccharoid Sandstone was seen reposing on the Second Magnesian Limestone in nearly horizontal beds. The layers are here quite thin, and many of them being indurated would answer well for flagging stones. This Sandstone was again observed resting on the bottom rock of the Second Magnesian Limestone in T. 30, R. 15, Sec. 28, in T. 30, R. 16, sections 19, 20, 29 and 30, and also in the north-east corner of the county, near the Osage Fork of the Gasconade.

I have not been able to see its thickness at any locality.

Second Magnesian Limestone.

This is the most important formation in the county. It presents a thickness of from 200 to 250 feet, and exists to a considerable extent in every township. The description I have given of it in Ozark county will pretty nearly apply to it here. Mr. Hough and myself made a great many sections of it in various portions of the county, from which I select the following one taken on the Gasconade near the mouth of Elk Creek. It gives a good view of the general features of the lower division of the formation in Wright:

No. 1. 35 feet slope; no rocks exposed.

No. 2. 6 feet perpendicular cliff of earthy, buff, Magnesian Limestone, containing calc-spar, passing downward into rather thick-bedded, gray Magnesian Limestone, with thin courses of dark and light chert and nodular masses of the same.

No. 3. 20 feet slope.

No. 4. 43 feet rough, broken chert and indurated Sandstone and Magnesian Limestone, the chert containing cavities occasionally lined with quartz crystals and chalcedony.

No. 5. 8 feet thin laminæ of greenish gray, fissile argillo-Magnesian Limestone, with thin bands of chert.

No. 6. 5½ feet Sandstone and Magnesian Limestone in alternating layers.

No. 7. 16 feet wall of compact Magnesian Limestone, containing chert and calc-spar.

No. 8. 55 feet slope, partly underlaid by Second Sandstone.

The upper part of the Second Magnesian Limestone everywhere consists of buff and cream-colored, earthy Magnesian Limestone (Cotton rock,) in even layers.

With these features the Second Magnesian Limestone may be constantly seen on the Gasconade and its branches, Wood's Fork, Lick Fork, Elk and Beaver creeks, and it is also occasionally finely displayed along the beautiful valleys of Parks, Stein's, Clark and Dove creeks, throughout nearly their entire extent. It is this formation that imparts to the bluffs of the streams in Wright their remarkable mural and picturesque appearance. The Cotton rock may, in general, be seen to the best advantage on the upper slopes and summits of the ridges.

Fossils.—The Second Magnesian Limestone of this county has not yielded fossils so abundantly as in Ozark. Nevertheless we have found them at a number of points, chiefly in the cherty debris of the formation. Near the mill on the Gasconade in T. 30, R. 13, Sec. 5, I found some thin, loose shales of calcareo-silicious rock, with *Straparollus bigranosus*,* *Chemnitzia*, and several specimens of the glabella and pygidium of *Arionellus* (?) *Missouriensis*. On Wood's Fork Mr. Hough found in the compact Magnesian beds with *Straparollus* and *Chemnitzia*, fragments of a trilobite, very similar to a species found by Mr. Broadhead in the Second Magnesian Limestone at Hermann, in Gasconade county.

SECOND SANDSTONE.

This rock presents the same lithological appearance in Wright county that it does in Ozark. It is well developed on the southern declivity of the Ozark range, where it is frequently seen beneath the Second Magnesian Limestone, presenting occasionally a thickness of one hundred feet and upward. The valley south of this range is also underlaid by this formation.

On Whetstone Creek this Sandstone first appears in T. 29, R. 13, Sec. 28, and thence continues uninterruptedly on both sides of the stream to its confluence with the Gasconade. As we approach the line between townships 29 and 30 it extends from a half to a mile east of Whetstone and on the west to Clark's Creek; but as we proceed north of this line it diminishes in width, and at the Gasconade receives a thick capping of Magnesian Limestone. Between Whetstone and Clark's Creek its thickness is about 130 feet. The lower part of the mass is in thick beds; the upper 30 feet is indurated, and in rather thinly laminated layers.

The Second Sandstone may also be frequently seen underlying the Second Magnesian Limestone in the bluffs of the Gasconade, Beaver, Lick Fork and Elk Creek. On these streams we scarcely ever find an exposure of more than fifty feet of the formation.

No fossils were discovered in the Second Sandstone in Wright county.

*This fossil is the most characteristic species of the Second Magnesian Limestone, both in this and Ozark county.

ECONOMICAL GEOLOGY.

SOILS.

In addition to what I have already said in relation to the soils of Wright county, when speaking of the Quaternary Deposits, I will merely observe, that under a proper system of cultivation, they are capable of supporting a large agricultural population, and are perhaps not inferior to those of any county in South-west Missouri. They are specially adapted to the raising of wheat, corn, oats and tobacco, and the prairie bottoms furnish excellent pasturage for cattle.

TIMBER.

The bottom lands of the streams bear often a thick growth of Hickory, Oak, Elm, Maple, Cottonwood and Black and White Walnut, and the uplands Black-jack, Post Oak, etc. There is therefore no lack of timber to supply the present and future demands of the county, and all the principal streams furnish water in abundance for mill sites.

IRON.

Masses of brown Hematite were observed in small quantities in the Second Magnesian Limestone on the Ozark Range and on the land in other portions of the county, but it was nowhere seen in sufficient quantity to justify the opinion that it could be worked to profit.

LEAD.

Galena has been found in small quantities at several localities in Wright county, always in the Second Magnesian Limestone.

In T. 29, R. 16, S. W. quarter of Sec. 11, Mr. J. P. Prock obtained about one hundred and fifty pounds of ore, in well-formed cubic crystals, from cavities in the Magnesian Limestone. The rock in which it occurs is compact, of sandy texture, and contains a good deal of calc-spar. This is the largest amount that has been obtained from any one place within the present limits of the county.* Mr. Prock also found small masses of *float mineral* in the S. E. quarter of Sec. 11, and N. E. quarter of Sec. 23, of same township and range.

On land belonging to Mr. Preston Prock, on a small branch of Wood's Fork, about a mile and a half east of the Webster county line, Lead occurs in the Cotton rock, and a half a mile both east and west

* Lead has been mined to a considerable extent in that part of the adjoining county of Webster which, at the last session of the Legislature, was separated from Wright county.

of this place it has been found in the same strata. At none of these localities does the ore occur in veins, but it is always found in bunches resting in cavities in the rock. On Mr. Sparks' land, in T. 29, R. 14, Sec. 23, Lead occurs in sandy Magnesian Limestone. About ten pounds of mineral have been obtained at this place.

COPPER.

In T. 28, R. 16, Sec. 23, Mr. Hough found small particles of the Green Carbonate of Copper disseminated through the calc-spar, which is here very abundant in Second Magnesian Limestone.

BUILDING MATERIALS.

The Second Magnesian Limestone and the Lithographic Limestone furnish good and durable rocks for building purposes, and the latter is abundant in nearly every part of the county.

THE COTTON ROCK

Of this county, as well as of Ozark, is a beautiful and excellent material for construction, while that composing the thicker and more compact Magnesian beds at the base of the formation, is especially adapted to the heavier kinds of masonry. The beds of the Second Sandstone may also be frequently found suitable for the construction of buildings, but as a general rule the Magnesian Limestones are to be preferred. The upper portion of the Second Sandstone on Whetstone Creek and the Gasconade exists often in thin, even layers, and these may be employed to advan-

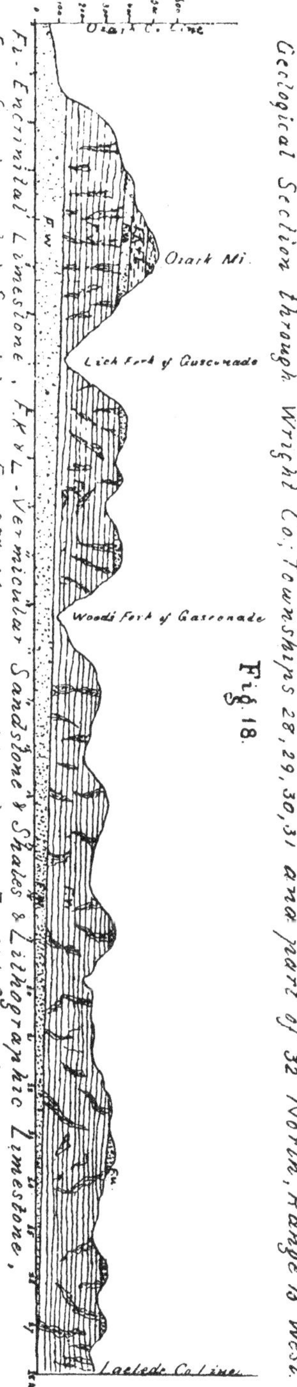

Geological Section through Wright Co. Townships 28, 29, 30, 31 and part of 32 North, Range 15 West.

Fig. 18.

tage for flagging stones and for hearths of furnaces and chimney places.

Materials for Brick-making

Of good quality are furnished by the sands and clays of the Quaternary formation, both on the uplands and in the alluvial bottoms.

Limestone.

The Lithographic Limestone of the Chemung will burn into a white, pure quick-lime, and is the best rock in the county for this purpose. When this rock can not be readily obtained, the compact beds of the Second Magnesian Limestone will answer a very good purpose. Some of the beds contain a good deal of calcareous spar, which is recognized by its glassy appearance, and these should be selected for burning in preference to the earthy-looking layers.

Hydraulic Lime.

Some of the Cotton rock strata apparently possess hydraulic properties.

Sand

For glass-making and mortar may be obtained in inexhaustible quantities from the Second Sandstone formation.

Buhr-Stone.

The large silicious masses which occur frequently on the tops of the high ridges in various parts of the county, often have the cellular and other appearances of a good quality of Buhr-stone.

CHAPTER XII.

LACLEDE COUNTY.

BY B. F. SHUMARD.

Laclede county has nearly 22 townships, and about 790 square miles. Its topographical features are very similar to those of Wright county, although it presents greater variety of surface. It varies from gently rolling prairie to rough and rugged hills, which are scarcely fit for cultivation. Generally, as we approach the larger water-courses, the land assumes a remarkably rough and broken character. In the vicinity of the Big Niangua, Gasconade, and its principal affluent, the Osage Fork, we find hills from 150 to 450 feet in hight, with abrupt, rocky slopes, and separated by deep and narrow valleys. But, after we leave these streams a short distance, the surface of the country loses its abrupt character, and as we reach the summit level between the Osage Fork and Gasconade and the upland east of the latter stream, we encounter moderately rolling lands and broad flats, bearing, chiefly, Post and White Oak, with some Black-jack and Black Hickory. Throughout these areas many excellent and productive farms may be selected. Between the Osage Fork and waters of the Gasconade, we find a broad and fertile district of undulating woodland, interrupted occasionally by extensive patches of beautiful prairie.

VALLEYS.

The valleys of Osage Fork and Gasconade, which are the largest in the county, vary from a fourth to a mile in width. They possess a rich soil, and are heavily timbered, chiefly with White and Sugar Maple, White and Black Walnut, White and Burr Oak, Buckeye, Shellbark and several other varieties of Hickory, Ash, Sycamore, Hackberry, Spicewood, Pawpaw and Dogwood.

Along the course of nearly all the smaller streams, we find valleys from 100 yards to half a mile wide. Some of them are extremely beautiful, presenting long undulating bands of rich prairie and woodland, bounded on either side by low hills, with gentle slopes, and often very graceful in outline. These valleys possess highly fertile soils, and afford some of the finest farms in the county. Among these the valleys of Goodwin Hollow, Dry Auglaize, Bear, Mill, Cobb's, Brush and Prairie Creeks are particularly worthy of being mentioned.

STREAMS.

Nearly every portion of Laclede county is well irrigated, as will be seen upon examining the map accompanying this report, which represents a multitude of streams meandering through all parts of it. The largest are the Gasconade, Osage Fork and Niangua Rivers. They are very crooked, the water remarkably clear, and their currents swift. They are capable of furnishing an abundance of the very best water-power.

QUATERNARY DEPOSITS.

Besides the superficial deposits, such as soil and detritus, we recognize in Laclede the "Bottom Prairie," and perhaps the equivalent of the Bluff formation.

The *Bottom Prairie*, wherever seen, presents the same characters as in Wright county, and therefore it need not be again described here. There is reason to believe that it exists in the valleys of many of the streams; but as few excavations of any considerable depth have been made for wells and other purposes in the county, its extent could not be determined. Very often it is covered with thick accumulations of comminuted chert derived from the destruction of the older strata.

Bluff Formation.—In this formation we are disposed to group the red Clays and Sand, which are everywhere met with beneath the soil and subsoil of the uplands of Laclede. It usually exists as tough, reddish loam, with courses of Sand occasionally interstratified, and remarkably free of coarser materials; at other times it abounds with small, angular fragments of chert. Its thickness was found to vary from 2 feet to 30 feet, and it was usually observed reposing on beds of flint. In a well sunk by Mr. Appling, in T. 32, R. 16, N. E. quarter of Sec. 13, we found the following Section:

No. 1. 4 feet soil and subsoil.
No. 2. 20 feet Brick-red Clay, very tough, and containing fragments of chert.
No. 3. 36 feet comminuted chert.

In a second well, also on Mr. Appling's land, the Section is—

No. 1. 4 feet soil and subsoil.
No. 2. 16 feet tough red Clay.
No. 3. 6 feet loose silicious Sand.

PALEOZOIC ROCKS.

The Paleozoic strata of Laclede county belong exclusively to the inferior part of the Lower Silurian system, or to the Magnesian Limestone series. The subdivisions of this series which we have observed here are the Saccharoid Sandstone, Second Magnesian Limestone, Second Sandstone and the Third Magnesian Limestone. The strata of these several formations present but little evidence of disturbance throughout the county. Occasionally we have observed local undulations, but usually the beds are found to maintain nearly a horizontal position.

Saccharoid Sandstone.

This formation prevails to a very limited extent in Laclede, and it was not anywhere seen in regular beds. Large fragments of it were found on the highest points of the dividing ridge between Osage Fork and Prairie Creek, and also on the high ridge east of the Gasconade, in T. 33, R. 12. At these places it is more indurated than we find it in the counties further east.

Second Magnesian Limestone.

The Second Magnesian Limestone is well displayed in Laclede. It occurs in almost every township excepting the half townships in the south-western part of the county. It is generally a buff, earthy Magnesian Limestone, sometimes soft and sometimes very compact in its texture, and usually breaking with a conchoidal fracture. Now and then the layers contain small crystals of calc-spar, and sometimes small, rounded masses of compact quartz. Near the junction of the formation with the underlying Second Sandstone, we most commonly find a few feet of alternations of hard Silico-magnesian Limestone and rough Sandstone, in thin layers, and deeply stained with iron. To these succeed from ten to twenty feet of soft, earthy Magnesian Limestone, above which we have the "Quarry Rock"—a tolerably compact, dark-gray, sub-crystalline Dolomite, mottled with small patches and veins of whitish, decomposing Dolomite, appearing on the weathered surface like fucoids. These beds vary from four inches to two feet in thickness, and are wrought somewhat extensively for building purposes. They are succeeded by thin and even-bedded, earthy Magnesian Limestone, which is generally of a uniform cream or buff color. The entire thickness of the formation has not been seen at any locality in Laclede county. The greatest development observed is on Cymblin Creek, in T. 35, R. 14, N. E. quarter of Sec. 28' where it presents a section of about one hundred and forty feet. Near the Gasconade, in T. 35, R. 14, S. W. of Sec. 10, it appears to the hight of ninety feet, and on the Osage Fork, in T. 34, R. 14, N. E. of Sec. 4, it is well exhibited to the hight of eighty-six feet.

The Second Magnesian Limestone occupies the highest parts of the county, and wherever it prevails we find a gently undulating country, well suited for farming purposes. The town of Lebanon is underlaid by this rock, and from thence it may be traced almost continuously in every direction for several miles. To the west and southwest it prevails to within a couple of miles of Spring, Hollow and Brush Creeks. It also occupies the higher parts of the country between those streams, and that between Bear and Mill Creeks. North of Lebanon, we find it developed in the prairies between Goodwin Hollow and the Dry Auglaize, and on the east side of the latter stream it extends to the Camden county line. Again, it forms all the higher parts of the ridge over which runs the line of the Pacific Railroad, and it is largely developed on the upland between the Osage Fork and Gasconade, and also on the upland east of the latter stream.

Fossils.—The Second Magnesian Limestone of Laclede has not yielded many fossils. They were only seen at a few points, and even then were so badly preserved as to not permit us to determine their specific character. They belong to the genera *Straparollus* and *Murchisonia*.

SECOND SANDSTONE.

This formation was frequently observed reposing on the Third Magnesian Limestone. It presents usually the same features described on pages 125 and 126 of the Second Geological Report. Its greatest development is in the vicinity of the Niangua, where it attains a thickness of from 60 to 70 feet. Its thickness is very variable in Laclede county, varying from 10 to 70 feet. It sometimes occurs in thin layers and sometimes in heavy massive beds. When well developed, as near the Niangua, we find the country much broken and the land sterile and scarcely fit for cultivation. The Second Sandstone is frequently exposed near the summits of the bluffs of the Gasconade and Osage Fork, where it is often found passing rapidly into compact and cellular chert. It is this rock, in connection with the Third Magnesian Limestone, that imparts to the bluffs of those streams their bold and abrupt character. This Sandstone occurs throughout the whole course of Mill Creek, and is quite common on Bear and Cymblin Creeks. It is also occasionally exhibited on Brush, Cobb's, Panther and Spring Hollow Creeks.

THIRD MAGNESIAN LIMESTONE.

This formation is largely developed, both vertically and horizontally, in Laclede county. In general lithological features it accords with those described in the Second Geological Report, on page 125. Nevertheless, we find some local variations of the beds at different points. The inferior part of the formation is usually an even-bedded, gray and buff Magnesian Limestone, of a sub-crystalline structure. Some of the beds are quite compact and fine-textured, and others are soft and of a sandy texture. The upper division of the formation consists for the most part of formations of chert and Magnesian Limestone, and occasionally beds of Sandstone. The chert and Magnesian Limestone frequently pass one into another in very short distances, so that sections of parallel beds, taken at points not far apart, present strongly marked differences. Thus, near Pine Creek, T. 33, R. 13, Sec. 34, Mr. Engelmann obtained a section as follows:

No. 1. 30 feet slope, covered with chert and cherty Sandstone.
No. 2. 2 feet compact, sub-crystalline Magnesian Limestone.
No. 3. 19 feet alternations of chert and gray sub-crystalline Magnesian Limestone.
No. 4. ½ foot fine-grained earthy Magnesian Limestone.

No. 5. 10 feet compact Magnesian Limestone; some beds coarse-grained; some cherty.
No. 6. 17½ feet hard Magnesian Limestone and chert.
No. 7. 7 feet thick-bedded, compact, light gray Dolomite.
No. 8. 8 feet cherty Magnesian Limestone.
No. 9. 10 feet Talus.

On the Gasconade, in T. 34, R. 13, Sec. 23, a section of the equivalent part of this formation is:

No. 1. 20 feet slope, strewn with chert and cherty Sandstone.
No. 2. 9 feet alternations of Sandstone and Dolomite, the latter sometimes oolitic.
No. 3. 20½ feet heavy beds of light gray, sub-crystalline Magnesian Limestone, Sandstone and chert, containing sometimes translucent quartz grains, which impart to the rock an oolitic structure.
No. 4. 33 feet cherty Magnesian Limestone.
No. 5. 6 feet sandy textured Magnesian Limestone.
No. 5. 50 feet alternations of chert and Dolomite.
No. 7. 1½ feet compact, silico-Magnesian Limestone, some of the layers passing into Sandstone.
No. 8. 9½ feet fine-grained, close-textured Dolomite.
No. 9. 3 feet bench of chert.

The Third Magnesian Limestone may be seen in the cuts of nearly all the streams of the county, but it is best displayed on the Niangua, Osage Fork and Gasconade rivers, and Mountain, Woolsey's, Stein's, South, Cobb's and Goodwin Hollow Creeks. On these streams it exhibits those bold and picturesque escarpments so characteristic of the formation wherever it occurs in Missouri.

On the Niangua it sometimes presents many vertical cliffs, from 200 to 300 feet high, and on the Gasconade and Osage Fork from 100 to 200 feet. In the bluffs of the smaller streams it exhibits a thickness of from 20 to 100 feet. Wherever the cherty beds of the formation lie near the surface, the country becomes very broken, and the soil is quite barren, from the immense quantity of fragments of this rock it contains. We often find accumulations of this broken material many feet in depth, and covering wide areas.

Fossils.—As far as our observations extend, organic remains are of uncommon occurrence in the Third Magnesian Limestone of Laclede county. On the Osage Fork, Gasconade and Mill Creek, we found *Straparollus acuto-carinatus*, and two or three species of *Murchisonia* identical with some that occur in the same formation in Ozark and Wright counties. They were observed only in the cherty beds of the mass.

ECONOMICAL GEOLOGY.

The soils of Laclede county present considerable variety. Those forming the alluvial bottoms of the streams are the richest in the county. They are derived partly from the destruction of the Third Magnesian Limestone and partly from the subjacent bottom prairie. They all contain a large admixture of vegetable mold. The soils of the larger water-courses are remarkable for their fertility, and support a heavy growth of the finest kinds of timber. They are capable of producing excellent crops of corn, hemp and oats, and after being under cultivation for several years, so as to exhaust them in part, they become excellent wheat lands. The bottoms of the smaller streams are not so heavily timbered, but are scarcely inferior in point of fertility. Among these we may cite the bottom lands of Goodwin Hollow, Dry Auglaize, Prairie, Bear, Brush, Stein's and Cobb's Creeks, as affording farms scarcely inferior to any to be found in the State.

UPLAND SOILS.

The soils overlying the Second Magnesian and the calcareous parts of the Third Magnesian Limestones come next to the bottoms in point of fertility. Some of the best upland soils are derived from the Quaternary red loam, which, as already stated, is extensively spread over the older rocks of the higher grounds of the county. These soils vary much in character. Sometimes they are light colored, clayey and wet in the spring, particularly in what are called the Post-Oak flats, but most generally we find them to possess the requisite proportions of Clay, Sand and vegetable matter to constitute valuable farming lands. Townships 33, 34, 35 and 36, of ranges 15, 16 and 17 west, contain large tracts of valuable upland, with timber in abundance for fencing and other purposes. These lands are capable of being vastly improved by deep and thorough subsoil plowing; and I do not hesitate to say that even the worst of the so-called wet Post Oak flats may be converted into valuable farms by one or two thorough subsoilings.

The poorest soils of the county are those overlying the Second Sandstone, and chert beds of the Third Magnesian Limestone. When these rocks reach the surface, the soil contains so much Sand or chert as to render it almost worthless.

IRON ORE.

Fragments of brown and specular Iron ore were observed at a number of points in the county, but only in small quantities, scattered over the surface of the hills occupied by the Third Magnesian Limestone and Second Sandstone. Mr. Engelmann observed large masses of brown Hematite near Bear Creek, in T. 36, R. 14, Sec. 25. On Fielding Clark's land, in T. 36, R. 16, Sec. 5, an impure earthy variety occurs, associated with Galena.

LEAD.

Although the Third Magnesian Limestone, which, in counties further east, has yielded such enormous quantities of Galena, is extensively developed in Laclede, we have observed it to occur only in a single locality—to wit: on Fielding Clark's land, in T. 36, R. 16, N. W. quarter of Sec. 5. At this place a few shallow excavations have been made in a soft variety of the Third Magnesian Limestone, and a few pounds of the Sulphuret of Lead got out. The ore occurs disseminated through an impure brown Iron ore, 200 yards distant from an igneous dyke of Granite. This locality is worthy of being further proved. It is not improbable that other deposits of this valuable metal will be found in Laclede county.

BUILDING MATERIALS.

The calcareous portions of the Third Magnesian Limestone furnish a good and durable building material, and this rock may be found in nearly every part of the county. The inferior part of the formation is usually the best, as it does not contain much silicious matter, and blocks from one to four feet thick may be got out. The Second Magnesian Limestone also yields excellent materials for construction. The dark-gray Dolomite, with vermiform bodies, near the base of the formation, is used somewhat extensively in the county for the underpinning of buildings, and for chimneys and hearths. It generally lies in even beds, from ten to eighteen inches thick; is easily quarried, and dresses well. Its texture and composition indicate that it is calculated to withstand the action of the weather for a long period.

Quarries have been opened in this rock on the divide near the head of Bear Creek, and near the Dry Auglaize, in T. 36, R. 15, Sec. —.

The entire thickness of the beds at these quarries is from twelve to fifteen feet. The Second Sandstone may also be used as a building rock, but it is inferior to the Dolomites.

FIRE-STONES, FLAGGING-STONES, ETC.

The quarry rock of the Second Magnesian Limestone furnishes a good material for the construction of the backs and jambs of chimney-places. The Second Sandstone may also be advantageously employed for this purpose. The latter is often quite refractory, and may be used for the hearths of iron and other furnaces. Some layers of this Sandstone are quite thin, and sufficiently indurated to answer very well for flagging and paving-stones.

MILL-STONES.

Very often we find the Second Sandstone composed of grains firmly cemented with a silicious paste, and this variety may be employed for mill-stones. At Cherry's grist-mill, on the Osage Fork, I saw a set of stones, made from this rock, that have been in constant use for upward of twenty years, and I am assured by Mr. Cherry that the farmers prefer the meal made by these stones to that made by the French Buhr. They were quarried in T. 34, R. 14, Sec. 16. The same rock exists also at a number of points on the Gasconade and Osage Fork Rivers.

LIMESTONE FOR LIME.

The Third Magnesian Limestone abounds in strata that may be burned for lime. The more crystalline portions should, of course, be employed for this purpose.

ROAD MATERIALS.

The comminuted chert which we find so abundant in the beds of nearly all the streams, and on the hill-sides, where the Third Magnesian Limestone prevails, is a most excellent material for macadamizing roads. It combines cheapness with durability, and should always be preferred to the Dolomites, which are more readily crumbled to powder. It can nearly always be found in fragments sufficiently small to be at once applied to the grades.

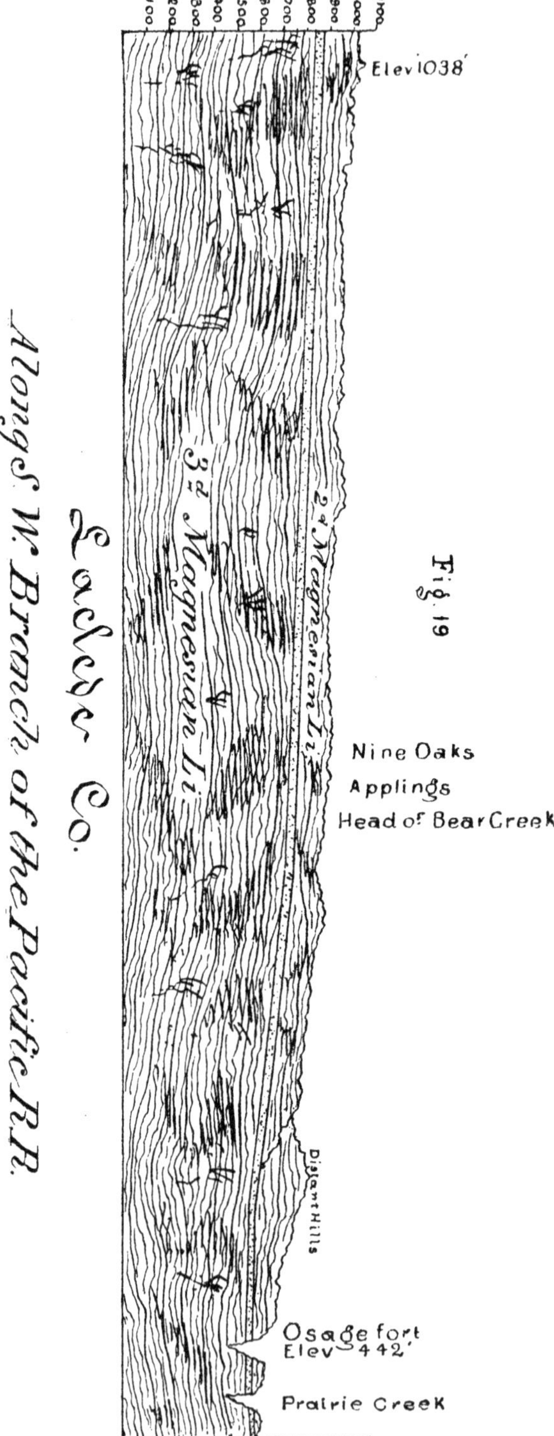

100
200
300
400
500
600
700
800
900
1000
1100
Elev 1038'
Fig. 19
2d Magnesian Li.
3d Magnesian Li.
Nine Oaks
Applings
Head of Bear Creek
Distant Hills
Osage fort
Elev 442'
Prairie Creek
Laclede Co.
Along S. W. Branch of the Pacific R.R.

CHAPTER XIII.

PULASKI COUNTY.

BY B. F. SHUMARD.

Pulaski county embraces an area of nearly six hundred and fifteen square miles. The county is in general very hilly and broken, but there are extensive districts of rich and productive agricultural lands in the alluvial bottoms of the streams, as well as in the uplands. The hills range from fifty to five hundred or more feet above the general level of the adjacent water-courses. Along the principal streams the scenery is remarkably bold and picturesque. The Gasconade and Big Piney Rivers, and Robideaux, Spring, Musgrove and Baldridge Creeks are often escarped with long lines of bluffs, which present occasionally perfectly perpendicular rocky faces more than two hundred feet in hight. If we travel back from the streams, avoiding the valleys of the smaller branches, we pretty constantly encounter at first very rough hills with rapid declivities, covered with chert and Sandstone; afterward the surface often becomes gently rolling, or expands into level plains, forming what are known in the county as "Post Oak Flats." These flats occur on the summits of most of the higher ridges. They have a width of from a hundred yards to a couple of miles, and bear a growth of chiefly Post Oak, Black-jack and Black Hickory. For a short time during the spring these lands are occasionally wet, but after they have once been effectually "broken up" by the plow, they are no longer so, but form good and very desirable farming lands. The most extensive flats are situated between the Gasconade, Robideaux and Big Piney, and to the east of the latter stream. They also occur on the dividing ridges of the small streams of the northern part of the county. The hills in the vicinity of the streams, though often exceedingly rough and unfit for cultivation, are still valuable on account of the heavy growth of excellent timber that is found upon them.

VALLEYS.

The valleys of the Gasconade, Big Piney Rivers and Robideaux and Spring Creeks are from a few hundred yards to a mile wide. They are remarkable for the richness and fertility of their soils throughout their whole extent in the county. They may be classed among the very finest soils of the State for the culture of corn, and after they are partially exhausted form the best of lands for raising wheat and other varieties of small grain. They bear a very heavy growth of White, Burr and Scarlet Oak, White and Sugar Maple, Shell-bark Hickory, White and Slippery Elm, Dogwood, Cottonwood, Ash, Linden, Elder, Grape, Hackberry and White and Black Walnut. The valleys of most of the small streams of Pulaski have also rich and productive soils, and some of the choicest farms in the county are to be found here. These valleys do not usually exceed a quarter of a mile in width, but often have a length of several miles. Their surface is for the most part level or gently undulating, and bounded on either side by gently rounded hills, which have sometimes a very beautiful and pleasing appearance. In Southern Missouri these narrow valleys are commonly known under the name of "Prairie Hollows."

STREAMS.

All parts of Pulaski are intersected by streams of the purest water. The largest is the Gasconade River, which first enters the south-western corner of the county, and after running a few miles in a general north-westerly course, enters Laclede, where it makes a curve easterly to re-enter Pulaski in the north-west corner of T. 35, R. 13, whence it pursues a general E. N. E. direction, traversing the entire length of the county. It has a swift current, and is exceedingly crooked throughout its entire course. It is capable of affording any quantity of the finest water power. The next in magnitude is Big Piney River, which enters the south-eastern portion of the county, and runs in a general course north through the western tier of townships to its confluence with the Gasconade. Although a crooked stream, the current is not so rapid as the Gasconade. It is navigable during certain periods of the year, and large quantities of lumber are annually rafted down this stream from Texas county. The Gasconade and Piney both receive a multitude of small confluents from all parts of the county.

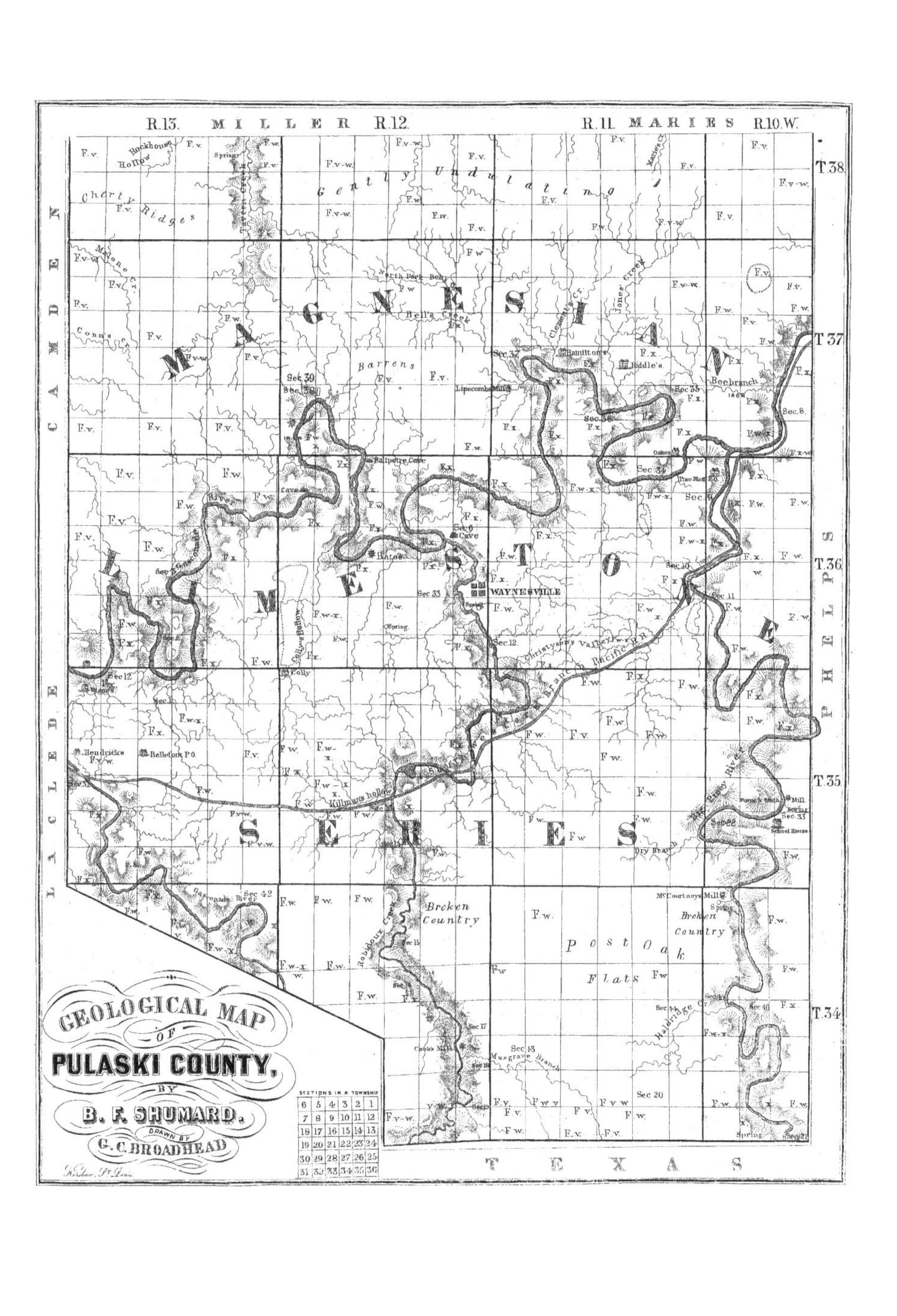
GEOLOGICAL MAP
OF
PULASKI COUNTY,
BY
B. F. SHUMARD.
DRAWN BY
G. C. BROADHEAD
SECTIONS IN A TOWNSHIP
6 5 4 3 2 1
7 8 9 10 11 12
18 17 16 15 14 13
19 20 21 22 23 24
30 29 28 27 26 25
31 32 33 34 35 36
R.13.
MILLER
R.12.
R.11.
MARIES
R.10.W.
T.38.
T.37
T.36.
T.35.
T.34.
CAMDEN
LACLEDE
PHELPS
TEXAS
MAGNESIAN
LIMESTONE
SERIES
Gently Undulating
Cherty Ridges
Barrens
Broken Country
Post Oak
Flats
WAYNESVILLE
Pacific R.R.
Gasconade River
Big Piney River
Roubidoux Creek
Bell's Creek
Jones' Creek
Saltpetre Cave
Lipscomb's Mill
McCourtneys Mill
Cook's Mill
Musgrave Branch
Dry Branch
Beebranch
Bellefont P.O.
Hendricks
Sec 33
Sec 12
Sec 42
Sec 20

QUATERNARY DEPOSITS.

The superficial deposits of Pulaski county may be classed as Alluvium, Bottom Prairie and Bluff. The Alluvium embraces the different varieties of soils, with their underlying clays and beds of comminuted chert, which are found both on the uplands and river bottoms. The soils of the larger bottoms contain a great deal of humus and decaying vegetable matter, and the beds of all the streams are generally covered with rolled and angular fragments of flint.

The subjoined section, taken in the valley of a small tributary of the Gasconade, in Sec. 4, T. 36, R. 13, forms a good example of the character of the surface deposits in other parts of the county:

No. 1. 3 feet dark soil and subsoil.
No. 2. 4 feet reddish Clay, containing a good deal of finely broken chert.
No. 3. 3 feet reddish arenaceous Clay.
No. 4. 5 feet bed of broken chert, with some reddish Clay.
No. 5. 2 feet reddish arenaceous Clay.
No. 6. 3 feet same as No. 4.
No. 7. 1 foot same as No. 3.
No. 8. 5 feet same as No. 4.
No. 9. 7 feet chert; the fragments larger than in upper beds, with some reddish Clay.
No. 10. 3 feet cherty beds of Third Magnesian Limestone.

Bottom Prairie.—Underneath the above deposits we sometimes find light gray and ash-colored loam and tough blue Clays, sometimes variegated, which, for the present, we place with the Bottom Prairie. They are rarely to be seen in the county, though it is probable they exist in the bottoms of most of the streams. In the few places where the formation has been seen, we have not been able to detect any fossils in it.

Bluffs.—In this county, as in Laclede, we generally find beneath the soil and subsoil of the hills and table lands, deposits of reddish Clay and Sand, the former being sometimes highly arenaceous, which we refer, provisionally, to the age of the Bluff formation. It sometimes attains a thickness of 30 feet.

PALÆOZOIC ROCKS.

There is but little variety among the older rocks of Pulaski county. The strata all belong to the Magnesian Limestone series, certain members of which are here strongly developed. We recognize the Second Magnesian Limestone, Second Sandstone and Third Magnesian Limestone.

Second Magnesian Limestone.

This formation is chiefly exhibited in the northern and eastern parts of the county, where it occurs generally on the highest parts of the hills. Mr. Engelmann describes it as a thin-bedded and even-bedded, dark gray Dolomite, with numerous small, irregular cavities, filled with light pulverulent Limestone, and underlaid by thick beds of fine textured, compact, light gray Magnesian Limestone. The entire thickness of the formation has not been seen at any locality in the county, the lower beds only being represented. It is constantly met with reposing on the Second Sandstone on the dividing ridges between the small streams on the north and west of the Gasconade. Whenever it constituted the surface rocks we find a gently undulating country provided with an arable soil. The best exposures are to be found near the northern boundary line of the county. The finest upland soils are to be found where this formation prevails. It is not improbable that the Post Oak Flats, between Robideaux and Piney, and those west of Piney, may be in part underlaid by this formation. This, however, can not now be determined, as no excavations have been made down to the older rocks in these situations.

Second Sandstone, F. *w*.

The Second Sandstone is an important formation in Pulaski; there is not a township in the county that does not contain a greater or less development of it. We find it capping nearly all the bluffs of the Gasconade, and frequently those of the Robideaux. It forms the surface rock over large areas between the Gasconade, Robideaux and Piney. In fact, as soon as we leave the valleys of these streams we find it everywhere strewn over the surface of the hills, on the slopes of which it is sometimes so abundant as to render the land sterile and unfit for cultivation. This formation is also frequently encountered on the north side of the Gasconade. It is this Sandstone, together with the cherty beds of the underlying Third Magnesian Limestone, which gives to portions of Pulaski county their exceedingly rough and broken character. The sections given below will convey a just idea of the lithological character of the different members of the formation as observed in the county.

Section taken on Robideaux Creek, T. 32, R. 12, Sec. 36.

No. 1. 15 feet alternations of Sandstone and chert projecting from a slope.

No. 2. 15 feet heavy bedded Sandstone, composed of coarse and fine crystalline grains, the weathered surface sometimes partially vitrified.

No. 3. 8 feet slope covered with heavy masses of Sandstone.
No. 4. 6 feet rough broken chert, with bands of Silicious Magnesian Limestone.
No. 5. 15 feet rough chert, in thick, irregular beds.
No. 6. 9 feet slope covered with rough masses of chert.
No. 7. 9 feet hard, firmly cemented Sandstone and chert.

On the Gasconade, in T. 35, R. 13, Sec. 19, Mr. Engelmann obtained the following section:

No. 1. 20 feet slope, covered with immense blocks of Sandstone.
No. 2. 2 feet bed of chert.
No. 3. 4 feet compact Magnesian Limestone.
No. 4. 18 feet alternation of Sandstone and sandy-textured Magnesian Limestone.
No. 5. Soft, heavy-bedded white Sandstone.
No. 6. 71 feet heavy-bedded Third Magnesian Limestone.

From the foregoing section, it will be seen that the Second Sandstone of Pulaski county contains some calcareous strata, as well as beds of chert. Indeed, it is very variable in its characters throughout the county, changing often very suddenly from pure Sandstone into chert, and from chert to Magnesian Limestone, in very short distances. It is rare to find two sections agree in all particulars, even when they are taken at points not far apart; the beds vary from three inches to several feet in thickness; some layers are quite soft, others approaching almost to quartzite in hardness. The thickness of the formation is also quite variable; it may be stated at from 20 to 100 feet, the most commonly observed thickness being from 50 to 60 feet. It is best developed near Cook's mill, in the S. W. part of the county, where it presented a thickness of upward of 100 feet.

THIRD MAGNESIAN LIMESTONE.

This formation is enormously developed in Pulaski county. It constitutes the bluffs of all the large streams, and presents a thickness which can not be estimated at less than 500 or 600 feet. The best exhibitions of it are to be found on the Gasconade and Piney, where it appears in a succession of elevated bluffs, first on one and then on the other side of the streams, presenting often perpendicular walls of more than 200 feet in hight. These bluffs are usually discolored by Oxide of Iron, and are often cleft from base to summit by deep, vertical fissures; they are also frequently cavernous, but we have not found the caves to be of any considerable magnitude, their length seldom exceeding 100 or 200 yards from the entrance. This formation is also exhibited in cuts of all the streams flowing into the Gasconade, and wherever the calcareous beds reach the surface we find a gently rolling country, well suited for cultivation; but on the contrary, where the silicious beds form the surface rocks, the country becomes very uneven and rocky.

No. 1. 2 feet rough and rugged chert.
No. 2. 57 feet compact and sandy-textured crystalline Magnesian Limestone, of a light gray color, in beds from a few inches to three feet thick.
No. 3. 2 feet band of chert.
No. 4. 39 feet sandy-textured, light gray, calcareo-Magnesian Limestone — a good building rock.
No. 5. 10 feet chert.
No. 6. 5 feet Magnesian Limestone.
No. 7. 30 feet chert, in rough, massive beds.
No. 8. 5 feet sandy-textured, light gray, calcareo-Magnesian Limestone.
No. 9. 2 feet chert.
No. 10. 51 feet Talus, probably underlaid by calcareo-Magnesian Limestone.

On Robideaux Creek, at Waynesville, Mr. Engelmann obtained the following section of the Third Magnesian Limestone:

No. 1. 20 feet slope, covered with rugged chert.
No. 2. 3 feet beds of chert.
No. 3. 7 feet sandy-textured Magnesian Limestone, with courses of chert.
No. 4. 5 feet alternations of chert and Limestone; some layers of oolite.
No. 5.
No. 6. 1 foot Sandstone.
No. 7. 30 feet cavernous, fine-textured, gray Magnesian Limestone, very much fractured.
No. 8. 25 feet, more crystalline, sandy-textured Magnesian Limestone; some layers highly granular.
No. 9. 13 feet compact, brecciated chert, and layers of compact and granular Magnesian Limestone.
No. 10. 15 feet sandy-textured Magnesian Limestone.
No. 11. 15 feet chert and Magnesian Limestone.
No. 12. 8 feet compact, light gray, sub-crystalline Magnesian Limestone.
No. 13. 2 feet band of chert.
No. 14. 50 feet sandy-textured Magnesian Limestone.

Fossils. — The cherty beds contain Gasteropoda, chiefly of the genus *Plutoromaria* and *Straparollus*; we found, however, only fragments, which are scarcely perfect enough to permit us to recognize their specific characters with certainty.

ECONOMICAL GEOLOGY.

SOILS.

But little more is necessary than to briefly recapitulate what has already been said in relation to the soils of this county. The richest soils are found in the valleys of the principal streams, including the Robideaux; throughout all their meanderings we find the excellent farms and farm sites, capable of supporting a dense agricultural population. The next soils in point of fertility are those of the smaller streams, which, though not so rich as those of the Gasconade and Piney, are still first rate soils, and produce well such crops as are adapted to the climate. The next best soils are those overlying the Second Magnesian Limestone, and are also quite productive; the land is usually just sufficiently undulating to allow easy drainage. Next in order comes the soil of the Post Oak flats, which are usually light colored and clayey, but when properly soiled, are capable of yielding well. The poorest soils are those overlying the Second Sandstone, and chert beds of the Magnesian Limestone; these generally prevail on the hills in the vicinity of the streams, sometimes extending back for a distance of one or two miles. But often where the Sandstone prevails, we find good, arable lands, as toward the heads of Robideaux and Spring Creeks.

IRON ORE.

This highly important mineral has been observed at a number of localities in Pulaski county; loose masses of it were frequently encountered scattered over the ridges, where cherty beds of the Third Magnesian Limestone and Second Sandstone prevail. Brown Hematite occurs in many places along the bluffs of the Gasconade and Piney. A large deposit of Specular Iron ore, of excellent quality, similar to that used at the Meramec Iron Works, in Phelps county, was examined by Mr. Engelmann, in T. 37, R. 12, Sec. 31; the ore was found thickly strewn over the surface in large and small masses, some of which were partly converted into brown Hematite. No workings have been carried on here, although it is probable the deposit is quite extensive.

About a mile and a quarter from Waynesville, in T. 36, R. 11, N. E. quarter of Sec. 30, is a large deposit of Iron ore in a declivity of a ridge composed of Third Magnesian Limestone, surmounted by Second Sandstone. The ore is chiefly brown Hematite, of fair workable quality. It occurs in the cherty beds of the Magnesian Limestone and Sandstone, and thickly covers a space of 50 or 60 square yards. Some of the masses are upward of three feet in diameter. Large masses of brown Hematite were also found on the hills of Bee Branch in T. 37, R. 10, and at Mr. Hamer's, on Big Piney, near the engineer s office on the Pacific railroad. Sulphate of Iron in small quantities occurs in a cave in T. 36, R. 8, Sec. 19. It is found also in abundance on Mr. Laquey's land, in T. 38, R. 13, Sec. 9, associated with brown Hematite. Small quantities of it were also observed at a number of points on the bluffs of the Gasconade.

LEAD

Has been found only at a few localities in the county, and in very small quantities. I am informed that in digging wells at Waynesville, fragments of Lead were thrown out with the chert. Judge Colly states that a few pieces of Lead were found several years since on his land, in T. 35, R. 13, Sec. 6. As the Lead-bearing Magnesian Limestone of our State (Third Magnesian) is so extensively developed in Pulaski county, and with the same lithological characters as in the best Lead districts, there can be no good reason why this mineral should not be found in workable quantities in various parts of the county.

NITER.

This mineral occurs disseminated through clays in several caves in Pulaski; and it is also found in the form of effervescenses on their walls. The most noted Niter cave is in the Third Magnesian Limestone, in T. 36, R. 12, Sec. 34. It has a wide entrance, which is situated about 30 feet above the level of the Gasconade. The Niter appears as an effervescence on the walls, and the dirt at the bottom of the cave is strongly impregnated with it. I am informed that Saltpeter was formerly manufactured in this cave.

SELENITE.

Crystals of Selenite occur imbedded in a red Clay, at the bottom of the last-mentioned cave.

MATERIALS FOR CONSTRUCTION.

The Second Magnesian Limestone furnishes an excellent rock for the construction of public works and buildings, for which purposes it is now somewhat extensively employed in the adjoining counties. The Third Magnesian Limestone affords also excellent and very durable building stone, which may be obtained along the streams and valleys of nearly every portion of the county. The compact and fine-textured varieties are most durable, and beds may frequently be found that will take a good polish. In selecting building rocks, the beds containing courses of chert should of course be avoided. The Second Sandstone may also be sometimes used for building purposes; but as a general rule this rock is inferior to the calcareous strata.

Limestones for Quick-lime

Are to be obtained wherever the Third Magnesian Limestone occurs. The best are the compact, light-gray layers, and the sandy-textured beds with facets of calc-spar disseminated.

Clay for Pottery.

Near the mouth of Spring Creek, at Spring Valley P. O., a Clay appears in a mill-race which seems to possess the characters of a potter's Clay. It will doubtless be found in other parts of the county.

Clay for Bricks.

The sandy, reddish Clay of the "Bluff" is frequently used for making bricks, and answers a good purpose. It is found on the higher grounds in all parts of the county.

ROAD MATERIALS.

No better material can be found for this purpose than the comminuted chert, which occurs abundantly in the beds of most of the streams, and it possesses the advantage of being broken up and ready to be at once applied to the grade.

MILL-STONES.

The compact layers of the Second Sandstone sometimes form a good substitute for mill-stones, and they may nearly always be obtained in the districts where this formation prevails. They are, however, objectionable on account of the frequent dressings they require. A better material is found near the Gasconade, in the vicinity of Bates' mill, examined by Mr. Engelmann. This is a bed of decomposing chert, traversed with seams of quartz, in the Third Magnesian Limestone. Mill-stones were obtained for several mills in the county at this locality, and they are said to answer a very good purpose.

SPRINGS.

Pulaski county abounds in springs, which generally issue from the Third Magnesian Limestone. Some of them are of astonishing size, and afford a plentiful supply of water to run the machinery of large saw and grist mills throughout the year. Indeed, nearly all of the mills in the county derive their water-power from these mammoth springs. One of the largest in the county is in the vicinity of Waynesville. It bursts out at the base of a high bluff of Magnesian Limestone, and runs off in a beautiful, transparent stream many feet in width. Springs of similar magnitude occur at Coppage's, Bell's, Cook's and Stone's mills, and near Piney, a short distance above the mouth of Dry Creek.

CHAPTER XIV.

PHELPS COUNTY.

BY B. F. SHUMARD.

[NOTE.—The introduction to this Report is wanting.]

QUATERNARY DEPOSITS.

In Phelps county the superficial deposits consist of alluvium, bottom prairie and bluff.

ALLUVIUM.

This formation includes, in addition to the soils and subsoils, those deposits of comminuted flint that are sometimes found beneath the soil and subsoil of the bottoms and uplands in those districts where the Third Magnesian Limestone prevails, and the rolled fragments that occur in the beds of some of the streams. Deposits of comminuted flint are quite common in the hills bordering Little Piney, Spring Creek and the Dry Fork of the Meramec.

THE BOTTOM PRAIRIE

Is supposed to exist in the bottoms of the larger streams, though no opportunities were afforded by means of wells or other excavations in favorable localities for inspecting it.

BLUFF FORMATION.

As in Laclede and Pulaski counties, we often find beneath the subsoil of the table lands and hills a deposit of reddish and light-colored clays and sands, with some courses of flint, extending sometimes to a depth of forty feet from the surface; the section given below will illustrate the usual characters of the deposit in this county.

Section of Mr. Lennox's well on upland, in T. 36, R. 7. Sec. 17:

No. 1. 7½ feet light gray loam.
No. 2. 28 feet tenaceous, reddish Clay, sometimes sandy and containing fragments of chert.
No. 3. 12 feet Second Magnesian Limestone.

Three and a-half miles beyond Wishon's, on the elevated ridge over which runs the Atlantic and Pacific Railroad, the section in a cut for the railroad is:

No. 1. 1¼ feet light ash-colored clayey soil.
No. 2. 2 feet reddish Clay, with some gravel.
No. 3. 1½ feet light ash-colored, tenacious Clay, mottled with dark purple and yellow.

On the upland, in T. 34, R. 8, S. 19, a well has been sunk to the depth of forty-seven feet without reaching the base of the deposit. The section here is:

No. 1. 2 feet soil and subsoil.
No. 2. 45 feet reddish, sandy, tough Clay, with beds of flint.

PALÆOZOIC ROCKS.

The geological structure of Phelps county, beneath the superficial deposits, is quite simple, all the rocks being of Lower Silurian age. The subdivisions of this system recognized here are Saccharoid Sandstone, Second Magnesian Limestone, Second Sandstone and Third Magnesian Limestone. On Lane's Prairie we found fragments of a Ferruginous Sandstone, filled with well-marked fossils of the Chemung Group, as *Orthis Michelini* and *Spirifer Marionensis*, but these do not constitute a part of the regular strata of the county, as the prairie here is underlaid by strata that belong unequivocally to the Saccharoid Sandstone.

Saccharoidal Sandstone.

This formation occupies the highest points of the county; it is exposed at a number of places on the dividing ridge over which the railroad passes, between Wishon's and Weber's, where, at a few localities, it may be seen overlying the Second Magnesian Limestone; it also appears at a number of points in the vicinity of Lane's Prairie, on the divide between the head of Little Bourbeuse and Spring Creek, on Robertson's Creek in T. 38, R. 6, Sec. 16, near the forks of the Bourbeuse in T. 38, R. 7, S. 19, and tumbling masses of it were found at the top of the railroad cut near Knob View P. O. It consists usually of moderately fine, transparent, rather slightly cohering quartz grains, in thin or massive beds; the color varies from white to ferruginous brown, the grains of the latter variety being sometimes strongly cemented with iron. The greatest thickness was observed in the vicinity of Lane's Prairie, where from forty to fifty feet are exposed. Immediately under the Saccharoidal Sandstone we find, at several localities, beds of marly ? Clay, presenting a variety of colors; these are well displayed in the subjoined section taken at the railroad cut, near Knob View P. O.:

No. 1. 3½ feet sandy loam.
No. 2. 5 feet purple and cream-colored, very tenacious Clay, with some flint scattered through it.
No. 3. 3 feet uneven-bedded, compact Sandstone, the grains firmly cohering.
No. 4. 1 foot variegated purple, cream-colored and greenish indurated Clay.
No. 5. 23 feet bed of broken massive chert, with a small proportion of purple Clay.
No. 6. 5 feet indurated Clay, beautifully variegated with cream color and dark purple.
No. 7. 12 feet very hard Sandstone, passing into quartzite.
No. 8. 15 feet green and variegated shale.

The beds of this section are strongly waved, and their thickness not uniform; the Sandsone is also much broken, and the whole mass has the appearance of being much disturbed. Mr. Engelmann reports the same beds at several localities in the county. In the western part of S. 14 of T. 39, R. 6, he found a yellow "Cotton rock," and near it, on the same level, an exposure of Sandstone, appearing like a dyke, the space between being occupied by rotten chert and purplish, indurated and soft shales, portions of which assume the characters of argillaceous Iron ore or red chalk. Mr. Engelmann also observed these beds in Sec. 28, of same township and range, together with a good deal of red Hematite, which he states is used by the people of the neighborhood as chalk and coloring material for thread, etc. In Sec. 33, of same township and range, he obtained the following section at a well:

No. 1. 7 feet light-colored, clayey soil and subsoil.
No. 2. 8 feet purple and variegated Clay, with large masses of Sandstone.
No. 3. 8 feet dark-yellow "Cotton rock."

Second Magnesian Limestone.

The Second Magnesian Limestone is pretty well developed in the higher lands of Phelps county. The best Section of the strata we have seen occurs at the railroad cut, near Weber's, (now Rolla,) in T. 37, R. 8, Sec. 8. It is as follows:

No. 1. 8 feet superficial deposits.
No. 2. 12 feet buff, earthy Magnesian Limestone, containing some chert.
No. 3. 16 feet variegated, yellow, buff and gray, fine-grained, earthy Magnesian Limestone.
No. 4. 6 feet light-gray, earthy Magnesian Limestone; "Cotton rock."
No. 5. 3 feet compact, gray Magnesian Limestone, containing small masses of iron pyrites, and some bands of chert.
No. 6. 2½-foot bed of earthy Magnesian Limestone, crumbling readily upon exposure.
No. 7. 18 inches earthy Magnesian Limestone, with nodules of chert.
No. 8. 8 feet alternations of hard, fine, granular, light-gray, silico-Magnesian Limestone, with flint nodules and chert.
No. 9. 18 inches blue argillaceous shale.
No. 10. 7 feet blue and buff Magnesian Limestone, very compact.
No. 11. 3 feet compact, earthy Magnesian Limestone.
No. 12. 30 feet slope, from which project even layers of sub-crystalline, silico-Magnesian Limestone.
No. 13. 31 feet gray, even-bedded Magnesian Limestone, in layers from six inches to two feet thick, containing vermiform markings, and used in the construction of bridges and culverts on Pacific Railroad.
No. 14. 13 feet gray, thin-bedded Magnesian Limestone, containing chert.

The strata of this Section present a dip of about 5° N. N. E. In T. 38, R. 8, Sec. 14, Mr. Engelmann found the lower part of the formation to consist of alternations of silico-Magnesian Limestone and Sandstone. With the characters above given, the Second Magnesian Limestone forms the surface rocks of the ridge separating the waters of the Bourbeuse from those of the Gasconade, save on the highest points, where, as already mentioned, Saccharoid Sandstone prevails. It is frequently exposed on the uplands and in the valleys of all the streams north of the dividing ridge, and also for some distance on the north side. The ridges to the north of the Dry Fork of the Meramec are likewise underlaid by this formation, and it is probable that it also exists beneath the superficial deposits of the highest parts of the plateau between Little and Big Piney Rivers.

SECOND SANDSTONE.

This Sandstone presents a greater vertical and horizontal range than either of the preceding formations; it has also a greater vertical development, obtaining sometimes a thickness of one hundred and fifty feet. A good Section, illustrating the lithological characters of the formation, is found near the head of Spring Creek, in T. 34, R. 9, Sec. 6, as follows:

No. 1. 9 feet heavy-bedded, white and brown Sandstone.
No. 2. 15 feet alternations of Sandstone and chert.
No. 3. 20 feet slope, covered with huge blocks of chert.
No. 4. 4 feet indurated Sandstone, passing into chert.
No. 5. 10 feet Sandstone and chert slope.
No. 6. 12½ feet soft, fine and coarse, yellow and white Sandstone.
No. 7. 5 feet calcareo-Magnesian Limestone, some of the layers silicious.
No. 8. 1 foot thin layers of Sandstone.
No. 9. 111 feet of Third Magnesian Limestone.

Another instructive Section is found on Little Piney, in T. 35, R. 8, Sec. 21, as follows:

No. 1. 15 feet slope, covered with large masses of angular chert.
No. 2. 52 feet heavy-bedded Sandstone, made up of rather fine crystalline grains.
No. 3. 3 feet sub-crystalline Magnesian Limestone.
No. 4. 20 feet rough chert, in thin layers.
No. 5. 25 feet heavy-bedded, white and yellow Sandstone.

The Second Sandstone is exhibited throughout the whole course of Spring Creek, in this county, where it is frequently seen reposing on the Third Magnesian Limestone; it likewise caps the bluffs of Little Piney, and occupies a large district between these streams. It is again largely developed on the Dry Fork of the Meramec, presenting there, occasionally, a thickness of a hundred and fifty feet; fine exhibitions of it are to be seen in the vicinity of Meramec Iron Works, and sometimes on the waters of the Bourbeuse. The country underlaid by this formation is often remarkably broken; in other localities, however, it forms slightly rolling and fine agricultural districts.

THIRD MAGNESIAN LIMESTONE.

This formation is also well developed in Phelps county. It has the same lithological and topographical features as in Pulaski, and, therefore, a further description is unnecessary. It may be seen throughout the whole length of Little Piney, Spring and Mill Creeks, where it is often displayed in bold, mural cliffs, extending from the water level to the hight, sometimes, of one hundred and fifty feet. It also constitutes the inferior beds of the bluffs of the Dry Fork of the Meramec, for a considerable distance above its confluence.

ECONOMICAL GEOLOGY.

SOIL.

The richest soils in the county are to be found in the valleys of the Little Piney, Meramec and Bourbeuse; they contain a large proportion of humus, with a proper admixture of clay, lime and sand, to constitute first-rate agricultural land, eminently adapted to the growth of corn, wheat, rye, barley, oats and other products suited to the climate. The timber growing upon them is heavy, of excellent quality, and almost inexhaustible. The soils of the small valleys, although not so heavily timbered as the large ones, possess great fertility, and support a large agricultural population. Scarcely an acre of worthless land is to be found in the valleys of any part of the county.

A large proportion of the uplands possess also excellent soils, particularly where the Second Magnesian Limestone is the underlying rock. Wherever this formation prevails in Phelps we find either moderately undulating woodland or beautiful level prairie, which, under proper cultivation, yields abundant and profitable crops. No one who has traveled in this county can have failed to admire its broad and fertile prairies, or the well-cultivated farms that stretch for miles along the Springfield road. Yet these lands are susceptible of great improvement from subsoiling, as is shown by experiments made by Mr. Lennox, who, for some years, has been in the habit of subsoiling his Post Oak land. He informed me that with surface plowing on a certain piece of ground he raised only from thirty to thirty-five bushels of corn to the acre. He then subsoiled to the depth of eighteen inches, and the following year the same land yielded from seventy to seventy-five bushels. He also found that the increase of his wheat crop amounted to about one-third from subsoiling. Even the rocky lands can be brought under successful cultivation by thorough subsoiling. The poorest soils of the county occur on either side of the valleys of Piney, Mill and Spring creeks and Dry Fork of the Meramec, in situations where the county is underlaid by the cherty portion of the Third Magnesian Limestone and Second Sandstone.

IRON ORE.

Iron ore of the best quality abounds at a number of localities. The oldest known and perhaps most valuable deposit in the county is the Meramec Ore Banks, situated about a half mile from the Meramec, on the west side. This bank was opened as early as 1826 by Messrs. Massey and James, who commenced the erection of a furnace, which was completed in the month of January, 1829, and has been in operation at intervals up to the present time. The ore, which is a rich, compact, *specular* variety, is wrought by Messrs. James, the present proprietors, with considerable profit. It occurs in large, rounded or angular masses, and appears to be almost inexhaustible. When the masses are broken they exhibit cavities filled with small, extremely beautiful, fibrous crystals, which are highly iridescent and sometimes perfectly transparent quartz crystals. In some parts of the bank the specular ore is imbedded in a soft purplish Hematite, which is quite soapy to the feel. It forms an excellent paint, for which purpose large quantities, I am told, are sent annually to the Eastern cities. The Sandstone in the neighborhood of the Iron bank contains masses of Iron pyrites.

In T. 37, R. 8, Sec. 32, Mr. Engelmann observed an extensive deposit of specular Iron ore, which is very similar in character to that of the Meramec Ore Bank. It belongs to the estate of Mr. James, but the ore has not yet been worked. In the north-west quarter of Sec. 27, T. 36, R. 7, large masses of specular and brown Iron ore are abundantly scattered over the surface. It is associated with the Second Sandstone. A shaft fifteen feet deep has been sunk at this place, from which a good deal of argillaceous red Hematite has been taken. A fine variety of red Hematite occurs in small quantities in T. 39, R. 8, Sec. 11. Some masses are quite pure and others are imbedded in chert. Hematite was also found scattered over the surface in T. 37, R. 7, Sec. 13, and at various other points in the county. Beautiful pseudomorphous crystals of Iron pyrites were found in large masses near the base of the railroad cut at Weber's, and fine specimens of it were saved and presented to the State collection by Mr. Churchill, one of the resident engineers at this place.

LEAD

Occurs in small quantity in a cave situated on a small branch of Little Piney, in T. 36, R. 8, S. 19. It is disseminated through a small seam of Barytes, which extends from the entrance of the cave back a distance of a hundred yards. Small fragments of lead have been obtained near the cave, a few feet above the level of the branch. Lead has been obtained on the hills in T. 36, R. 9, S. 35. Several excavations have been made here in the sandy-textured Third Magnesian Limestone, but only a few pounds of mineral have been collected. Small pieces have also been picked up on the surface in T. 39, R. 7, Secs. 24 and 32, the largest lumps weighing about a half of a pound. At all the above localities the lead is found in the Third Magnesian Limestone. In T. 39, R. 8, S. 8, Mr. Engelmann reports the occurrence of lead in Second Magnesian Limestone. In 1856 about 350 pounds of mineral were obtained here, and on Rocky Branch of Spring Creek upward of 2,000 pounds have been raised from the same formation in one season. Small pieces have also been picked up on the waters of Robertson's Creek, and in various other parts of the county.

COPPER

Has been observed only in very small quantities in the lead cave on Piney, above mentioned.

BARYTES

Occurs in a seam from one to three inches thick in the same cave, and forms there the gangue of the lead and copper.

COAL.

A local bed of impure Cannel Coal, with some bituminous Coal, occurs on Robertson's Creek in T. 38, R. 6 W., S. 9. It seems to be located in a depression of the Saccharoidal Sandstone, and is one of those irregular circumscribed deposits, such as are mentioned in the Second Report as occurring in strata inferior to the true Coal Measures. This Coal was mined about thirteen years ago by Mr. Samuel Massey, and was abandoned after a level had been driven into the hill a distance of about forty feet, and several shafts sunk on the slope of the hill, one of them twenty feet deep. This Coal seems to be of very poor quality, and of very limited extent.

BUILDING MATERIALS.

Phelps county abounds in excellent materials for construction. The Second Magnesian Limestone furnishes a good rock for bridges, culverts and the foundations of houses. The beds, No. 13 of the section near Weber's, on the railroad, are to be found at a number of points where this formation prevails; these can be readily quarried and dressed, and are quite durable. In the districts where the Third Magnesian Limestone occurs, good quarries of fine building rocks may also be opened.

Fire Stones

Of the best quality occur in the Second Sandstone. A quarry in this rock, near the Meramec Iron Works, furnishes the stack and hearth-stones for the furnace at this place, and I am informed by Mr. James, one of the proprietors, that it is preferable in every respect to hearth-rocks that have been used here from a distance. It exists here in beds of from one to twelve feet thick, and is made up of rather coarse and fine grains of translucent and milky quartz, rather loosely cemented with silicious matter. The Second Sandstone also furnishes a durable rock for hearths and chimney-places.

Limestone.

Both the Second and Third Magnesian Limestone will furnish good rock for quick-lime, though that made from the latter is generally the best.

Clay for Bricks

Is found abundantly in nearly every part of the county, both in the bottoms and on the ridges.

SPRINGS

Of purest water are abundant, particularly in those parts of the county where the Third Magnesian Limestone prevails. A magnificent spring issues from the base of a bluff of this formation at the Meramec Iron Furnace, furnishing an abundant supply of water for all operations at the works.

A chalybeate spring was observed by Mr. Engelmann on a small branch of Mill Creek, in T. 39, R. 8, Sec. 14. The water, however, is not strongly charged with iron.

Gasconade Bluffs
Little Piney
Mill Creek
Little Beaver
Beaver
Maries Co.
Webers
Wishons
Little Prairie P.O.
Springfield Road
Steelville Road
3rd Magnesian Li.
2d Sandstone
Phelps Co.
Along S. W. Branch of the Pacific R.R.

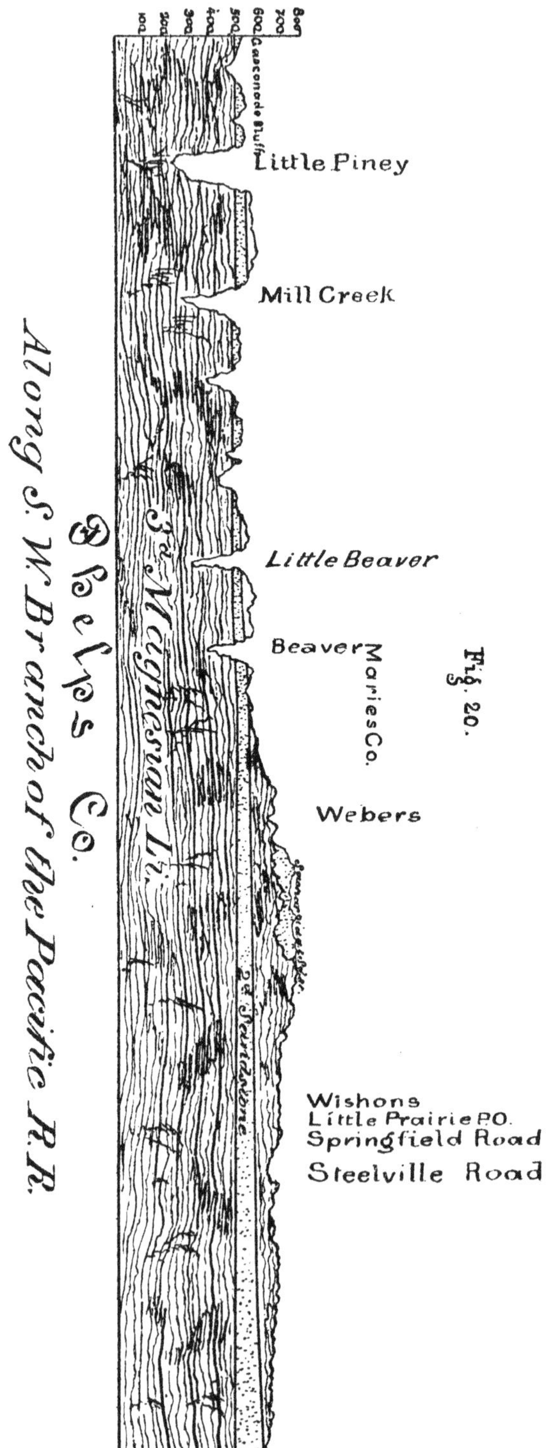

Fig. 20.

CHAPTER XV.

CRAWFORD COUNTY.

BY B. F. SHUMARD.

The area occupied by this county, since a portion of Phelps has been separated from it, is rather more than 700 square miles. Within its boundaries we find great variety of surface, from level to slightly rolling prairie and oak openings, to hills with rocky and precipitous sides. The soil, too, varies from alluvial bottom land to productive or nearly sterile upland. For purposes of description, the county may be divided into two unequal portions by the level plateau upon which the Atlantic and Pacific Railroad is located. On the north side of this ridge, the country consists of moderately rolling or level oak openings and prairie, intersected in every direction by numerous beautiful prairie valleys, limited by gentle hills from eighty to one hundred and fifty feet high—the whole presenting a most desirable region for the agriculturist. On the south side of this ridge, the topographical features are quite different. In the immediate neighborhood of the Meramec River and its principal branches, (Húzza, Crooked and Dry Creeks,) the land is often quite broken and rocky, and the hills rise from one hundred to four hundred feet in hight; but we also frequently find between these rough ridges extensive tracts of level Post and Black Oak and Hickory lands. The valleys of the streams here are broad, extremely productive, and frequently heavily timbered with White and Burr Oak, White and Black Walnut, White and Sugar Maple, Shell-bark Hickory, Pawpaw, Dogwood, Linden, Basswood, Grape and Haw.

In T. 36, 37 and 38, R. 4 and 5, we often find on the uplands narrow prairie valleys, bounded by low hills branching out in all directions. These valleys afford many handsome and highly productive farms. Steelville, the county seat of Crawford, is situated on one of them.

STREAMS.

Crawford county is, in general, pretty well watered by the Meramec and Little Bourbeuse Rivers, and their affluents. The Meramec enters near the middle of the western boundary line, runs with a serpentine course in a direction north of east, and leaves the county a little south of the north-east corner. It is capable of furnishing an abundance of water-power at all seasons of the year to supply the wants of the inhabitants.

GEOLOGICAL STRUCTURE.

In this county we have both igneous and stratified rocks. The first consists of Granite, which is confined to a very limited space, and the second of Quaternary and Lower Paleozoic strata.

GRANITE.

An outburst of Granite occurs in Secs. 9 and 16 of T. 35, R. 2 W., on one of the head branches of Huzza Creek. It projects in the form of huge, rounded knobs from the sides and summit of an isolated hill two or three hundred yards in circumference, and with a hight of about eighty feet above a small valley which encircles it. The rock consists of rather coarse crystals of flesh-colored feldspar and translucent quartz, with here and there some scales of mica—feldspar being the predominating ingredient. The mass resembles, in nearly every respect, that observed by Prof. Swallow in T. 34, R. 3 E., (Iron county,) described in the Second Annual Report; and the Granite of Ste. Genevieve and Wayne counties presents, for the most part, the same characters. On the south-west side of this protrusion there is a heavy deposit of argillaceous Hematite, and the Second Magnesian Limestone is inclined at an angle of about 35°. The hills in the vicinity rise to the hight of at least two hundred and fifty feet, and are composed of Third Magnesian Limestone capped with Second Sandstone.

QUATERNARY.

The superficial deposits in this county are the same as in Phelps. On the table-lands, we usually find, beneath the soil, red or ash-colored loam, with irregular layers of chert and sand, extending down sometimes to the depth of fifty feet. In the rough hills bordering the main streams, this deposit is often very thin or entirely wanting, and we find only fragments of chert, Sandstone or Magnesian Limestone. We give the following sections in illustration of the most constantly observed character of the superficial deposits of the uplands. The first is taken at Mr. Spencer's, about fifty feet above the level of the streams, in T. 39, R. 5, Sec. 2:

No. 1. 1 foot ash-colored, sandy soil.
No. 2. 5 feet bed of comminuted chert.
No. 3. 15 feet tenacious red clay, somewhat sandy.
No. 4. 2 feet comminuted chert imbedded in dark red clay.
No. 5. 1 foot bed of chert.

The second was taken by Mr. Engelmann at Mr. Parsons' well, in T. 39, R. 3, N. E. quarter of Sec. 5, as follows:

No. 1. 6 feet tenacious clay.
No. 2. 2 feet irregular masses of white Sandstone.
No. 3. 45 feet alternating beds of light-colored clay and tumbling Sandstone.

PALÆOZOIC ROCKS.

All the older stratified rocks of this county belong to the base of the Lower Silurian system, or the Magnesian Limestone series. We have the Saccharoidal Sandstone, Second Magnesian Limestone, Second Sandstone and Third Magnesian Limestone.

Saccharoidal Sandstone.

This formation is well represented, but, as far as our observations extend, it is confined almost exclusively to the highest points of the dividing ridge between the waters of the Meramec and the Bourbeuse, and the country lying north of this ridge. The rock occurs in massive beds, and in thin, laminated layers, which vary in compactness from soft, crumbling Sandstone to almost a quartzite; its colors are snow-white, brown and red. The rock, as it appears in this county, can not generally be distinguished from the Second Sandstone, save by its stratigraphical relations—the lithological characters of the two formations being almost precisely the same. It is frequently exposed on the Bourbeuse and branches; and wherever we find it capping the hills they are characterized by gentle declivities. The greatest development of it is in the vicinity of the great bend of the Bourbeuse, where it is seen reposing on the Second Magnesian Limestone, presenting a thickness of from one hundred to one hundred and twenty feet. On the waters of Brush Creek, in the neighborhood of McDade's Spring, it occurs in bold cliffs, with an exposed thickness of about seventy feet. And on Pigeon Roost Creek, in T. 39, R. 4, Sec. 14, it exhibits a thickness of from fifty to sixty feet.

The purple and variegated clays, with argillaceous Hematite, described in the report of Phelps county as lying at the base of the Saccharoidal Sandstone, have been observed at a few points in Crawford. They appear in T. 39, R. 4, Sec. 2; near Kinney's, in T. 39, R. 5, Sec. 32, and a short distance south of Amanda Postoffice. They do not seem to be so well developed as in Phelps.

Second Magnesian Limestone.

This formation, like the preceding one, is confined chiefly to the dividing ridge between the Meramec and Bourbeuse waters and the country north of it. It is found, except on the higher points of this ridge, whenever the superficial deposits are removed, and at some few points may be seen lying in nearly horizontal beds, beneath the Saccharoidal Sandstone. Excellent exposures of it occur on the Bourbeuse and most of its branches; when it is the surface formation we find beautiful hills with gentle slopes, of neatly rounded outlines. Usually the formation consists of even-bedded, fine-textured, light gray Dolomite, sometimes clouded with buff, and in beds from six inches to one foot thick. Some of the strata contain a large proportion of calcareous matter, and sometimes we find intercalated beds of chert, but, as a general rule, the formation is remarkably free from silex.

Second Sandstone.

The Second Sandstone is better developed in this county than either of the formations just described. Its range is limited chiefly to the country south of the main dividing ridge. It is finely displayed n Meramec River, and Crooked, Benton and Huzza Creeks, where it may be seen capping most of the bluffs; it is also largely developed on the uplands between these streams. We also saw some exposures of it, surmounted by Second Magnesian Limestone, on Pigeon Roost Creek, near the northern boundary of the county in T. 39, R. 4. But the finest exposures of this formation observed in the county are on Crooked Creek, in T. 36, R. 4 W.; it presents here a vertical thickness of at least 150 feet, and exists in bold and often rugged cliffs. The rock is made up of fine quartz grains, sometimes moderately coherent, and sometimes passing into true quartzite. Occasionally it presents the appearance of a quartz breccia. In this region the beds have a southerly dip of from 35° to 40°. The country in the vicinity is broken, and in places unfit for cultivation. In fact, as a general rule, wherever the rock approaches the surface it imparts to the country a rough aspect.

Third Magnesian Limestone.

The Third Magnesian Limestone is a very important formation in Crawford, as it has a wide geographical as well as vertical range, and in portions of the county is highly galeniferous. It has not been observed on the north side of the main dividing ridge, but on the south it prevails on nearly all of the streams. It is especially well exhibited along the Meramec River, Huzza, Crooked and Benton Creeks, where it often appears in bold and picturesque bluffs, with mural faces to the streams. These bluffs are often characterized by vertical fissures, and some of them are penetrated with caverns of considerable size. The formation consists of sandy textured, hard, close-grained, light and dark-gray Magnesian Limestone, with chert in thick beds, and disseminated through the calcareous portions. Whenever the cherty beds reach the surface, they impart a very rough character to the country.

In the eastern portion of the county the formation contains a great deal of cellular chert, which is scattered profusely over the hills in rugged masses. The cavities in the rock are frequently lined with bluish or whitish, mammillated chalcedony, covered with small, transparent quartz crystals, affording beautiful specimens for the cabinet.

Toward the head of Huzza Creek, near Wisdom's mill, this formation exhibits a thickness of 300 feet; and here the creek runs through a narrow channel to form one of the finest mill sites I have ever seen. On the Meramec, in T. 39, R. 3, the exposed thickness of the formation is even greater than in the vicinity of Wisdom's mill.

ECONOMICAL GEOLOGY.

SOILS.

Crawford county can boast of soils that for productiveness are surpassed by none in the State. The alluvial bottoms of the Meramec, Bourbeuse, and, indeed, of all the streams, are as rich as could be desired, and annually yield to the farmer abundant crops to reward him for his labor. The soils of the uplands, underlaid by the Second Magnesian Limestone, are likewise of excellent quality, and under proper management are well adapted to the growth of corn, wheat, rye, oats, hemp and tobacco. Frequently very beautiful and arable farms are to be found on the uplands. It is only on the hills of the larger streams, where the cherty beds of the Third Magnesian Limestone and the Second Sandstone reach the surface, that the soils are poor, and too rocky for successful cultivation.

IRON.

Iron ore of excellent quality has been found at a number of localities in this county; generally associated with the Second Sandstone and cherty parts of the Third Magnesian Limestone. The varieties observed are brown Hematite, specular and sulphuret or Iron pyrites. A deposit of brown and specular Iron occurs in T. 37, R. 4, S. E. N. E. Sec. 5, on land owned by Mr. Collins. The ore appears in a hill elevated from 60 to 70 feet above the level of a small valley, and is thickly strewn over the surface; the soil is of a deep cherry color. No work has been done here to prove the extent of this deposit, although the prospect is that ore exists in workable quantity.

Brown Hematite occurs at a number of points in T. 36, R. 3. In Secs. 15 and 36 it is most abundant, commingled with pseudomorphous crystals of pyrites, chert and crystalized quartz. At Bleeding Hill Copper Mines, according to Mr. Engelmann's observations, there seems to be a rich deposit of specular ore of excellent quality. A great deal of ore is here scattered over the top of a hill, composed of Third

Magnesian Limestone and Second Sandstone. A shaft has been sunk here, at the bottom of which was on one side compact chert, and on the other a solid mass of specular Iron, while the intervening space was filled with gravel and red Clay, with some Copper. At the bottom of another shaft near by, which was sunk through 37 feet of red Clay and comminuted chert, the miners encountered a 4-foot bed of soft, purple Iron ore, greasy to the touch, and like the paint ore at the Meramec Iron Works in Phelps county. Workable beds of Iron ore were examined in T. 38, R. 6, S. half of S. E. qr. in Sec. 29, T. 38, R. 3, Sec. 1, and in T. 36, R. 5, Sec. 32, belonging to the estate of Mr. James. These will doubtless prove valuable deposits.

In T. 37, R. 7, N. W. corner of Sec. 13, Mr. Engelmann found specular ore abundantly scattered over the surface, together with pseudomorphous crystals of pyrites. Specular ore of fine quality also occurs abundantly on the summit of a high hill in T. 35, R. 5, S. E. qr. of S. W. quarter of Sec. 32; in T. 37, R. 3, Sec. 4, and at various places in this township.

Very little work has been done at any localities in this county, but the surface indications are such as to lead to the opinion that most of the deposits above spoken of are worthy of being more fully tested, in order to ascertain the probable quantity of ore.

LEAD.

The eastern part of Crawford constitutes a part of that vast Lead district, for which our State has become so famous. The mines that have perhaps yielded the greatest quantity of lead in this county are those of Mineral Hill, in T. 40, R. 2, Sec. 32 and 33, the property of Mr. Hubert Taylor. This hill was examined by Mr. Engelmann, who described it as an isolated eminence, extending from the N. E. quarter of Sec. 32 to the N. E. quarter of 33. It is the highest hill in this vicinity, and is composed of Third Magnesian Limestone, thickly covered on the summit with fine chert, imbedded in red clay. The whole side of the hill is covered with shallow diggings, from which immense quantities of ore have been obtained. These mines have been known for more than twenty years, during which period upward of a million pounds of ore have been raised, and nearly all of it from surface diggings. I am informed by Mr. Williams that five hundred men were engaged in mining on this hill at one time. No systematic mining operations have yet been attempted here, notwithstanding the prospective richness of the locality.

East of this place, in Sec. 33 of same township and range, Mr. Engelmann reports that a crevice, bearing E. N. E., was struck in the Third Magnesian Limestone, containing Lead, Iron and chert, imbedded in red clay, and in N. E. N. W. of same section, a sheet of mineral was found bearing in the same direction. The lead was attached directly to the Magnesian Limestone, without any gangue, and formed a vertical sheet from five to six inches wide. It was only followed for a short distance horizontally and to the depth of about ten feet. In N. E. quarter of N. E. quarter of same section another crevice was found, bearing E. or E. N. E., and dipping vertically. This ore was wrought for the distance of about 200 yards horizontally and to the depth of 60 feet at one point. This crevice is from three to four feet wide, and contains, besides Lead, Iron, with a good deal of ocher. In places, cherty rock sets in across the crevice, closing it entirely, but the soft Magnesian Limestone interstratified with this chert still contains Lead ore, and continues beyond the walls of the crevice. Mr. Engelmann entertains the opinion that these crevices are not true fissures or lodes, as they do not penetrate the chert layers, but are mere "openings" or "chimneys." In the same section there is a cave in the Magnesian Limestone, with its floor thickly covered with red clay. At the mouth of this cave a shaft was sunk, from which a considerable quantity of mineral was raised, and it is probable that much more lead could be procured by sinking shafts through the clay in other parts of the cave.

Williams' Mines, located west of Mineral Hill, in T. 40, R. 2, Sec. 32, were first opened by Samuel Williams, the present proprietor, in 1851, who soon associated with him Mr. Jas. Funk. These gentlemen worked the mines with from three to twelve hands, until the month of April, 1854, up to which time they had raised 202,183 pounds of ore, all of which was smelted at Hibler's Furnace, three miles distant. From April to the end of the year 1854, they were worked by Williams, Casey & Clancy, with from four to six hands, during which time 145,000 pounds of mineral were raised. They have been worked by numerous shafts and several tunnels, on the declivity of a hill, and on a line running at nearly N. E. and S. W. Along this line the mineral was first encountered, at a depth of 25 feet from the surface, and the workings were continued to the depth of 75 feet. The greatest amounts of ore have been obtained principally from three fissures, situated from 25 to 30 feet apart. These do not maintain any regular dimensions, but vary, usually, from 2 to 8 feet in width, and from 3 to 4 in hight. One of them was found to have a width of 40 feet at one point, with a hight of 18 feet. The mineral runs in regular ranges through red clay, and is associated with brown Hematite, pyrites and ocher. During the last three years but little work has been done at these important mines.

Nearly every portion of Sections 32, 33 and 34 of T. 40, R. 2, contains more or less lead. Mr. Williams informed me that in the N. E. corner of Sec. 1 of same township and range, he has obtained about 3,000 pounds of mineral, and that altogether 10,000 pounds have been raised here.

Wein's Diggings are situated on Courtois Creek, in T. 38, R. 2, S. E. of S. E. of Sec. 3. About 13,500 pounds of ore were raised here during the winter of 1856 and the spring of 1857. This ore was smelted at Hill's Furnace, in Washington county.

Montre's Diggings are situated directly north of Wein's, and in the same 80-acre tract. A great deal of lead has been obtained at these mines at various times by surface diggings, but they have not been worked for several years.

On McKane's land, in S. E. quarter of S. E. quarter of T. 37, R. 2 W., several shallow excavations have been made, and a couple of hundred pounds of ore obtained.

Halbert's Diggings, situated in S. E. corner of Sec. 1, of T. 37, R. 4; from 3,000 to 4,000 pounds of ore were raised here, in 1844, from surface workings.

Evans' Diggings, located in N. E quarter of Sec. 3, T. 37, R. 3; some surface-work was done here in 1856, and about 300 pounds of mineral obtained.

Ransom's, formerly Hopkins' Diggings, examined by Mr. Engelmann, are situated in T. 38, R. 2 W., Sec. 15. They occur in the sandy-textured beds of the Third Magnesian Limestone, a few feet from their junction with the Second Sandstone. These mines were opened by Mr. Hopkins, who accidentally struck a sheet of mineral while quarrying rock for building his chimney. The sheet of ore was about five inches thick, and about three feet wide; it was followed in an easterly direction for only a few feet. Mr. Hopkins procured from these mines some 40,000 pounds of mineral, and Mr. Ransom, since he has owned the property, has raised about 14,000. No regular mining has been done here; but Mr. Engelmann is of opinion that the prospect at this place is a good one, and worth a further trial. He supposes the ore to occur in thin, horizontal sheets, which extend in all directions, and connect with pockets.

Hinch's Lead Diggings, located in T. 38, R. 2, Sec. 3. Only five or six hundred pounds of mineral have been obtained here. Small quantities of Lead are found in this neighborhood, wherever excavations have been made.

Trask & Garrison's Diggings, located near the middle of west line of Sec. 5, T. 36, R. 2 W., have yielded from 10,000 to 15,000 pounds of mineral.

Isgrig's Diggings, situated in T. 39, R. 2, S. E. of N. E. of Sec. 4. A little surface-mining has been done here; the ore is found in little veins, traversing the Magnesian Limestone.

Sappington's Diggings, situated in T. 39, R. 2, N. W. quarter of Sec. 1. They were opened in the spring of 1857, and have yielded 55,000 pounds of mineral.

Clarke's Diggings, in same section, were opened in 1853, and have been worked only at intervals. They have yielded 25,000 pounds.

Darby's Diggings, also in the same section, were opened in 1855. About 7,000 pounds of ore have been obtained, although but little work has been done.

The three mines last mentioned are situated on the same hill. Mr. Engelmann, who examined them, describes the rock as sandy-textured Magnesian Limestone, with courses of chert. The mineral occurs in small crevices and pockets, in the Magnesian Limestone, and disseminated as float mineral, through the red clay. It is sometimes found adhering to masses of sulphuret and brown oxide of Iron, and at one point occurs in a thin sheet in the Magnesian Limestone.

Railroad or Coffee Diggings are located on the spur of the same ridge, in S. W. quarter of Sec. 36, on land belonging to the Pacific Railroad. The occurrence of Lead here was first observed in 1857, and some five or six thousand pounds have been raised by persons in the neighborhood.

Rutledge's Diggings, in T. 39, R. 2, N. E. quarter of Sec. 21, have been occasionally worked with good success, but only surface-ore has been obtained.

Red Hill Diggings are situated in T. 40, R. 2, N. E. of S. W. of Sec. 23, and owned by Mr. Sullivan. They have yielded about 400,000 pounds of lead. The underlying formation here is the sandy-textured beds of the Third Magnesian Limestone, which are covered with a thick deposit of red Clay, whence most of the mineral has been procured; a few small veins, however, have been found in the Magnesian Limestone. The surface of this hill is penetrated in every direction by numerous shallow pits.

Hibler's Diggings, in T. 40, R. 2 W., N. E. of N. W. of Sec. 35, have been worked occasionally by Mr. Hibler, who has obtained about 10,000 pounds of ore from them. The ore occurred as float mineral in the Clay, in crevices or pockets, and in the form of thin sheets penetrating the Magnesian Limestone.

Lead, in small quantities, has also been obtained in Secs. 26 and 27, T. 40, R. 2, and not far from Bredell's copper furnace.

At all the above described localities, the Lead has been derived from the Third Magnesian Limestone. In the Second Magnesian Limestone, Lead has also been found at a number of points, but only in small quantities.

Carbonate of Lead occurs in small particles at Williams' mines, and at Mineral Hill.

COPPER.

The Copper mines of this county have formed the subject of a special report by Dr. H. King, who had opportunities of inspecting them about the time they were being worked, and has given us a very minute account of them.* As no work has been done at these mines for some years, and consequently little was to be seen at the time of Mr. Engelmann's visit, who was detailed to examine them, we will have to avail ourselves largely of Dr. King's observations.

Hinch's Copper Mine is located on the side of a high hill, near the center of Sec. 4, T. 38, R. 2 W., and is owned by Messrs. Hinch, Harrison, Anderson and King. It was discovered in 1849, and several thousand pounds of ore have been raised here. According to Dr. King, the ore, near the surface, is a carbonate and oxide, but deeper it assumes the character of a sulphuret of excellent quality. Dr. King also states that 800 pounds of the ore were sent to the furnace and produced 273 pounds of good pig Copper.

*Report on the Rives, Hinch, Bleeding Hill and Blanton Copper Mines in the State of Missouri, by H. King, M. D.

The holes or shafts have been sunk chiefly in loose, red surface Clay and comminuted chert, but the walls of some of them are in the Magnesian Limestone. The Copper ore was found with brown Hematite in small fragments disseminated through the Clay, and filling fissures in Sandstone. Small scales of native Copper were found occasionally with the carbonate and oxide.

Mr. Engelmann states that very little has been done here toward investigating the real character of this mine, owing to the very irregular manner in which the work has been carried on. He considers the mine analogous to that of Copper Hill.

Rives' Copper Mine is located in the north-east quarter of Sec. 13, T. 39, R. 3 W., at the head of a small ravine. The formation here is the cherty portion of the Third Magnesian Limestone and Second Sandstone. This mine was worked to some extent in 1849, and a number of pits were sunk through the superficial deposits, consisting of Iron. At the time of Mr. Engelmann's visit nothing could be gathered concerning the character of this mine. According to Mr. King's report, some twelve or fifteen holes have been sunk, and in nearly all of them more or less Copper in some condition was found. The chief amount raised, however, was from two or three shafts on the west side of the eastern hill. Here, at the depth of about twenty feet, a mass of ore was struck several feet in thickness, or which was penetrated to this extent without passing through it. Dr. King further states that "a large pile, probably some hundred thousand pounds, of this ore was brought to the surface, where it has since been left exposed to the rains and other atmospheric influences. It is chiefly an oxide and sulphuret of Iron and Copper, but not very rich in this latter metal."

"In most of the other shafts sunk at this mine the ore was found in the state of green carbonate; but this was generally in a deposit of fragmentary chert."

The conclusions which Dr. King arrived at from his examinations of this locality are that this would be an extremely valuable Copper mine if properly worked.

Copper Hill.—No work has been done at this mine since Dr. Litton examined it. I beg, therefore, to refer to the report of that gentleman on the mines, in the Second Geological Report, which gives a full account of all that we know concerning it.

Bleeding Hill.—This mine is situated in T. 38, R. 2 W., south-west quarter of north-west quarter of Sec. 4, and is owned by Messrs. S.

Reed & Co. Mr. Engelmann, who examined it, reports that only a few shallow shafts have been sunk here, chiefly through red Clay and chert. In some instances they have been extended into the underlying strata. The ores found here occur in small fissures in the Second Sandstone, and consist of green and blue carbonate, sulphuret, and some scales of virgin Copper, commingled with a great deal of earthy brown Hematite. Much irregular and useless labor has been expended here, without developing any practical results, and we know nothing certainly concerning the value of this mine, although the surface indications are favorable.

On Hibler's land, in T. 40, R. 2. W., Sec. 22, some excavations have been made for Copper, but only small fragments of blue and green carbonate have been found. A few pieces have also been found at several points on Huzza and Crooked creeks.

COBALT AND MANGANESE.

Dr. H. King cites the occurrence of black oxide of Cobalt and Manganese at Rives' mine (*Rep. on Rives, Hinch, etc., Copper Mines*, p. 19,) but we have not met with any indications of these metals in the county.

COAL.

Irregular deposits of Coal have been found at two localities, not far apart, in Crawford county. One of these, situated in T. 36, R. 4, Sec. 21, near Crooked Creek, was worked as early as 1844, by Mr. Samuel Massey. Several shafts have been sunk here on the western declivity of a hill, which consists mainly of Third Magnesian Limestone and Second Sandstone; an adit also runs from the base to intersect the shafts. Immediately at the bank, we have a Section as follows:

No. 1. 30 feet slope.
No. 2. 6 feet dark argillaceous Sandstone.
No. 3. 10 feet dark tenacious fire Clay.
No. 4. 4 feet impure Coal, containing much pyrites.

Mr. James, of the Meramec Iron Works, informs me that between 25,000 and 30,000 bushels of Coal were hauled from here to the works, shortly after the bank was opened. It was found, however, to contain

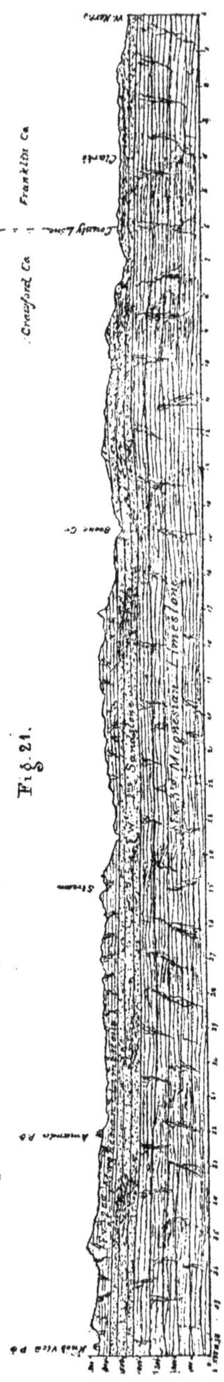

Fig. 21.

Geological Section through Crawford Co. along South West Branch of the Pacific Rail Road.

too much Iron pyrites to answer a good purpose for the manufacture of Iron, and the mine was abandoned.

This Coal, like all similar deposits found in strata below the regular Coal Measures, is confined to a very limited area, and undoubtedly could be worked out in a very short time.

A deposit of the same kind occurs on Taft Branch, in T. 36, R. 4 W., Sec. 30, in the Second Sandstone. Several shafts were sunk here some twelve years ago, from which a few bushels of Coal were obtained. The material penetrated by these shafts seems to have been a dark ash-colored shale, with some carbonaceous matter disseminated through it. The hills in the vicinity exhibit frequent exposures of Second Sandstone, lying in nearly horizontal beds.

BUILDING MATERIALS,

Of fine quality, exist in nearly every part of the county. In the northern part, the even-bedded Second Magnesian Limestone is to be found in about every township. This rock is readily quarried, dresses well, and possesses durability. In the southern and middle portions the Third Magnesian Limestone will, at numerous localities, yield a good building material. The workable beds are perhaps not so easily quarried, in general, as those of the Second Magnesian, but they are more durable, and better suited for heavy masonry.

The Granite we have described in the first pages of this report, and located in T. 35, R. 2 W., is a very valuable material for the construction of public buildings. It combines beauty with durability, and is situated very favorably for quarrying. This Granite would also furnish an excellent rock for mill-stones.

ROAD MATERIALS.

The broken chert which is so frequently found on the hill-sides and beds of the streams of the Third Magnesian Limestone districts is an invaluable material for this purpose. It sometimes forms natural gravel roads in this county that are almost equal to the best macadamized roads.

LIMESTONES,

Of good quality, abound wherever the Second and Third Magnesian Limestone prevails.

SPRINGS

Of pure, crystal water are abundant in many sections of the county, particularly in the Magnesian Limestone regions.

A chalybeate spring was found in Sec. 21, of T. 36, R. 3 W. It breaks out a little above the level of Dry Creek, and contains a thick, gelatinous precipitate of Iron. It has rather a strong chalybeate taste, and doubtless possesses considerable tonic properties.

CHAPTER XVI.

CAPE GIRARDEAU COUNTY.

BY B. F. SHUMARD.

This county contains about 530 square miles, and as there is much variety in the character of its underlying strata in different sections, we find a corresponding variety in its topographical features. The surface is generally hilly, except within a very limited area in the southern part of the county, marked on the maps Quaternary, which is nearly level and often wet and swampy. The hills rise to the hight of from 50 to 500 feet above the adjacent water-courses. The main ridge separating the streams running northwardly into Apple Creek from those flowing in an opposite direction, commences near the north-western corner of the county, and bears south-east toward the Mississippi. This water-shed, at some points, attains an elevation estimated at about 600 feet above the bed of the Mississippi. In the two middle ranges of townships, the hills are, for the most part, characterized by moderately gentle slopes, and we have here an extensive district of desirable farming land furnished with an abundant supply of good timber. The valleys of many of the streams are remarkable for their richness and fertility.

In that part of the county where the Lower Helderburg rocks prevail (see map) we find usually a broken country, the hills high and marked with abrupt declivities often thickly covered with chert. The bluffs of the Mississippi are here remarkably bold and picturesque, presenting sometimes perpendicular faces to the river of from 100 to 150 feet. Over a considerable portion of this area, however, the older rocks are covered with an extensive accumulation of Quaternary deposits, and we find an abundance of highly arable land, sustaining often a growth of excellent timber.

In the western range of townships, underlaid by the Third Magnesian Limestone and Second Sandstone, the country is, in some respects, similar to that just described, but the hills are not so high, and the valleys of the streams are broader. These latter are from a hundred yards to three-fourths of a mile wide, and their soils are generally extremely rich and fertile. Many good farms are also to be found on the uplands, but the slopes in some places are so thickly covered with chert as to render them unfit for ordinary cultivation.

STREAMS.

Every part of Cape Girardeau is bountifully supplied with streams of excellent water. The Mississippi forms the eastern boundary line, Apple Creek the northern line, and the Whitewater passes in a remarkably tortuous course through the eastern range of townships. These main channels have numerous affluents, which reach almost every section in the county, as will be seen by consulting the map.

TIMBER

Is abundant throughout the county. The bottoms of the Mississippi River and Whitewater and Cedar Creeks support a heavy growth of forest trees, among which Black and White Walnut, White and Sugar Maple, American and Slippery Elm, Pawpaw, Dogwood, Cottonwood, Buckeye, Shell-bark Hickory and Ash are the kinds most commonly met with. In the southern portion of the county, in the neighborhood of the swamp lands, we have, in addition, Black and Sweet Gum, Tulip Tree, Beech, and in the swamps, Cypress. The poorer lands sustain a growth chiefly of Post Oak, Black Oak, Black-jack, White Oak and Black Hickory. About one mile above the mouth of Indian Creek, Mr. Hough saw a few trees of Yellow Pine, but they have not been noticed elsewhere in the county.

GEOLOGY.

The formations of this county may all be referred to the Quaternary and Silurian systems.

QUATERNARY SYSTEM.

As this system includes all the deposits beneath the soils down to the regularly stratified rocks, it is, of course, almost universally spread over the county.

The Alluvial Bottoms of the streams consist of clays, marls, sands and vegetable matter combined in various proportions, and the soils formed from them possess all the elements of fertility in a great degree. They cover the valleys sometimes to the depth of twenty or even fifty feet. In the districts underlaid by the Third Magnesian Limestone, Second Sandstone and Helderburg rocks, the deposits of which we are speaking occasionally abound with fragments of chert, but most generally they are quite free from coarse materials.

Bluff.—This formation is well developed, and we encounter it beneath the soil and subsoil in almost every part of the county. The general character of the deposit is shown from the following sections:

In a well sunk by Mr. Holcomb, in T. 31, R. 14, Sec. 27, the section is—

No. 1. 10 feet tough yellow clay.
No. 2. 20 feet red clay.
No. 3. 15 feet alternations of red, blue and yellow clay, containing sometimes fragments of Niagara Limestone.

At Mr. McLain's well, in Appleton, the materials passed through were—

No. 1. 30 feet extremely tough red clay.
No. 2. 18 feet yellow, white and red clay, with masses of Trenton Limestone.

Interesting exhibitions of these deposits are to be found in the hills bordering the swamp lands in the southern part of the county. Here they are exposed occasionally to the hight of forty feet, and sometimes are weathered in such a manner as to appear like moraines.

SILURIAN SYSTEM.

All the strata of Cape Girardeau county, beneath the Quaternary deposits, belong to the Silurian System, and we here find the most instructive and complete series of the different members of this system hitherto observed in the State. In order to illustrate the stratigraphical relations of these formations as they occur in this county, we have constructed a vertical section, somewhat similar to that of the general section published in the Second Annual Report.

UPPER SILURIAN.

This system occupies the eastern part of the county, and covers an area of about 120 square miles. Its boundaries are laid down on the accompanying geological map. It is represented in this county by the Delthyris Shale, (Lower Helderburg,) Niagara Group and Cape Girardeau Limestone.

DELTHYRIS SHALE.

The beds referred by us to this formation are confined to the north-eastern part of the county. They consist chiefly of alternations of buff and bluish gray, compact, calcareo-silicious Limestone and ferruginous chert. They generally occur in thin layers, and contain numerous irregularly rounded masses of silex, which vary in size from an inch to a foot in diameter, and sometimes exhibit a well-marked concentric structure. These masses impart to the weathered faces of the strata an exceedingly rough appearance.

Wherever this formation prevails we find a remarkably rough and broken country, sometimes entirely unfit for cultivation. The hills are separated from each other by deep and narrow valleys, and their sides are frequently covered with thick accumulations of chert. It is finely displayed on the Mississippi, between the mouth of Apple Creek and Bainbridge. Near Vancil's Landing it forms picturesque and nearly vertical escarpments from 100 to 150 feet high, with faces marked in every direction by deep fissures. According to the observations of Mr. Hough, this formation prevails throughout nearly the whole course of Indian Creek and its branches. Near the Mississippi he found an exposure of upward of 200 feet, consisting mainly of silicious beds. This formation constitutes likewise the main body of the hills both north and south of Indian Creek, for distances varying from one to seven miles west of the Mississippi. The entire thickness of the formation has not been seen here at any single locality. In the accompanying vertical section 350 feet is given as its thickness, but from examinations in an adjoining county it is highly probable that this estimate is from fifty to a hundred feet below its actual development.

Fossils.—The most characteristic species are *Dalmania tridentifera, Leptaena depressa, Orthis elegantula* and *Phacops* and *Platyostoma*, (several species.)

NIAGARA GROUP.

This formation succeeds in descending order the strata just described. In its lithological features it differs widely from the same formation as observed in other portions of the Mississippi Valley. In Iowa and Illinois, according to the recently published work of Prof. Hall on the Geology of the former State, it is described as a "nearly pure Dolomite, having a crystalline structure and light, yellowish gray color."* Whereas, in South-eastern Missouri it is composed of

*Extract Silliman's Journal, vol. 27, p. 111.

variegated purple, yellow and drab, compact, argillaceous Limestones and soft indurated shales of various colors.

On the Mississippi, about one mile above Shepherd's Landing, we have the following section, which illustrates very well the usual characters of the upper part of the formation:

No. 1. 3 feet slope, covered with chert.

No. 2. 75 feet Lower Helderburg, consisting of rough chert and thin bands of gray, argillaceous Limestone, the whole containing numerous silicious nodules.

No. 3. 5 feet gray, argillaceous Limestone, Niagara Group.

No. 4. 5 feet purple and yellow, fine-textured Limestone, handsomely variegated, and containing *Striatopora flexuosa*—(Hall.)

No. 5. 30 feet crumbling, earthy, bluish-gray and yellow Limestone, highly charged with fossils, as follows: *Cheirurus Missouriensis*, *Encrinurus punctatus*, *Calymene rugosa*, *Calymene* allied to *C. senaria*, *Phacops*, (two species,) *Dalmania*, (2 species,) *Orthoceras gracile*, (Portlock,) *Terebratula*, *Leptæna depressa*, *Tellinomya*, *Platyostoma*, *Murchisonia*, *Bellerophon*, *Striatapora flexuosa* and *Poteriocrinus*.

No. 6. 10½ feet dark, carbonaceous, fissile shale, filled with *Graptolites* and arborescent fucoid-like markings.

No. 7. 5 feet gray Limestone, with *Dalmania*, *Orthoceras* and columns of a *Crinoid*.

No. 8. 3 feet bed of gray, yellow and purple, variegated, impure marble.

No. 9. 82 feet alternations of purple, yellow, buff, blue and gray, compact and earthy Limestone, capable of being split readily into layers from a-half to an inch thick, the whole forming a beautiful, variegated cliff.

On a small branch, about two miles north of Cape Girardeau, in T. 31, R. 14, Sec. 24, we find the following section of the inferior members of the formation:

No. 1. 44 feet slope, covered with fragments of chert.

No. 2. 26 feet laminated beds of brick-red, sandy textured, earthy Limestone, with *Cyathophyllidæ*.

No. 3. 32 feet very hard, fine-textured, red and purple Limestone, clouded with yellow and green, forming an elegant variegated marble. It contains *Calymene Blumenbachii?* *Striatopora flexuosa* and *Columnaria inequalis*.

No. 4. Thick beds of bluish gray, hard, brittle Limestone, containing *Halysites Catenularia*.*

No. 5. 35 feet Cape Girardeau Limestone, with its characteristic fossils.

No. 6. 50 feet slope, covered with debris extending to the base of the hill.

With the characteristics here given, the Niagara Group occupies a greater area in the county than the Lower Helderburg, as will be seen by consulting the geological map, where its general boundaries are indicated. It is well displayed along the bluffs of the Mississippi from a point about three miles below the mouth of Indian Creek,

*A single specimen only of this interesting fossil was found by Mr. Hough among some loose fragments of this rock at the base of the exposure.

where it first appears cropping out from beneath the Lower Helderburg strata, to within a short distance of Caney Creek. The extreme southern limit of the formation is in the north-west quarter of fractional T. 30, R. 14. It is the surface rock over the greater part of T. 31, R. 14; the southern sections of T. 32, R. 14; the eastern part of T. 31, R. 13; thence it extends diagonally through the middle portions of townships 32 and 33, R. 13, and crosses Apple Creek into Perry county.

The thickness of this group of strata, as ascertained from measurements made by Mr. Hough and myself, is 216 feet. The greatest development observed at any one place in the county was on the Mississippi, about one mile above Shepherd's Landing, where 140 feet are exposed.

Cape Girardeau Limestone.

The next formation in descending order is the Cape Girardeau Limestone, which constitutes the lowest member of the Upper Silurian series yet found in the State. It is well separated from the Niagara Group, both by lithological and palæontological characters, notwithstanding its limited vertical development. It is composed of bluish-gray Limestone, in layers from two to six inches thick, marked by numerous vertical joints. The rock is very compact, and breaks with a smooth conchoidal fracture.* The weathered surfaces are usually coated with a thin ferruginous crust, and the upper part of the mass contains bands and nodules of flint.

The best exposure of this member of the series is at the mouth of Cape Creek, on the Mississippi River, two miles above Cape Girardeau. Its entire thickness is to be seen here, amounting to 60 feet. In T. 31, R. 13, S. 24, Mr. Hough found an exposure of it of about 30 feet, and he also observed the same beds in Sec. 12 of the same township and range.

Fossils.—The strata at the mouth of Cape Creek abound in fossils, none of which, as far as our observation extends, range into the formations above or below. The most characteristic species are *Glyptocrinus fimbriatus*, *Glyptocrinus* (two undescribed species,) *Tentaculites incurvus*, *T. Major*, *Homocrinus flexuosus*, *Protaster*, *Acidaspis Halli*, *Proetus depressus*, *Encrinurus deltoideus*, *Cyphaspis Girar-*

* An analysis of this rock gives, as its composition:

Insoluble residue	8.60
Alumina and peroxide of iron	1.93
Carbonate of lime	86.00
Carbonate of magnesia	3.70
	100.23

deauensis, *Orthis Missouriensis*, *Leptæna mesacosta*, *Rhynconella* (several species,) and *Stictopora*, *Cladopora* and *Retepora* ——.

LOWER SILURIAN SYSTEM.

HUDSON RIVER GROUP.

Under this general name we include, provisionally, a series of beds interposed between the Trenton Limestone and Cape Girardeau Limestone. Its subdivisions are designated Upper and Lower Hudson River shales and Receptaculite Limestone. In Cape Girardeau this group possesses considerable interest in an economical point of view, as it furnishes an inexhaustible supply of excellent building material.

Upper Hudson Shales.—These form the beds of passage between the Upper and Lower Silurian, and consist of about 45 feet of bluish-gray and yellow silico-argillaceous shales, in which we have not been able to detect any organic remains. They are placed in the series under examination merely from their strong lithological resemblance to the lower shales, which contain highly characteristic Hudson River fossils. An exposure of 18 feet occurs on the Mississippi about three-quarters of a mile below Cape Creek, and their entire thickness was measured on a farm belonging to Mr. Stout, in T. 31, R. 13, S. W. qr. of Sec. 2. At this place they are exposed on the bank of a small creek to the hight of 20 feet, and have been penetrated 25 feet further down to the Sandstone, in a fruitless search after Coal. Indeed, although the resemblance between these shales and those of the Coal Measures is not at all striking, pits have been sunk in them for Coal, at various points in the county, at the cost of considerable money and labor, and in one case resulting in the death of the miner from suffocation with carbonic acid gas while working in the pit. It is scarcely necessary to say that these shales occupy a geological position far below the Coal strata, and that any search for valuable beds of Coal in them, or in fact in the strata of any part of the county, will certainly result in a loss of both time and money.

Cape Girardeau Sandstone.—Under this name we designate a formation which comes next in descending order, and which, on account of its stratigraphical position between the Upper and Lower Hudson shales, we have classed with the Hudson River Group. It usually appears as a dull, yellowish, silico-argillaceous Sandstone, composed of rather fine silicious grains.* It occurs in thin and heavy

* An analysis of this rock, by Dr. Litton, gives, for its composition:

Silica	87.58
Alumina and peroxide of iron	9.67
Lime	Not determined.
Water	1.35

beds, and its entire thickness may be estimated at about 100 feet. When first quarried it is usually quite soft, but hardens from exposure to the atmosphere. This Sandstone is found capping the hills in the vicinity of Cape Girardeau. Near the Mississippi, a mile above the town, a thickness of about 40 feet is exposed. It also occurs in the river bluffs in T. 31, R. 14, S. 14, and at other points in this township. Along the western outcrop of the Upper Silurian it appears at a number of localities, and at a quarry near the head of Shawnee Creek a thickness of about 60 feet was measured by Mr. Hough.

Although we have searched diligently for fossils at every locality of this Sandstone we have visited in the county, no traces of any have been found. It is, therefore, not without much hesitation that we include the mass, together with the overlying shales, in the Lower Silurian.

Lower Hudson Shales.—This formation is seen directly beneath the Sandstone, in a small branch a mile above Cape Girardeau. About 12 feet is exposed above the bed of the branch, and it has been penetrated to the depth of 30 feet further for Coal. It consists of dark-bluish, calcareo-argillaceous shale, with intercalated bands of bluish-gray flattened nodules of tough earthy Limestone. These seem to be confined to the upper part of the formation. The total thickness of the beds can not be less than 60 feet. Fossils are quite abundant, and generally they are in fine state of preservation. The most characteristic species are *Asaphus gigas*, *Strophomena deltoidea*, *Leptæna sericea*, *Rhynconella capax*, *Turbo bilex*, and remains of an undetermined Crinoid. The trilobites occur chiefly in the Limestone nodules.

Receptaculite Limestone. —This is the next member of the series in Cape Girardeau, and, economically considered, the most important of the group. The lines of division separating it from the formations above and below are strongly marked by lithological characters. It consists, for the most part, of white crystalline Limestone, occurring usually in thick beds. At Cape Girardeau, where it may be seen to best advantage, we find two varieties; one, bluish white and somewhat coarse textured, forms a handsome and durable building stone, and is largely employed for burning into lime; the other, a pure white and more compact variety, answers all the ordinary purposes of marble.* The Receptaculite Limestone has a thickness in Cape Girardeau of not less than 130 feet, which is, I believe, a greater development than has been found elsewhere in the State. On the Cape Girardeau and

* The proportions of the different constituents of this marble, according to the analysis made by Dr. Litton, are:

Carbonate of Lime, 99.57.
Silica, *a trace*.
Alumina, *a trace*.

Jackson road it appears in a number of localities, until we arrive within a couple of miles of the latter place. It is also exhibted at several points on the Perryville road, and on the head-waters of Randall's, Cane, Shawnee and Flat Rock Creeks.

In our description of the Mississippi River section, published in Second Annual Report, this formation was grouped as a subdivision of the Trenton. Since then, however, a more thorough study of its palæontology has caused us to alter our opinion, and we now think that its proper place is with the Hudson River. This view is based upon the fact that its most characteristic fossils are Hudson River species, as for example *Orthis lynx*, *Strophomana alternata*, *Stroph. deltoidea*, *Rhynconella capax* and *Asaphus gigas*. The association of *Receptaculites* with the group of fossils just mentioned, leaves no doubt that the formation we are considering is the precise equivalent of the Galena or "Lead-bearing Limestone" of Iowa and Illinois, notwithstanding their great dissimilarity of lithological character. We have chosen the term Receptaculite Limestone to designate it, in preference to that of Galena Limestone, for the reason that although well developed in our State, it is not galeniferous; while the genus *Receptaculites* is everywhere regarded as its most characteristic fossil.

Trenton Limestone.

This formation extends over a considerable area in Cape Girardeau, and here, as in other parts of the State, consists of thick and thin beds of bluish-gray and drab Limestone, very compact in texture, and often emitting a ringing sound when struck with a hammer. It forms a belt from three to seven miles wide, which commences near the middle of the northern boundary line, and traverses in a south-eastern direction the entire length of the county. It is spread over an area of more than 100 square miles, and its thickness is estimated at about 250 feet. The greatest thickness seen at any one point was on Cape LaCruche Creek, not far from Cape Girardeau, where it exists in perpendicular bluffs from 70 to 100 feet high. It is also well displayed on Apple Creek, at the town of Appleton, and on Hughes', Buckeye, Flat Rock and Shawnee Creeks.

Fossils occur in all parts of the formation, but they are most abundant in the superior strata. Just under the Receptaculite Limestone, at Cape Girardeau, the beds are densely crowded with *Strophomena filitexta*, *Leptæna sericea*, *Orthis subæquata* and *Chætetes lycoperdon*. Fossils also abound in the bluffs of Cape LaCruche Creek and at Appleton.

Black River and Bird's-eye Limestones.

These formations are represented in Cape Girardeau, though we can not separate them here into two distinct groups, nor is it easy, by lithological features, to separate them from the overlying Trenton. In the bluffs bordering the swamp in T. 30, R. 13, Sec. 14, I obtained the following section of their beds, in descending order:

No. 1. 70 feet perpendicular wall of bluish-gray Trenton Limestone, containing *Pleurotomaria lenticularis*, *Leptæna fililexta*, and other Trenton fossils.

No. 2. 30 feet Black River and Bird's-eye Limestone, consisting of alternations of light and dark brittle Limestone, of very fine texture, and resembling lithographic Limestone.

Some of the more compact layers of No. 2 contain an abundance of small, crystalline prints, which appear to be the extremities of a fossil similar to *Stictopora ramosa*, so characteristic of the Bird's-eye of New York and Kentucky. In T. 33, R. 12, I found near the brow of the hills the same beds, and after a search of a few minutes, obtained examples of this delicate *Bryozoon*, finely weathered out on the surface of some masses of the rock. On a small branch of Hubble's Creek, near Jackson, Mr. Hough found the uppermost layers to be an exceedingly compact, brittle, bluish-gray Limestone, handsomely variegated with dark, bluish lines. On the west side of Hubble's Creek, T. 30, R. 12, S. 13, bands of quartzose Sandstone occur, interstratified with the dark Limestone containing *Cythere*.

CALCIFEROUS SAND GROUP AND POTSDAM SANDSTONE.

In Cape Girardeau the Magnesian Limestone series occupies about 250 square miles, forming nearly the entire western half of the county. We here recognize the several subdivisions of the mass from the First Magnesian down to the Third Magnesian Limestone, inclusive.

First Magnesian Limestone.

The beds referred to this formation consist of gray, calcareo-Magnesian Limestone and buff, earthy Dolomite. In T. 30, R. 13, S. 14, we find a section as follows:

No. 1. 30 feet slope.

No. 2. 6 feet dark, compact, brittle Limestone, containing *Cythere*, and alternating layers of banded Limestone (Bird's-eye Limestone.)

No. 3. 42 feet gray, calcareo-Magnesian Limestone and buff, earthy Dolomite.

But the best display of the strata of this formation occurs on Apple Creek, near the county line, in T. 33, R. 11, Sec. 3, as follows:

No. 1. 1 foot of cream-colored, earthy Magnesian Limestone, with vermicular markings.
No. 2. 3-feet bench of hard, quartzose Sandstone.
No. 3. 3 feet cream-colored, earthy Magnesian Limestone.
No. 4. 1-foot bench of compact Sandstone, of fine texture.
No. 5. 8 inches of dark-gray Dolomite, some of the layers brecciated.
No. 6. 9 feet light-gray Magnesian Limestone, breaking with a conchoidal fracture; occurring in heavy beds.
No. 7. 8-inch bench of Sandstone.
No. 8. 22 feet thick and thin beds of earthy, cream-colored Magnesian Limestone and compact Dolomite.
No. 9. 1½ feet hard, gray Magnesian Limestone, with masses of Sandstone disseminating through it.
No. 10. 5 feet hard, fine-grained Sandstone,
No. 11. 6 inches Magnesian Limestone, with silicious grains, giving it an oolitic appearance.
No. 12. 2½-foot ledge of Sandstone.
No. 13. 2 feet silico-Magnesian Limestone.
No. 14. 1½ feet dark and light-gray Magnesian Limestone, in thin layers.
No. 15. 4 feet slope.

From the point where this Section was taken, the First Magnesian Limestone prevails, along the course of Apple Creek, for the distance of two and a half miles, and then dips beneath the Black River and Bird's-eye. Mr. Hough found it exposed on the hills at the head of Byrd's and Cane Creeks, and also traced it for several miles down these streams. The formation under notice is remarkable for its cavernous character, the surface of the country being often marked by sink-holes where it prevails. These are usually of an inverted conical shape, from ten to thirty feet in diameter, and sometimes thirty feet in depth. Occasionally, they are so numerous as to render it difficult for one to travel over the surface on horse-back. No fossils have been found in the formation in this county.

Saccharoidal Sandstone.

This member of the series presents the same lithological features in Cape Girardeau as in other parts of the State. It attains a thickness of about 100 feet, and may be seen to best advantage near the county line, in the N. W. corner of T. 33, R. 12, where a thickness of about 80 feet is exposed. It is frequently visible in heavy beds along the bluffs bordering the swamp lands between Hubble's and Whitewater Creeks, preserving here its usual form of massive cliffs of nearly pure white Sandstone composed of pure silicious grains, well adapted to the manufacture of glass.

SECOND MAGNESIAN LIMESTONE.

It is sometimes difficult in this county to distinguish this from the First Magnesian. The strata composing it are, as a general rule, darker colored than in the equivalent beds further north. In the bluffs bordering the swamp lands, between Hubble's and Whitewater Creeks, the formation is frequently exhibited, and at one point we find an exposure of about 70 feet, consisting of compact, dark-gray Dolomite and earthy, buff, impure Magnesian Limestone, with bands of chert occasionally interstratified, and the whole surmounted with Saccharoid Sandstone. On Apple Creek, in the north-west portion of the county, it is also well displayed at several localities.

SECOND SANDSTONE.

This member of the Magnesian Limestone series presents here the same character as observed elsewhere in the State. It is found capping the higher hills between Whitewater River and the western boundary of the county, and also frequently occurs on the hills for a short distance east of this stream.

THIRD MAGNESIAN LIMESTONE.

This constitutes the base of the series in this county, and is confined chiefly to the western tier of townships. Fine exhibitions of it may be seen at various points along the course of Whitewater River and its branches, where it appears in bluffs from 50 to 80 feet high. The entire thickness of the formation has not been seen at any locality examined by us. The superior beds usually consist of alternations of gray Dolomite, chert and Sandstone; below these, we have light and dark-gray, thick-bedded Magnesian Limestone, compact in texture and traversed occasionally in all directions by spar veins. Many of the beds of this formation furnish valuable and very durable building materials.

Fossils are not abundant In the S. W. portion of the county, near Crooked Creek, Mr. Hough found, in the cherty beds, *Straparollus*, *Orthoceras* and *Murchisonia*.

ECONOMICAL GEOLOGY.

SOILS.

This county contains an unusually large proportion of arable soils. Those spread over the valleys of the Mississippi River, Whitewater, Apple, Hubble's, Randall's, Cape LaCruche and Flora Creeks, as well as a number of the smaller branches, produce plentiful crops of corn, wheat, oats and other kinds of grain adapted to the climate. The swamp lands, too, in the northern part of the county, possess soils of great richness, requiring only a thorough system of drainage, based on scientific principles, to convert them into the finest and most productive lands to be found in the county, and not inferior to the best in the State. The time is, I think, not far distant when these swamp lands will be occupied by a thriving agricultural population. The uplands of the district occupied by the Niagara, Hudson River, Trenton and First and Second Magnesian Limestone, constituting nearly the whole of the two middle ranges of townships, possess soils of excellent quality, while a large portion of the country is just sufficiently undulating to secure free drainage. In those portions of the county underlaid by the Third Magnesian Limestone, Second Sandstone and Lower Helderburg, the soils are really of good quality, but sometimes they contain so much chert as to render them unfit for cultivation. This is particularly the case near the streams.

IRON ORE

Of good quality occurs at several localities in Cape Girardeau. On land owned by Mr. Williams, in N. W. quarter of Sec. 10, T. 31, R. 13, a deposit of brown Hematite occurs on the declivity of a hill. It may be traced over a space of about a hundred yards, and exists in rough, irregular masses, some of which would weigh upward of fifty pounds. In a few specimens, the ore exists in thin scales, assuming the form of iron mica, and in others it contains a large proportion of silex in small grains. No work has been done to test the probable extent of the deposit at this locality, but the appearances are favorable that the ore exists in considerable quantity. The formation in the immediate vicinity of the deposit is the Cape Girardeau Limestone.

Argillaceous Iron ore, of good quality, was observed associated with the Second Magnesian Limestone, in T. 30, R. 12, N. E. quarter of Sec. 10, and with the Cape Girardeau Sandstone, two miles east of

Jackson. But at neither of these localities does the ore occur in sufficient abundance to justify working.

Sulphuret of Iron has been noticed at nearly all the localities where the shales of the Hudson River group occur.

A chalybeate spring exists on Flat Rock Creek, a short distance above its mouth. The water yields a copious, gelatinous precipitate, and possesses a strong taste of Iron. It may be employed with benefit in diseases requiring a tonic course of treatment.

LEAD.

Fragments of this ore have been picked up at several localities in the county, but only in very small quantities. But as the Third Magnesian Limestone, the most productive Lead-bearing rock in the State, is largely developed in the western townships, it is not improbable that this important ore will yet be found in workable quantity.

BUILDING MATERIALS.

Cape Girardeau county possesses an inexhaustible supply of the finest kind of building materials. In this respect, it is perhaps more highly favored than any county in the State; for nearly every township is abundantly supplied with good and valuable materials for this purpose. The Receptaculite Limestone furnishes the well-known Marble of Cape Girardeau. The principal quarries are situated back of the town, and about three-quarters of a mile from the Mississppi, where a thickness of about 40 feet of the marble has been laid bare by the quarrymen. We find here two distinct varieties: one, of a bluish tinge, and somewhat coarse texture, affords an excellent and apparently durable building stone; the other, a finer, white and more compact variety, answers all the ordinary purposes of marble. It is extensively used for tomb-stones in the vicinity of the town of Cape Girardeau, and, if judiciously selected, takes a tolerably good polish. This rock was used in the construction of the State-house of Louisiana, and has been, and still is, shipped extensively to New Orleans and other southern points, as well as to St. Louis. Good quarries of this rock may be opened at many of the localities in the county, where we have indicated the existence of the Receptaculite Limestone.

A handsome variety of Marble occurs near the base of the Niagara group at several localities in the county. The best quarry of this Marble is on the branch of a small creek, about two miles N. E. of Cape Girardeau, and but a short distance from the Mississippi. It is an exceedingly fine textured, brittle Limestone, of a purplish color, clouded with green and yellow, and is exposed in heavy masses on the declivity of a hill. No work had been done at this quarry at the time we visited it; but the appearances were that the rock might be obtained in considerable quantity. We obtained specimens for the State cabinet that are susceptible of an excellent polish, and which would answer a good purpose for ornamental work.

The same strata occur on the Mississippi, about one mile above Shepherd's Landing, but the rock contains more argillaceous matter, and is therefore inferior to the beds at the quarry above described.

Mr. Hough reports a quarry of this Marble in T. 32, R. 13, N. W. quarter of Sec. 22. He describes it as a finely variegated Marble, very compact in texture, and with numerous fossils of the Niagara group. It is used for tomb-stones, and has been quarried for shipment to St. Louis, Memphis and other places.

Another variety of Marble exists in the strata referred by us to the Black River and Bird's-eye Limestone. This rock was examined by Mr. Hough, and subsequently by myself. It is a compact, fine textured, bluish-gray Limestone, containing bluish vermicular markings. It is very similar in appearance and texture to the McPherson Marble of Jefferson county, and occupies precisely the same stratigraphical position. It is susceptible of a tolerable polish, and appears to be a durable rock.

The First, Second and Third Magnesian Limestones all yield building materials of more or less value, but the beds of the Third Magnesian are to be preferred, on account of their greater durabilty and beauty. The Cape Girardeau Sandstone may be used to advantage for the coarser kinds of masonry, chimneys, walling and the outside work of lime-kilns. This rock, when first quarried, is quite soft, but hardens rapidly from exposure to the atmosphere.

Fire and Flagging Stones.

The Second Sandstone furnishes an excellent rock for the construction of hearths, for chimneys and furnaces, and other purposes requiring a rock of a refractory character. It may be obtained abundantly from the hills near Whitewater Creek. Excellent flagging stones may also be obtained here.

ROAD MATERIALS

Of the very best quality occur abundantly in different parts of the county. The chert of the Delthyris shale and Third Magnesian Limestone affords an excellent material for this purpose. In the districts occupied by these formations we find, along the streams, this chert in the greatest abundance, and generally in a sufficiently comminuted state to be ready to be applied at once to the grades. The gravel road between Cape Girardeau and Jackson was constructed of this comminuted material, at a comparatively small cost, and it is one of the finest roads to be found in the State.

POTTERS' AND PIPE CLAYS.

In the bank of a small creek in T. 31, R. 14, Sec. 21, is a deposit of yellow Clay which is very plastic and quite free from gritty substances. This has the appearance of being a good potters' Clay. On Mr. Mavens' land, in N. part of Sec. 12, of same township and range, there is a valuable deposit of nearly pure white pipe Clay exposed in a bed about four feet thick. A similar Clay also appears near Cape Girardeau, on the Jackson road, a short distance west of Williams' mill; and near by is a deposit of very plastic, ferruginous Clay, which answers well as a paint, and for which purpose it is frequently employed by persons in the neighborhood.

SAND FOR GLASS-MAKING.

The Saccharoid Sandstone furnishes an excellent quality of nearly pure Sand, which is well adapted for this purpose.

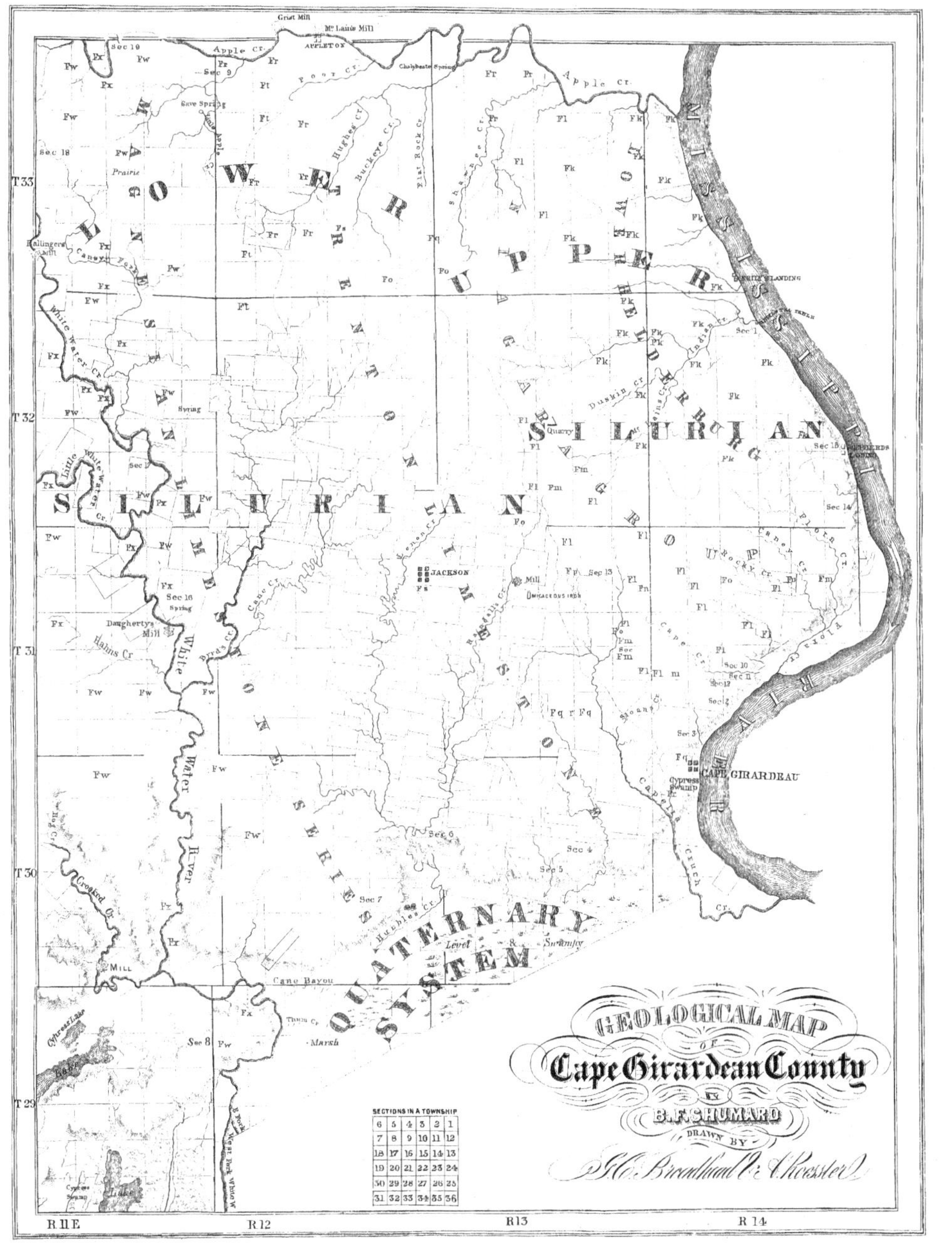
GEOLOGICAL MAP
OF
Cape Girardeau County
BY
B. F. SHUMARD
DRAWN BY
J. C. Broadhead & A. Roessler
SECTIONS IN A TOWNSHIP
CAPE GIRARDEAU
JACKSON
MISSISSIPPI RIVER
SILURIAN
QUATERNARY SYSTEM
Apple Cr.
White Water River
Cape Bayou
R 11 E
R 12
R 13
R 14
T 33
T 32
T 31
T 30
T 29

Fig. 22.

GEOLOGICAL SECTION of the BLUFFS of the MISSISSIPPI in CAPE GIRARDEAU CO.

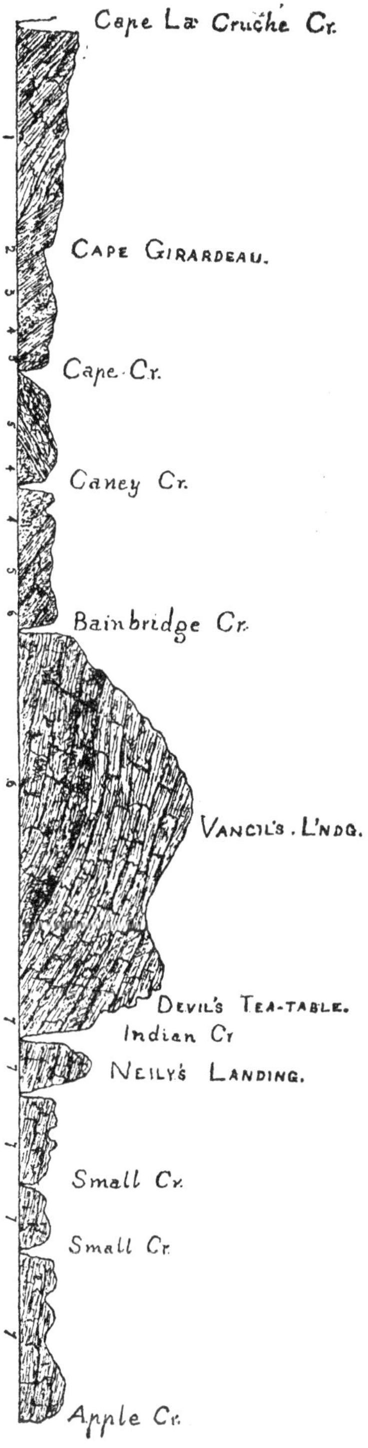

Cape La Cruche Cr.
Cape Girardeau.
Cape Cr.
Caney Cr.
Bainbridge Cr.
Vancil's L'ndg.
Devil's Tea-table.
Indian Cr
Neily's Landing.
Small Cr.
Small Cr.
Apple Cr.

1 2 3 4 5 5 4 4 5 6 6 7 7 7 7 7

No. 1. TRENTON LIMESTONE, 2 RECEPTACULITE LIMESTONE, 3 HUDSON RIVER GROUP, 4 CAPE GIRARDEAU SANDSTONE 5 SHALE (HUDSON RIVER), 6 NIAGARA GROUP, 7 LOWER HELDERBURG or HITHERIS SHALE.

Fig. 23.

VERTICAL SECTION OF THE SILURIAN STRATA OF CAPE GIRARDEAU Co.

BY B. F. SHUMARD

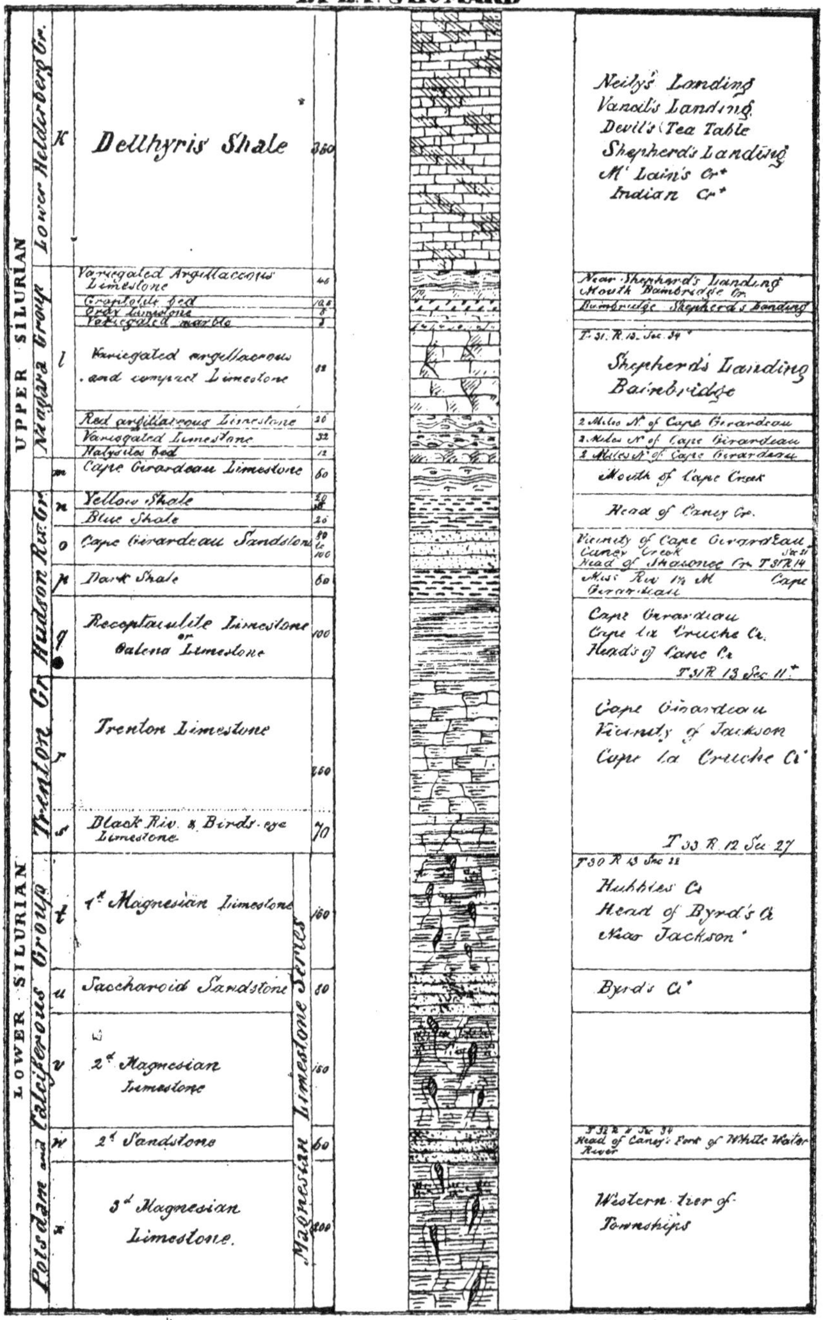

System	Group		Formation	Feet	Localities
UPPER SILURIAN	Lower Helderberg Gr.	k	Delthyris Shale	350	Neily's Landing Vancil's Landing Devil's Tea Table Shepherd's Landing McLain's Cr.* Indian Cr.*
	Niagara Group		Variegated Argillaceous Limestone	46	Near Shepherd's Landing Mouth Bainbridge Cr.
			Graptolite bed	10.5	Bainbridge Shepherd's Landing
			Gray Limestone	8	
			Variegated marble	3	
		l	Variegated argillaceous and compact Limestone	88	T. 31. R. 13. Sec. 34* Shepherd's Landing Bainbridge
			Red argillaceous Limestone	26	2 Miles N. of Cape Girardeau
			Variegated Limestone	32	2 Miles N. of Cape Girardeau
			Halysites bed	12	2 Miles N. of Cape Girardeau
		m	Cape Girardeau Limestone	60	Mouth of Cape Creek
LOWER SILURIAN	Hudson Riv. Gr.	n	Yellow Shale	20	Head of Caney Cr.
			Blue Shale	26	
		o	Cape Girardeau Sandstone	80 to 100	Vicinity of Cape Girardeau Caney Creek Head of Shawnee Cr. T. 31 R. 14 Sec. 31
		p	Dark Shale	60	Miss. Riv. 1½ M. Cape Girardeau
	Trenton Gr.	q	Receptaculite Limestone or Galena Limestone	100	Cape Girardeau Cape la Cruche Cr. Heads of Cane Cr. T. 31 R. 13 Sec. 11.*
		r	Trenton Limestone	250	Cape Girardeau Vicinity of Jackson Cape la Cruche Cr.
		s	Black Riv. & Birds-eye Limestone	70	T. 33 R. 12 Sec. 27
	Potsdam and Calciferous Group — Magnesian Limestone Series	t	1st Magnesian Limestone	160	T. 30 R. 13 Sec. 22 Hubbles Cr. Head of Byrd's Cr. Near Jackson*
		u	Saccharoid Sandstone	80	Byrd's Cr.*
		v	2d Magnesian Limestone	150	
		w	2d Sandstone	60	T. 32 R. 9 Sec. 34 Head of Caney's Fork of White Water River
		x	3d Magnesian Limestone	200	Western tier of Townships

* This locality Examined by Warwick Hough

CHAPTER XVII.

PERRY COUNTY.

BY B. F. SHUMARD.

This county is of an irregular triangular form, and contains about four hundred and sixty square miles. In general, the surface features resemble those of Cape Girardeau. The district of country west of the Saline, and also that for a short distance on the east side of that stream, is frequently quite broken. The hills are marked with steep declivities, covered often with chert and fragments of Sandstone, and sometimes attain an altitude of from 300 to 350 feet above the adjacent water-courses. We find here, however, both on the uplands and in the valleys, extensive tracts of good land for farming purposes. In the south-east corner of the county, there is also a small space that is exceedingly rough, the hills attaining here a hight of 500 feet above the Mississippi, and being separated from each other by deep and narrow valleys.

But the greater portion of the county, comprising the central and eastern districts, is moderately rolling, and possesses good and often highly arable soils. The highlands are sometimes densely covered with heavy forest trees, and at other times sparsely wooded with Black-jack, Post Oak and Black Hickory—forming what are termed oak openings or barrens.

The valleys of the streams in nearly every part of the county are remarkably fertile. The alluvial bottom of the Mississippi, in the north-east, is from two to five miles wide, and bears a heavy growth of valuable timber—Black and White Walnut, several varieties of

Elm, Burr, Red and White Oak, White and Blue Ash, Pig-nut and Shell-bark Hickory, Pawpaw, White and Sugar Maple, Sycamore, Hackberry, and Fox and Summer Grapes, are the kinds most commonly met with. The valleys of the Saline, Cape Cinque Hommes, Apple, Dry and Indian Creeks, are from fifty yards to a half mile wide, and sustain nearly all the varieties of trees that occur on the Mississippi bottoms.

GEOLOGY.

In Perry county we have recognized the Quaternary, Carboniferous, Devonian, and Upper and Lower Silurian systems. It is also highly probable that the eruptive rocks exist at or near the surface, since we have found, a short distance from Wittenburg, a loose mass of Granite that would weigh several tons, while the Palæozoic rocks in this vicinity present evidences of very considerable disturbances. In fact, the strata composing the bluffs of the Mississippi from Grand Tower to the Bois Brule, and those of the latter stream to its sources, exhibit frequent abrupt foldings and flexures the whole distance. Near McClennahan's Creek, the strata are almost vertical, and at various points, are inclined at an angle varying from 25° to 60°. The area of greatest disturbance seems not to have extended very far west of the above-mentioned streams, although we find that the formations throughout the county have a general inclination toward the Mississippi.

QUATERNARY SYSTEM.

The formations of this system developed in Perry are Alluvium and Bluff. They present here the same lithological features as in Cape Girardeau, and it is, therefore, unnecessary to again describe them. Good sections of the Alluvium are displayed along the shores of the Mississippi, Apple, Saline, Bois Brule and Cape Cinque Hommes, while the Bluff is met with beneath the soil of the uplands in almost every part of the county. We have not been able to detect in it any terrestrial or fluviatile shells at any of the localities examined.

CARBONIFEROUS SYSTEM.

The subdivisons of the Carboniferous system recognized in Perry are Ferruginous Sandstone, Archimedes Limestone and Encrinital

Limestone. These rocks occupy but a limited horizontal space in the county. They enter the northern part from Ste. Genevieve, where they constitute the "Mississippi Bluffs," and extend eastwardly, forming a narrow strip eight or nine miles long, and from a quarter to two miles broad. They also form the bluffs of the Mississippi from a point about one and a-half miles below Bailey's Landing to the town of Wittenburg. Their greatest width here scarcely exceeds two miles.

Ferruginous Sandstone.

This member of the Carboniferous is well developed. On the Mississippi it first appears capping hills of Archimedes Limestone, a short distance below Williams' Run, and thence extends almost uninterruptedly to Wittenburg. Its greatest development is exhibited about two miles below Williams' Run, where it constitutes nearly the whole mass of hills, 200 feet high. The lower part of this Sandstone exists in heavy beds, but the upper layers are schistose. The rock is sometimes very hard; usually, however, the particles are so loosely coherent that a blow with the hammer reduces the rock to fine sand. The color varies from white to ferruginous brown. The Ferruginous Sandstone was also observed resting on the Archimedes in the northern part of the county, and also at several points on the Bois Brule.

Archimedes Limestone.

This formation succeeds, in descending order, the Sandstone just described. It consists of beds of gray Limestone, which are very variable in thickness, and alternating bands of blue and yellow marl, and sometimes intercalated beds of Sandstone. The thickness of the mass can not be less than 250 feet in the county under examination.

The boundaries of the formation are laid down in the Geological map. It is finely displayed on the Mississippi, between Wilkinson's Landing and Wittenburg, on the Bois Brule about a mile above McClennahan's Creek, and again on the Mississippi in the northern part of the county.

Fossils—Are exceedingly abundant, particularly in the blue and yellow marls of the formation, from which they may be obtained in great perfection. The most characteristic species are: *Archimedipora Swallovana* and *Meekana*, *Pentremites Godonii*, *P. pyriformis*, *P. sulcatus*, *Agassizocrinus dactyliformis*, *Poteriocrinus mani-*

formis, *Acrocinus Shumardi*, *Spirifer Leidyi*, *S. trigonalis*, *Spiriferina spinosa*, *Athyris subtilita* and *Spirigera hirsuta*.

This assemblage of fossils indicates that the Archimedes Limestone of Perry is the equivalent of the Chester and Kaskaskia beds of Prof. Hall's section of the Carboniferous rocks of the Mississippi Valley, and therefore that they occupy a position above the St. Louis Limestone.

The St. Louis Limestone and inferior Archimedes Limestone we have not been able to recognize as distinct formations in Perry. The next succeeding member of the Carboniferous observed here is the Encrinital Limestone. This group we have found at only a single locality in the county, namely: on the Bois Brule, a short distance above McClennahan's Creek, where we find it resting in a highly inclined position upon the Devonian rocks. It presents here the usual lithological characters of the formation, and shows a thickness of about 150 feet.

DEVONIAN SYSTEM.

The rocks of this system follow next in descending order, and all of them may, we think, be referred to the age of the Hamilton Group of the New York series. The beds consist of gray and bluish-gray calcareo-silicious Limestone, with bands of flint interstratified. They cross the Mississippi from the Devil's Oven on the Illinois shore, and appear on the Missouri side about a half mile above the Grand Tower. They dip at a rapid rate north-eastwardly, and in a few hundred yards pass beneath the Archimedes Limestone. The same beds again appear on the Mississippi a mile below Bailey's Landing, where a few feet were seen reposing upon the Delthyris Shale; on Williams' Run about three-quarters of a mile above its confluence, and on Brazeau Creek a mile and a half from the Mississippi. They also occur in the northern part of the county, namely: on the Bois Brule above the mouth of McClennahan's Creek, and thence extend eastwardly in a very narrow belt into Ste. Genevieve county.

Fossils.—On the Mississippi, near the Grand Tower, the group abounds in fossils. We find here *Dalmania calliteles*, *Phacops bufo*, *Spirifera mucronata*, *S. sculptilis*. *S. congesta*, *S. medialis*, *Spirigera reticularis*, *Chonetes nana?* *C. carinata*, *Productus subaculeatus*, *Favosites reticulata*, *F. basaltica*, *Cyathophyllum panciradiatum*, and various other undetermined fossils.

UPPER SILURIAN SYSTEM.

The Upper Silurian rocks of Perry all belong to the Delthyris Shale and Niagara Group, and they occupy but a narrow belt in the northern and south-eastern parts of the county.

Delthyris Shale.

This formation presents the same lithological characters as in Cape Girardeau. It possesses considerable interest in an economical point of view, as all the workable beds of iron occurring in the county are found in it. It forms the bluffs of the Mississippi from the Grand Tower to the mouth of Apple Creek, and in this part of the county extends west from one to four miles. Just above Grand Tower the formation leaves the river, passes north-west in a narrow strip from a fourth to a half mile wide and eight to ten miles long, reaching the river again about one mile below Bailey's Landing. It also appears at intervals along the southern margin of the Devonian rocks, in the northern part of the county. The thickness of the mass is, perhaps, not less than 400 feet. The best exposures of it occur on the Mississippi between Grand Tower and Apple Creek, where it exists in high perpendicular bluffs, and imparts to the scenery of this part of the river its peculiar, wild and picturesque features. Wherever this formation prevails the surface of the country is extremely hilly and broken.

Fossils.—Many of the beds of Delthyris Shale are almost destitute of organic remains, but occasionally we find layers in which they are quite abundant. On the Mississippi, one mile below Bailey's Landing, and near Birmingham, are the best localities. We have collected here *Leptæna depressa*, *Leptæna* of several undetermined species, *Orthis hybrida?* *Orthis elegantula?* *Rhynconella camura?* *Platyostoma* of several species, *Dalmania tridentifera*, *Phacops*, *Cheirurus*, and a *Hapeocrinus* which is identical with a species that we have found in the Upper Silurian strata of Tennessee. At the Birmingham Iron works we have found, also, with some of the foregoing species, an undescribed Pentremite.

Niagara Group.

The rocks of this group show themselves at a number of localities along the western margin of the Delthyris shale in the eastern part of the county, and also skirt the southern border of the same formation in the northern part. They present here nearly the same characters as in Cape Girardeau, although they are not as well developed, either vertically or horizontally. The best exposures we have seen occur near Lick Creek, T. 34, R. 13, Secs. 34 and 3, on Williams' Run, T. 35, R. 13, S. 19, and at Meredith's mill, on the Bois Brule. At Williams' Run they exhibit a section as follows:

No. 1. 40 feet slope, covered with fragments of chert.
No. 2. 37 feet alternations of gray and purple Limestone.
No. 3. 60 feet slope, from which project at intervals beds like those of No. 2.
No. 4. 10 feet variegated, compact, brittle Limestone of purple and yellow colors.
No. 5. 10 feet gray, compact Limestone.
No. 6. 30 feet yellow and buff calcareo-Magnesian Limestone of Hudson River Group, appearing at intervals in slope.
No. 7. 10 feet Receptaculite Limestone.

The fossils do not differ from those characterizing the Niagara in Cape Girardeau county.

LOWER SILURIAN SYSTEM.

The rocks of this system are spread over almost five-sixths of the entire county, and they range from the Hudson River Group down to the Third Magnesian Limestone.

Receptaculite Limestone. (Hudson River Group.)

The Cape Girardeau Sandstone, and the shales that we find above and below it, in Cape Girardeau, are replaced in this county, so far as observed, by yellow and buff beds of hard, Calcareo-magnesian ? Limestone, containing *Asaphus*, *Leptæna sericea*, *Orthis lynx* and *Strophomena alternata*. They form the beds of passage between the Niagara and Receptaculite Limestone, as shown in the section last described. These beds have a thickness of about 30 feet. The Receptaculite Limestone proper has been observed only at a few localities in Perry. On Brazeau Creek, two miles from Wittenburg, a thickness of 50 feet is exposed. The rock exists here in heavy beds, and is composed of a coarse, white semi-crystalline Limestone, the particles of which in some of the layers are so loosely coherent as to be readily crumbled with the hand; others, however, are sufficiently firm to afford a good building rock. Good exposures of this rock may also be seen on the Bois Brule, a short distance above Meredith's mill.

TRENTON LIMESTONE.

This group has a wide horizontal range, and is confined chiefly to the eastern half of the county. It prevails along Apple Creek, from the mouth of Lick Creek to Kimmell's mill, in the S. W. corner of S. 32, T. 34, R. 12. On the west it is limited by the First Magnesian Limestone. Commencing at Kimmell's mill, its boundary line passes north-westwardly near Abernethy's mill, and crossing Cape Cinque Hommes Creek two and a-half miles from Perryville, reaches Blue Spring Creek in N. W. qr. of S. 24, T. 36, R. 10; thence it turns nearly west and enters Ste. Genevieve county. From this line the Trenton Limestone extends east for distances varying from eight to twelve miles, reaching the Mississippi, however, only at one point, namely: a short distance below the mouth of Cape Cinque Hommes Creek. The best exposures to be found in the county are on Apple, Indian, Cape Cinque Hommes and Brazeau Creeks. It presents here for the most part the same lithological characters as observed in other parts of the State: a fine textured, brittle Limestone, of a drab or bluish-gray color, with bands of bluish marl occasionally interstratified. Caves are not uncommon in the district occupied by the Trenton Limestone, and the strata are often traversed by deep fissures, which sometimes lead down to streams of running water, abounding in a variety of fishes. No locality in the county has afforded us a view of all the beds of the formation. The greatest thickness we have seen is on Indian Creek, near Wilkinson's mill, where Mr. Hough measured 130 feet.

Fossils are found more or less abundantly over the whole of the district occupied by the formation. They may be collected in considerable variety, and handsomely weathered out, on the Bois Brule in T. 36, R. 12, S. W. qr. of S. 31. At this place we found *Strophomena filitexta*, *Leptœna sericea*, *Orthis occidentalis*, *O. subæquata*, *Rhynconella capax*, *Subulites elongata*, *Scalites*, *Murchisonia*, *Straparollus* and *Orthoceras* (three species.)

BLACK RIVER AND BIRD'S-EYE LIMESTONE.

The rocks which we refer to these formations possess the same characters as in Cape Girardeau. They are exposed in T. 34, R. 11, near the middle of S. 24, and in T. 35, R. 13, S. 32. At the latter locality we found in association with *Orthis disparilis* and *Leptæna sericea*, a well-marked specimen of *Maclurea magna*, a very characteristic fossil of the Chazy Limestone of the New York system.

Magnesian Limestone Series.

The rocks of this series cover an area of 260 square miles. They occupy nearly the whole of the western half of the county, and also crop out on the Mississippi and at several points on the Bois Brule.

First Magnesian Limestone.—This subdivision of the group consists for the most part of thin beds of buff and cream-colored, earthy Magnesian Limestone, alternating with beds of compact, brittle Limestone. It occupies a belt of country from two to four miles wide, extending in a north-westerly direction from Apple Creek to the Ste. Genevieve line, being limited on the east by the Trenton Limestone and on the west by the Saccharoidal Sandstone. The town of Perryville is underlaid by this formation. It likewise appears on the Mississippi, near Bailey's Landing, and on the Bois Brule, not far from its mouth, where it may be seen resting in a highly inclined position on the Saccharoidal Sandstone. In the district where this formation prevails we usually find a gently rolling country, and sometimes rocky glades covered with Cedars. Sink-holes are of common occurrence, particularly where the upper part of the formation approaches the surface. These have been formed from the falling in of the roofs of caves which have been hollowed out from the strata by means of subterranean springs and streams. In the vicinity of the road leading from Perryville to St. Mary's, in Ste. Genevieve county, these holes are quite numerous, and some of them were observed to be 50 feet in diameter and 40 feet in depth.

Saccharoidal Sandstone.—This member attains a greater thickness in Perry than in any county we have examined in South-east Missouri. On the Mississippi it occurs a short distance below Cape Cinque Hommes Creek, forming rugged cliffs 150 feet high. On Cape Cinque Hommes it extends from its mouth to the Bois Brule, appearing in a succession of bold, perpendicular escarpments, some of them nearly 200 feet high. The rock in this part of the county occurs usually in heavy beds, and consists of moderately fine quartz grains, loosely cemented with a silicious paste; some of the strata are intersected in every direction by veins of quartzite. In the western part of the county we find this Sandstone prevailing along Muddy Branch, and it also caps the hills on both sides of the Saline and North Fork of Apple Creek, appearing frequently on the high points two or three miles east of these streams.

Second and Third Magnesian Limestones.—It was found impossible to draw a line of separation between these two formations, nor were we able to recognize the Second Sandstone as a distinct member in Perry; we have, therefore, to consider them together. The mass is largely developed, occupying nearly the whole western third of the county. The upper 100 feet or more presents the usual characters of the Second Magnesian Limestone, being composed of buff and cream-colored, earthy Magnesian Limestone (Cotton rock,) in even beds, from a few inches to two feet thick, forming glades with gentle slopes on which the strata appear sometimes in a succession of low step-like terraces. Exposures of from 60 to 80 feet, presenting the above characters, were observed by Mr. Hough in T. 34, R. 10, Sec. 7, and in T. 35, R. 9, Sec. 35, he got a section as follows:

No. 1. 50 feet even beds of earthy Magnesian Limestone, projecting in benches from slope.
No. 2. 5 feet coarse, sandy-textured, gray Magnesian Limestone.
No. 3. 12 feet slope.
No. 4. 4 feet dark, bluish-gray, sub-crystalline Dolomite.
No. 5. 20 feet slope.
No. 6. 20 feet fine-textured, compact Dolomite.

On Cedar Creek, near its head, I saw upward of 100 feet of the same beds exposed in a glade, and they are exhibited also on the hills of the Saline, in T. 35, R. 10, and at several points on North Apple Creek. Below these beds we find fine-grained, hard and sandy-textured gray, bluish-gray and buff Dolomites, with a great deal of chert and occasionally thick bands of Sandstone interstratified. These strata are finely displayed in the south-western townships, particularly on Whitewater and Saline creeks and their branches. Near the head of Cedar Creek we saw a thickness of 150 feet, and in Sec. 6, T. 35, R. 10, they present a thickness estimated at not less than 250 feet. Wherever these beds occur the surface of the country is very rough, and often thickly strewn with chert and Sandstone.

ECONOMICAL GEOLOGY.

LEAD.

This important mineral occurs in the Magnesian Limestone group at several localities in Perry.

Rozier & Wilkinson's Diggings are located on the north side of Saline Creek, in T. 35, R. 9, north-east quarter of Sec. 29, on the declivity of a ridge 300 feet high. They were first opened by Messrs. Wilkinson, Brown & Pratte in 1827, and were worked at intervals until the fall of 1828, during which period, as I am informed by one of the present owners, they yielded about 40,000 pounds of ore, which was smelted in the neighborhood of the workings by means of a log furnace. The mines were then abandoned until the year 1839, when they were worked by Mr. Pratte, who obtained in a short time a considerable amount of ore. Operations were again suspended until a few weeks previous to the time of our visit (1856,) when they were reopened by Mr. H. Dodd, who worked them to some profit. The ore is a sulphuret, and occurs in masses disseminated through red Clay in "openings," the walls of which consist of bluish-gray, sandy-textured Magnesian Limestone. Lead has also been found near the surface, a short distance west of the above diggings, on land owned by F. Valle.

Horn's Diggings are situated on the north side of a ridge 250 feet high, in north-east quarter of Sec. 12, T. 35, R. 9, and have yielded about 700 pounds of surface ore. No work has been done here since 1853. Lead ore has also been found in small quantities on the Byrd tract in T. 35, R. 9, Sec. 6.

IRON ORE.

In the district occupied by the Magnesian Limestone group, we frequently find masses of brown Hematite scattered over the surface of the flint hills, but all the valuable deposits observed by us occur in the south-eastern part of the county, in the Lower Helderburg and Delthyris shale, and on lands owned chiefly by the St. Louis and Birmingham Iron Mining Company. They have formed the subjects of special reports by Dr. Henry T. King and Prof. J. D. Whitney, both of whom concur in opinion respecting the value and great abundance of the ore. The principal deposits occur in a group of high hills, situated near Apple Creek, west and north-west of the town of Birmingham. But the most prominent locality for the ore exists at what is termed "the Iron ridge," about one mile and a half northwest of Birmingham. This ridge has a direction nearly north and south, and an elevation estimated at about 300 feet above the Mississippi. The ore is here brown Hematite, which thickly covers a space on the summit of a ridge of perhaps more than an acre in extent. Toward the southern extremity several excavations have been made, some of them to the depth of 20 feet. The material constituting the upper five or six feet is compact, brown Iron ore, and is a kind of Iron breccia, composed of pure Hematite and angular fragments of chert, firmly cemented with a ferruginous paste. Below this ore we have beds of comminuted chert, which in the bottom of the excavation passes into white Sandstone. Lower down the declivity of the ridge, say 25 feet, are other excavations in which brecciated Iron ore was again encountered, commingled with sandy Iron ore. Toward the northern part of the ridge, the ore is of purer quality, and from indications upon the surface, it is probable that good, workable Hematite may be obtained in abundance. About a third of a mile south of the Iron ridge, and from 50 to 60 feet above the valley of Gray's Branch, a bed of Hematite occurs between strata of chert, in the Delthyris shale. The ore is from six inches to a foot thick, and varies in quality, some portions of the bed containing a large proportion of silicious matter, while other portions are remarkably free from foreign substances of any kind.

Deposits of Hematite ore exist also near Birmingham, on Apple Creek; in fact, nearly all the hills in the vicinity contain more or less of the ore.

About one mile below Wittenburg, and a quarter of a mile west of the Mississippi, is another deposit of brown Hematite, on the summit of a ridge from 250 to 300 feet high. This ore is of good quality, and occurs in large masses, which are thickly strewn over a space of fifty yards or more.

As comparatively little work has been done anywhere in the Iron districts of the county, it is not possible to arrive at a certain conclusion in regard to the quantity of good workable ore that these lands are capable of yielding; but if we may be permitted to judge from surface indications merely, the appearances are sufficiently flattering to justify an opinion that ore of excellent kind may be procured in abundance. It is likewise worthy of remark that the ores occupy the same geological position as the Iron deposits of Decatur county, Tennessee, which have been worked with so much profit for a series of years.

MANGANESE.

This ore was found on the Mississippi, in T. 34, R. 14, Sec. 9. It occurs in small masses disseminated through a deposit of silicious Clay, which at this locality is interstratified with the Delthyris shale.

BUILDING MATERIALS

Of good and durable kinds are abundant in nearly every part of the county. The Dolomites of the western portions furnish a most excellent material for the construction of buildings; the inferior beds occur in thick layers and possess great durability, being well adapted for heavy structures, while the superior beds, known as "Cotton rock," may be easily wrought, and yield a handsome stone for dwellings.

In the central portion of the county we have the Trenton Limestone passing downward into the Black River Limestone, both of which formations yield a good material for construction. In the east and the north we find the Niagara Limestone, which furnishes occasionally a good variety of Marble.

FIRE-STONES.

The Sandstone which frequently occurs in the hills in the western part of the county may be employed to advantage for the hearths of chimney places, and layers may also be obtained that are sufficiently refractory in their nature to answer well for the hearths of iron furnaces.

LIMESTONE FOR QUICK-LIME.

The Receptaculite Limestone is the best Lime rock to be found in the county, and is to be preferred above all others when it can be procured; but the Trenton, Black River, Archimedes and the inferior members of the Magnesian group, all furnish rock that may be advantageously used for this purpose.

Sand for Mortar and Glass-Making.

The Ferruginous and Saccharoidal Sandstones both answer well for mortar, but the Saccharoidal is best adapted for the manufacture of glass, as it is frequently made up of fine, transparent, silicious grains, and is almost entirely free from admixture of foreign matter.

ROAD MATERIAL.

The comminuted chert which we find so abundant in Saline, Apple. Whitewater and other streams, as well as throughout the whole district occupied by the Delthyris shale, is a most valuable material for macadamizing roads.

BUHR-STONE.

A short distance west of Grand Tower, on the very highest points of the hills, we saw large masses of extremely hard, cellular and brecciated silex, which apparently possess all the characters of a good Buhr-stone.

POTTERS' CLAY.

On Mr. Thompson's land, in T. 34, R. 8, Sec. 22, is a bed of pink, white and yellow, variegated Clay, which has all the qualities of a good Clay for potters' use. Part of the bed contains too much sand, but the largest proportion is quite free from grit. Potters' Clay also occurs on the Mississippi a short distance below the Grand Tower, where we likewise find a bed of pipe Clay.

SPRINGS

Of purest water prevail in almost every part of the county, but in the Magnesian Limestone and Delthyris shale districts they are particularly numerous, and often give forth large volumes of water.

TIMBER,

Of the most useful kinds, is found everywhere in the county, and in quantities sufficient to supply all the wants of a dense population for a great many years. In the western part, near the Grand Tower, is a small pinery, from which, however, most of the finest trees have been cut to supply a saw-mill located in the neighborhood.

CHAPTER XVIII.

STE. GENEVIEVE COUNTY.

BY B. F. SHUMARD.

This county contains about 486 square miles, and embraces within its limits considerable diversity of surface. In general terms, it may be described as hilly; the hills rising sometimes to the hight of 500 feet above the Mississippi, and from 50 to 300 feet above the adjacent streams. The general direction of the main ridges is N. E. and S. W. Many good farms are to be found on the high lands of different parts of the county; but there are some districts in which the surface is very uneven, and the soil too light and sandy for successful cultivation. In the vicinity of the Junca and the head branches of the Aux Vases, the country is remarkably rough and broken. We find also some broken country bordering the valleys of the Mississippi, Saline and Establishment. The alluvial bottoms of the streams throughout the county possess soils of great fertility, and well adapted to the growth of all the staples of the country. There are many fine farms to be seen along the Saline and its branches, the Aux Vases below the Junca, North and South Gabouri, Fourche Polite, Establishment, Fourche Duclos and Isle le Bois Creeks.

TIMBER.

Nearly every part of Ste. Genevieve is supplied with timber in abundance. The valleys of the large streams are covered with a heavy growth of forest trees, as are also frequently the hill-sides in their vicinity. On the head branches of the Aux Vases, Establishment and Terre Bleu, there are heavy forests of excellent Pine, but the prevailing growth over a large portion of the high lands is Black Oak, Black-jack, Post Oak and Black Hickory.

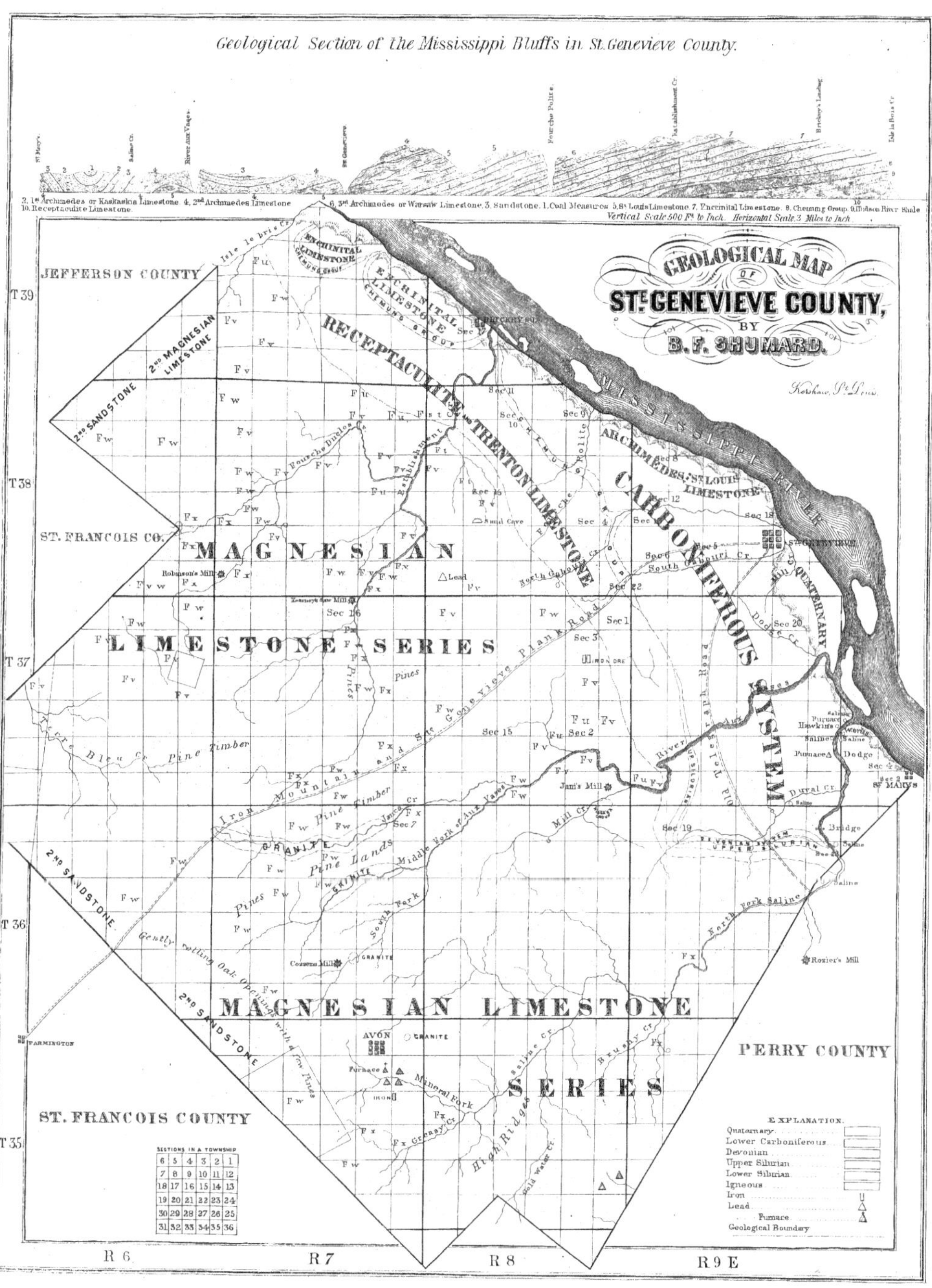
Geological Section of the Mississippi Bluffs in St. Genevieve County.
2. 1st Archimedes or Kaskaskia Limestone. 4. 2nd Archimedes Limestone 6. 3rd Archimedes or Warsaw Limestone. 3. Sandstone. 1. Coal Measures. 5. St. Louis Limestone. 7. Encrinital Limestone. 8. Chemung Group. 9. Hudson River Shale 10. Receptaculite Limestone.
Vertical Scale 500 Ft. to Inch. Horizontal Scale 3 Miles to Inch.
GEOLOGICAL MAP OF STE. GENEVIEVE COUNTY, BY B. F. SHUMARD.
JEFFERSON COUNTY
ST. FRANCOIS CO.
ST. FRANCOIS COUNTY
PERRY COUNTY
MAGNESIAN LIMESTONE SERIES
CARBONIFEROUS SYSTEM
RECEPTACULITE AND TRENTON LIMESTONE
ENCRINITAL LIMESTONE CHEMUNG GROUP
ARCHIMEDES & ST. LOUIS LIMESTONE
QUATERNARY
2ND SANDSTONE
2ND MAGNESIAN LIMESTONE
GRANITE
MISSISSIPPI RIVER
STE. GENEVIEVE
ST. MARYS
AVON
FARMINGTON
T 39
T 38
T 37
T 36
T 35
R 6
R 7
R 8
R 9 E
SECTIONS IN A TOWNSHIP
EXPLANATION.
Quaternary
Lower Carboniferous
Devonian
Upper Silurian
Lower Silurian
Igneous
Iron
Lead
Furnace
Geological Boundary

STREAMS.

Nearly all parts of Ste. Genevieve are well watered. The Mississippi forms the north-eastern boundary of the county, and receives a multitude of small streams, which rise chiefly in the western townships.

GEOLOGY.

The Quaternary, Coal Measures, Carboniferous and Upper and Lower Silurian Systems are all more or less developed. The accompanying vertical Section exhibits the thickness and relative position of the different members composing these systems, which we have recognized in Ste. Genevieve county.

QUATERNARY SYSTEM.

ALLUVIUM.

This formation presents the usual characters of Sand, Clay and Humus, and good sections of it may be seen on the banks of most of the streams. The best Section seen in the county is on the Saline, T. 36, R. 9, S. W., of Sec. 1, where we find—

No. 1. 5 feet soil, with a great deal of Humus.
No. 2. 30 feet yellow, arenaceous Clay.
No. 3. 15 feet plastic, blue Clay.

Near this place Mr. B. Pratte, of St. Mary's, obtained, in a well, 18 feet below the surface, a fine molar tooth of a Mastodon. The specimen was presented by Mr. Pratte to the Academy of Science of St. Louis, and is now preserved in the museum of that Institution.

BLUFF.

This member is well developed on the high lands throughout the county, and consists of Clay, Sand and Marl. At Ste. Genevieve from thirty to fifty feet of it is exhibited on the Gabouri, and at Brickey's Landing, on the Mississippi, a thickness of near sixty feet was measured.

PALÆOZOIC ROCKS.

UPPER CARBONIFEROUS OR COAL MEASURES.

The Coal Measures are but sparingly represented in Ste. Genevieve. The inferior beds cap the hills a half mile above St. Mary's, on the Mississippi. At this place excavations have recently been made for Coal to the depth of about thirty-five feet, and we find here the following section:

No. 1. 134 feet slope, covered with soil.
No. 2. 8 feet blue and dark shale.
No. 3. 2 feet purple, arenaceous shale.
No. 4. 28 feet fine-grained, yellowish, micaceous Sandstone, containing carbonaceous matter and vegetable remains.

A few hundred yards from this place, the shales of this Section present a thickness of twenty-five feet, and are surmounted by ten or twelve feet of hard, silicious Limestone. It is not at all probable that any valuable seams of Coal will be found in this neighborhood, as the strata dip rapidly toward the river.

LOWER CARBONIFEROUS (MOUNTAIN LIMESTONE.)

THE UPPER ARCHIMEDES. (KASKASKIA LIMESTONE of Professor Hall's Section of the rocks of the Mississippi valley,)

Succeeds, in descending order, the beds above described. It occurs at only a few points in the eastern corner of the county, and nowhere has its entire thickness been seen. It crops out on the bank of the Mississippi, just above St. Mary's, and on the Saline, near its mouth. At these places it consists of thin beds of gray Limestone and bluish marl, highly charged with fossils, among which *Pentremites pyriformis*, *P. sulcatus, Agassizocrinus dactyliformis*, *Spiriferina spinosa*, *Spirifer trigonalis*, and several species of *Archimedipora*, are the forms more commonly observed.

FERRUGINOUS SANDSTONE.

This formation comes next, and consists of thinly laminated quartzose Sandstone, passing downward into thick-bedded Sandstone, sometimes assuming the character of a coarse gritstone, or even conglomerate, with rounded pebbles of silex and jasper. It is exhibited along the bluffs bordering the alluvial bottom of the Mississippi, from a point about three miles from Ste. Genevieve, to the mouth of the Aux Vases. Near the upper end of the exposure we find a thickness

VERTICAL SECTION OF STRATA OBSERVED IN STE. GENEVIEVE CO.

by B. F. Shumard

System	Group		Formation	Thickness	Locality
QUATERNARY SYSTEM		a	Alluvium	50	
		c	Bluff	60	Brickeys Landing & Ste. Genevieve
CARBONIFEROUS SYSTEM	Coal Measures	e	Hard Silicious Limestone	10	½ M. above St. Marys
			Blue purple and Drab Shale	25-40	
			Micaceous Sandstone	30	¼ M. above St. Marys
	Archimedes Group	h	Archimedes Limestone or Kaskaskia Limestone.	200	Near St. Marys
		f	Sandstone	80	Near St. Marys. Mississippi R. below Ste. Genevieve
		h'	Archimedes Limestone	50	St. Marys. Mississippi Bluff below Ste. Genevieve
		g	Saint Louis Limestone	150	
			Oolitic Limestone	20	2 M. W. of Ste. Genevieve
		h''	Archimedes Limestone or Warsaw Limestone	80 100	Gabouri Cr. Ste. Genevieve Plank Road
		i	Encrinital Limestone	200 300	Mississippi River 18 M. above Ste. Genevieve
DEVONIAN	Chemung Group	j	Chouteau Limestone	90	Gabouri Cr. Towns. 38, R. 8. 5 2
		k	Vermicular Sandstone & Shale	25 30	Brickey's Landing Gabouri Cr.
		l	Sandstone	25	Little Saline Cr.
		p	Hamilton Group	25	Little Saline Cr.
		m	Oriskany Sandstone		Saline Cr
SILURIAN — UPPER		m	Lower Helderburg	100	
		n	Niagara Group	150	St. Marys & Farmington Rd.
	Hudson River Gr.		Hudson River Shales	30	Mississippi River
		q	Receptaculite Limestone	130	Mississippi River Gabouri Cr.
SILURIAN — LOWER		r	Trenton Limestone	250	Gabouri Creek Isle Bois Creek
	Magnesian Limestone Series	t	1st Magnesian Limestone	150	Head of Gabouri Cr.
		u	Saccharoidal Sandstone	80	White Sand cave
		v	2d Magnesian Limestone	250	Middle portion of County
		w	2d Sandstone	150	Western part of County
		x	3d Magnesian Limestone	200	Headbranches of Aux Vases, Establishment & Saline Crs.

These localities reported by Warwick Hough Esq.

of about forty feet resting on a Limestone next to be described. Just above St. Mary's, it again occurs on the Mississippi, dipping at a high angle, and surmounted with the Upper Archimedes Limestone. We have estimated the thickness of the formation in Ste. Genevieve at from eighty to one hundred feet, but we have not seen more than forty feet exposed at any one locality.

Immediately beneath the Ferruginous Sandstone we have a second Archimedes Limestone, which, for the sake of convenience, we may designate the

Ste. Genevieve Limestone.*

This member has been observed reposing on the St. Louis Limestone at several points in the county under examination. It is very analogous in its lithological features to the Upper Archimedes Limestone, occurring, however, in thick beds, and the inferior part shades almost imperceptibly into the St. Louis Limestone. It is exhibited in the bluffs of the Mississippi, commencing a mile or two below Ste. Genevieve, and from thence extends almost uninterruptedly to the mouth of Aux Vases Creek, receiving at several points a capping of Ferruginous Sandstone. It likewise occurs on the hills a short distance west of St. Mary's, and on the Saline, a mile or so above its mouth.

The St. Louis Limestone,

Which next succeeds, is not as well developed as in St. Louis county, and it also differs somewhat in physical characters. It is this rock that forms the cliffs along the gravel road above Ste. Genevieve, and of the Mississippi till we get about three miles above the town. At the lower end of this exposure, the strata are more or less oolitic; but in a short distance they assume the character of a heavy-bedded gray Limestone, and present a thickness of from 60 to 100 feet. On Gabouri Creek, this formation prevails from the mouth to a point about three miles above, where it is succeeded by a Third Archimedes

*This group is well displayed on the Illinois side, a short distance above Prairie du Rocher, where it was first recognized by my colleague, Dr. J. G. Norwood, with whom I visited the locality last summer. During our visit, we collected from these beds an interesting suite of fossils, some of which prove to be new; others are species of the Kaskaskia Limestone, but most of them are identical with forms that occur in the Second Archimedes or Warsaw Limestone of Prof. Hall's section. Among the species which have been recognized by us in these beds, we may mention *Rhynconella trinuclea*, *R. Wortheni*, *Spirigera hirsuta*, *Retzia Marcyi*, *Spiriferina spinosa*, *Spirifera Leidyi*, *Productus elegans*, *P. biseriatus*, *Murchisonia vermicula*, *Pentremites florealis*, and one or more species of *Archimedipora*.

We have likewise recognized these strata on the Illinois shore, below the mouth of Mary's River, where they contain a large *Pentremite*, which has been described by Mr. S. S. Lyon, of the Kentucky survey, under the name of *P. obesus*. The Archimedes beds are here surmounted by eighty feet of Ferruginous Sandstone.

Limestone. At the oolitic quarries on the plank road, about two miles from Ste. Genevieve, we get the following instructive section of the lower beds of this formation:

No. 1. 50 feet slope, strewn with chert and some masses of silicified *Lithostrotion* (*L. mammillare.*)

No. 2. 60 feet light gray, sandy-textured Limestone, containing *Lithostrotion mammillare*, *Syringapora*, fragments of *Melonites multipora* and *Archæocidaris.*

No. 3. 20 feet white highly oolitic Limestone, with *Lithostrotion*, *Archæocidaris* and *Pentremites conoideus.*

The oolitic beds, which here constitute the base of the St. Louis Limestone, form a handsome building material, for which purpose they have been somewhat extensively quarried here.

Below Ste. Genevieve, the formation under examination is again finely exhibited near the mouth of the Aux Vases, and enters largely into the composition of the cliffs for some distance above. It likewise appears in the bluffs of Saline Creek, in the vicinity of Saline Springs.

The entire thickness of the formation in this county has not been precisely ascertained, but it may be estimated at from 150 to 200 feet.

Third Archimedes Limestone.

This comes next in descending order, and is the Second Archimedes or Warsaw Limestone of Prof. Hall's section. It also holds the same position as the Archimedes Limestone of Barrett's Station, on the Pacific Railroad, in St. Louis county, which has been used for building the custom-house at St. Louis. The formation is made up of gray and bluish gray Limestone, and the beds contain numerous columns of *Crinoids*, *Pentremites laterniformis*, *P. conoideus*, and a small, undescribed species of *Pentremites*, *Dichocrinus simplex*, *Archimedipora*, *Spirigera hirsuta*, *Productus Indianensis*, *Rhynconella subcuneata*, and *Holopea Proutana.*

This formation may be seen on the Mississippi, below the mouth of Establishment Creek, extending to within a couple of miles of Ste. Genevieve. Two miles from Ste. Genevieve, on the plank road, it is seen directly under the oolitic beds of the St. Louis Limestone, and it is also well displayed on Gabouri Creek, three and a-half miles from Ste. Genevieve, where it reposes on the Encrinital Limestone. Its thickness is from 100 to 150 feet.

The Encrinital Limestone,

Which terminates the Carboniferous, presents the same characters as in other parts of the State. It forms the principal part of the hills of the Mississippi, in the northern part of the county, between the Establishment and Isle le Bois, where it may be seen reposing on the

Chemung Group, and exhibiting a thickness of 200 feet. It crops out on Gabouri, four miles above the mouth, and on the plank road, four and a-half miles from Ste. Genevieve. Mr. W. Hough also observed it on Saline Creek, about three miles above its confluence, and on the Riv. Aux Vases near the point where the old telegraph road crosses it.

CHEMUNG GROUP.

There are two well-marked subdivisions of this group in Ste. Genevieve, the superior of which corresponds to the Chouteau Limestone, and the inferior, perhaps, to the Vermicular Sandstone and shale.

THE CHOUTEAU LIMESTONE

Is made up of rather thin beds of buff and gray Silico-magnesian Limestone, containing nodules of silex and bands of chert, and marked with *Orthis Michelini* and *Spirifer Marionensis.* At the base we usually find *Fucoides Cauda-galli.* These beds are exhibited in a ravine a short distance from the Mississippi, in T. 38, R. 8, N. W. qr. of S. 2, where we have measured a thickness of 64 feet. On Gabouri Creek, five miles from Ste. Genevieve, we have a thickness of near 90 feet exposed. On Little Saline Creek, in T. 36, R. 9, S. 2, Mr. W. Hough found about 70 feet of this formation resting upon 25 feet of Silicious Sandstone. The terminating beds of the Chemung, in Ste. Genevieve, consist of brick-red, purple and greenish shales and variegated Limestones, which might readily be mistaken for the Niagara rocks of Cape Girardeau, Perry and the southern part of this county, to which they bear a strong lithological resemblance. The fossils are, however, well-marked Chemung species, and the beds are doubtless on a parallel with the Vermicular Sandstone and shales of the general section. They are well seen at Brickey's Landing, on the Mississippi, in T. 39, R. 7, S. 11. At this place the Chouteau Limestone is wanting, and we find a thickness of 25 feet of purple and red argillaceous beds, directly under the Encrinital Limestone. The same strata again appear on Gabouri Creek, five miles from Ste. Genevieve. Fossils are not abundant in this part of the Chemung. The species most frequently observed were *Orthis Michelini ?* and *Spirifer Marionensis.*

The next member met with, in the descending order, is a Sandstone. It was observed at only a single locality in the county, by Mr. Hough, who found it resting immediately upon the Devonian rocks on Little Saline Creek, in T. 36, R. 9, S. 2. He describes it as a thick-bedded Silicious Sandstone, in appearance very similar to the Saccharoidal, and presenting a thickness of about 25 feet. So far as observed it is destitute of fossils, and, therefore, it is not possible to say whether it should be grouped with the Chemung or the Devonian.

DEVONIAN SYSTEM.

Two formations belonging to this system have been recognized in Ste. Genevieve, namely: the Hamilton Group and the Oriskany Sandstone. They were observed occupying a very limited area near the Big and Little Saline Creeks.

Hamilton Group.

This formation was found at only one locality, namely: on the Saline, in T. 36, R. 9, S. 2, where it was examined by Mr. Hough, and by whom it is described as a white and flesh-colored crystalline Limestone, with fossils like those occurring in the Hamilton, near Wittenburg, in Perry county. Mr. Hough gives 25 feet as its thickness.

Oriskany Sandstone.

This member of the New York series has not been previously recognized in Missouri, or, in fact, in any of the Western States. In Ste. Genevieve county it crops out on Saline Creek about four miles S. W. of St. Mary's. The beds present here a southerly dip of about 75°, and consist of nearly pure, light gray Limestone, with a somewhat granular structure.

The fossils here are *Spirifer arenosa*, *Spirifer** ——, *Orthisina (Hemipronites) umbraculum ? Leptæna depressa*, *Chonetes*, *Illænus* and *Lichas*.

UPPER SILURIAN.

Lower Helderburg.

Mr. Hough found a thickness of 100 feet of this formation exposed in T. 37, R. 8, S. 1. I have not seen it in the county. Its lithological characters, according to Mr. Hough, are the same as in Perry and Cape Girardeau.

Niagara Group.

This member occupies a narrow zone, scarcely a quarter of a mile in width, extending from a point near the Saline, about five miles above the mouth, nearly west to Janis' mill, on Mill Creek. It is entirely wanting in the northern half of the county. The beds are well displayed on the St. Mary's and Farmington road, about a mile west of the Saline. They present here a thickness of not less than 150 feet,

*This Spirifer is Fig. *a*, by Prof. Hall, with other Oriskany fossils in Pl. 97 of the Third Vol. of the Palæontology of New York.

and consist of compact Calcareo-magnesian and Argillaceous Limestone, with *Caryocrinus ornatus*, *Eucalyptocrinus* and *Haplocrinus*. At Janis' mill, the formation is inclined at an angle of from 80° to 90°, and the beds have been considerably altered by volcanic ? agency, being converted into an extremely beautiful, variegated marble of remarkably fine texture, and quite brittle. The rock passes through various shades of flesh, yellow, green, pink, purple and chocolate, and in some masses the different colors are exquisitely and harmoniously blended.

LOWER SILURIAN.

Hudson River Shale.

In descending the Mississippi, this formation was first observed about five miles above the mouth of Establishment Creek. A thickness of five feet is here exposed in a ravine, a short distance from the river. It has been here penetrated to the depth of 25 feet down to the Receptaculite Limestone, in search of Coal. It is a dark, bluish-gray argillaceous shale, and contains a small *Lingula*. The same beds again appear in a ledge three feet high, at the mouth of the Establishment. It has not been recognized elsewhere in the county.

Receptaculite Limestone.

The upper ten or twelve feet of this formation in Ste. Genevieve consists of thin layers of blue argillaceous and sub-crystalline limestone filled with *Orthis Occidentalis*, *Rhynconella capax*, *Leptæna sericea;* below these it is usually a thick-bedded, white and highly crystalline Limestone, in which *Receptaculites*, *Illænus*, *Asaphus* and *Orthis lynx*, are the most common fossils met with. On the Mississippi it occupies the lower part of the bluffs from the Isle le Bois to the Establishment, being well displayed at Brickey's Landing, and at several points between this place and Salt Point. If we travel back from the river in this part of the county, we find it reaching the tops of the hills at distances of from one-half to three miles. South of the Establishment it occupies a narrow zone, extending southwardly, crossing the Fourche a Polite about three miles, and the North and South Gabouri Creeks about six miles above their mouths. On Mill Creek, near Janis' Mill, it again appears, dipping at an angle of about 50° N. N. E. The thickness of this formation in Ste. Genevieve is about 130 feet.

Trenton Limestone.

This formation, in the county under notice, presents the same characters as in Jefferson and Perry. On the Isle le Bois, it appears a short distance above the mouth, and from thence extends south-eastwardly, occupying a belt of country from one to two miles wide; this belt crosses the Establishment two miles, and the Gabouri about six and a half miles from the Mississippi.

Black River and Bird's-Eye Limestone.

These formations have not been recognized in this county as distinct from the Trenton.

Magnesian Limestone Series.

The rocks of this series are extensively developed, being spread over the whole middle and western third of the county.

First Magnesian Limestone.—This member in Ste. Genevieve consists usually of thin, even-bedded, buff, and cream-colored silico-magnesian Limestone, passing sometimes into a nearly pure dolomite. It forms for the most part smoothly rounded hills, with gentle declivities, from which the strata project at intervals in long parallel lines. The surfaces of some of the layers are marked with vertical points, intersecting each other in every direction, which have been formed from the shrinking of the strata while in a soft condition, and subsequent filling of the cracks with fine mud.

The first Magnesian Limestone forms the prevailing rock of the hills at the heads of Fourche a Polite, and North and South Gabouri, and extends north-west in a narrow belt into Jefferson county, crossing the Establishment below the mouth of the Fourche Duclos. It is also exposed on the Aux Vases below the mouth of Mill Creek, and on the Saline, near the line of Perry county. Its thickness in Ste. Genevieve I have estimated at 150 feet.

Saccharoidal Sandstone.—This important formation consists of white and ferruginous sandstone, occurring, usually, in massive beds. Its lithological and chemical characters in this county have been fully described by Dr. Litton, in the Second Annual Report (part 2, page 85.) It extends south-west in a narrow strip, from a half to three-quarters of a mile wide, from the head branches of the Isle le Bois to the Aux Vases, which it strikes below the mouth of Mill Creek. The best exhibitions of it to be found in the county are at the "White Sand Cave," eight miles nearly due west of the town of Ste. Genevieve, and on Kaufman's land in T. 37, R. 8, S. 3. At the former locality a thickness of about twenty-five feet of the pure white variety is exposed in heavy beds. This locality furnishes the white sand so justly celebrated for the manufacture of the purer varieties of glass. Thickness from thirty to eighty feet.

The *Second Magnesian Limestone* occupies a large area chiefly in the central and north-western portion of the county. If we draw a line passing south-eastwardly from the sources of the Isle le Bois to a point on Mill Creek, about a mile and a half above its confluence with Aux Vases, and thence extend this line to the Saline, a short distance below the mouth of its North Fork, we shall have pretty nearly the line separating this formation from the Saccharoidal Sandstone; west and south of this line it ranges from one to three miles, forming, like the First Magnesian, neatly rounded hills with gentle declivities.

The *Second Sandstone* constitutes the surface rock over a larger portion of the county than any other formation, and it also presents a greater vertical development than we usually find in other counties of this portion of the State. It is constantly encountered on the high ridges at the sources of the Establishment, Terre Bleu, Aux Vases and Saline. We find it also occupying the highlands of nearly every section in T. 36 and 37, R. 7. The rock varies in lithological character in different parts of the county, but usually appears in thin beds of white, yellow or reddish colors, and made up of moderately fine silicious grains. Near Cozzens' mill, on the South Fork of the Aux Vases, a thickness of about eighty feet is exposed, and here the rock is curiously weathered into huge conical and dome-shaped masses that rise from ten to twenty feet above the surface, some of them standing quite isolated, and others joined at different hights from their bases. In this vicinity the rock occurs in heavy beds, and passes from a fine-grained Sandstone to a coarse gritstone containing large pebbles of milky and translucent quartz. North of this place, near Junca Creek, the Sandstone is very much indurated, and sometimes passes into conglomerate. On the Mineral Fork of the Saline it is a coarse gritstone of a dirty, gray color, and contains Galena and much Sulphuret of Iron. The thickness of the Second Sandstone, in this part of the county, may be safely stated at 150 feet, although we have not seen a greater thickness than eighty feet exposed at any one point. Nearly the whole pine district of this county is underlaid by the Second Sandstone.

The *Third Magnesian Limestone* is principally met with in the cuts of the streams in the western and southern portions of the county. It is the prevailing rock of the North Fork of the Saline and tributataries throughout nearly their entire course. We find it also well developed on the upper part of the Establishment and its branches, and likewise in the head waters of the Fourche Duclos. On all these streams it presents the usual lithological characters of the mass, frequently forming bold escarpments, with mural faces, and sometimes exposed to the hight of 150 feet.

ERUPTIVE ROCKS.

These consist chiefly of Granite and Greenstone, and occur on the upper branches of the Aux Vases, and near the Mineral Fork of the Saline.

GRANITE.

This rock differs but little from the Granite exposed in the vicinity of the Iron Mountain. Feldspar of the flesh-colored variety predominates greatly over the quartz and mica, and often the latter ingredient is entirely wanting. Sometimes it is coarse-grained, the feldspar being in moderately large crystals; but at other times it possesses a fine texture, is quite hard, and may be dressed in almost any desirable form. It is best developed along the course of the Junca Creek, a tributary of the Aux Vases, being constantly exposed in the bed of this stream, from the N. E. quarter of Sec. 2, T. 36, R. 7, to its very head. Not far from the lower extremity of the exposure, it rises in rugged cliffs to the hight of 175 feet, forming here a narrow gorge, through which the creek passes. At this place veins of quartz traverse the Granite in various directions; the largest of these veins that I saw was about four inches thick, and its bearing N. 20° E.

On the Middle Fork of the Aux Vases, the Granite commences about a mile above the mouth, and may be traced along its course for a distance of about three miles, projecting above the surface in large dome-shaped masses. On the South Fork it occupies a very limited space in the N. W. quarter of Sec. 25, T. 36, R. 7.

Small fragments of red Granite were also observed scattered over the top of a high ridge about a mile N. E. of Avon. The fragments thickly cover a space of about 80 square yards, and mark the existence of a granitic dyke near the surface at this point.

GREENSTONE.

Mr. Hough found fragments of this rock, mingled with masses of Granite, near the lower extremity of the Granite protrusion on the Junca, but the direction of the dyke could not be ascertained.

ECONOMICAL GEOLOGY.

LEAD.

The only mining for Lead in Ste. Genevieve has been done at Avon mines, owned by Messrs. Kaufman & Blackledge. These mines are situated in the southern part of the county, on the Mineral Fork of Saline Creek, in T. 37, R. 7, N. E. quarter of Sec. 12. The ore, which is a Sulphuret, occurs in a thin, nearly horizontal sheet, and disseminated through coarse-grained, dark Sandstone, of the age of the Second Sandstone of the general Section. About five feet of this dark Sandstone is exposed here, and it contains, besides the Lead, nearly vertical seams of Sulphuret of Iron, and bands of yellow Ocher. The principal workings here have been on the north side of the creek. From Mr. Blackledge I learn that up to the time of our visit (November, 1856,) these mines yielded about 150,000 pounds of ore, of which amount 16,000 pounds were received previous to 1849, by the former proprietors; the remainder in the winter of 1849–50, and the fall of 1854, by the present owners. The Lead obtained in 1849–50, amounting to about 85,000 pounds, was smelted at Mine la Motte, and there still remained on hand 60,000 pounds, which Messrs. Kaufman & Blackledge were preparing to smelt at a furnace recently erected by them at Avon, in the vicinity of the mines.

Small quantities of Lead have also been picked up in T. 36, R. 8, Sec. 31.

COPPER,

In the form of Sulphuret, occurs sparingly with the Lead at the Avon mines.

IRON ORE.

A valuable deposit of brown Hematite occurs in T. 37, R. 8, Sec. 11, on land belonging to the estate of the late Col. Kaufman. The ore occurs in the Second Magnesian Limestone, and is to be seen in large masses both on the summit and declivity of a high ridge. A number of shallow excavations have been made here, and at nearly all of them more or less Iron ore was encountered. The surface indications warrant the opinion that ore of good quality exists here in workable quantities.

Another deposit of Limonite exists in the same geological position on the summit of a hill, a short distance south of Avon mines. This ore is very similar to that above described, and excavations should be made here in order to ascertain the extent of the deposit. Hematite in small quantities was also observed by Mr. Hough in T. 35, R. 8, S. 7.

Sulphuret of Iron has already been mentioned as occurring in the Second Sandstone at the Avon Mines.

BUILDING MATERIALS

Of good kinds occur in nearly every part of the county. Among the Carboniferous rocks we have, at the base of the St. Louis Limestone, the oolitic beds, which are nearly pure white, and form a handsome, but at the same time not durable rock for building. The principal quarry is on the plank road, two miles west of Ste. Genevieve; but it may be had at various other places in the neighborhood.

The Third Archimedes Limestone, which is the same as has been used for the custom-house at St. Louis, may be procured on the Mississippi above Ste. Genevieve, and on the plank-road, near the oolitic quarry.

The St. Louis, Encrinital, Niagara, Receptaculite and Magnesian Limestones all furnish material of more or less value for construction. The Second Sandstone may likewise be employed for this purpose. It is also frequently an excellent fire-rock, being well adapted for the hearths and jambs of chimneys and hearths of furnaces.

The altered Niagara rocks at Janis' mill furnish a most beautiful variegated Marble, which is susceptible of a high polish, and may be used for vases, mantels, etc.

ROAD MATERIALS.

For flagging stones the Second Sandstone may be employed, and the First Magnesian Limestone is at present used somewhat extensively for this purpose at Ste. Genevieve.

Silicious gravel for roads occurs abundantly on the Saline, Establishment and Aux Vases, and generally in a sufficiently comminuted state to be applied at once, without further preparation, to the grades.

SAND FOR MANUFACTURE OF GLASS.

The white sand occurring eight miles west of Ste. Genevieve has already been described. This valuable material may also be obtained on the Kaufman estate, in T. 37, R. 8. Sec. 23, and at other points along the outcrop of the Saccharoid Sandstone.

SALINE SPRINGS.

The brine springs of this county are found chiefly on Saline Creek. They occur along this stream from the mouth to a point about two miles above, appearing at intervals of from a few yards to a quarter of a mile.

They issue from the base of bluffs composed of Archimedes and St. Louis Limestone, which sometimes reach the hight of 150 feet. Some of the springs are highly impregnated with saline matter, and bubbles of suphureted hydrogen constantly escape from their surfaces. I am informed by Mr. Pratte, of St. Mary's, who kindly accompanied me to the Salines, that salt was manufactured here to a considerable extent while the country was under the Spanish Government. Up to the year 1812, they were known as the "Perouse Salt Works."

Subsequently, large quantities of salt were annually made at these springs by Messrs. Scott & Hempstead, from whom they were purchased by Gen. Dodge, who continued the manufacture with considerable profit until the year 1820, at which time the works were abandoned.

CHAPTER XIX.

JEFFERSON COUNTY.

BY B. F. SHUMARD.

This county occupies a superficial area of about 550 miles. Its surface is for the most part hilly, the highest ridges attaining an elevation of about 450 feet above the Mississippi, and from 200 to 300 feet above the general level of the adjacent water-courses. The highlands of a large portion of the county are moderately rolling, possess good soils and a growth chiefly of Black, White, Post and Black-jack Oaks and Black Hickory. In the northern and western townships, the ridges are very narrow at their summits and separated from each other by deep ravines. The hills bounding the valleys of the larger streams are also frequently marked with steep declivities, but sometimes they rise by a succession of gentle slopes or terraces to the general level of the table lands.

Nearly every part of the county is well watered. The Mississippi and Meramec form its eastern boundary; Big River passes in a remarkably serpentine course through the western portion, while the central townships are traversed by the Plattin, Joachim, Sandy, Grand Glaize, Little Rock, Saline and numerous smaller creeks. The valleys of these streams are generally broad, affording many highly cultivated farms, possessing soils of remarkable fertility, and which sustain a heavy growth of excellent kinds of timber.

QUATERNARY SYSTEM.

The Alluvium of this county possesses the same characters as in St. Louis, and the Mississippi, Meramec and Big River afford many interesting sections, in which we find occasionally fresh water and land shells in great abundance. Mastodon remains have also been disinterred from it near the Sulphur Springs, on Little Rock Creek, by Drs. Koch and McDowell of St. Louis. The bones were found in a dark loam, mixed with a great deal of humus, at the base of some high bluffs of Receptaculite Limestone.

Bluff.—This formation is extensively spread over the table lands of a large portion of the county, presenting occasionally a thickness of more than 50 feet, as shown in excavations for wells and in the cuts of the Iron Mountain Railroad in the southern part of the county. Some of the best soils of the county have been derived from this formation.

CARBONIFEROUS SYSTEM.

Third Archimedes or Warsaw Limestone.

This formation constitutes the newest of the Palæozoic series observed in Jefferson, and occupies a small district in the north-east corner, forming here the bluffs of the Meramec, and extending a mile or two west of that stream. Its characters are the same in Jefferson as at Barret's Station in St. Louis county, being a dark gray and bluish-gray Limestone, in moderately thick beds, with bands of argillaceous Limestone interstratified. *Pentremites conoideus*, *P. laterniformis*, and a species of *Archæocidaris*, seem to be most characteristic fossils. The entire thickness of this member has not been seen at any of the localities examined by us in the county.

The Encrinital Limestone

Is also confined to the north-eastern portion of the county. It here exhibits the characteristic lithological and palæontological features of the formation as described in the Second Annual Report. The best exhibition of it occurs on the Mississippi, between the Meramec and Rattle-snake Creek, where we find it capping the hills and presenting a thickness of upward of 60 feet. Its relations with the underlying Chemung rocks may be satisfactorily seen along this line of exposure. Back from the Mississippi the Encrinital Limestone appears chiefly in narrow strips on the summits of the highest ridges in townships 42 and 43, R. 5, and the eastern half of T. 43, R. 4.

CHEMUNG GROUP?

The rocks of this group are sparingly developed both vertically and horizontally in Jefferson, the entire formation being represented by about 25 feet of reddish argillaceous Limestone, surmounted with five or six feet of compact Limestone, the whole, probably, corresponding in age to the Vermicular Sandstone and shales of general section. The whole thickness of the group is to be seen on the Mississippi, near Sulphur Spring Landing, and below the mouth of Rattle-snake Creek. The Chemung beds were also noticed cropping out on the hills near the mouth of Big River, and at several points in T. 43, R. 5.

The fossils most frequently found were *Orthis Michelini* (Var. *Vanuxemi*—Hall,) *Spirifer Marionensis*, and a *Cyrtia* belonging to an undetermined species.

DEVONIAN SYSTEM.

This system in Jefferson county is represented by a few feet of brown quartzose Sandstone, usually occurring in a single thick bed. It may be seen on the Mississippi, underlying the rocks above described, at Sulphur Spring Landing and at the quarry near the mouth of Rattle-snake Creek. At these places its whole thickness does not exceed eight feet, but on the dividing ridge between Little Rock and Bear creeks, T. 42, R. 5, Sec. 12, I saw a thickness of about twenty feet. We could not find fossils at any of the localities where this rock is exposed, although careful search was made for them.

LOWER SILURIAN SYSTEM.

The Upper Silurian rocks which are so well developed in Cape Girardeau, Perry and Ste. Genevieve, are entirely wanting in Jefferson, as are also the Hudson River Shales; and we therefore find the Devonian Sandstone, above described, resting immediately upon the *Receptaculite Limestone*. A particular description of this formation as it occurs on the Mississippi in this county has already been given in my description of the Mississippi River Section, in the Second Annual Report, under the name of Crystalline or Upper Trenton Limestone. It is therefore only necessary to mention here its range in the interior. We have found it capping the hills in the N. W. part of frac. T. 43, R. 4, and appearing at intervals along a narrow belt, extending south-east, chiefly on the south side of Little Rock Creek to the Mississippi. It is finely displayed on the former stream, particularly as we approach the mouth, where it forms perpendicular bluffs, from 40 to 80 feet high, and abounding in fossils.

TRENTON LIMESTONE.

This member is better developed, both horizontally and vertically, than any of the formations above described. Commencing on Isle le Bois Creek, in the south-east corner of the county, we find it ranging along the Mississippi in a narrow band from one to two miles wide until we reach a point two miles above Herculaneum; it there leaves the river, passes north-west to the Meramec, and at the same time expands suddenly to the width of five or six miles, receiving sometimes on the higher elevation a capping of Receptaculite, Chemung and Encrinital Limestone. The best exposures of this rock are to be seen on the Mississippi between Herculaneum and Rush Tower, on the Meramec, in the north-western part of the county, and on Big River, from Sec. 12, T. 42, R. 3, to its confluence, and throughout the whole course of Bear Creek. Its lithological and palæontological features have been detailed with sufficient minuteness in the Second Annual Report. (Part 2, pp. 145, 147.)

BLACK RIVER LIMESTONE.

This formation is represented in Jefferson county, although, as elsewhere stated, it is always difficult to draw a distinct line of separation between it and the Trenton. On the Mississippi, two miles below Rattle-snake Creek, we have found in it, at the foot of the bluffs, *Gonioceras anceps* and *Ormoceras tenuifilum*—species which are, I believe, restricted to the Black River Group in New York. We have also observed fragments of the same fossils in T. 43, R. 3 E., S. 27, in bluish-gray Limestone, associated with *Orthis tricenaria* and *Leptæna filitexta.*

BIRD'S-EYE LIMESTONE.

The beds which I refer to this formation are well exposed at Selma, on the Mississippi; on the hills in T. 39, R. 7, S. 8, and at McPherson's marble quarry, two miles from the Mississippi, in T. 42, R. 6. At the second of these localities a thickness of nearly 100 feet is exposed, resting on the First Magnesian Limestone. The layers here contain *Cythere sublævis*, and a small filiform coral, which resembles a *Syringapora* that occurs in the Bird's-Eye Limestone of Kentucky. At McPherson's marble quarry we find the section as follows:

No. 1. 15 feet compact, fine-textured, bluish-gray, brittle Limestone, with numerous Trenton fossils.

No. 2. 20 feet Black River Limestone, filled with vermiform cavities.

No. 3. 2½ feet compact, even-bedded, light bluish Limestone, with dark bluish cloudings, and containing chert, nodules and crystalline points.

No. 4. 2½ feet light drab, brittle Limestone, with bluish cloudings, forming a handsome and durable building rock (McPherson marble.)

No. 5. 30 feet slope.

Magnesian Limestone Series.

The rocks of this series form a conspicuous part of the geology of the county under notice. They constitute the surface rocks of about two-thirds of its entire area, and contain all the important deposits of Lead and Iron discovered within the district.

First Magnesian Limestone.—This subdivision of the group presents its usual features in Jefferson, consisting of buff Dolomite, in thin beds, with thin partings of blue and greenish shales. It may be satisfactorily examined on the Mississippi at Selma, and at Plattin Rock, where a thickness of 130 feet is exposed. In the interior of the county it is exposed at a number of points along the southern and western outcrop of the Trenton Limestone, exhibiting a thickness of from 100 to 140 feet, and imparting to the hills a gently rounded outline.

Fossils are very scarce in the First Magnesian Limestone. The most characteristic is a minute species of *Cythere*, which we have found toward the base of the formation, and which seems to be distinct from *Cythere sublævis* of the Black River and Bird's-eye Limestone.

The *Saccharoidal Sandstone* attains its full development in Jeffer son, reaching a thickness of from 80 to 100 feet. On Big River, in T. 42, R. 4, S. 27, the pure white variety is finely displayed toward the base of the bluffs, and may be traced for the distance of a mile or more, exhibiting a thickness of from 60 to 80 feet. Along this exposure an inexhaustible supply of pure silicious sand may be obtained for glass-making. Good exposures of this rock may also be seen in T. 43, R. 3, S. 27; on the Springfield road in T. 41, R. 5, S. 22, at Rockfort and a mile west of Rush Tower; but at some of these localities the rock is stained with oxide of iron. On the Mississippi this Sandstone first appears at the foot of the bluffs at Plattin Rock, and thence extends a couple of miles down the river in exposures 15 or 18 feet high.

The *Second Magnesian Limestone* is spread over a larger district in the county than any other formation, becoming here an important mass, as it contains valuable deposits of Lead and Iron. Sandy, Rankin's, McClennahan's, How's, Yankee, McCormick, and, in fact, all the important Lead mines in the eastern half of the county, occur in the Second Magnesian Limestone. Hillsborough, the county seat, is located upon this formation, and thence it is the underlying rock of the county for a number of miles in every direction. It is constantly encountered on the higher grounds of T. 40 and 41, R. 4 and 5, T. 39, R. 4, 5 and 6, and the western parts of T. 41 and 42, R. 3. We also find frequent exposures of it on Big River, between Maddox and Eastwood's mill, and on Sandy, Joachim and Plattin Creeks.

Fossils were found quite abundantly in some of its cherty layers on the summit of a hill in T. 39, R. 6, Sec. 2. These consist of *Gasteropoda*, and belong chiefly to the genera *Straparollus* and *Murchisonia*. They appear to be distinct from any hitherto found in these rocks, and, so far as I know, belong to undescribed species.

Second Sandstone.—This rock is sparingly developed in Jefferson county. It occupies the summits of the hills immediately adjacent to Big River, between the mouth of Dry Fork and the southern line of the county. We have also observed loose masses of it scattered over the surface in the vicinity of the lead mines, in T. 38, R. 4 and 5. It generally occurs in thin layers, and may be distinguished from the Saccharoidal by its brick-red color and more indurated character.

THE THIRD MAGNESIAN LIMESTONE

Occurs chiefly in the South-west, and its presence is usually indicated, even where the strata are hidden from view, by the roughness of the country, the numerous fragments of chert that cover the surface, and the peculiar red character of the soil. Big River has cut its bed deep into this formation between Morse's mill and the southern boundary line of the county, and it ranges from one to three miles on either side of this stream. The Lead mines of the southern and western townships are in this formation, and here the rock contains a great deal of porous chert, the cavities of which are frequently lined with beautiful crystals of quartz and chalcedony. In general, the mass has the same lithological features as in Franklin, Crawford and Pulaski counties; but at the tunnel for the railroad, at Big River, bands of blue argillaceous shale, containing a small *Lingula*, alternate with the Dolomite beds. The section at this place is—

No. 1. 40 feet thick, uneven-bedded, grayish-buff Magnesian Limestone.
No. 2. 10 feet alternations of blue shale and rough Magnesian Limestone.
No. 3. 8 feet rough, dark, hard Magnesian Limestone.
No. 4. 10 feet bluish-gray shale, breaking with a conchoidal fracture, and containing *Lingula*.

ECONOMICAL GEOLOGY.

In Jefferson county, Lead, chiefly in the form of sulphuret, occurs at a number of localities, both in the Second and Third Magnesian Limestones.

Gopher or Herculaneum Mines are located on a high ridge of Second Magnesian Limestone, in S. E. quarter Sec. 34, T. 41, R. 5 E. They were worked by a company, and yielded about 120,000 pounds of ore. A great deal of heavy and calc-spar was found mingled with the lead at most of the shafts and excavations.

Tarpley Mines, situated in N. E. quarter of Sec. 11, T. 38, R. 43, have been fully described by Dr. Litton, in the Second Report of the Geological Survey. Since his visit, however, during the year 1855, about 123,000 pounds of ore were raised at these mines, and in the spring of 1856, they were worked with eight hands, yielding 35,000 pounds. These mines are in the Third Magnesian Limestone.

Poston & Tyler's Mines, located in the W. half of Sec. 11, T. 38, R. 4 E., yielded, during the year 1855, upward of 90,000 pounds of ore. According to Mr. Daly, to whom the survey is much indebted for valuable information respecting the mines of Southern Missouri, every part of Sec. 11 contains more or less galena. At the Daly Diggings, at the head of the Plattin, 60,000 pounds of ore were obtained from a single shaft, in 1856–7.

Mammoth and Sandy Mines have yielded large amounts of Lead, and a particular account of them has been given by Dr. Litton in the Second Report of the Geological Survey. Sandy Mines have been purchased recently by a company, and I am informed that preparations are being made to work the lode in a systematic manner.

How's Diggings, located in Secs. 3 and 4, T. 39, R. 6 E, are in the Second Magnesian Limestone, and were discovered in 1840. They have yielded about 150,000 pounds of ore, most of which was obtained from shallow excavations. It was smelted chiefly at the furnace of Sandy Mines.

Yankee Diggings are situated in Sec. 6, T. 39, R. 6 E. The ore exists here in a fissure, whose direction is nearly north and south, and which contains a great deal of heavy and calc-spar, with some Sulphuret of Iron. Most of the ore obtained here was from a shaft 70 feet in depth.

McCormick's Diggings, situated about three-fourths of a mile south of Yankee Diggings, yielded 13,582 pounds of ore during the year 1855. A number of shafts have been sunk here, some of them more than thirty years ago.

Lead has also been found at several other localities in this vicinity; on Mr. Berry's land, upward of 550 pounds of ore have been raised.

Garrity & Butcher's Diggings, in Sec. 12, T. 38, R. 4 E., have not been worked for some years, but are regarded as being excellent mines.

Bisch & Daly's Mines are located in Sec. 7, T. 38, R. 5 E. One shaft has been dug here to the depth of 80 feet, and a considerable quantity of Lead obtained.

Bogy's Diggings, located in E. half of S. W. quarter of Sec. 12, T. 38, R. 4, have yielded considerable Lead; but workings have been suspended here for several years.

Lee's Diggings, south of Mammoth mines, in Sec. 13, T. 39, R. 3 E., were wrought to some extent about twenty years ago, but no work has been done here recently.

Robinson's Diggings, in Sec. 16, T. 39, R. 4 E., on land owned by General Hunt; about 50,000 pounds of ore have been raised here.

Kelly's Diggings, in Sec. 5, of same township and range, have yielded considerable amounts of Lead.

Frissel's Mines, in N. W. quarter of Sec. 30, T. 40, R. 3 E., are in the Third Magnesian Limestone. According to Mr. Frissel, these mines were discovered in 1842, and they have yielded 125,000 pounds of Sulphuret of Lead, of which amount 100,000 pounds were raised during the years 1842-3. They have not been wrought to any great extent for several years.

Nashville Mines, in N. E. quarter of Sec. 33, T. 40, R. 3 E., have been worked at intervals since 1827, and have yielded, up to the present time, about 100,000 pounds of ore.

Gray's Mines, located in Sec. 4, T. 39, R. 3 E., were discovered nearly forty years ago, and have been worked at different periods up to the present time, (1856.) A few shafts have been sunk here, but most of the Lead was obtained from surface diggings. The ore was formerly smelted on the spot, by means of a log furnace, the remains of which are still to be seen. No memoranda have been kept to show the amount of Lead that has been raised at these mines, but from Mr. Frissel I learn that some years ago they were wrought with great profit.

Rocky Diggings, situated in S. E. quarter of Sec. 5, T. 38, R. 5 E., have yielded some ore, but they have not been worked for several years.

Miller's Diggings, situated in the same section as Rocky Diggings are yielding Lead in small quantity.

IRON ORE

Occurs in several localities in Jefferson, chiefly in the form of brown Hematite and Sulphuret. The principal deposit examined occurs in the Second Magnesian Limestone, in N. E. quarter of Sec. 4, T. 39, R. 4 E., on land belonging to Mr. Prentiss. The ore is brown Hematite, of good quality, and remarkably free from foreign matter. It cccurs in large, botryoidal and irregular masses, which thickly cover the surface. The indications are decidedly favorable that ore exists here in workable quantity.

Masses of argillaceous Hematite were also observed on Isle Bois Creek, in T. 39, R. 6 E., Sec. 13, but not in sufficient quantity to justify working.

Sulphuret of Iron is associated with the Lead at Sandy mines and Yankee Diggings.

COPPER.

The only locality for this ore that has come under our observation in the county, is in T. 39, R. 4 E., Sec. 17, known as Skewes & Valle's Copper mines.* These mines were first discovered in 1844, and were wrought during the years 1845-6-7 by Dr. Cooley and Mr. Cross, and in 1849-50 by Messrs. Skewes & Valle. The ore consists of a mixture of Sulphuret and blue and green carbonates of Copper. Some ten or twelve shafts have been sunk, varying from 60 to 120 feet in depth. I could not obtain information in regard to the quantity of ore mined here. It was conveyed to Mine la Motte, and there smelted.

ZINC.

This ore, in the form of Sulphuret, occurs sparingly at Sandy mines.

SULPHATE OF BARYTA

Pretty constantly accompanies the Lead ores at nearly all the mines examined in the county. On Mr. Frissel's land, in T. 40, R. 3 E., S. W. quarter of Sec. 28, it almost completely fills an extensive fissure in the Third Magnesian Limestone several yards wide. This fissure has been traced upward of a mile in a direction a little north of west, but it diminished very rapidly in width toward the western extremity.

BUILDING MATERIALS.

There is abundance of good rock for construction in every part of the county, and generally in accessible positions. The First, Second

* For information concerning these mines, I am indebted to Gen. Hunt, of Jefferson county.

and Third Magnesian Limestones all furnish rock of more or less value for buildings. The Third Magnesian is the most durable, but can not be wrought with as much facility as the First and Second. The Bird's-eye Limestone, of McPherson's quarry, and other localities, is a very handsome rock, occurs in very regular beds, and may be quarried with ease. It has been used in the construction of the McPherson buildings, in St. Louis, which are among the handsomest structures in the city. The Receptaculite Limestone occurs in remarkably thick beds in this county, and has been employed for the columns of the court-house at St. Louis; but owing to the numerous cavities it contains, is inferior to the Cape Girardeau Marble, which is of the same geological age. The Encrinital and Archimedes Limestones furnish good and durable building rocks.

ROAD MATERIALS.

The chert of the Third Magnesian and Encrinital Limestones is an excellent material for roads, and may be obtained in abundance in the districts where these rocks prevail.

PIPE AND POTTERS' CLAY.

A pure white silicious pipe Clay occurs at Gray's Lead Diggings. It forms a good substitute for lime as a white-wash, for which purpose it is frequently used in the neighborhood. Potters' Clay of good quality may also be found at Gray's mines, as well as at the Nashville mines.

SPRINGS

Of pure water abound over a large portion of the county. The most remarkable one is Big or House's Spring, situated in T. 43, R. 4, Sec. 33; this spring issues from the base of a high bluff of Trenton Limestone, and discharges an immense volume of water, which forms a beautiful, clear stream, abounding in a variety of fishes.

Saline springs occur near the Meramec, in the north-east corner of the county. The water possesses a moderately saline taste, and is strongly impregnated with sulphureted hydrogen, which constantly rises from the surface of the springs. Salt was manufactured here during the early settlement of the county.

There are two Sulphur springs in the county, both of them situated a short distance from the Mississippi—one on Little Rock and the other on Grand Glaize Creeks. They issue from the lower part of the Receptaculite Limestone. The water is slightly saline, possesses a strong taste of sulphureted hydrogen, and deposits a somewhat copious white precipitate of sulphur.

CHAPTER XX.

CLARK COUNTY.

BY B. F. SHUMARD.

This county contains about 535 square miles, and is capable of supporting a large agricultural population. There are but few counties in the State of the same extent that can boast of a larger area of arable land than this one.

The bottoms of the Mississippi and Des Moines, as well as those of the smaller streams, are rich and fertile, and sustain a heavy growth of timber. The kinds most commonly met with are Cottonwood, Sycamore, Shell-bark and Pig-nut Hickory, Red, Scarlet and Pin Oaks, Black and White Walnut, White Ash, Linden, Buck-eye and Birch.

The upland soils are derived mainly from the Bluff, and though not so rich as those of the alluvial bottoms, yield excellent crops, and besides are capable of great improvement from deep and thorough subsoiling.

By reference to the accompanying geological map, it will be seen that the prairie occupies a much greater area in the county than the timbered lands. In general, however, the two can be so proportioned that each prairie tract may have a sufficient amount of wood land to furnish timber for fences and other needful purposes.

The surface of the country, for the most part, varies from that of a nearly level plain to gracefully rounded hills. Occasionally, in the immediate vicinity of the streams, it is somewhat broken, but never too much so for cultivation. The highest elevations scarcely ever exceed 150 feet, while the general hight is from 75 to 120 feet above the adjacent water-courses.

The principal streams are the Mississippi, Des Moines and North Fabius Rivers, and Fox, Little Fox, Big and Little Wyaconda, Honey and Sugar Creeks. The first two form the eastern boundary line of the county; the others course through the interior and flow into the Mississippi. An inspection of the map will show that every township is watered by one or more of these streams or their tributaries.

Natural springs are of rather unfrequent occurrence, especially in the upland prairie, the inhabitants here deriving their supplies of water either from cisterns or wells. Excellent water may usually be obtained at depths varying from thirty to eighty feet beneath the surface.

QUATERNARY SYSTEM.

The formations of this system in Clark are: Alluvium, Bottom Prairie, Bluff, and Drift or Boulder formation.

The Alluvium presents the same characters as observed in the counties already reported upon. It is well displayed in the valleys of the streams, forming sometimes perfectly level and beautiful plains, extending along their courses for several miles, and having a breadth varying from a hundred yards to half of a mile. With this formation we include the remarkable river terrace, which commences at St. Francisville and extends southwardly through T. 65, R. 6, and from thence into the northern part of T. 64, R. 6. This terrace is from a half of a mile to a mile broad, and rises somewhat abruptly from the lower prairie, to the hight of from 40 to 60 feet. It is nearly level on the summit, and consists of fine and coarse silicious sand, with small, rounded pebbles of quartz, trap and porphyry scattered through it.

The Bottom Prairie is only to be recognized in the bottoms of the Mississippi and Des Moines, south of St. Francisville. It presents the same characters as observed in Marion county, and therefore need not be again described here.

The Bluff formation constitutes an important part of the geology of Clark county. It is present everywhere beneath the soil of the upland prairie, and also of a large proportion of the timbered lands. In the western tier of townships it effectually conceals the older formations from view, even in the deepest cuts of the streams, and hence the citizens of this part of the county are compelled to haul stone for building and other purposes a distance of six, and sometimes even fifteen miles.

The following section, obtained at a well sunk on the high prairie, in T. 66, R. 7, near Chambersburg, will convey an idea of the general character of the formation as observed in this county:

No. 1. 3 feet dark vegetable mold.
No. 2. 3 feet light-colored, loose subsoil.
No. 3. 16 feet tough, yellow Clay.

No. 4. 16 feet yellow, arenaceous Clay, containing small rounded pebbles and scales of mica.
No. 5. 1 foot dark Clay and sand.
No. 6. 3 feet ferruginous and ash-colored Clay, with masses of ocher disseminated.
No. 7. 4 feet coarse sand, containing pebbles and boulders of granite and green-stone.
No. 8. 1 foot tough, yellow Clay.

At Mr. Carson's, in T. 65, R. 8, S. 27, the section is:

No. 1. 5 feet soil and subsoil.
No. 2. 14 feet tough, blue Clay, (Potters' Clay.)
No. 3. 22 feet yellow Clay, with boulders.
No. 4. 1 foot 6 inches fine silicious sand.
No. 5. 4 feet yellow Clay, with large boulders.

At Mr. Newman's, near the Iowa line, in T. 67, R. 8, Sec. 16, a well was sunk to the depth of 80 feet, of which 75 feet was through alternations of white, yellow and blue clay and sand, and 5 feet through the Boulder formation, consisting of beds of pebbles and boulders, chiefly green-stone. From the above sections it appears that the Bluff formation of Clark contains much more argillaceous matter than hitherto observed in other parts of the State. In fact, in lithological character, it is very analagous to the bottom prairie of St. Joseph, as described in the Second Annual Report.

The Drift or Boulder formation is probably co-extensive with the Bluff. In the beds and along the valleys of the streams, boulders are frequently met with, sometimes four or five feet in diameter, and with their angles well rounded. They consist chiefly of green-stone, porphyry, and several varieties of granite. The best exhibition of the formation that we have seen is near a mill on Fox Creek, in T. 67, R. 9, Sec. 20. At this place about 50 feet of coarse sand, containing pebbles and boulders, are exposed in a slide on the right bank of the stream.

CARBONIFEROUS SYSTEM.

The formations of Clark county beneath the above described deposits all belong to the Carboniferous System, namely: Coal Measures, Ferruginous Sandstone, St. Louis Limestone and Archimedes Limestone.

Coal Measures.

We have found it impossible to determine with as much accuracy as desirable the precise area occupied by the Coal formation in the county under examination, from the circumstance that over a large district the strata are completely concealed from view by a thick accumulation of Quaternary deposits. This is particularly true of the western townships, where one may travel for hours without encountering a single rock exposure. At localities, however, where the strata are well exhibited, we have found the dip to vary but slightly from horizontality, and to be quite regular, so that we can form a tolerably correct opinion with reference to those parts of the county where no rocks reach the surface. An inspection of the geological map will show that the coal measures are supposed to be spread over more than one-half the whole county, or about nine townships. On the west they pass into Scotland and Knox counties, on the south into Lewis county, and on the north into the State of Iowa. In the N. E. part of the county they extend to within a short distance of the Des Moines River. The best exhibition of the coal strata that we have observed in the county is at Gray's bank, about two miles west of Des Moines River, in T. 68, R. 8, S. W. qr. of S. 23, where three distinct seams of coal are visible. The section at this place is as follows:

No. 1. 40 feet slope, probably underlaid by bluff.
No. 2. 10 inches impure Coal.
No. 3. 3 feet dark, impure Fire-Clay.
No. 4. 1 foot 6 inches bituminous Coal.
No. 5. 1 foot one inch dark Fire-Clay.
No. 6. 10 inches bituminous Coal.
No. 7. 12 feet blue ferruginous shale.
No. 8. 50 feet arenaceous Limestone, very thin-bedded, passing downward into St. Louis Limestone.

This bank has been wrought to some extent on the north side of a hill by means of a level, which, at the time I was there, was about 100 feet in length. The middle seam is of tolerable quality, and is used by the blacksmiths in the neighborhood; the upper and lower seams are too thin and impure for use.

At Mitchell's bank, situated near the Des Moines, in T. 66, R. 7, S. 4, we find the following section:

No. 1. 20 feet bluff and soil.
No. 2. 15 feet dark ferruginous shale, containing *Lingula* and Coal plants, chiefly *ferns.*
No. 3. 1 foot, three inches bituminous Coal.
No. 4. 15 feet dark clay and slope.
No. 5. 15 feet hard arenaceous Limestone, with bands of brown Sandstone interstratified.

In the north part of S. 4, T. 66, R. 7, we find an instructive section, showing the connexion of the Coal Measures with the formations beneath. The order here, in descending series, is:

No. 1. 80 feet slope, no rocks exposed.

No. 2. 18 feet dark, fissile shale, with leaf-like partings of calcite. The shale contains *Productus splendens*, *Chonetes mesoloba* and *Coal plants*.

No. 3. 25 feet brown micaceous Sandstone, with *Coal plants*.

No. 4. 8 feet compact, buff calcareo Magnesian Limestone.

No. 5. 6 feet argillaceous shaly Limestone and thin seams of sandy Limestone.

No. 6. 50 feet St. Louis Limestone, containing *Lithostrotion Canadense* and *Echinocidaris*.

No. 7. 20 feet geodiferous beds of Archimedes Limestone.

On Mr. Deming's land, located near the edge of the high prairie, in T. 67, R. 8, S. E. qr. of Sec. 25, the Coal has been wrought more extensively than at any other point in the county. The mining has all been done on the north side of a low range of hills, about thirty feet below their summits. Some ten or twelve openings have been made here, but none of them have been carried more than a few fe et into the hills. The Coal is of the bituminous variety, and contains a good deal of iron pyrites. The thickness of the seam is from fifteen to eighteen inches. It is surmounted by dark fissile shale, filled with *Calamites*, *Lepidodendron* and *ferns*.

On land owned by Mr. Devance, on Fox Creek, three-fourths of a mile below the mouth of Little Fox, a twelve-inch seam of Coal crops out on both sides of and in the bed of the stream. It is overlaid by blue Fire-Clay, containing masses of dark, hydraulic (?) Limestone, with fossils, chiefly *Productus splendens* and *Chonetes mesoloba*.

Bituminous Coal likewise crops out on a small branch in the S. W. qr. of S. 24, T. 67, R. 9, and indications of it have been observed at various other points in the county.

Cannel Coal.—On Mr. Bennett's land, on Fox Creek, T. 66, R. 8, N. W. qr. of S. E. qr. of S. 16, is a bed of Cannel Coal, about five feet thick, surmounted by three feet of dark shale. This shale shows itself in a horizontal stratum for a distance of one hundred yards on the right bank of the creek, just above the water level. It is underlaid by dark clay, which rests directly upon the St. Louis Limestone. This coal has a dull luster, and breaks out in quadrangular blocks. As very little mining has been done here, we can only form an opinion of the quality of the coal from inspecting the bed where it has been exposed for some time to the action of the weather. It appears to contain a large proportion of earthy matter, but when the bank is well opened, a better quality of coal may be obtained. It has been mined mainly to supply the furnace of a steam mill in the neighborhood, the proprietors of which, I am informed, greatly prefer it to wood.

At Mr. Conway's, on the same land section, and about a half mile north of Beckett's, there is another exposure of Cannel Coal in a ravine, ten feet above the level of Fox Creek. This is probably a continuation of the bed observed on Beckett's land, which it strongly resembles in lithological appearance.

LOWER CARBONIFEROUS OR MOUNTAIN LIMESTONE.

The Lower Carboniferous rocks are well represented in Clark, and their boundaries are laid down on the geological map. They constitute the bluff of the Des Moines from the Iowa line to St. Francisville, and also the range of hills, which in the eastern portion of the county mark the former limit of the Mississippi.

The subdivisons of this system observed here are the Ferruginous Sandstone, St. Louis Limestone and Archimedes Limestone. The subjoined sections give the general character of the strata that make up these several formations:

Section No. 1, taken near St. Francisville.

No. 1. 20 feet gray, fine-grained Limestone of sandy texture, in layers from a-half of an inch to six inches thick, and containing silicious masses of *Lithostrotion Canadense.*

No. 2. 18 feet concretionary buff, light-gray and drab, brittle Limestone, forming bold cliffs.

No. 3. 4 feet very hard, fine-grained Limestone, of a buff color, with *Lithostrotion Canadense.*

No. 4. 20 feet buff, magnesio-calcareous Limestone, soft above but rather compact at base, containing casts of *Spirifera*, *Rhynconella*, *Fenestella*, *Chœtetes* and *Pentremites.*

No. 5. 35 to 40 feet blue, argillaceous shale, with geodes from two to eighteen inches in diameter, and occasionally bands of buff, earthy limestone.

No. 6. Yellowish, sandy limestone, with bands and nodules of chert, and containing *Actinocrinus Mississippiensis* and *Actino. Americanus.*

No. 7. 8 feet bluish-gray, moderately coarse texture, sub-crystalline Limestone, in thin beds abounding in fossils.

The following section taken on the Des Moines, about five miles north of St. Francisville, T. 66, R. 7, Sec. 24, exhibits arenaceous strata not observed in the preceding section:

Section No. 2.

No. 1. 10 feet Ferruginous Sandstone.

No. 2. 50 feet thin-bedded, sandy Limestone, passing downward into fragmentary Limestone, appearing in rough and nearly perpendicular escarpments.

No. 3. 4 feet blue, argillaceous shale, with rounded masses of buff, calcareo-magnesian (?) Limestone imbedded.

No. 4. 3 feet buff Limestone, moderately compact.

No. 5. 2½ feet gray, compact, sandy Limestone, with fine scales of mica, *Spirifera* and *Fenestella.*

No. 6. 9 feet soft micaceous Sandstone, made up of fine grains.
No. 7. 1 foot blue, very fine-grained, soft, argillaceous Sandstone.
No. 8. 7 feet soft, fine-grained, gray, micaceous Sandstone, in layers from six inches to a foot thick.
No. 9. 40 feet slope, covered with debris.
No. 10. 12 feet gray Archimedes Limestone in thin beds.

FERRUGINOUS SANDSTONE.

This formation has been recognized at only a few places in Clark, and nowhere presents a great thickness. It was observed capping the hills on the Des Moines, five miles above St. Francisville and about two miles below Athens. At these localities the rock is a soft, thin-bedded, silicious Sandstone, of a reddish-brown color. On Honey Creek, in T. 64, R. 7, Sec. 16, is an exposure of sixteen feet, reposing on the St. Louis Limestone. The layers are quite thin, even-textured, and lighter colored than those seen on the Des Moines.

ST. LOUIS LIMESTONE.

This formation is largely developed in the county. In lithological features, however, it is strikingly different from the St. Louis Limestone of St. Louis county, though it contains pretty nearly the same assemblage of organic remains. In Clark it consists for the most part of massive and rough strata of compact, gray and drab Limestone, surmounted with thin, even layers of light gray, sandy-textured Limestone. In this formation we include the beds from one to four inclusive of Sec. No. 1, and the beds from two to five inclusive of Sec. No. 2. The inferior arenaceous strata of the last section are limited to a few localities, and must be regarded as beds of passage between the St. Louis and Archimedes Limestones. The entire thickness of the St. Louis Limestone in the county under consideration may be estimated at about 140 feet.

It is well displayed along the bluffs of the Des Moines from St. Francisville to the Iowa line, where it constitutes those bold and rugged escarpments that give to this part of the river its picturesque character. It prevails extensively on Fox Creek, from a point four or five miles below Waterloo to the eastern margin of the Coal formation, and is also well exhibited on Honey Creek in the vicinity of Winchester. Near Judge Lowrie's, in T. 64, R. 7, Sec. 26, the upper part of the formation appears as a light-colored Limestone in even beds, well adapted for tomb-stones and door-sills.

Fossils.—The most common species are *Lithostrotion Canadense*, *Orthisina* (*Hemipronites*,) *umbraculum*, *Productus cora* and *Spirifer*, *Rhynconella*, *Syringopora*, *Melonites*, and an *Archæocidaris* belonging to an undescribed species. The white Limestone near Judge Lowrie's contains several minute shells of the genera *Conocardium*, *Arca*, *Avicula*, *Athyris* and *Bellerophon.*

ARCHIMEDES LIMESTONE.

In Clark we recognize three well-marked subdivisions of this formation. The superior beds consist of buff-colored calcareo-magnesian Limestone, of various degrees of hardness, with bands of blue shale intercalated. Some of the layers are replete with casts of *Archimedipora*, *Spirifer* and *Athyris.* We also find here a *Pentremite* which resembles very nearly *P. conoideus*—(Hall.) This part of the formation corresponds to the *Archimedes* Limestone of Barrett's Station of St. Louis county, and the Warsaw Limestone of Prof. Hall's Mississippi River section. The several parts of the mass are well displayed in the vicinity of St. Francisville, and at a number of other localities on the Des Moines. They are also exhibited near Waterloo, on Honey Creek, and in the neighborhood of Winchester, where about seventy feet are exposed. The middle part of the formation constitutes the well-known geodiferous beds of Dr. Owen, and is composed of blue marls, with geodes and some bands of earthy, buff Limestone. It prevails on Honey Creek between Winchester and the bluffs, limiting the Mississippi bottom, on the Des Moines, at St. Francisville and other points, and on Fox Creek, near Waterloo, where a thickness of more than twenty feet is exposed. At St. Francisville and other localities on the Des Moines, geodes are often extremely abundant. They vary from a couple of inches to two feet in diameter, and when broken open are found lined with chalcedony and transparent crystals of quartz. Some contain also elegantly formed crystals of carbonate of lime, which occupy nearly the entire cavity of the geode, while others are furnished occasionally with beautiful crystals of blende and Iron pyrites.

The inferior division of the formation comprehends what is called by Professor Hall the Lower Archimedes, or Keokuk Limestone. It consists of gray and bluish-gray Limestone, splitting readily into thin layers, beds of shale and sometimes chert. The uppermost layers also contain chert nodules of irregular shape. Some of the beds abound with *Spirifer trigonalis* Martin, (*S. incrassatus* Eich.) and fish teeth. We find also *Platycrinus Saffordi*, Troost, *Actinocrinus Humboldtii*, Troost, *Amphoracrinus Americanus*, Rœmer, and occasionally an *Archimedipora*, with a very slender axis, described by Professor Hall under the name of *Fenestella Owenana.* This part of the formation appears on the shore of the Des Moines, at St. Francisville, where it displayed a thickness of ten feet. But it is best exposed on Fox Creek, about four miles below Waterloo, at which place a thickness of forty feet is exposed. The beds here abound with the characteristic fossils of the mass.

ECONOMICAL GEOLOGY.

BUILDING MATERIALS

Of good quality exist at a number of localities in Clark. A handsome and very superior Limestone for construction occurs in the upper part of the St. Louis Limestone, on the north side of Honey Creek, in T. 64, R. 7, Sec. 26. This rock, which is quarried near the top of a hill, is of a light color, breaks with a conchoidal fracture, and possesses a finely granular texture. The bed generally preferred is two feet four inches thick, and remarkably free from joints, so that blocks may be readily procured of almost any required length and breadth. At Waterloo I saw some very neat tombstones which had been cut from this rock, and I am told that it is susceptible of being lettered and ornamented. Some of the buff magnesio-calcareous beds of the Archimedes and St. Louis Limestone likewise furnish a valuable and apparently very durable rock for building purposes, and the heavier kinds of masonry. The inferior part of the St. Louis Limestone, near St. Francisville, furnishes the material for the construction of the public works on the Des Moines. This rock is said to possess the property of hardening from exposure to the atmosphere.

FIRE-STONES.

For hearths and chimneys, the arenaceous beds of passage between the St. Louis and Archimedes Limestones supply a good material. The Ferruginous Sandstone may likewise be advantageously employed as a fire-rock.

ROAD MATERIALS.

For paving streets the Boulder formation furnishes a most excellent material. Boulders may be obtained in abundance, and of almost any required size, along the shores and in the beds of the Wyaconda, Musgrove Branch, Fox Creek and other points in the county. Coarse and fine pebbles, for gravel roads, may also be procured at the same localities.

GRINDSTONES.

The Sandstone we have described as occurring on the Des Moines, about five miles above St. Francisville, is used for this purpose. The beds of the Section at this locality, designated No. 3, furnish the best material. They consist of micaceous Sandstone, made up of fine silicious grains, and the layers are from six inches to a foot thick. When first taken from the quarry, this Sandstone is soft, but after exposure for some time to the air, it becomes indurated. Near Bill's mill, on Fox Creek, a thin-bedded Sandstone of light hue occurs, that may also be wrought into grindstones, of tolerable quality.

LIMESTONES,

Suitable for quick-lime, may be obtained from the inferior Archimedes and the superior members of the St. Louis Limestone.

FIRE-CLAY,

Apparently of good quality, occurs directly under the dark shale of the Coal Measures, on Mr. Clarke's land, in T. 67, R. 7, S. W. quarter of Sec. 32. We find this substance also on Devance's land, on Fox Creek, about a mile below the mouth of Little Fox. It is highly probable that this important material will be found also at other localities in the county, when the Coal seams are more extensively worked.

POTTERS' CLAY.

At various points where the "Bluff" exists, a very tenacious Clay occurs directly under the subsoil, generally known under the name of Joint Clay. This possesses all the external characters of a good Clay for potters' use, and it abounds in almost every part of the county.

EXPLANATORY NOTE.—The cuts for this volume, excepting maps, were all engraved in New York. They were received at too late a day to return those imperfectly executed.

G. C. B.

ERRATA.

On p. 28, in No. 2 of Sec. 50, for "Third Magnesian" read "Second Magnesian."
On p. 30, in No. 5 of Sec. 59, for "Third Magnesian" read "Second Magnesian."
On p. 9, in 17th line from bottom, in word "Drifts," omit final "s."
On p. 275—plate—for "Hitheris" read "Delthyris."

INDEX.

INDEX TO MAPS AND ILLUSTRATIONS.

www.ingramcontent.com/pod-product-compliance
Lightning Source LLC
LaVergne TN
LVHW020212110826
845151LV00003B/682

9781425534677